THE MIND'S EMPIRE

MYTH AND FORM IN GEORGE CHAPMAN'S NARRATIVE POEMS

RAYMOND B. WADDINGTON

THE JOHNS HOPKINS UNIVERSITY PRESS
BALTIMORE AND LONDON

This book has been brought to publication with the
generous assistance of the Andrew W. Mellon Foundation.

The Johns Hopkins University Press, Baltimore, Maryland 21218
The Johns Hopkins University Press Ltd., London

Library of Congress Catalog Card Number 74-6841
ISBN 0-8018-1546-0

Library of Congress Cataloging in Publication data
will be found on the last printed page of this book.

The title page illustration is taken from an engraving
in Alciati's *Emblemata*, printed in Padua in 1621.

FOR LINDA,
RAY, AND TED

CONTENTS

Acknowledgments ix

I. Chapman's Poetics 1

II. Mythic Form: The Example of *Bussy D'Ambois* 19

III. *The Shadow of Night* 45
    Orphic Hymns 45
    Luna 51
    Diana 72
    Hecate 91
    De Guiana 108

IV. An Unnatural Perspective: *Ovids Banquet of Sence* 113

V. An Ovidian Epic: *Hero and Leander* 153

VI. Articulate Clocks and a Splendid Recovery 181

    Index 215

ACKNOWLEDGMENTS

My title borrows a phrase from Chapman's well-known description of the *Odyssey*. I had to discard Fred Cassidy's title suggestion ("On First Looking into Chapman's Poems") simply because I could no longer even guess what look I was on, let alone claim to remember the first one. Although my involvement with Chapman began in a single chapter of a 1963 doctoral dissertation, this book really commenced to take shape in 1965–66, when I was a postdoctoral fellow in the Humanities Center of The Johns Hopkins University. I am grateful to Charles S. Singleton, director of the center, to the Samuel S. Fels Foundation for funding the fellowship, and to the Hopkins English department—where there were giants in the earth in those days—for its hospitality. Some of the final writing was done in 1971–72, while I was a visiting fellow in the Institute for Research in the Humanities at the University of Wisconsin, Madison. I am indebted to the institute's director, E. David Cronon, and to my companions at the Old Observatory for many kindnesses. I have been assisted also by generous financial support from the American Philosophical Society, the Henry E. Huntington Library, and the Graduate School of the University of Wisconsin, Madison.

A study of this kind makes one fully conscious of the extent to which scholarship is a cooperative venture. Carroll Camden, among other favors, answered questions about Elizabethan astrology; Emmett Bennett and Fritz Solmsen, resident classicists at the Humanities Institute, were unfailingly helpful; Albert J. Loomie, S.J., guided my reading in Elizabethan political history; Tim Heninger lent his expertise in numerology and kindly permitted me to read some of his book manuscript; Milos Velimirovic shared his knowledge of musicology; and Philipp Fehl, the only art historian whose asides always illuminate, made me understand better what I was trying to do in chapter 4. I am grateful to my friends and colleagues, Alex Chambers, Madeleine Doran, Mark Eccles, and Joe Wittreich, for their constant support and encouragement. Individual chapters have been improved by Carol Kagay, Bob Presson, Andy Weiner, Bill and Camille Slights, and Kim Veltman, who also showed me how to construct a perspective picture. The two graces of the University of Wisconsin English department, Diane Boland and Jane Renneberg, typed the whole thing; and Ray the young helped assemble the manuscript. John Wallace and John Shawcross must be singled out for special thanks.

Portions of chapters 2 and 6 were published in different form in *ELH*, *PMLA*, and the *Journal of the Warburg and Courtauld Institutes*. They are reprinted by permission of the editors, the Modern Language Association of America (for *PMLA*), and The Johns Hopkins University Press (for *ELH*). The illustrations are reproduced by permission of the Milton S. Eisenhower Library of The Johns Hopkins University, the Scolar Press Ltd., the Glasgow University Library, and the Folger Shakespeare Library.

My greatest professional obligation is to Jackson Cope. He first suggested writing this book and had faith in it even before I was convinced of its reality. I regret, selfishly, that my slowness in completing it has deprived me of four valued readers—Bob Presson; Rosalie Colie; Don Allen, who would be glad to escape reading another book; and Earl Wasserman, who could never read enough of them.

THE
MIND'S
EMPIRE

ONE
CHAPMAN'S
POETICS

Jonson once thought "that Done himself for not being understood would perish."[1] He could not have anticipated the phenomenon of twentieth-century taste that for some three decades would elevate Donne's poetry to an enormous popularity, in large part because of its difficulty. One of the side effects of this now-receded Donne boom was to lend a satellite reputation to George Chapman, Donne's older contemporary, who has been described as "perhaps the most complex author of his age."[2] In a famous ricocheting definition T. S. Eliot pronounced, "In Chapman especially there is a direct sensuous apprehension of thought, or a recreation of thought into feeling, which is exactly what we find in Donne."[3] Eliot's imprimatur has proved a mixed blessing. While the metaphysical aura has caused Chapman to be read more widely than at any time since the enthusiastic appreciation of the Romantics, it also established a mental set which ensured that much of the reading was a misreading.

Only since Donne's greater light has faded to the point that "now his flasks / Send forth light squibs, no constant rayes," has it been possible to see that Chapman belongs to an entirely different poetic constellation. The shift in attitude can be measured by a pair of comprehensive Chapman studies: in 1951 Jean Jacquot found it necessary to devote half a dozen pages to the question of "Chapman et Donne"; fifteen years later Donne all but vanishes from the index to Millar MacLure's book as MacLure, with a regretful bow to Eliot, concludes that Chapman's verse "is not like anything we have come to understand as 'metaphysical' poetry."[4] Nevertheless, old habits of thought change slowly. One may assent intellectually to the proposition that "The King is dead," while

---

[1]C. H. Herford, Percy and Evelyn Simpson, eds., *Ben Jonson*, 11 vols. (Oxford, 1925), 1: 138.

[2]S. K. Heninger, Jr., *A Handbook of Renaissance Meteorology, With Particular Reference to Elizabethan and Jacobean Literature* (Durham, N.C., 1960), p. 183.

[3]T. S. Eliot, "The Metaphysical Poets," *Selected Essays, 1917-1932* (London, 1949), p. 286. Originally published in 1921. Eliot's lead is followed by, *inter alia*, Elizabeth Holmes, *Aspects of Elizabethan Imagery* (Oxford, 1929), pp. 97–101; George Williamson, *The Donne Tradition* (Cambridge, Mass., 1930), chap. 3; and Mario Praz, *The Flaming Heart* (Garden City, N.Y., 1958), pp. 192–94.
   Eliot's attraction to the metaphysicals has been placed in historical perspective by Frank Kermode, *The Romantic Image* (New York, 1957); Joseph E. Duncan, *The Revival of Metaphysical Poetry: The History of a Style, 1800 to the Present* (Minneapolis, 1959); and Arnold Stein, "Donne and the 1920's: A Problem in Historical Consciousness," *ELH*, 27 (1960): 16–29.

[4]Jean Jacquot, *George Chapman (1559–1634): sa vie, sa poésie, son théâtre, sa pensée* (Paris, 1951), pp. 249–54; and Millar MacLure, *George Chapman: A Critical Study* (Toronto, 1966), p. 228. It must be remarked that Jacquot, whose study remains the most original book on Chapman, finds as many differences as similarities between Chapman and Donne. In his

still finding it very difficult to give up lifelong royalist attitudes. We have ceased to find the metaphysical label very pertinent or illuminating for Chapman's poetry; yet, because the preoccupation with style generated by Eliot so drastically narrowed our perception of the poetry, the mental set remains in force, even though we have declared the central premise invalid.

As a case in point, consider a recent article by Charles K. Cannon, which seems representative in its wrongness.[5] According to Cannon, Chapman's "major contribution to poetic theory in the English Renaissance" was the recognition that "sense is immanent in sound; meaning begets the shape of a poem's language and vice versa" (p. 249). Since he can adduce no evidence that Chapman intended to contribute anything of the sort, Cannon is forced to denigrate and explain away Chapman's own critical comments. By focusing upon a post-Renaissance conception of style Cannon understandably fails to perceive any larger poetic structure that Chapman himself might recognize. The *Hymnvs in Noctem* is like "a surrealist painting" with symphonic "movements" and "crescendoes" (p. 256), but also manages to suggest "an Hegelian dialectical progression" (p. 258). For Cannon, describing Chapman's "alogical progression through association" (p. 259), Rosemond Tuve might never have lived. Rejecting the idea of Chapman as a metaphysical, Cannon rather pretentiously invokes Joseph Frank's concept of "Spatial Form in Modern Literature" to arrive at the conclusion: "The poet can only express this dark matter in a dark style. Style and meaning become aspects of a unity" (p. 262). By this reading not only is Chapman not a metaphysical, he becomes an anachronistic modern who eschews the rhetoric and logic to which he gives lip service.[6] Ironically, the aesthetic which Frank abstracted from the creative works of Eliot, Pound, Joyce, and Djuna Barnes here substitutes for Eliot's own critical formulation. One brand of twenties impressionism simply replaces another.

In this chapter I wish to disinter the Donne comparison, but only to prevent the spirit from walking any further. By extending the comparison beyond the largely accidental and superficial stylistic resemblances, I want to emphasize how thoroughly different the two poets are; and, by so doing, to better establish Chapman's own poetic identity. If Chapman

---

conclusion, pp. 280–81, he uses Eliot's description of the metaphysical learned sensibility—"their mode of feeling was directly and freshly altered by their reading and thought"—to vitiate the source-scholar's depreciation of Chapman's originality.

[5]Charles K. Cannon, "Chapman on the Unity of Style and Meaning," *Journal of English and Germanic Philology*, 68(1969): 245–64.

[6]My quarrel is not with the application of a modern aesthetic to Renaissance poetry, but with the failure to make that application historically plausible. Jackson Cope has adapted Frank's theory in a reading of Milton; first, however, he troubles to establish a consonance between the twentieth-century and the seventeenth-century context of ideas; see *The Metaphoric Structure of Paradise Lost* (Baltimore, 1962). See also Joseph Frank, "Spatial Form in Modern Literature," *Sewanee Review*, 53(1945): 221–40, 433–56, 643–53.

can be twinned with any one of his contemporaries, a far better case could be made for Edmund Spenser than for John Donne.[7]

Let us begin with the celebrated obscurity. Donne's obscurity, to summarize the obvious, is the cumulative result of syntactic distortion, logical density, ellipsis and compression, learned allusions, farfetched conceits, harshness in diction and metrics. The style largely derives from satiric tradition, in which such writings are supposed to be rough, "dark," and displeasing; and it receives personal reinforcement from Donne's anxiety not to be mistaken for a professional poet, for someone who sweats to make his verse ingratiating.[8] Donne apparently began his career writing satiric epigrams and verse satires, and the training stuck when he graduated to other kinds of poetry. Rosemond Tuve observed that "Donne's 'sonets' and elegies are many of them virtually short satires, combining the conventions of philosophical dialectic (*genus humile*) with the *energia* and diminishing figures of rhetoric's demonstrative 'dispraise,' and both with the conventionally harsh tone of satire."[9]

In analyzing the imagery of *Hero and Leander,* Tuve isolated two reasons for Chapman's obscurity—his fondness for "introducing an unexpected logical complication into an image" and his frequent assumption of technical learning on the reader's part.[10] He also uses heavily figures of substitution (such as periphrasis and antonomasia); makes a single image carry multiple rhetorical functions; tends to compress rather than amplify or reiterate; and organizes frequently by contraries, antitheses, and paradox. Most of these characteristics could be associated with Donne as easily as with Chapman. Language, therefore, serves as a more clearly differentiating tool. Whereas Donne's diction has a persistent tendency toward "lowness," the satirist's deflating, undercutting "realistic" vision, Chapman's "idealism" nudges his diction in the opposite direction, toward inflation or grandiloquence, the "full and haightned stile" praised by Webster.[11]

---

[7]MacLure, too, perceives some Spenserian affinities; see his Index entry, p. 241. Of course, the answer one gets depends on the question one asks. Concentrating upon ethical attitude, rather than poetic style or mode, Douglas Bush connects Chapman with Greville and Daniel; see *English Literature in the Earlier Seventeenth Century, 1600–1660,* rev. ed. (Oxford, 1962), pp. 96–97.

[8]On the pose of amateur, see A. Alvarez, *The School of Donne* (London, 1961), pp. 27–40. This study, while valuable in parts, mainly is interesting as a belated attempt to revive the Eliot thesis.

[9]Rosemond Tuve, *Elizabethan and Metaphysical Imagery* (Chicago, 1947), p. 243. See also pp. 136–37, 228–30, 242–43; and a pair of articles by Arnold Stein, "Donne's Harshness and Elizabethan Tradition," *Studies in Philology,* 41(1944): 390–409; "Donne's Obscurity and the Elizabethan Tradition," *ELH,* 13(1946): 98–118.

[10]Tuve, pp. 267–68.

[11]I have adapted some conclusions from an unpublished paper by Janet Gemmill. On the thought by contraries and elevation of language, see MacLure, pp. 225–28. For Webster's

But the distance between the two poets becomes fully apparent when we define the ends which the stylistic obscurity is meant to serve, its function as one particular technique in a larger poetic mode. Chapman predominantly wrote allegorical poetry; Donne did not. Consequently Chapman employed "allegorical rhetoric" or—to borrow Edgar Wind's more graceful phrase—"the language of mysteries." Michael Murrin has very helpfully distinguished the differing rhetorical situations presupposed by allegorical and oratorical poets:

> The allegorical poet served the truth which he had received under inspiration, and this truth exercised the primary operative control over his rhetoric. He did not really cater to his audience but tried to preserve his truth intact and communicate it to those capable of understanding it. This requirement forced him to deal with two different audiences: the many who could never accept his revelation and the few who could. He had, therefore, simultaneously to reveal and not to reveal his truth, and for this double purpose he cloaked his truth in the veils of allegory. The many reacted with pleasure to his symbolic tales, and the few knew how to interpret them.[12]

Murrin argues that the orator's concern with an immediate audience dictates that he will derive his arguments from the popular beliefs of the audience and strive for clarity of presentation. The allegorist, in contrast, begins with an absolute truth, which creates a presentational dilemma; while he must protect his truth from the unworthy multitude by concealing it, he must conceal in such a way as to reveal it to the few prepared to understand and accept.[13] Accordingly, whereas the orator aims at lucidity of style, the allegorist darkens his by recourse to any one of several accepted devices—riddle, enigma, parable, fable, myth, irony, ambiguity.

The mode of Donne's poetry falls somewhere between the two extremes. His deliberate difficulty and his disdain for the general audience parallel the allegorist's desire to save his message for the few initiates. But Donne's whole manner of truth-telling smacks more of shared commonplaces than of wisdom handed down from above; and a consideration of the Donne circle leads A. Alvarez to believe that the poems were not obscure to its members: "They had too much in common, they used

---

remark, see the Preface to *The White Devil*, in Joel E. Spingarn, ed., *Critical Essays of the Seventeenth Century* (1908; reprint ed., Bloomington, 1957), 1: 66.

[12]Michael Murrin, *The Veil of Allegory: Some Notes toward a Theory of Allegorical Rhetoric in the English Renaissance* (Chicago, 1969), p. 168.

[13]Why must the allegorist conceal his message? Both to protect his truth and to protect himself. Murrin suggests that prophets in antiquity presupposed rejection by the many and set out to be deliberately divisive. See *The Veil of Allegory*, pp. 21–32; on the differences between allegory and oratory, see especially pp. 3–20. For the connection with religious mysteries, see also Edgar Wind, *Pagan Mysteries in the Renaissance* (New Haven, 1958).

the same shorthand."[14] Donne, it would seem, assumes the oratorical situation but radically narrows his audience to a select coterie.

Consistent with his professed refusal to take poetry seriously, Donne left us no poetics, critical commentaries, or even conversations with a Drummond. With the exception of the forced *Ivstification of Andromeda Liberata*, Chapman's only critical remarks are scattered in the prefaces, dedications, epistles, and commendations which he wrote for specific occasions over the course of his career. The high degree of consistency in theory and attitude permits us to read these serial proclamations as a coherent and fully articulated statement of a poetics. He separates his audience into the many and the few, always expressing contempt for the former and admiration for the latter: "I rest as resolute as *Seneca*, satisfying my selfe if but a few, if one, or if none like it."[15] "The prophane multitude I hate, & onlie consecrate my strange Poems to these serching spirits, whom learning hath made noble, and nobilitie sacred" (*Poems*, p. 49). Chapman states the obvious with admirable succinctness in an epistle "To the Understander": "You are not every bodie."[16] The elite to whom he looks for understanding are elevated to that position by learning and nobility, with the emphasis on the former; the vulgar, "the base, ignoble, barbarous, giddie multitude" (*Poems*, p. 329), are characterized by ignorance and passion, addicted to rumor and opinion rather than to learning and judgment. The undertone of satisfaction in Chapman's defense of *Andromeda Liberata* arises not merely from an Elizabethan enjoyment of a good quarrel but from the pleasure, after a twenty-year career, of having been proved *right*—the vulgar rabble by maliciously misinterpreting his poem have demonstrated what he believed all along, that they are incapable of comprehending an allegory.

In his justification Chapman advances the argument, quoting Plato, that poetry inherently is ambiguous: "*Est enim ipsa Natura vniuersa Poesis aenigmatum plena, nec quiuis eam dignoscit.*"[17] The context, however, makes it certain that he is speaking of allegorical or mythological poetry, the "misteries and allegoricall fictions of *Poesie*." At various

[14]Alvarez, p. 40. Murrin, pp. 189–95, also assigns Donne a middle position, but for different reasons. Stein, "Donne's Obscurity," pp. 107–8, notes that satiric figures and tropes are related to allegory and that in a few poems Donne does use allegory.

[15]Phyllis Brooks Bartlett, ed., *The Poems of George Chapman* (1941; reprint ed., New York, 1962), p. 19 (cited hereafter as *Poems*).

[16]Allardyce Nicoll, ed., *Chapman's Homer* (New York, 1956): 1.548. The *odi profanum volgus et arceo* formula originates with Horace (*Carmina* 3. 1.1), but the platonic adaptation puts it to a use which Horace seems not to have intended. See Steele Commager, *The Odes of Horace* (New Haven, 1962), pp. 16–20.

That Chapman is sincere in his devotion to learning and nobility of the spirit may be inferred from the several poems which he dedicated to commoners—Matthew Roydon, Thomas Harriot, Henry Jones.

[17]*Poems*, p. 327. He quotes from the spurious *Alcibiades II*. See the Loeb edition, trans. W. R. M. Lamb, rev. ed. (Cambridge, Mass., 1955), p. 261.

times Chapman endorses all the standard justifications for poetic obscurity.[18] He wishes to keep the "base and prophane *Vulgare*" from debasing his truth: "Poesie is the flower of the Sunne, & disdains to open to the eye of a candle. So kings hide their treasures & counsels from the vulgar, *ne euilescant*."[19] The obscurity exists only in the mind of the reader who is incapable of understanding the truth: "it may perhaps seeme darke to ranke riders or readers that have no more soules than burbolts: but to your comprehension and in it selfe I knew it is not."[20] And, finally, the obscurity enhances the value of the truth by creating obstacles to be overcome by the understanding: "rich Minerals are digd out of the bowels of the earth not found in the superficies and dust of it" (*Poems*, p. 49). In his commitment to allegorical obscurity, Chapman seems unusually acute in grasping implications of the stylistic opposition to the oratorical mode which this commitment creates. Rather than perspicuity or clarity, which is the stylistic ideal of a Jonson, Chapman maintains "That, *Enargia*, or cleerenes of representation, requird in absolute Poems is not the perspicuous deliuery of a lowe inuention; but high, and harty inuention exprest in most significant, and vnaffected phrase" (*Poems*, p. 49). He associates the attack upon *Andromeda Liberata* with Demosthenes' slur upon the Delphic Oracle (*Poems*, p. 329); and he believes that the oratorical standard of audience-oriented poetry runs counter to the true nature of poetry:

> But that Poesie should be as peruiall as Oratorie, and plainnes her speciall ornament, were the plaine way to barbarisme: and to make the Asse runne proude of his eares; to take away strength from Lyons, and giue Cammels hornes. [*Poems*, p. 49]

In fact, if we use Murrin's description as a standard, Chapman's poetics read like a program illustration to the theory of allegorical poetry. It begins and ends with truth. "Nor is this all-comprising *Poesie*, phantastique, or meere fictiue; but the most material, and doctrinall illations of *Truth*" (*Poems*, p. 407):

> Yet euer held in high Reuerence and Aucthority; as supposed to conceale, within the vtter barke (as their Eternities approue) some sappe of hidden Truth: As either some dimme and obscure prints of diuinity, and the sacred history; Or the grounds of naturall, or rules of morall Philosophie, for the recommending of some vertue, or curing some vice in generall. [*Poems*, p. 327]

---

[18]See Murrin, pp. 10–12. In the fullest study of the matter Margaret Bottrall argues that Chapman had a "natural tendency" toward obscure expression which determined his adoption of obscurantist literary theories (an unilluminating chicken-or-egg question); but she, too, finds a consistent defense in his statements. See "George Chapman's Defense of Difficulty in Poetry," *Criterion*, 16(1936–37): 638–54.

[19]*Critical Essays of the Seventeenth Century*, 1: 68.

[20]*Chapman's Homer*, 1: 548.

Because Poetry is an epiphany of Truth, Chapman persistently associates her with learning and wisdom; "*Philosophy* retirde to darkest caues / She can discouer" (*Poems*, p. 384). Although poetry can fulfill any number of particular instructional or doctrinal purposes, the simplest and most accurate description of its function would be that it disseminates the exact pattern or form of truth:

> And, as in a spring,
> The plyant water, mou'd with any thing
> Let fall into it, puts her motion out
> In perfect circles, that moue round about
> The gentle fountaine, one another, raising:
> So Truth, and Poesie worke; so Poesie blazing,
> All subiects falne in her exhaustlesse fount,
> Works most exactly; makes a true account
> Of all things to her high discharges giuen,
> Till all be circular, and round as heauen.

[*Poems*, p. 387]

The poet receives this truth by inspiration, a "*Diuinus furor*" which Chapman describes as "a perfection directly infused from God" (*Poems*, p. 408).[21] As Chapman explains the process in *The Teares of Peace*, by exacting mental preparation and arduous study the poet readies himself for the silent moment of spiritual illumination which he likens to the Hermetic *gnosis* and to Pythagoras's inner perception of the music of the spheres. Paradoxically, the poet's job is to transform this silent transfiguration into human speech in order to ravish other men with the desire for this truth. Poetry "Erect[s] him past his human Period / And heighten[s] his transition into God" (*Poems*, p. 306). Because of this platonized conception of "diuine infusion," Chapman associates himself with the biblical prophets, who are for him, as was Moses for Pico della Mirandola, poets.[22]

Although Franck L. Schoell long ago proved Chapman's large and direct indebtedness to the writings of Marsilio Ficino, it remained for Jacquot to demonstrate the pattern to the pieces, the centrality and consistency of Renaissance platonism to Chapman's thought and his poetics.[23] Ficino's massive effort to prove the philosophic harmony of

[21]See also Chapman's comments on his *Memorable Maske*, in T. M. Parrott, ed., *The Comedies* (1914; reprint ed., New York, 1961), 2: 444. Jacquot, p. 235, and MacLure, pp. 34–35, discuss the *furor poeticus*. For the background, see Robert V. Merrill with Robert J. Clements, "The Four Furies," *Platonism in French Renaissance Poetry* (New York, 1957), pp. 118–44.

[22]*Critical Essays*, 1: 67. For Pico see "Oration," *On the Dignity of Man, On Being and the One, Heptaplus*, trans. C. G. Wallis, Paul J. W. Miller, Douglas Carmichael, Library of Liberal Arts, no. 227 (Indianapolis, 1965), pp. 12–14, 29–30; "First Proem," *Heptaplus*, pp. 67–75.

[23]Franck L. Schoell, *Études sur l'Humanisme continental en Angleterre a la fin de la Renaissance* (Paris, 1926); Jacquot, pp. 199–231, 233–41. Jacquot states, "Cependant, c'est à Chap-

Plato and Christ had, as well, aesthetic and stylistic consequences that were perhaps most explicitly stated by Pico in the *Heptaplus*, his commentary upon the book of Genesis.[24] According to Edgar Wind, the "hidden mysteries" concept was disseminated mainly from Plato's fanciful notion that a true philosopher is like one who has undergone a religious initiation and passed beyond the level comprehended by the vulgar populace. Thus inspired by Plato and later systematized by Plotinus, a figurative use of religious terminology and imagery became a staple of philosophic discourse. Armed with this historical precedent, the Renaissance platonists—particularly the Florentine group and their followers— as a matter of course figured their profound truths in poetic myths which were deliberately expressed in exotic styles.[25] We should not be surprised that, when they turned to the Bible, they read with the same vision.

Pico tells us that "Plato himself concealed his doctrines beneath coverings of allegory, veils of myth, mathematical images, and unintelligible signs of fugitive meaning." But Plato was only a "Moses Atticus." Pico believes that Christ chose to use the parable because it is an exclusive mode of discourse: "he proclaimed [the Gospel] to the crowd in parables; and separately, to the few disciples who were permitted to understand the mysteries of the kingdom of heaven openly and without figures. He did not even reveal everything to those few, since they were not fit for everything. . . ."[26] If Plato was an Attic Moses, the converse holds true. Moses was an Hebraic Plato, who learned the secrets of the Egyptians and who wrote Genesis according to the pattern of creation he learned on Sinai, thereby secretly imparting to skilled readers, like Pico, the mysteries of all things. Pico, of course, modeled his own style of writing, described by Wind as "contrived" and "conceited," to conform to the

---

man que la litterature anglaise de la Renaissance doit l'exposé le plus complet de la théorie platonicienne de la poésie" (p. 234). On the platonism, see also Ennis Rees, *The Tragedies of George Chapman: Renaissance Ethics in Action* (Cambridge, Mass., 1954), pp. 13–19. I disagree flatly with Ruth Wallerstein's conclusion: "He is not touched at the core by his neo-Platonism." *Studies in Seventeenth-Century Poetic* (Madison, 1950), p. 89.

Since Frances A. Yates's important study, *Giordano Bruno and the Hermetic Tradition* (Chicago, 1964), requires us to reassess our conception of Renaissance platonism, I should specify that I use the term "platonism" to include both neoplatonism and Hermeticism. I am aware of the strong Hermetic element in Chapman, who advised a potential patron to "Heare Royall *Hermes* sing th'Egyptian Lawes" (*Poems*, p. 396). But it seems unprofitable, if not impossible, to differentiate the two, and perhaps "platonism" has the broader utility as a label.

[24]See Murrin, pp. 119–29, and passim; Maren-Sofie Røstvig, "*Ars Aeterna*: Renaissance Poetics and Theories of Divine Creation," *Mosaic*, 3 (1970): 40–61; R. B. Waddington, "The Sun at the Center: Structure as Meaning in Pico della Mirandola's *Heptaplus*," *Journal of Medieval and Renaissance Studies*, 3(1973): 69–86; also E. N. Tigerstedt, "The Poet as Creator: Origins of a Metaphor," *Comparative Literature Studies*, 5(1968): 455–88. For the aesthetic consequences of Florentine platonism more generally, see André Chastel, *Marsile Ficin et l'Art* (Geneva, 1954).

[25]Wind, pp. 13–23.

[26]"First Proem," *Heptaplus*; quotations, pp. 68–69.

theory: "In attempting to mark the disparity between verbal instrument and mystical object, Pico made his own language sound at once provocative and evasive, as if to veil were implicitly to reveal the sacred fire in an abundance of dense and acrid smoke."[27] The persona selected to speak this "language of mysteries" will be the very antithesis of the orator with his stance of apparent openness and candor. The role assumed by the allegorical rhetor or poet partakes of the biblical prophet, the wise man, the oracle, but usually it goes beyond this to the hierophant and mystagogue. Henry Reynolds speaks of how

> those old wise *AEgyptian* Priests beganne to search out the Misteries of Nature (which was at first the whole worlds only diuinity), they deuized, to the end to retaine among themselves what they had found, lest it should be abused and vilefied by being deliuered to the vulgar, certaine markes they called *Hieroglyphicks* or sacred grauings. And more then thus they deliuered little; or what euer it was, yet alwaies *dissimulanter*, and in Enigma's and mysticall riddles, as their following disciples also did. And this prouizo of theirs those Images of *Sphynx* they placed before all their Temples did insinuate, and which should by riddles and enigmaticall knotts be kept inuiolate from the prophane Multitude.[28]

The image of the sphinx before the temple is not a bad one for figuring the rhetorical situation of the allegorical poet—always forbidding, yet tantalizing enough to entice the potential Oedipus who just may solve the meaning of his riddle.

In the poems where Chapman most directly addresses himself to issues of poetic and religious inspiration, *The Shadow of Night* and *The Teares of Peace*, he adapts personae which both Pico and Reynolds would have recognized as appropriate for the stance of the platonic mystagogue. With the first he wraps himself in the mythology of Orpheus, *priscus theologus* as well as *poeticus*, and in the second he suggests an identification with a peculiarly Renaissance Hercules, not the strong man but the wise man, the god of eloquence whom he conflates with Hermes Trismegistus. Wind has remarked the elements of irony and mockery present in Plato's original identification of the philosopher with the heirophant of the mystery cults; and, although the humor was largely missed by the platonic exegetes of the Renaissance, playfulness at least fitfully reappeared in the spirit of *serio ludere*.[29] But the mysteries of which Chapman is custodian permit no such lightness. To approach poetic "skill" with understanding requires an initiation of the spirit: "Now what a supererogation in wit this is, to thinke skil so mightilie

---

[27]Wind, p. 18.

[28]*Mythomystes*, in *Critical Essays*, 1: 156. For Chapman's view of the relations of hieroglyphics and enigma to poetry, see his *Ivstification* (*Poems*, p. 327).

[29]Wind, pp. 14–15 on Plato; and pp. 179–88 on *serio ludere*.

pierst with their loues, that she should prostitutely shew them her secrets, when she will scarcely be lookt vpon by others but with inuocation, fasting, watching; yea not without hauing drops of their soules like an heauenly familiar" (*Poems*, p. 19). And woe betide the reader who approaches Homer with unlaundered mind:

> Lest with foule hands you touch these holy Rites;
>   And with preiudicacies too prophane,
> Passe Homer, in your other Poets sleights;
>   Wash here. In this Porch to his numerous Phane.
> Heare ancient Oracles speake, and tell you whom
>   You haue to censure.

[*Poems*, p. 390]

The entire role of vatic poet and the religious analogy of the inspired prophet/priest who simultaneously protects his sacred trust from the many and imparts it to the fit few, has significant ramifications for the question of poetic form. Put very simply, when the afflatus descends upon the prophet, he loses his human identity, becoming instrumental to the voice of God, no more than a conveyance to the Word which transiently inhabits him. When Ananias questioned Saul's worthiness, the Lord replied, "Go thy way: for his is a chosen vessel unto me" (Acts 9:15); and the Lord touched the mouth of Jeremiah telling him "Behold, I have put my words in thy mouth" (Jer. 1:9). Saul and Jeremiah have far more in common as prophets than they had as private men; they assume a conventionalized role that prepares the audience to expect a certain kind of message, but the message always takes priority in interest over the particular vessel chosen as mouthpiece. The Lord instructed Jeremiah to "speak . . . all the words that I command thee to speak unto them; diminish not a word" (Jer. 26:2).[30] But, just as the personality of the appointed individual is effaced by the conventional figure of the prophet, so that containing vessel inescapably shapes the words which he speaks. Prophetic utterance assumes standard forms which are themselves a reflex of the prophetic persona. Presumably Jeremiah tried to heed very strictly the Lord's admonition to "diminish not a word"; ironically, though, even people who do not have the remotest idea of what Jeremiah prophesied are aware that he gave his name to a conventional literary structure, the jeremiad. To borrow the words of a tiresome latter-day prophet, here the medium really is the message.

What does this mean for the prophetic poet or the allegorical poet? First, I would suggest, it means that for them, as for the public oratorical poet, the question of genre occupies a position of fundamental importance. The selection of a poetic genre as the vessel for his word immedi-

---

[30]Murrin, pp. 29–30, comments on the Jeremiah quotations.

ately accomplishes two things for the poet: it supplies him with a formal organizational principle for his matter; and it guarantees at least a generally appropriate level of response from his audience. The concept of poetic genres arises from a vision which orders human experience in a hierarchy. Public poets, whether political or religious, tend to work in the upper range of the hierarchy. Once again the difference between Donne and Chapman may be instructive.

The mode of Donne's poetry is primarily private, aimed at a small audience of intimates or particular individuals;[31] his stylistic level gravitates to the low, for satiric or instructional purposes, and the middle, the vehicle for the familiar epistle. In consequence genre means relatively little to Donne; and with the bulk of his verse ascertaining the correct generic provenance appears to be a less valuable starting point than it is with most Renaissance poets. As Donald Guss observes, "In general, Donne seems to write as courtier rather than *vates*, and to be simply careless of genre."[32] When he does not ignore genre, frequently he stands it on its head, parodies it, or distorts it beyond recognition. There are no sonnets in his *Songs and Sonets*.[33] As innumerable readers have attested, Donne's remarkable simulation of a direct, colloquial, speaking voice overpowers other elements and tends to level out formal distinctions in the poems, which is merely another way of saying that genre does not hold a large place in his poetic strategy. Trying his hand at the epithalamion, the most relentlessly conventional of poetic forms, Donne produced two insipid specimens with which he seems uncomfortable; only by burlesquing the form in the *Epithalamion Made at Lincolnes Inne* was he able to put his usual stamp of identity upon it.[34] Any good poet, however, must be a Gulliver whom the ropes of Lilliputian critics cannot successfully immobilize. The two *Anniversaries* are the conspicuous exception to his antigeneric bent—formal, allegorical, elevated, vatic. The persona of the first is the Mosaic lawgiver (457–66); of the second, a prophet of grace: "Thou art the Proclamation; and I ame / The Trumpet, at whose voice the people came."[35]

[31]For the "symptoms" of private and public modes, see Earl Miner, *The Metaphysical Mode from Donne to Cowley* (Princeton, 1969), pp. 4–5.

[32]Donald L. Guss, *John Donne, Petrarchist* (Detroit, 1966), p. 196, n. 1.

[33]The so-called *Sonnet, The Token* has an extra quatrain, though the *Holy Sonnets* show that he could compose more conventional ones when he wanted to.

[34]See David Novarr, "Donne's 'Epithalamion Made at Lincoln's Inn': Context and Date," *Review of English Studies,*" 7(1956): 250–63.

[35]I quote from Donne, *The Complete Poetry*, ed. John T. Shawcross (Garden City, N.Y.: Anchor Series, 1967). The fact that the major studies of the *Anniversaries* have been rhetorical and allegorical lends implicit support to my description. For the former, see Louis L. Martz, *The Poetry of Meditation*, rev. ed. (New Haven, 1962), pp. 211–48, and O. B. Hardison, Jr., *The Enduring Monument* (Chapel Hill, 1962), pp. 162–86; and the latter, e.g., Marjorie Nicolson, *The Breaking of the Circle*, rev. ed. (New York, 1960), pp. 81–106. See also Hardison, pp. 69–71, on "The ranking of genres."

Chapman's very strong preoccupation with genre may be most noticeable in his dramatic works; particularly in comedy he seemed to try ceaseless modulations of form to give an audience just the desired perspective upon the story material. We have from him a commedia dell'arte parody of Marlowe, possibly the first humors comedy, a "New" comedy, tragicomedy, satiric comedy, attempts to blend serious platonic love with farce. They are far from uniformly successful; but they evidence a very up-to-date knowledge of comedic theory and practice, both in London and on the continent, and, possibly because comedy was a less serious genre to Chapman, a willingness to venture an almost avant-garde experimentalism. In his nondramatic verse—with a single and deliberate exception, *Ovids Banquet of Sence*—Chapman published nothing that did not have a distinct generic identity, permitting his audience at once to recognize the general type of a poem and from there to ascertain its particular properties. Often a generic precisian, he gives us not plain funeral elegies, but epicedes, epitaphs, and anniversaries.

Whereas Donne's "voice" is primarily confined to poetry appropriate to the middle and low styles, Chapman descends to the middle style in his dedicatory epistles and sonnets, normally inhabiting the top register of epic and heroic poem, religious hymn, public ceremony. He left no pastoral, disclaimed being a satirist (*Poems*, p. 330), and his invective against Ben Jonson was never published. Chapman works consciously in a public mode. The meditative voice did not affect him; *Goodfriday, 1613. Riding Westward* can cast little light on *A Hymne to our Sauiour*. His religious poems are private only in the sense that the actions of the hierophant at the altar are, while fully displayed, inscrutable and isolated. Chapman's most private poems are his translations of Petrarch's *Penitential Psalms*, but even these are exercises in a long tradition. His only love poems assume the viewpoint of society rather than of a participant. Genre and voice in this way interact to establish the public, ceremonial character of most of the verse.

Where necessary, conventional genres are tailored to suit the special requirements of the hierophant's role. In *The Teares of Peace* the medieval dream-vision form oddly subsumes the revelation of Pimander to Hermes Trismegistus; and the two hymns which comprise *The Shadow of Night* are not merely religious but Orphic. Henry Reynolds said, paraphrasing Pico's judgment on the *Orphic Hymns*:

> There is nothing of greater efficacy then the hymnes of *Orpheus* in naturall Magick, if the fitting musick, intention of the minde, and other circumstances which are knowne to the wise, bee considered and applyed. And againe,— *that they are no lesse power in naturall magick*, or to the vnderstanding thereof, *then the Psalmes of Dauid* are in the *Caball*, or to vnderstand the *Cabalistick* Science by.[36]

---

[36]*Mythomystes*, in *Critical Essays*, 1: 166.

As we shall see, Chapman exploits fitting music, intention, and "other circumstances" to invest his hymns fully with the aura of Orphic magic.

To complete the running comparison: by and large Donne's poetry is linear, dramatic, a mimesis of particular psychological states. Chapman's poetry is iconic, narrative, and presents universals, as he says himself, *"non Socratem sed Hominem"* (*Poems*, p. 327). Chapman's true poetic peers are Spenser and Milton, both vatic, public, ceremonious poets as conscious of form and genre as Chapman. The pernicious consequence of the Eliot-Donne-metaphysical syndrome has been the tendency to look upon Chapman primarily as a stylist. The microscopy of style analysis conditioned Chapman's critics not to expect any large organizational principles, such as mode, genre, structure, so they have seldom noticed any. The very title of Havelock Ellis' essay, *George Chapman; With Illustrative Passages* (Bloomsbury, 1934), proclaims a critical assumption; one can detach and appreciate the purple passages without being too concerned about the poems as wholes. The "anthology of passages" approach even has its survivals with MacLure, who is wont to praise a poem as being "not without an occasional felicity."[37] The grounds underlying such judgments have been best articulated by Heninger:

> Chapman's greatest asset was a sensitivity to words comparable to Marlowe's, and he retained much of the energetic forcefulness that enlivens the best Elizabethan poetry. . . . Chapman's inattention to form, in both his poems and plays, is no doubt the major defect that accounts for his failure to please succeeding generations. His most readable works are the translations of Homer and Hesiod, where the form was already provided and he needed to supply only words. Chapman lacked the ability to order his materials into well-organized entities—but throughout his works . . . there are isolated passages of surprising beauty and power.

Heninger concludes:

> Chapman never learned to arrange his images so that the completed poem has a well-ordered structure. As a rule, his compositions are long and formless . . . we might wish that he had learned structural discipline for his poems.[38]

I have no dispute with Heninger's acute discussion of imagery; but the partiality of his examination leads, I believe, to mistaken conclusions about the poems as wholes. On the contrary, Chapman was very keenly attentive to the larger elements of form, structure, overall organization;

[37]MacLure, p. 70. Concerning genre, he remarks that Chapman "was anti-Aristotelian in his notion of poetic creation" (p. 9), and that "for Chapman the genres are instrumental, to be spoken through, dislocated, rather than rested in" (p. 229). I quite agree that his use of genre is instrumental, that it is a preliminary organizational feature and less significant than what I shall speak of as the "inner form"; but I am not sure I see the dislocation.

[38]Heninger, pp. 183, 199.

and in his best works, as I will seek to demonstrate, his imaginativeness and control of them allow him to fashion poems of a high order. Indeed, one could maintain that the frequent unevenness of surface texture or style results from a sometimes too exclusive devotion to form in the larger sense.

We have been considering outer form, i.e., conventional form or genre, as an extension of the persona adopted by the poet. The form of prophetic utterance in this way is as revelatory as the actual content, which of course we know from the Delphic oracles. Milton also was highly conscious of the tradition that we have described. While at school he delivered a speech on Pythagoras, who "followed the example of the poets—or, what is almost the same thing, of the divine oracles—by which no sacred and arcane mystery is ever revealed to vulgar ears without being somehow wrapped up and veiled." Later Milton finely epitomized the desired harmony of form between speaker and speech by remarking that a poet "ought himself to be a true poem."[39] Such an intimate adjustment of the two will not often be achieved by outer form alone, since genre can do no more than establish a basic frame of reference—what kind of thing it is, how it is like other examples.

Chapman works to achieve this refinement by turning to an inner form, shaping the poem to a directly symbolic purpose. A Hymne to Hymen, for instance, opens and closes with the same couplet, thus describing the form of a circle. This "circle" symbolizes the temporal progression through the wedding day which goes full circle; Hymen's embrace ("in Hymens armes, / His Circkle holds, for all their anguish, charms"); and the union of the lovers ("Two into One, contracting"; "These two, One Twyn are"). More complexly, A Coronet for his Mistresse Philosophie interweaves ten sonnets with the first line of each sonnet repeating the last line of the preceding one, the whole describing the shape of the coronet, the circle believed to be the perfect geometric form, which Chapman awards to Philosophy. In any lengthy or complicated narrative, however, the technique of symbolic ordering by manipulation of formal units and direct verbal repetitions obviously becomes less tenable, since such patterning will become either mechanically obtrusive or forgettably remote.[40] As this study will seek to demonstrate, Chapman's significant narrative poems all have in common the use of mythic form as a structuring device. Since the next chapter will develop the argument in full, I shall only outline the procedure now.

The mythic narratives function in two general ways: first, as a structure of ideas or meaning. Chapman knows thoroughly the traditional

---

[39]Quotations from Prolusion II, "On the Music of the Spheres," and An Apology for Smectymnuus, in Merritt Y. Hughes, ed., John Milton: Complete Poems and Major Prose (New York, 1957), pp. 603, 694.

[40]The device of ending a work where it began, by "commodius vicus of recirculation," survives as late as Finnegans Wake.

interpretations of the classical myths and the systematic allegorical commentaries of the Renaissance platonists and mythographers. He recognizes a consonance of meaning, a similarity in the core of truth, between the myth and matter he has selected for his narration. Second, acting upon that recognition of essential likeness, he brings it to the fore by selecting, ordering, shaping the raw narrative material in conformity with the typology of the myth. Mythic form, therefore, both describes the structure of the narrative within the conventional mold of genre and points to a transcendent form, the realm of ideas or truth which Chapman believed to be inherent in the myth. Chapman's terms for these two functions of myth within the poem are "body" and "soul." Discussing the moral and ethical truths of Homer's epics, he explains:

> To illustrate both which, in both kinds, with all height of expression, the Poet creates both a Bodie and a Soule in them. Wherein, if the Bodie (being the letter, or historie) seemes fictiue, and beyond Possibilitie to bring into Act: the sence then and Allegorie (which is the soule) is to be sought. [*Poems*, p. 407]

The body and soul analogy is commonplace, of course, in Renaissance writings, as were most of the critical *topoi* which we have discussed; but the precision with which Chapman argues it and again the consistency with which his various critical statements dovetail in a full platonic poetics suggest that he makes the analogy not because it is familiar but because for him it is true.[41] Chapman, too, would resist the inference that the poet imposes mythic form upon the hapless story by an act of will and ingenuity. He attacks the concept of poetic license, the poet being strictly confined to the laws of eternal truth, and explains poetic creation by the Plotinian concept of the release of indwelling form: using the tools of his learning the poet frees the form and soul of the myth from its imprisonment in the matter of the formless story.[42]

The anthropomorphic analogy of body and soul runs through Chapman's critical commentaries. Here the poem's fictive body offers local habitation for the soul of its truth; but, at the same time, just as the pulse of the human body indicates its state of health, so poetry acts as the "Soules Pulse" (*Poems*, pp. 305–6). Elsewhere the analogy operates on the cosmic plane: "For, as the Sunne, and Moone, are figures giuen / Of [God's] refulgent Deitie in Heauen: / So, Learning, and her Lightner, Poesie, / In earth present his fierie Maiestie" (*Poems*, p. 386). The implicit assumption of likeness between the several realms of experience

[41] I would argue that the strictness of Chapman's platonism serves to prevent the casual confusions which creep into Jonson's similar-sounding formulation: "Hence, hee is call'd a *Poet*, not hee which writeth in measure only; but that fayneth and formeth a fable, and writes things like the Truth. For, the Fable and Fiction is (as it were) the forme and Soule of any Poeticall worke, or *Poeme*" (*Discoveries*, Herford and Simpson, 8: 635).

[42] For poetic license, see *Critical Essays*, 1: 68; for Plotinian creation, see *The Teares of Peace*, 366–84, first commented upon by Elizabeth Holmes, pp. 76–77.

or planes of nature helps to explain how Chapman expected his mythic narratives in all their riddling obscurity to be penetrated by the learned few.

Wind and Murrin have shown how the Renaissance allegorists, artists, and poets preeminently chose to conceal their meaning in the veil of myth, following the model of the hierophants from the mystery religions. This, however, creates the further dilemma of how to make the myth intelligible to the approved audience. Murrin postulates the poet's solution:

> He found an answer to his rhetorical problem in his own subject matter. If the poet expresses the action of the gods in the cosmos and in the human soul, he can at least assume that the educated elite will share the same general theory about the universe as microcosm to macrocosm. It follows then that a *single* theory of the cosmos will serve to explicate the poet's allegories, even on the psychic level, and restrict the kinds of interpretation possible to any given myth. The poet's allegories can serve as a true and precise mode of communication between the few.[43]

In just this way the unvarying correspondence between microcosm, geocosm, and macrocosm acts as a principle of interpretative control in Chapman's allegorized myths. The conception, both of world vision and allegorical principle, is exactly the one which governs the *Heptaplus*. Pico states the theory underlying the entire exposition explicitly at the beginning: "Bound by chains of concord, all these worlds exchange natures as well as names with mutual liberality. From this principle (in case anyone has not yet understood it) flows the science of all allegorical interpretation."[44] If the relational pattern is constant, the reader faced with an unknown can interpret meaning confidently by recourse to the corresponding known.

At the risk of seeming deliberately perverse, I will use Donne to illustrate the poetic procedure I have presented as Chapman's. In the *Anniversaries* Donne assumes the persona of biblical prophet, first an Old Testament prophet of law and then a New Testament prophet of grace. The serious funeral occasion and the questions it provokes, the state of the world after the subject's loss and the new life of the subject's soul, dictate choice of the public, conventional, and highly rhetorical outer form; for the inner form of the narratives, Donne takes the platonic myths of the World Body and the World Soul, performing a medical anatomy upon the dead body in the first and describing the ascent of the soul to union with God in the second. The principle of cosmic allegory by which Donne expands from the microcosm of Elizabeth Drury to geocosm and macrocosm serves as interpretative control, keeping the explanations of, e.g., Ben Jonson, Marjorie Nicolson, and Frank Manley at least generally

---

[43]Murrin, p. 47; see also pp. 33–34, 47–50, 98–101.

[44]*Heptaplus*, trans. Carmichael, pp. 78–79.

consistent with Donne's own explanation that Elizabeth described "the Idea of a Woman."[45]

Donne's exception will prove to be the rule for Chapman; but the passing similarity described here will, I hope, serve to emphasize the larger differences. Chapman usually draws his myths, whether directly or indirectly, from *The Metamorphoses*; in fact, all the major poems from the 1590s are stimulated by Chapman's dislike for the changing taste in Ovidian poetry, from the mythological to the erotic. Since Donne was a force in the newer vogue for Ovidian eroticism, Thomas Carew's prediction of poetic regression after Donne's death could describe the kind of poetry Chapman had written:

> They will repeale the goodly exil'd traine
> of gods and goddesses, which in thy just raigne
> Were banish'd nobler Poems, now, with these
> The silenc'd tales o'th'Metamorphoses
> Shall stuffe their lines, and swell the windy Page,
> Till Verse refin'd by thee, in this last Age,
> Turne ballad rime, Or those old Idolls bee
> Ador'd againe, with new apostasie.[46]

Chapman's kind of poetry is old-fashioned in comparison to Donne's; but, like many late practitioners of an art, he gains greatly in sophistication because of that. The strategems which the winds of change moved Chapman to deploy result in complexities, tensions, and density that make his best work extremely interesting technically, as well as remarkable poetry. One recurring example of such sophistication would be his skill at typological adaptation of myths. As he explains in the *Ivstification*, poets "haue enlarged, or altred the Allegory, with inuentions and dispositions of their owne, to extend it to their present doctrinall and illustrous purposes" (*Poems*, p. 327). Understanding Chapman's handling of myth never is merely a matter of having read the same books, although admittedly that helps. Rather, it is necessary to appreciate the flexible systemization of myths that had evolved by Chapman's time, enabling the commentators, emblematists, and poets to adapt freely among typological equivalents, a procedure at which Chapman was a master.

All flat maps ("and I am one") are reductive, necessarily omitting attractive way stations and interesting bypaths. So the present chapter has done with the object of plotting a primary journey from Hitchin to Firenze. Many of the omissions will be restored as the subsequent chapters examine Chapman's narrative poems in full from the perspective established here. But first we shall explore his use of mythic form by looking at a great dramatic poem.

[45]For Donne and Jonson, see Herford and Simpson, 1: 133; Nicolson, pp. 81–106; and Frank Manley, ed., *John Donne: The Anniversaries* (Baltimore, 1963), pp. 10–50.

[46]"An Elegie upon the death of the Deane of Pauls, Dr. Iohn Donne," 63–70, quoted from Shawcross's Donne edition.

TWO
MYTHIC FORM: THE EXAMPLE OF BUSSY D'AMBOIS

Bussy D'Ambois will serve as our introduction to Chapman's way with mythic form. I choose his greatest tragedy as a demonstration piece for several reasons: first, despite the lapse of a decade and the difference in medium, *Bussy* exhibits a close thematic and imagistic bond to the early poetry.[1] Second, in a number of plays Chapman employs a mythological structure to shape the dramatic action and its meaning; the technique by which the "fictive bodies" of dramatic and nondramatic narratives are formed remains the same, thereby permitting the opportunity for mutual illumination.[2] And finally, since the poems examined in this study will be familiar in varying degrees to most readers, it seems helpful to start with what must be the best-known work in Chapman's canon.

Bussy D'Ambois opens with the isolated hero soliloquizing upon the condition of man and upon the necessity of virtue as a guide. His physical situation is significant, for his neglect of the light, until Monsieur enters to announce "the sun shines on thee," does more than set into play the complex light-dark imagery. The contrast between Monsieur's world of the court and Bussy's "green retreat," consanguinean to the "green world" of Renaissance comedy,[3] establishes a familiar thematic opposi-

---

[1]For connections between *Bussy* and *The Shadow of Night*, see pp. 21–22 of R. B. Waddington, "Prometheus and Hercules: The Dialectic of *Bussy D'Ambois*," *ELH*, 34 (1967): 21–48, an essay from which the body of this chapter has been adapted; also, Peter Bement, "The Imagery of Darkness and of Light in Chapman's *Bussy D'Ambois*," *Studies in Philology*, 64 (1967): 51–77.

[2]For mythic structure in *The Gentleman Usher* and *The Widow's Tears*, see Jackson I. Cope, *The Theater and the Dream: From Metaphor to Form in Renaissance Drama* (Baltimore, 1973), pp. 29–76. A. P. Hogan, "Thematic Unity in Chapman's *Monsieur D'Olive*," *Studies in English Literature*, 11 (1971): 295–306, discusses another comedy from the *Bussy* period.

[3]See Northrop Frye, "The Argument of Comedy," *English Institute Essays*, ed. D. A. Robertson, Jr. (New York, 1948), pp. 58–73, and Frye's *Anatomy of Criticism* (Princeton, 1957), pp. 182–84.

tion. Bussy is shown in and, hence, allied with prelapsarian, Golden Age nature at the outset; but for postlapsarian man, however innocent, living in such a state is not a viable choice. As in comedy, the green retreat can be only a temporary refuge; man must make his peace by transforming his society, not by fleeing it.

Despite Bussy's initial scorn of Monsieur's offer, the audience has been prepared for its ultimate acceptance by the first soliloquy, implying the speaker's readiness to venture forth upon his life's journey. The idea controlling the last half of the speech is the sea of fortune and the course of the individual life as a voyage upon it. This *topos* has been particularly associated with the epic and the epic hero.[4] If the messenger speech of 2.1 elevates Bussy to epic status by an inflated treatment of his duel, the elevation is not unexpected; it trumpets his choice of behavior entertained at the outset. Bussy concludes that as "great seamen" who have sailed "In tall ships richly built and ribb'd with brass, / To put a girdle round about the world" must call upon a "poor staid fisherman" to guide them into port,

> So when we wander furthest through the waves
> Of glassy Glory and the gulfs of State,
> Topp'd with all titles, spreading all our reaches,
> As if each private arm would sphere the world;
> We must to Virtue for her guide resort,
> Or we shall shipwrack in our safest Port.[5]

[*Bussy* 1. 1.28–33]

Thus Bussy charts a course of action for his life, not as virtuous guide to the great Monsieur but as himself a great man guided by a code of virtue.

Given the opportunity to put his plans into effect, Bussy enters the court (1.2), quarrels with established favorites, fights the duel and receives pardon (2.1), and consummates a love affair with Tamyra (2.2 and 3.1). Act 3, scene 2 begins with Bussy at the height of his success and power as the King's favorite; the middle segment of the long scene discloses the conspiracy of Guise, Monsieur, and Montsurry, now allied against Bussy, and the act closes with a confrontation of nearly open hostility between Bussy and Monsieur. The dramatic action of the play conforms to the rising-and-falling fortune pattern, with Bussy reaching the apex of his worldly achievement at the exact center of the play as forces already gather against him. Act 2 really concerns Bussy's emergence in his chosen role. Determined to rise to greatness as a courtier, he

[4]On the sea of fortune see Howard R. Patch, *The Goddess Fortuna in Medieval Literature* (Cambridge, Mass., 1927), pp. 101–7; the development of "nautical metaphor" from Virgil to Spenser is discussed by E. R. Curtius, *European Literature and the Latin Middle Ages*, trans. W. R. Trask (New York, 1953), pp. 128–30.

[5]I quote from Nicholas Brooke, ed., *Bussy D'Ambois*, in *The Revels Plays* (Cambridge, Mass., 1964).

establishes his preeminence in the two spheres of the courtier's existence—honor and love. With the emergence of Bussy in this role, Chapman commences by a series of allusions to reveal the mythic structure of the play. He implies Bussy's situation in the developing tragedy through reference to the related myths of Prometheus and Hercules.

The Prometheus analogy is employed most prominently in acts 3 and 4 and, as a host of commentators have noted, the identification of Bussy with Hercules is pervasive in the last scene of act 5.[6] The Hercules myth does appear earlier in the play, but in such a way that the relation to Bussy remains only potential until near the end. The offenses of the characters opposed to Bussy are associated with several of the labors of Hercules: in the political conflict Bussy connects the Lernaean Hydra with both Guise (3.2.74) and Monsieur (3.2.400). The hydra is a symbol of legalistic excess in The Republic; Boccaccio treats the hydra as sophistry, and its death at the hands of Hercules signifies intelligence discovering and destroying fraud.[7] The use here to illuminate the struggle for influence between Bussy, an honest courtier, and the corrupt alliance of Guise and Monsieur is apposite. Similarly, in the sexual conflict between Monsieur and Bussy for Tamyra's favor, Bussy foresees the struggle as that of Hercules and Antaeus: "I would . . . from your whole strength toss you into air" (4.1.88–90). This familiar struggle of reason and passion or spiritual and physical later defines the agon of Christ and Satan in Paradise Regained.[8] Likewise, for Tamyra Monsieur's lust becomes "the Augean stable of his foul sin" (4.1.179–80) in her anticipation of Bussy's protection. But, it should be emphasized, these allusions serve to measure the quality of Bussy's failure. Monsieur and the Guise win the political struggle; Tamyra's protector proves ineffectual. The Herculean mantle which embraces Bussy in the final scene does not belong to the conqueror Hercules of the labors.

Properly we must begin with the order in which the myths enter the play. In 2.1 Henry pardons Bussy at the behest of Monsieur, while signifying that he considers the sentence—"this merited death"—justified. Maintaining his innocence, Bussy in effect refuses the pardon, seeking

---

[6]See particularly A. S. Ferguson on the allusions to Hercules Oetaeus, "The Plays of George Chapman," Modern Language Review, 13 (1918): 1–24; and Brooke, Appendix B, pp. 149–52. Brooke sees an early Hercules allusion in 2.1.25–27 (p. xl), but the reference to "Atlas or Olympus" probably belongs to the Prometheus context of Titanic rebellion. Jean Jacquot, Bussy D'Ambois, Collection bilingue des classiques etrangers (Paris, 1960), cv–cvi, and Eugene M. Waith, The Herculean Hero in Marlowe, Chapman, Shakespeare, and Dryden (London, 1962), pp. 88–111, have asserted the importance of the mythic dimension, but ignore the interaction of Prometheus with Hercules.

[7]Republic, 4.426E; Boccaccio, Geneologie Deorum Gentilium Libri, Scrittori d'Italia (Bari, 1951), 13.1. See also Salutati, De Laboribus Herculis, ed. B. L. Ullman (Zurich, 1951), 3.9.

[8]PR 4.562–68. Milton's version has been traced to Comes (a favorite source for Chapman) and to the redaction in the dictionary of Charles Stephanus. See D. T. Starnes and E. W. Talbert, Classical Myth and Legend in Renaissance Dictionaries (Chapel Hill, 1955), p. 238.

rather to be placed beyond the law: "since I am free / (Offending no just law), let no law make / By any wrong it does, my life her slave." The nobility of Bussy's behavior sufficiently impresses Henry that he elevates Bussy to a position of highest favor with the intention of using the natural greatness he perceives in Bussy to benefit the court:

> Speak home my Bussy, thy impartial words
> Are like brave Falcons that dare truss a fowl
> Much greater than themselves; flatterers are Kites
> That check at nothing; thou shalt be my Eagle,
> And bear my thunder underneath thy wings.
>
> [Bussy 3.2.1–5]

The designation of Bussy as Jupiter's eagle has the effect of implying Henry's recognition of Bussy's various qualities—imperiousness, pride, majesty as well as virtuous, elevated thought.[9] The thunder borne by the eagle empowers Bussy to act as messenger of Henry's own will, for, as Chapman tells us in Eugenia, "The soule Mythologisd is the Eagle which is said to beare the thunder vnder her wings. . . . The word, intended by the Thunder; which diuine Scripture call[s] Gods voice" (Poems, p. 289). Vaulting from his initial position as Monsieur's favorite to favorite of the King himself, Bussy is only too eager to accept the "surname of mine Eagle"; yet the notion of Bussy acting as Jupiter's eagle has conflicting implications. "Shew me a Great Man," Bussy announces, "That affects Royalty, rising from a clapdish; / That rules so much more than his suffering King, / That he makes kings of his subordinate slaves" (3.2.28–30). With such a man as target

>   let me but hawk at him,
> I'll play the Vulture, and so thump his liver,
> That (like a huge unlading Argosy)
> He shall confess all, and you then may hang him.
>
> [Bussy 3.2.36–39]

The speech is a telling one. Clearly the "Great Man" affecting royalty, rising from the beggar's dish to outrule his King is Bussy himself, complete to the ship figure which he first launched. Bussy's allusion to Prometheus arises naturally from the association of Jupiter and eagle, stemming from the legend that Jupiter saw as portent of victory a flying eagle just before his war with the Titans.[10] Yet, if Bussy is correct in his

---

[9]See Guy de Tervarent, Attributs et Symboles dans l'Art Prophane, 1450–1600 (Geneva, 1958–59), 1: 4–8.

[10]Vicenzo Cartari, Imagini delli Dei de gl'Antichi (1647), ed. Walter Koschatzky (Graz, Austria, 1963), p. 87. The similarity of the myths of Prometheus and Tityus led to an interchangeable use of eagle and vulture. On this see Erwin Panofsky, Studies in Iconology (1939; reprint ed., New York, 1962), pp. 216–17 and n. 149.

unconscious identification of himself with the rebellious Titan, he cannot also function as Jupiter's eagle.

This is demonstrated in the quarrel following, precipitated by Guise's question, "Where will you find such game as you would hawk at?" and Bussy's insolent reply, "I'll hawk about your house for one of them." The two men exchange bitter taunts until Bussy beseeches Henry, "let me fly, my Lord." The King replies, "Not in my face; my Eagle, violence flies / The Sanctuaries of a Prince's eyes." Thus denied, Bussy provokes Guise to continue the quarrel out of the King's presence on the dueling field; but Henry forestalls this, too, and in an emblematic scene commands their reconciliation. Although Henry rebukes Guise for his intolerance of Bussy, we may reflect that in view of Bussy's martial prowess it is Guise who gains by Henry's intervention. In the same way Henry's glowing praise of Bussy as a man upholding the original state of nature has a double-edged effect; the praise is genuine, yet it serves to call attention to the discrepancy between the ideal described and the reality:

> Kings had never borne
> Such boundless eminence over other men
> Had all maintain'd the spirit and state of D'Ambois;
> Nor had the full impartial hand of Nature
> That all things gave in her original,
> Without these definite terms of Mine and Thine,
> Been turn'd unjustly to the hand of Fortune—
> Had all preserv'd her in her prime, like D'Ambois;
> No envy, no disjunction, had dissolv'd
> Or pluck'd out one stick of the golden faggot
> In which the world of Saturn was compris'd,
> Had all been held together with the nerves,
> The genius and th' ingenuous soul of D'Ambois.

> [*Bussy* 3.2.95–107]

The fact is that, since men have not maintained the spirit and state of D'Ambois, D'Ambois is a threat to the equilibrium of the state that has evolved. It might have been better if kings had never borne "boundless eminence," but they do. Henry's role is that of Jupiter (or Jove) which in comparison with Saturn implies something other than total justice: "But when that into *Lymbo* once *Saturnus* being thrust / The rule and charge of all the world was under Jove unjust."[11] The "enchanted glass" of the court has replaced the Saturnian "golden faggot" and its ambiance is the policy of Monsieur, the violence of Guise. What is natural in another context becomes monstrous within the frame of their world, and to them D'Ambois is a sport of nature, "Fortune's proud mushroom shot up in a night."

[11]W. H. D. Rouse, ed., *Shakespeare's Ovid: Being Arthur Golding's Translation of the Meta-morphoses* (Carbondale, Ill., 1961), 1.129–30.

Henry's association of Bussy with man of the Saturnian Golden Age, ominous as it might be in emphasizing Bussy's distance from effective participation in the Iron Age, serves to clarify the way Chapman uses the Prometheus myth. Reference to the Golden Age directs our attention to the earliest civilization of man; the source of classical and postclassical treatments of both the myth of the Golden Age and the myth of Prometheus is Hesiod.[12] Chapman's 1618 translation of the *Works and Days*, entitled *The Georgicks of Hesiod*, is dedicated to Bacon, commending in the dedication and in a long note on Prometheus the expositions of mythology in *De Sapientia Veterum*. Charles W. Lemmi summarizes the dominant allegorical treatments of Prometheus and their relevance to Bacon:

> Fulgentius interprets Prometheus as the providence of God which, having created man's body, breathed into it the heavenly spark of the soul. Servius, instead, and Augustine, regard Prometheus as an enlightened leader and reformer who, so to speak, invented civilization. Boccaccio combines both views, attributing to Prometheus a two-fold symbolism. Natalis Comes, . . . agrees rather with Servius than with Fulgentius, but explains Prometheus and Epimetheus as human forethought and thoughtlessness more than as individuals. Bacon is indebted both to Comes and to Boccaccio, and interprets the whole myth as a history of mankind which, having described the creation of the first human beings, traces the progress of civilization in a course marked by forethought and intelligence, and yet by thoughtlessness and rashness also.[13]

The laudatory statements which Chapman directs to *De Sapientia Veterum* should not be dismissed as patronage puffery. Chapman's translation of Hesiod is a late work, but this does not indicate that his acquaintance with Hesiod is similarly late; *The Shadow of Night* contains five direct references to Hesiod, while several conceptions—for instance, chaos as the original parent of the world and a primal harmony of elemental strife—proclaim obvious Hesiodic origins. In these hymns the Hesiodic elements could be entirely derived through the intermediary

[12]For the Golden Age see *Works and Days* (105–125); for Prometheus *Works and Days* (42–104) and *Theogony* (521–616). The Golden Age is most usefully discussed by Panofsky, pp. 20–21; Charles S. Singleton, *Journey to Beatrice*, Dante Studies 2 (Cambridge, Mass., 1958), 189–201; and Harry Levin, *The Myth of the Golden Age in the Renaissance* (Bloomington, Ind., 1969). Irving Ribner has stressed the importance of the Golden Age myth in *Bussy*; see "Character and Theme in Chapman's *Bussy D'Ambois*," *ELH*, 26 (1959): 485–88; reprinted in his *Jacobean Tragedy: The Quest for Moral Order* (London, 1962), pp. 24–29.

For consideration of Prometheus, see Raymond Trousson, *Le Thème de Prométhée dans la Littérature Européenne*, Vol. 1 (Geneva,1964); Panofsky, *Studies*, pp. 50–51; with Dora Panofsky, *Pandora's Box* (1956; reprinted, New York, 1962), pp. 3–13; Olga Raggio, "The Myth of Prometheus," *Journal of the Warburg and Courtauld Institutes*, 21 (1958): 44–62.

[13]Lemmi, *The Classical Deities in Bacon* (Baltimore, 1933), pp. 128–29. On Bacon's indebtedness to Comes, see also Barbara Carman Garner, "Francis Bacon, Natalis Comes and the Mythological Tradition," *Journal of the Warburg and Courtauld Institutes*, 33 (1970): 264–91.

handbook of Comes. But whether or not Chapman knew Hesiod firsthand this early in his career is irrelevant; the point remains that his understanding of Hesiod is from the outset filtered through Comes. Like any literate Elizabethan Chapman knows various applications of the Prometheus myth, using in the *Hymnvs in Noctem* the notion of the poet as Promethean creator, and in a note to the Hesiod, interpreting the theft of fire as abuse of knowledge. But his larger response to the myth is formed not by his usual platonic sources, Ficino and Plotinus, who read it as an allegory of spiritual awakening and yearning for union with the divine beauty;[14] rather, it comes from the Servius-Boccaccio-Comes branch of exposition with its emphasis upon the social and civil implications. This application of the myth conforms to his use of the Orpheus myth, also derived from Comes, to symbolize the process of civilization and the establishment of justice.[15] Chapman's approval of the interpretation in Bacon's treatise probably should be understood as the approbation of a reader who has employed the same major source books and already has arrived at much the same conclusions himself.

Like Orpheus, Bussy too hopes "To draw men growne so rude / To ciuill loue of Art, and Fortitude." He goes to court proclaiming, "I am for honest actions, not for great: / If I may bring up a new fashion, / And rise in Court with virtue, speed his plough." From the eminence of his newly attained position as Henry's favorite, Bussy vows to cleanse the court of flattering sycophants, to expose the lawyers, clergymen, authoritarians who turn "sacred Law" into a rapacious Harpy, perverting "Blood into gold, and Justice into lust." Bussy's proposed campaign to reform the court is well intended, just as his original motives are blameless; in *De Guiana* Chapman himself had urged Elizabeth to "create / A golden worlde in this our yron age." The problem for Bussy arises with the necessary choice of means. Lacking Hamlet's gift of introspection, Bussy fails to realize that by acting in the world one inevitably becomes a part of that world and is "a little soil'd i' th' working."[16] Bussy can gain access to the court only on its terms, as "great man"; by accepting those terms, however, he becomes like the objects of his attack, thus losing his moral initiative. Moreover, the means to power are not without inherent risk: "A Prince's love is like the lightning's fume, / Which no man can em-

[14]See Plotinus, *Enneads* 4.3.14; Ficino, *Opera* (Basel, 1576), pp. 680, 1232, 1298; also Celio Calcagnini, *Super Prometheo et Epimetheo epitoma*, discussed by Trousson, pp. 96 and 101. For Chapman's borrowings from Ficino, see Franck L. Schoell, *Études sur l'humanisme continental en Angleterre a la fin de la renaissance* (Paris, 1926), pp. 1–20.

[15]For Chapman's borrowing from Comes, see Schoell, pp. 179–97. Cf. the relations between the Golden Age and the idea of justice, analyzed by Singleton, pp. 189–201, and Frances A. Yates, "Queen Elizabeth as Astraea," *Journal of the Warburg and Courtauld Institutes*, 10 (1947): 27–37, 62–70.

[16]I am indebted to the perspective provided by Maynard Mack, "The World of Hamlet," *Yale Review*, 41 (1952): 502–23.

brace, but must consume." Bussy is threatening to his enemies by virtue of his difference from them, vulnerable by erroneously allowing himself to become similar to them.

The trap which the gods prepared for Prometheus was the creation of Pandora, and this episode of the myth underlies Monsieur's plotting:

> When the most royal beast of chase, the Hart
> (Being old, and cunning in his lairs and haunts)
> Can never be discover'd to the bow,
> The piece or hound: yet where (behind some queich)
> He breaks his gall, and rutteth with his hind,
> The place is mark'd, and by his venery
> He still is taken.

[*Bussy* 3.2.152–58]

The metaphor of the stag hunt is nicely appropriate to the full activity of the play in several ways: in Chapman's period the hunt as symbol of man destroyed by his passions ordinarily connotes the Actaeon myth, a type of the fall; as Monsieur states, the hart is particularly the "royal beast," making the hunt a suitable figure for the disposal of a king's advisor or favorite;[17] at the same time imaging Bussy as stag recalls his "natural" affinities as a creature of the forest. Like the old hart, Bussy has been impervious to direct clashes of force and must be taken by stealth. Monsieur intends to bring down his royal beast by relying upon that side of his nature characterized by, in Sir Thomas Browne's phrase, "immoderate salacity, and almost unparallel'd excess of venery."[18] When his quarry is "mark'd," Monsieur "takes" Bussy by his venery—that is to say, by making "horns" at Montsurry, he triggers the cuckold's revenge. While Monsieur enunciates his plot in these terms, Chapman maintains the general role of Bussy as the rebel Titan: "and as this doting hand, / Even out of earth (like Juno) struck this giant, / So Jove's great ordnance shall be here implied / To strike him under th' AEtna of his pride" (3.2.136–39). The specific reference is to Typhon, but the consistent Hesiodic orientation serves to hold in our minds the Promethean reformer. Chapman's use of the myth is sparing; he does not, for instance, directly allude to Tamyra as a Pandora. But he does manipulate the plot against Bussy to conform to Pandora's role in the myth. Bussy's misconstruction of his own part creates the occasion for Monsieur's amused taunt: "your great Eagle's beak / (Should you fly at her) had as good encounter / An Albion cliff, as her more craggy liver" (4.1.54–56). As

---

[17]In *The Gentleman Usher* the variant of a boar hunt is used as the occasion of a near-successful assassination attempt upon Strozza. See also the allegorical stag hunt in *Cooper's Hill*, and the discussion by Earl R. Wasserman, *The Subtler Language* (Baltimore, 1959), pp. 72–76.

[18]Sir Thomas Browne, "Of the Deer," *Pseudodoxia Epidemica*, in *Works*, ed. Geoffrey Keynes, rev. ed. (Chicago, 1964), 3.9.

Monsieur already knows from the gossipy maid, Tamyra's "liver," phys-iologically the seat of the passions, is only too susceptible to Bussy.

The nature of the affair between Bussy and Tamyra has been some-what obscured by the changes in the 1641 text.[19] There Bussy, while new to the court, implausibly announces that his love "hath long been vow'd in heart" to Tamyra; the earlier printed version parallels more closely the relations of the mythic prototypes. The woman initiates the liaison and the physical fact of adultery is made more explicit than in the later text. "So, of a sudden," Tamyra reveals, "my licentious fancy / Riots within me: not my name and house / Nor my religion to this hour observ'd / Can stand above it" (2.2.42-45). Bacon comments, "Pandora has been generally and rightly understood to mean pleasure and sensual appetite, which after the introduction of civil arts and culture and luxury is kindled up as it were by the gift of fire."[20]

Remembering Chapman's use of the "banquet of sense" topos in the poem of that name, we may note that the banquet motif likewise appears in Bussy in a strategic way.[21] Pero, Tamyra's maid, tells Monsieur how at midnight she had stolen forth to spy upon her mistress, "I saw D'Ambois and she set close at a banquet." Monsieur knows well what kind of ban-quet: "is this our Goddess of Chastity?" Chapman uses a symbolic setting in the scene of Bussy's first court appearance, creating audience perspec-tive by playing the tensions developed in the foreground of the scene against the chess game between Henry and Monsieur. In 4.1 the action is framed through a similar device, the banquet which goes so ill that Henry detects "the dim ostents of Tragedy" and calls the feast to a close: "come, my brave Eagle, let's to covert fly." Here Bussy makes his impor-tant speech upon women as "patterns of change to men":

For as the Moon (of all things God created)
Not only is the most appropriate image
Or glass to shew them how they wax and wane,
But in her light and motion, likewise bears
Imperial influences that command
In all their powers, and make them wax and wane;
So women, that (of all things made of nothing)
Are the most perfect images of the Moon.

[Bussy 4.1.10-16]

[19]On the integrity of the 1607 quarto, see especially Robert P. Adams, "Critical Myths and Chapman's Original Bussy D'Ambois," Renaissance Drama, 9 (1966): 141-61; also the textual introductions by Brooke and by Maurice Evans, Bussy D'Ambois, New Mermaid edition (New York, 1966).

[20]Quoted by Lemmi, p. 130.

[21]See Frank Kermode, "The Banquet of Sense," Bulletin of the John Rylands Library, 44 (1961): 68-99; reprinted in his Shakespeare, Spenser, Donne; Renaissance Essays (London, 1971), pp. 84-115. Chapman also works the device in The Blind Beggar of Alexandria (sc. 3). D. K. Anderson provides some further background and contemporary analogues; see "The Banquet of Sense in English Drama (1595-1642)," Journal of English and Germanic Phi-lology, 43 (1964): 422-32.

The direct implication, that Tamyra in her mutability now rules Bussy, should be seen in context of Bussy's relation to the general theme of nature; this most perfect image of the moon now controls his ebbing fortunes in the sublunary world just as surely as her original guides the movement of the tides. Both understand that Tamyra is herself subject to the vicissitudes of her nature—"None can be always one," Bussy says—which descend thence to her lover. The individual nature participates as much in the fallen as the unfallen, court as well as country, and Bussy, while recognizing the dangers attendant upon his position, is powerless to retrieve his mistress from the effects of her passion (3.1.43–48; 4.1.34–38).

Monsieur quickly acts upon his nearly open threat (4.1.66 ff.) to reveal his knowledge of the adultery to Montsurry. Informed by Tamyra of this turn of events, Bussy cries rhetorically, "What insensate stock, / Or rude inanimate vapour without fashion, / Durst take into his Epimethean breast / A box of such plagues as the danger yields, / Incurr'd in this discovery?" (4.2.9–13). The Epimetheus to whom Bussy refers is, in an obvious sense, Monsieur ("keep fire in your bosom," Montsurry had told Monsieur in first rejecting his secret). Like the two Titans, Bussy and Monsieur are "brothers" in this play—in their political rivalry, in their sexual rivalry for Tamyra's favors, in the curious hate/love attraction between them. This last quality is best exemplified by the insultingly affectionate tenor of Monsieur's language when addressing Bussy. After Bussy's scathingly brutal assessment of Monsieur's character (3.2.375 ff.), the latter responds, "Why now I see thou lov'st me, come to the banquet." Certainly jealousy for Bussy as well as Tamyra underlies Monsieur's reaction to the affair: "Sweetheart: come hither, what if one should make / Horns at Montsurry?"

The two men are "brothers," moreover, in the sense of each being a reverse image of the other. Nonetheless, like many of the other mythological allusions in the play, this one has to be refracted to be fully understood. According to the longstanding etymological interpretation, subscribed to by Comes,[22] Prometheus represents forethought and Epimetheus afterthought. Bussy presumably thinks of his graphic warning to Monsieur to beware his own Herculean wrath and is enraged to find it ignored. Yet, as the Renaissance mythographers well knew, each god or legendary figure carries within the potentiality to become its own opposite—Prometheus always implies the possibility of becoming Epimetheus.[23] This has been Bussy's pattern of behavior throughout the play: despite his foreknowledge of great men and the court, he opts to become a courtier; despite the justice of his quarrel with the mocking courtiers, the excess of his wrath in the duel renders him indistinguishable from

---

[22]Lemmi, p. 130, translates Comes, 4.6.

[23]See Edgar Wind, *Pagan Mysteries in the Renaissance* (New Haven, 1958), pp. 158–75.

them—"As one had been a mirror to another."[24] Having made bitter and powerful enemies who are sure to watch for the weakness they can seize upon, Bussy again surrenders forethought in taking upon himself the Pandora's Box of his affair with Tamyra. Chapman explains:

> For man's corporeal part, which is figured in Epimetheus, signifying the inconsiderate and headlong force of affection, not obeying his reasonable part or soul, nor using foresight fit for the prevention of ill, which is figured in Prometheus, he is deceived with a false shadow of pleasure.[25]

Although in the logic of Bussy's actions Prometheus consistently has become Epimetheus, Chapman gives the theme greatest emphasis in the penultimate scene, as if to ensure audience comprehension of the reasons for Bussy's doom, by having Bussy make a symbolic rejection of the powers of foreknowledge. In this scene he is visited by the ghost of Friar Comolet who commands, "Note what I want, my son, and be forewarn'd." Bussy is perplexed by the enigmatic words: "Note what he wants? he wants his utmost weed, / He wants his life, and body: which of these / Should be the want he means, and may supply me / With any fit forewarning?" (5.2.15–18). Bussy recalls Behemoth's promise that "when the voice / Of D'Ambois shall invoke me I will rise, / Shining in greater light: and shew him all / That will betide ye all" (4.2.134–37). Summoning Behemoth, Bussy learns from the spirit of darkness that the hand of his mistress shall kill him "If thou yield / To her next summons." The symbolic expression of foreknowledge and its rejection could be rendered no more explicitly than through Bussy's attendance by demonic agents of prophesy. As Milton attests, the typology of the story of Prometheus and Pandora corresponds to the Christian truth of original sin, and the loss of the Golden Age is a pagan analogue to the expulsion of our first parents from Eden.[26] Bussy chooses to reject the foreknowledge offered by Behemoth:

> I must fare well, how ever; though I die,
> My death consenting with his augury;
> Should not my powers obey when she commands,
> My motion must be rebel to my will:

[24]For this particular point and helpful discussion of the entire play, I am indebted to Professor Roy Roussel.

[25]Chapman, *The Georgicks of Hesiod*, in *Homer's Batrachomyomachia*, ed. Richard Hooper, 2d ed. (London, 1888), p. 155.

[26]Henry Reynolds argues, "What other can Hesiod's Pandora, the first and beautifullest of all women, by whome all euils were dispersed and spred vpon the earth, meane then Moses his Eue? What could they meane by their Golden-Age . . . But the state of Man before his Sin?" *Mythomystes*, reprinted in Joel E. Spingarn, ed., *Critical Essays of the Seventeenth Century*, 1 (1908; reprint ed., Bloomington, 1957): 175–76. On Milton's use of the analogy see Panofsky and Panofsky, *Pandora's Box*, p. 71; also D. C. Allen, *The Harmonious Vision* (Baltimore, 1954), p. xiv.

My will, to life: if when I have obey'd
Her hand should so reward me, they must arm it,
Bind me and force it: or I lay my soul
She rather would convert it many times
On her own bosom, even to many deaths.

[*Bussy* 5.2.68–76]

The speech is more than reminiscent of Adam's first abuse of human foreknowledge in electing to make his lot with Eve, although he knows this resolution means death. Milton's Adam expresses it, "I feel / The Link of Nature draw me: Flesh of Flesh, / Bone of my Bone thou art, and from thy State / Mine never shall be parted, bliss or woe" (9.913–16). Adam and Bussy in this situation decide in favor of their human rather than their suprahuman tendencies, and this choice, of course, is the essence of the tragic dilemma. Northrop Frye observes, "Prometheus, Adam, and Christ hang between heaven and earth, between a world of paradisal freedom and a world of bondage. Tragic heroes are so much the highest points in their human landscape that they seem the inevitable conductors of the power about them, great trees more likely to be struck by lightning than a clump of grass."[27]

After he has received his death wound Bussy slips into the shroud of the mythical Hercules; the speech on fame, concluding with "And tell them all that D'Ambois now is hasting / To the eternal dwellers," is a rather close adaptation from Seneca's *Hercules Oetaeus*.[28] Bussy seems consciously to be taking upon himself the role of the Christian Hercules, that of the heroic man patiently enduring his sufferings through Christian fortitude.[29] Chapman first explored this conception dramatically in *The Gentleman Usher* in which Strozza, suffering the torment of a dangerous arrow wound, wishes for death, only to be chided by his wife:

Oh, hold, my lord! This is no Christian part,
Nor yet scarsely manly . . . .
Patience in torment is a valour more
Than ever crown'd th' Alcmenean conqueror.

[*Gent. Usher* 4.1.48–49, 56–57]

Strozza heads his wife's advice—"My free submission to the hand of Heaven / Makes it redeem me from the rage of pain"—and is rewarded with a miraculous cure accompanied by the attainment of visionary powers and a belief, similar to Henry's view of Bussy, in the natural

[27]Frye, *Anatomy*, p. 207. Cf. the pattern of tree imagery in *Bussy*, especially 5.3.42–46, and 66–68.

[28]"Dic sub aeternos properare manes / Herculem et regnum canis inquieti, / unde non umquam remeabit ille" (1525–27). See Brooke, p. 150.

[29]See Jacquot, *Bussy D'Ambois*, pp. cv–cvi, and Marcel Simon, *Hercule et le Christianisme* (Paris, 1955).

nobility of man: "Had all been virtuous men, / There never had been prince upon the earth, / And so no subject; all men had been princes: / A virtuous man is subject to no prince, / But to his soul and honour" (5.4.56–60). This is the part implicit in Bussy's borrowing of Hercules' death speech and in his behavior—his forbearance and forgiveness of his murderers, his appeal to Montsurry to be reconciled with Tamyra.

But Bussy is premature in assuming the Hercules role. Weakening from his wound, Bussy spurns the assistance of Tamyra and props himself with his sword: "I am up / Here like a Roman statue; I will stand / Till death hath made me marble: O my fame / Live in despite of Murder!" (5.3.143–45). The conscious heroics of the pose and the concern with fame seem truly the last infirmity of a noble mind, ironically clashing with Bussy's initial, contemptuous assessment of great men as "colossic statues, / Which, with heroic forms without o'er-spread, / Within are nought but mortar, flint, and lead" (1.1.15–17). Bussy's posturing reveals the extent to which his assumed role has taken possession of him, as he tries to salvage something of his shattered aspirations by playing the part of the "great man" to the end. His refusal of Tamyra's movement to help him as he stands wounded denies the participation in common humanity that he earlier asserted in responding to her letter. But Tamyra unwittingly jars Bussy out of his complacent renunciation, driving him to acceptance of responsibility for the human suffering he has caused. She asks him to forgive her for writing the letter which lured him to the ambush, exposing, as she speaks, her wounds in mute testimony to the torture that she has undergone. The effect upon Bussy is simple and direct: "O, my heart is broken." The sight of Tamyra's maimed body destroys the composure forged from a stoic acceptance of death and a comfort in heroic reputation. Now Bussy sees his life and death as a bitter object lesson upon man's presumption and folly:

> My sun is turn'd to blood 'gainst whose red beams
> Pindus and Ossa (hid in endless snow),
> Laid on my heart and liver, from their veins
> Melt like two hungry torrents: eating rocks
> Into the Ocean of all human life,
> And make it bitter, only with my blood:
> O frail condition of strength, valour, virtue,
> In me like warning fire upon the top
> Of some steep beacon, on a steeper hill;
> Made to express it like a falling star
> Silently glanc'd—that like a thunderbolt
> Look'd to have stuck, and shook the firmament.
>
> [*Bussy* 5.3.182–93]

This remarkable speech justly has been singled out to examine the manner in which Chapman richly interweaves both source material and psychological patterns developed in the course of the play;[30] for present purposes, however, it is more important to notice the function of the speech in bridging stages of the mythic structure. "My sun is turn'd to blood" does not refer primarily to Tamyra; Chapman remains consistent in his cosmological symbolism. Rather, it alludes to the sun of greatness that shone upon him and, like Montsurry's "earth moves, and heaven stands still" apostrophe, it epitomizes the destruction of an accepted order through the familiar "nature inverted" *topos*. Pindus and Ossa, Chapman understood from Seneca, are the mountains under which the rebellious Titans were buried. He points the general context of the reference into a specific Promethean allusion by having Bussy describe the mountains as laid on his "heart and liver," the two organs which interchangeably were the objects of torture in the myth.[31] The mountains, Bussy imagines, will melt "like two hungry torrents" into the "Ocean of all human life," making it bitter with his blood. The implication is not that his greatness will destroy nature; instead it admits a recognition of his destructive effect upon humanity. In so doing the imagery further implies that Bussy acknowledges his humanity: returning to the sea-of-life trope, initiated by Bussy but sustained by other speakers through the play,[32] indicates his awareness that without virtue as guide he has "shipwracked"; that he, like ordinary man, is mortal. So it is with a new-found humility that Bussy sees in himself, "O frail condition of strength, valour, virtue," a warning beacon for others, "a falling star," to express the gap between aspiration and achievement.

Jean Jacquot has argued that the description of the mountains falling into a bloody sea represents a fusion of the biblical destruction of the world (Rev. 8:8–11) with a reference to the destruction of the Titans in *Hercules Oetaeus*. It would seem also to owe something to Chapman's recollection of accounts relating the liberation of Prometheus. Valerius Flaccus, for example, describes how Hercules' assault upon Mount Caucasus causes the snowy mountain summit to fall into the sea, blocking the mountain streams from the sea; the passing Argonauts gaze in wonder at the snow-strewn beaches, the fallen boulders, the gore-saturated air.[33] The association is not a gratuitous one, for Hercules' legendary voyage across the ocean to free Prometheus is directly relevant to the symbolic pattern Chapman develops in transforming Bussy from a Prometheus to a Hercules. Again Bacon's extensive explications of the myth are helpful

[30]See Brooke, pp. xxxii–xxxiii, and Jacquot, p. xcviii–ci.

[31]The substitution was widespread because it occurred in some of the most influential commentaries—for example, those of Servius and Fulgentius. See Raggio, pp. 51 and 53. Although she does not mention the point, plates illustrating her article show the variation plainly; see especially 7f, from Cicero's *Tusculanae Quaestiones*, and 8d–e, from Alciati's *Emblemata*.

[32]Note especially the sea imagery in 1.2.138–46; 3.2.286–89; and 5.3.21–25, 49–56.

[33]*Argonautica*, 5.154–76.

and suggestive for Chapman's play. The aid of Hercules represents, Bacon tells us, "fortitude and constancy of mind":

> It is worth noting too that this virtue was not natural to Prometheus, but adventitious, and came by help from without; for it is not a thing which any inborn and natural fortitude can attain to; it comes from beyond the ocean, it is received and brought to us by the Sun; for it comes of Wisdom, which is the Sun, and of meditation upon the inconstancy and fluctuations of human life, which is the navigation of the ocean. . . .[34]

Bussy's bitter wisdom, too, comes from the sun in the figure of his death speech, as he completes his epic voyage upon that ocean which is simply "the inconstancy and fluctuations of human life."

Bacon returned twice to his exegesis of this mythic episode, each time in directly Christian terms. His second account in *De Sapientia Veterum* manipulates the pagan-Christian correspondence with suitably pious caution:

> It is true that there are not a few things beneath which have a wonderful correspondency with the mysteries of the Christian faith. The voyage of Hercules especially, sailing in a pitcher to set Prometheus free, seems to present an image of God the Word hastening in the frail vessel of the flesh to redeem the human race. But I purposely refrain myself from all licence of speculation in this kind, lest peradventure I bring strange fire to the altar of the Lord.[35]

Bacon continued to think about the myth and by the time he composed his essay *Of Adversity* he was both less rigid in detail and more confident about Christian typology: "Hercules, when he went to unbind Prometheus (by whom human nature is represented), sailed the length of the great ocean in an earthen pot or pitcher; lively describing Christian resolution, that saileth in the frail bark of the flesh thorough the waves of the world." Lemmi, noting Bacon's divergence from Comes in his reading of Prometheus's rescue, comments that, while Bacon might have known a specifically Christian allegorization, he just as easily could have arrived at it from his own knowledge of the Prometheus typology.[36] Perhaps so; however, Lemmi seems to underestimate the currency of this Christian reading in the Renaissance period. Raymond Trousson states, "Hercule fut, dès le Moyen Age, entendu comme l'équivalent païen du Sauveur; en conséquence, Prométhée devint l'appellation antique d'Adam, lui-même archétype de la nature humaine, racheté par le Fils de Dieu." Within this tradition Ronsard composed his *Hercule chrestien*:

---

[34]Quoted by Lemmi, p. 138.

[35]Ibid., p. 140.

[36]Lemmi, pp. 134, 140.

> qu' est-ce de Prométhé
> Dessus Caucase aux aigles garrotté,
> [Lequel] Alcide affranchit, hors de peine
> Le delivrant, sinon Nature humaine
> (J' entends Adam) que Christ a détaché
> Par sa bonté des liens de péché,
> Lors que la Loy comme une aigle sans cesse
> Luy pincetoit son ame pecheresse,
> Sans nul espoir, avant que par la foy
> De Christ la grace eust combatu la Loy?[37]

These are some of the connotations that accrue to the Hercules-Prometheus legend as Chapman exploits it in the play. Like Prometheus and Epimetheus, the two figures symbolize aspects or phases of the total human spirit that is Bussy D'Ambois; Chapman knows, as well as Donne, the ambivalent nature of postlapsarian man: "Look, Lord, and finde both *Adams* met in me." Bussy's entrance in the final scene is prefaced by the friar's ghost in a speech which unites the motifs of Bussy's Titanic presumption, final submission to fate, and original sin:

> 'Tis the just curse of our abus'd creation,
> Which we must suffer here, and 'scape hereafter:
> He hath the great mind that submits to all
> He sees inevitable; he the small
> That carps at earth, and her foundation-shaker,
> And rather than himself, will mend his maker.
>
> [*Bussy* 5.3.69–74]

Bussy's death speech brings Prometheus or "human nature" down from the mountain peak to end the voyage "in the frail bark of the flesh thorough the waves of the world." In recognizing his own excesses, his own follies, his substitution of valor for virtue, and in presenting himself as an exemplum, Bussy submits to what he "sees inevitable" and thus attains something of the Christian resolution that he heretofore lacked. Bussy fears that his life expresses no more than a shooting star, but the friar's curtain speech accords him a place in the mythological galaxy:

> Look up and see thy spirit made a star,
> Join flames with Hercules: and when thou set'st
> Thy radiant forehead in the firmament,
> Make the vast continent, crack'd with thy receipt,
> Spread to a world of fire: and th' aged sky,
> Cheer with new sparks of old humanity.
>
> [*Bussy* 5.3.269–74]

---

[37]Trousson, 1:123; see also Frances A. Yates, *The French Academies of the Sixteenth Century* (London, 1947), pp. 191–93, on the medievalism of Ronsard's typology.

Kathleen Williams has shown that *The Faerie Queene*, Books 3 and 4, presents the theme of concord through the use of mythological characters whose relations illustrate various types of false concord as well as, ultimately, the attainment of true concord by the reconciliation of opposites.[38] Although Spenser's epic employs overtly a mythic technique that, because of the difference in medium, can assert itself only as an allusive structure in Chapman's play, Williams's exposition is pertinent, since Chapman develops in *Bussy D'Ambois* a thematic exploration of true and false concord similar to Spenser's. The contrast of harmony and dissonance, concord and discord, is manifested through the large symbolic oppositions which create the framework for the dramatic action. The ideal of the Golden Age, the harmonious natural world in which Astraea or Justice herself dwelt, Chapman evoked in the placeless "green retreat" of Bussy's "natural" milieu, a source of appeal thereafter in the speeches of Bussy and King Henry. Bussy's own mettle will be tested by the Iron Age court, conventional foil to the pastoral ideal; and, just as Bussy presents himself as a microcosm of that lost ideal, so the court is an epitome of the confusion Astraea has fled: "The King and subject, Lord and every slave / Dance a continual Hay; our rooms of State, / Kept like our stables; no place more observ'd / Than a rude market-place" (1.2.28–31). Although an enlightened and effective monarch can restore to a court something like the lost order, it is Bussy's misfortune to attempt to bring justice to a court ruled by a man who wants either power or will to effect change. The French cannot imitate the English, Henry argues, "Because in Kingdoms, / Where the King's change doth breed the subject's terror, / Pure innovation is more gross than error."

Henry's choice of metaphor in describing the way he and all his people "dance a continual Hay" derives from the imagery of *The Shadow of Night*. There, in a long simile Chapman had used the confused action of "rude rurall dances" to amplify an important argument:

> So our first excellence, so much abusd,
> And we (without the harmonie was vsd,
> When Saturnes golden scepter stroke the strings
> Of Ciuill gouernement) make all our doings
> Sauour of rudenesse, and obscuritie,
> And in our formes shew more deformitie
> Then if we still were wrapt, and smoothered
> In that confusion, out of which we fled.
>
> [*Noct.* 193–200]

---

[38]Kathleen Williams, "Venus and Diana: Some Uses of Myth in *The Faerie Queene*," *ELH*, 28 (1961): 101–20; and her *Spenser's World of Glass: A Reading of "The Faerie Queene"* (Berkeley and Los Angeles, 1966), pp. 79–91, 122–31.

Dancing connoted, as Sir John Davies' *Orchestra* so fully evidences, a ceremony or social ritual ordered to the tune of that earthly music which expresses, in little the cosmic harmony of the celestial spheres.[39] Chapman could think of no more encompassing a figure for man's corruption than this antimasque—a perverse and grotesque aping of that cosmic dance. He incorporates this imagery to describe Bussy's behavior at his court presentation: Bussy's deliberate provocation of the Guise is "one of the best jigs that ever was acted" to the rival courtiers, who mockingly challenge, "Come sir, we'll lead you a dance." For them it becomes a dance of death; but more important than the irony is the fact of Bussy's participation in the dance. Who, indeed, can tell the dancer from the dance?

Because he lacks the temperamental balance to maintain personal harmony, Bussy's efforts to establish civil harmony by returning justice to France are diverted into false channels. Particularly this is enacted in two incidents in which the antagonists bend to a false reconciliation, first on the political, then on the personal plane. Alarmed at the burgeoning quarrel between Bussy and the Guise, Henry forbids the conflict, invoking the power of the caduceus: "Let my hand therefore be the Hermean rod / To part and reconcile, and so conserve you, / As my combin'd embracers and supporters" (3.2.108–10). Jacquot traces Chapman's use of the caduceus as an emblem of concord to Cartari, one of his favorite authorities.[40] This symbolic reading gained wide favor, and the legend of Mercury separating with his rod the two fighting serpents certainly is pertinent for Henry's purposes. Both men of course submit, Guise expressing the hope that "the manly freedom / That you so much profess, hereafter prove not / A bold and glorious license to deprave." Bussy on his part counters with the wish that "your worthy greatness / Engender not the greater insolence, / Nor make you think it a Perogative, / To rack men's freedoms with the ruder wrongs." The qualifications convey the crux of the issue neatly. If we accept Tamyra's evaluation of her affair with Bussy, ignoring his airy dismissal, "Sin is a coward, Madam," it is evident that his freedom has proved a "license to deprave," as surely as Guise's insolence results in a tyranny wronging individual freedoms. The reconciliation of opposites that Henry hopes to accomplish is the classic golden mean of government, a balance of freedom and authority; instead, he creates a false union of license and tyranny. In Samuel Johnson's words, this is the yoking together of disparate qualities by violence, and it lasts only until Henry goes offstage.

[39]For the background of dance as symbol of cosmic order, see J. C. Meagher, "The Dance and the Masques of Ben Jonson," *Journal of the Warburg and Courtauld Institutes*, 25 (1962): 258–65; also 265–77 on dancing as moral instruction.

[40]See Jacquot's notes in *Bussy* to 3.2. Alastair Fowler, *Spenser and the Numbers of Time* (London, 1964), pp. 156–66, explores the symbolism of the caduceus.

The second mistaken attempt to effect a reconciliation occurs when the wounded Bussy, with the friar's prompting, urges Montsurry to "be reconcil'd / With all forgiveness to your matchless wife" (5.3.169–70). The gesture is futile, displaying again Bussy's failure to comprehend his impact upon their lives. The extremes of Montsurry's reaction have implied his inability to adapt to the situation, and his torture of Tamyra— unknown at this point to Bussy—nullifies her obligation to him. But the friar persists after Bussy's death in pleading for this "Christian reconcilement." Montsurry offers forgiveness, explaining in the complicated image of a candle consuming itself why reconcilement to his love is impossible. Although the candle "looks" upward, like their love, it must burn down. The candle wax, gathered from bees, suggests to him a comparison of diminishing sweetness:

As having lost his honey, the sweet taste
Runs into savour, and will needs retain
A spice of his first parents, till (like life)
It sees and dies; so let our love.

[*Bussy* 5.3.254–57]

Nicholas Brooke comments that "the phrase 'first parents' (for the bees) also indicates Adam and Eve as the image ends in a generalized reference—'like life'—to the values of their story, and to original sin from which the escape is a final clarity of vision in the moment of death (hence the use of 'sees' for the shining of the candle)."[41] The theme of man's original state and its relevance to his condition in the present world indicates that the speech illuminates the value of Bussy's story as well. Bussy is the Adamic man whose self-imposed exile from the higher nature of the green world in favor of the court and knowledge of sin follows the pattern of the Christian myth. Without being in opposition, the images of tree and ship or nature and artifice, country and court, have served to keep in the foreground the ambivalence of Bussy's, and man's, nature. "Like life," like Bussy, the candle "sees and dies," implying that the final clarity of vision which he achieves justifies the apotheosis that the now-wiser friar perceives Bussy to have undergone.

The religious poetry of John Donne reveals a persistent fascination with the *concordia discors* that is possible in the concept of Christianity.[42] The occasion of the *Annunciation and Passion falling upon one day* yields a lesson:

---

[41]Brooke, note to 5.3.254 ff. On possible emblematic sources for the image of the candle extinguishing itself, see A. R. Braunmuller, "The Natural Course of Light Inverted: An *Impresa* in Chapman's *Bussy D'Ambois*," *Journal of the Warburg and Courtauld Institutes*, 34 (1971): 356–60.

[42]On *concordia discors* in Donne's writings, see Wind, pp. 174–75.

> this day hath showne,
> Th' Abridgement of Christs story, which makes one
> (As in plaine Maps, the furthest West is East)
> Of the 'Angels *Ave*,' and *Consummatum est*.

The paradox of *Goodfriday, 1613. Riding Westward*—"that I am carryed towards the West / This day, when my Soules forme bends toward the East"—is resolved in a *Hymne to God my God, in my sicknesse* with the understanding that "As West and East / In all flatt Maps (and I am one) are one, / So death doth touch the Resurrection." The directional metaphor impressed Donne as such an effective expression of the coincidence of opposites that he used it for his own epitaph: "Hic licet in occiduo cinere aspicit eum cuius nomen est oriens";[43] however, he was not without other metaphors to convey the theme. In a poem of congratulation *To Mr. Tilman after he had taken orders* Donne figures the knowledge that "Gods graces, mens offences," necessarily meet in the clergyman by recourse to a staple of platonic mythology: "Both these in thee, are in thy Calling knit, / And make thee now a blest Hermaphrodite."[44] When Donne frames the theme against the ordinary Christian's situation, his most effective image is undoubtedly that of the two Adams:

> Looke Lord, and finde both *Adams* met in me;
> As the first *Adams* sweat surrounds my face,
> May the last *Adams* blood my soule embrace.

The concept is that of man's redemption by grace which, through the agency of Christ's sacrifice, fuses both natures, bestial and angelic, in the microcosm of man's spirit. It expresses the true concord that Chapman shadows in the death of Bussy D'Ambois through the myth of Hercules and Prometheus. In Chapman's use of the myth, as in Ronsard's, "Prométhée libere par Hercule, c'est la nature humaine, c'est Adam, affranchi du péché par le Christ."[45] Unlike Ronsard in his external exposition of the myth, however, Chapman uses the mythic heroes to symbolize stages of process in the transmutation of the human spirit. Much like the speaker of Donne's poems, Chapman seeks symbols to embody the true concord of the Christian mind and, finding them in the traditions of allegorized mythology, he selects mythic patterns to shape the structure of the play into thematic revelation of Bussy's spiritual voyage. Through

---

[43]A. H. Bullen, ed., *Walton's Lives* (London, 1884), p. 76.

[44]Ficino uses the myth of the Androgyne to theorize that man's nature originally contained both the natural and the supernatural; see *Commentary on Plato's Symposium*, Speech 4. See also Fowler's discussion of the hermaphroditic Venus as symbol of concord in *The Faerie Queene*, pp. 163–66.

[45]Simon, p. 182. For emphasis on the aspects of the myth suggesting a typological atonement, cf. the version of Apollodorus, *The Library*, in which Hercules binds himself with a crown of olive before releasing Prometheus (2.5.11) and finds a substitute, Chiron, to die in place of Prometheus (2.5.4).

these traditions the friar's apostrophe, "Look up and see thy spirit made a star, / Join flames with Hercules," may be properly understood.

As one of the recurrent thematic words in Chapman's poetic vocabulary, *form* takes on a variety of meanings and receives a generous spectrum of local applications: the *Hymnvs in Noctem* analyzes the formless condition of the fallen world, and the *Hymnvs in Cynthiam* reveals the goddess, "Forme her selfe," as soul to the body politic of England; *Hero and Leander* considers violations of social forms, offering a corrective myth to explain that "loue is forme." *The Teares of Peace* posits learning as the informing principle of man's soul; *A Hymne to our Sauiour on the Crosse* lauds Christ for "perfecting the forme thou didst infuse / In mans creation"; *Eugenia* praises Death as "A shining Christall; since through him we see / The louely forms of our felicitie." And in *Peristeros: or the male Turtle*, Chapman's contribution to the *Loves Martyr* volume, it is the merit of the Phoenix "That is my forme, and giues my being, spirit."[46] But, rather than discuss direct thematic instances of this sort, I wish to discriminate what poetic form must have meant to Chapman, drawing inferences both from his own comments on poetry and from the cumulative example of the writings themselves.

At the most external level Chapman's concern with form manifests itself in the already noted sensitivity to generic vehicle. The choice of a conventional form to serve as container for the "history" or "matter" must be made by gauging its appropriateness to the occasion, to the audience addressed, and to the "spirit" or burden of meaning it should convey. In *The Shadow of Night* and *A Hymne to our Sauiour* the hymn seems the inevitable formal choice for the deities addressed, for the history recounted in the former, and for the solemn occasion of the latter, as well as in respect to the conceptual thrust upon the reformation of man's spirit through the agency of the subject deity.[47] Similarly, *A Coronet for His Mistresse Philosophie* implies a direct comment on a current literary fashion, even before one reads a line, by the choice of a sonnet sequence as the formal vehicle, although the linking of the sonnets into a crown extends generic into symbolic forms.[48] Perhaps less obviously, with *Hero and Leander* Chapman's veneration for Musaeus and his decision to focus upon the idea of justice predicate an elevation to epic.

[46]D. J. Gordon, "Chapman's *Hero and Leander*," *English Miscellany*, 5 (1954): 65–85, discusses the philosophic antecedents of Chapman's "form." On "Peristeros" see William H. Matchett, *The Phoenix and the Turtle: Shakespeare's Poem and Chester's Loues martyr* (The Hague, 1965), pp. 91–95.

[47]On "A Hymne to our Sauiour" see Millar MacLure, *George Chapman: A Critical Study* (Toronto, 1966), pp. 78–79; and the rhetorical analysis by O. B. Hardison, *The Enduring Monument* (Chapel Hill, 1962), pp. 159–62.

[48]Louis L. Martz, *The Poetry of Meditation*, rev. ed. (New Haven, 1962), pp. 107–8, discusses the sonnet "corona."

For all Chapman's attention to generic distinctions, however, a more profound, "inward" significance was assigned to mythic form or the "fictive body" of the poem. This "fictive body" should not be confused with the total narrative content or with the unshaped "history" from which it is constructed. Chapman's prefatory epistles to his Homer translations make it apparent that he regarded those epics as totally mythic, as he confidently alludes to "my Poeme of the mysteries / Reueal'd in Homer" (Poems, p. 393)—the absence of which almost causes one to wish for a larger Chapman corpus—and vigorously defends Homer's allegorical mode: "Why then is Fiction, to this end, so hatefull to our true Ignorants? Or why should a poore Chronicler of a Lord Maiors naked Truth, (that peraduenture will last his yeare) include more worth with our moderne wizerds, then Homer for his naked Vlysses, clad in eternall Fiction?"[49] Mere body in itself does not constitute form: "Am I this truncke? It is my painted sheath" (Eugenia, 551). But spirit acting upon matter or body can instill order and thereby create significant form. Ficino describes the creation of the world: "It is that still formless substance which we mean by Chaos; that first turning toward God we call the birth of Love; and the giving of the forms, the completion of love. This composite of all the Forms and Ideas we call in Latin a mundus, and in Greek, a cosmos, that is, Orderliness."[50] And, just as World Soul creates World Body, so the soul of man informs his body: "A man, all Center is, all stay, all minde, / The bodie onely, made her instrument: And to her ends, in all acts must consent, / Without which order, all this life hath none, / But breeds the other lifes confusion" (Eugenia, 633–37). By the same principle of correspondence, the soul or spirit of the poem imposes form upon the "allegorical fiction."

Beyond the mythic form exists what Chapman variously calls truth, soul, or "the universal"—in other words, something very like the realm of platonic ideas, universals, or forms. His reference in Eugenia to "The Louely forms of our felicitie" that we perceive through death would, in fact, seem to justify describing the abstract "truths" of the poems in precisely such terms. Chapman's persistence in describing the body's form as the imprint of the soul upon chaotic matter plainly reveals the extent to which his poetics originate in Renaissance platonism, wherein myth,

---

[49]Poems, pp. 407–8. The Lord Mayor's "naked Truth" is a fine example of what Northrop Frye calls "naive allegory"; see Anatomy, pp. 90–91. Chapman's disapproval of "word-for-word traductions" (Poems, p. 393) further suggests his distance from mimetic interpretation of Homer.

[50]Marsilio Ficino's Commentary on Plato's Symposium, trans. Sears R. Jayne, University of Missouri Studies, 19 (Columbia, Missouri, 1944), 1.3. The Florentine platonists believed that the creation of the world established the model for all literary creation. See Michael Murrin, The Veil of Allegory: Some Notes Toward a Theory of Allegorical Rhetoric in the English Renaissance (Chicago, 1969), pp. 119–28; and R. B. Waddington, "The Sun at the Center: Structure as Meaning in Pico della Mirandola's Heptaplus," Journal of Medieval and Renaissance Studies, 3 (1973): 69–86.

fable, and icon are perceived as the incarnation of essences. As E. H. Gombrich has explained regarding the platonic theory of visual symbols:

> They are the forms which the invisible entities can assume to make themselves understood to the limited human mind. In other words, the Idea of Justice—be it conceived as a member of the celestial Hierarchy or as an abstract entity— is inaccessible to the senses. At best we can hope to grasp it in a moment of ecstasis and intellectual intuition. But God has decreed in His mercy (as Giarda reminds us) that these entities may accommodate themselves to our under- standing and assume visible shape. Strictly speaking these allegorical images neither symbolize nor represent the Platonic idea. It is the Idea itself, con- ceived as an entity, which through these images tries to signal us and thus to penetrate through our eyes into our mind.[51]

Another key to this belief may be found in Chapman's effort to associate his poetic mode with hieroglyphics, which causes him to assert that poetic myths are an *Ur-Hieroglyphica*:

> So hath [learning] pleased her selfe with no disguise more; then in misteries and allegoricall fictions of *Poesie*. These haue in that kinde, beene of speciall reputation; as taking place of the rest, both for priority of time, and prece- dence of vse; being borne in the ould world, long before *Hieroglyphicks* or Fabels were conceiued: And deliuered from the Fathers to the Sonnes of Art; without any Aucthor but *Antiquity*. [*Poems*, p. 327]

Underlying the passage is the Renaissance discovery of Horapollo and Ficino's mistaken interpretation of the heiroglyphics: "When the Egyp- tian priests wished to signify divine mysteries, they did not use the small characters of script, but the whole images of plants, trees or animals; for God has knowledge of things not by way of multiple thought but like the pure and firm shape of the thing itself."[52] In actual practice of course, however devoutly an artist or poet held to the essential theory of sym- bolism, a heavy reliance upon the conventional was inevitable, as we know from Chapman's own compositional habits. Since no one can attain a constant state of divine illumination, the prudent writer consults his predecessors, the poets and wise men who did have something to say about the shape and meaning of a particular myth or image.[53] This ex- plains the emphasis on transmission "from the Fathers to the Sonnes of Art"; the recurrent demand for a learned audience; the existence of the poetic anatomies of learning itself; and the reliance upon Plutarch, Comes, Cartari, and the emblem books. Nevertheless, if the effort to com- prehend such poems requires Herculean learning, the possible reward

---

[51]E. H. Gombrich, *Symbolic Images: Studies in the Art of the Renaissance* (New York, 1972), p. 177; see pp. 139–80; and, for the assimilation of the theory from art to poetics, pp. 157–60.

[52]Quoted by Gombrich, pp. 158–59.

[53]See, e.g., Gombrich, pp. 175–76.

justifies the labor. As the angelic mind through love "lowers" the forms to accommodate them to man's sensory world, so the forms of poetic myth can raise man from his present estate:

This little Soules Pulse, *Poesie*, panting still
Like to a dancing pease vpon a Quill,
Made with a childes breath, vp and downe to fly,
(Is no more manly thought); And yet thereby
Euen in the corps of all the world we can
Discouer all the good and bad of man,
Anatomise his nakednesse, and be
To his chiefe Ornament, a Maiestie:
Erect him past his human Period
And heighten his transition into God.

[*Poems*, p. 306]

To return to the example of *Bussy D'Ambois*: in this drama Chapman gives us heroic tragedy at the level of generic form; in turn, Chapman creates the mythic form of the tragedy from the interacting myths of Prometheus and Hercules, a sensible manifestation of the idea or form of *concordia discors*. The strategy of endowing a play with a mythic structure brilliantly solves a problem inherent in the dramatic medium. Since he is deprived of the convention of direct utterance, except for relatively ineffectual prologues and epilogues, how is the dramatic poet to compensate for the oracular persona which in nondramatic poetry serves notice that he speaks of mysteries? Chapman succeeds in speaking an "allegorical rhetoric" even without that persona, by recourse to mythic structures in a number of his plays. As Michael Murrin observes, "The allegorist, dividing truth from morality by the veil of myth, achieved both ends—at least in theory. The people learned morality from the story of the poet, and the wise understood it."[54] By analogy *Bussy D'Ambois* can be read virtually on two levels. Superficially, it presents engrossing, sensational melodrama, based on scandalous events only a generation past and exploiting all the devices of current popular theatre; but "inwardly" the mythic form heightens the story to something far more meaningful for the initiates. That the play permits or even encourages two simultaneous levels of response explains critical confusion disseminated by the academic Polyphemus; still, a number of modern readers have been sensitive to the presence of its removed mysteries. Maurice Evans has commented, "The effect of this subtle interrelation of image and action is to add a dimension which lifts the whole level of the play almost to that of mythology."[55]

To anyone who is not a Renaissance platonist (myself included), the "ideas" in Chapman's poems will seem far less engrossing than the means of evoking them, the mythic narratives themselves, and the par-

[54]Murrin, p. 50.

[55]Evans, *Bussy D'Ambois*, p. xxvii.

ticulars of poetic process. But they deserve to be considered with respect. The ideas of Justice from *Hero and Leander*, Learning from *The Teares of Peace*, and Form from *The Shadow of Night* are not simple ones, as the following chapters will attempt to demonstrate. Although the thematic concerns of Chapman's narratives do overlap—Justice, for instance, enters marginally into the *Hymnvs in Cynthiam*, gets extended treatment in *Hero and Leander*, and reappears at the center of *The Teares of Peace*—more than any other "idea," his poems are preoccupied with the concept which informs *Bussy D'Ambois*—that of *concordia discors*.

Whereas *Bussy* embodies *concordia discors* in the Prometheus and Hercules myths, *Hero and Leander* presents it in the exemplary, inset myth of Hymen. The god of marriage again symbolizes the concept in *A Hymne to Hymen*, written for the marriage in 1613 of Princess Elizabeth to the Elector Palatine. Presumably that train of associations caused Chapman to create his *Memorable Maske of the Middle Temple and Lyncolns Inn*, written for the same occasion, upon the same idea, which this time was presented as the reconciliation of riches and honor.[56] The following year another court wedding evoked his most complex treatment of *concordia discors* in *Andromeda Liberata*, figured now by the myths of Perseus-Andromeda and Mars-Venus. Any post-Renaissance reader might fairly complain that *concordia discors* is itself a myth or metaphor and has no business being categorized as a platonic "form." Yet Edgar Wind's study of the iconography of *concordia discors* has demonstrated how fundamentally the idea expresses the vision of Renaissance platonists; and Earl Wasserman has shown its importance to English poetry, describing it as "one of the great controlling patterns of thought and of literature in this period."[57] As much as any of the other forms and ideas, *concordia discors* expresses Chapman's perception of the nature of reality, his own comprehension of the best ordering of man, nature, and society, which may be as essential a revelation as one can ask.

If we step back from the mythic forms which embody Chapman's ideas, we can generalize about the characteristic radical components in the various narratives. Recently Angus Fletcher has fruitfully described the two "great archetypes" or "cardinal images" of temple and labyrinth upon which Spenser organized the "overall shaping" of *The Faerie Queene*. Fletcher particularly associates these archetypes with the prophetic mode of literature, commenting that "a dialectic of the temple and the labyrinth enables the poet to develop a mythological grammar, whereby he can combine myths from various matrices in a large, loose, yet harmonious syncretic union."[58] This account of method splendidly characterizes Chapman's usual compositional procedure in the mythic

[56]See D. J. Gordon, "Le *Masque Mémorable* de Chapman," *Les Fêtes de la Renaissance*, ed. Jean Jacquot (Paris, 1956), 1: 305–15.

[57]Wind, especially pp. 78–88; Wasserman, pp. 53–61; quotation, p. 53, n. 7.

[58]Angus Fletcher, *The Prophetic Moment: An Essay on Spenser* (Chicago, 1971), p. 6; see also pp. 11–12.

narratives. Moreover, the dialectic of temple and labyrinth illuminatingly describes the allegorical narrative of Chapman's most prophetic poem, the *Hymnvs in Cynthiam*, wherein a tormenting hunt through thickets conveys the reader from one building named "Pax Imperij" to another called "Cynthiaes Temple." Elsewhere in Chapman (with the notable exception of *An Epicede*) the particular images of temple and labyrinth are less relevant, but the concepts which they represent are basic enough to the poet's mind to be constantly pertinent: on the one hand, the image of order, stasis, being, intimating always the presence of a higher level of reality; on the other, chaos, flux, process, intimating the human condition of error and uncertainty.[59] Chapman's "templar" images consistently are iconic, female figures at the center of the narrative spatially or of the narrator's consciousness psychically—Cynthia, Ceremony in *Hero and Leander*, Justice in *The Teares of Peace*, Religion in *Eugenia*. Rather than the condition being externalized as wandering in a maze, human imperfection and error usually occur as a problem of perception; the narrator or society generally "sees crookedly," misapprehending the nature of the female goddess, and must learn to view her correctly, which means from the right moral perspective.[60] Chapman complicates the perceptual dilemma in *Ovids Banquet of Sence* in which he creates his one "white goddess" figure, Corynna, whom the self-deluded protagonist never does see aright. Seeing correctly and so understanding the perfect order of the temple is logically prior to acting upon that understanding, whether action takes the practical form of applying the principles of order to one's own life, or the mystical form of union with the One. Spenser's knights learn from the House of Holiness and the Castle of Alma, then return to the quest. Similarly, Chapman's *concordia discors* poems, with their obvious implications of transcendent union and concord of body and spirit, do not present their narrators and protagonists with the dilemma of seeing through the labyrinth. That problem symbolizes an earlier stage of progress, and the obstacles are externalized— Fever, who kills Prince Henry in *An Epicede*; the monster slain by Perseus in *Andromeda Liberata*. Typologically the *concordia discors* myths are presided over by bisexual figures, avatars of Hermaphrodite or Aristophanes' Androgyne.[61] Hymen, Perseus, and Prince Henry all symbolize a dialectic of corresponding male and female attributes, celebrating not the sport of nature or the carnival freak connoted to our demythologized age, but wholeness, harmony, mortal perfection.

[59]See Fletcher, pp. 14–34, for a full discussion of the qualities symbolized by temple and labyrinth.

[60]Fletcher, p. 23 n., associates his idea of the temple with the development of perspective theory in art. For a full account of perspectivism in Chapman's poems, see chapter 4.

[61]In addition to n. 44 above, see Wind, pp. 172–75; and Marie Delcourt, *Hermaphrodite: Mythes et rites de la Bisexualité dans l'Antiquité classique* (Paris, 1958), especially pp. 104– 29; *Hermaphroditea: Recherches sur l'être double promoteur de la fertilité dans le monde classique*, Collection Latomus, 86 (Brussels, 1966).

THREE
THE
SHADOW
OF
NIGHT

ORPHIC HYMNS

The obvious contemporary model for Chapman's *The Shadow of Night*, with its intimidating dedicatory epistle and ostentatiously learned glosses, might be *The Shepheardes Calendar*; yet the resemblance is more apparent than actual. While E. K.'s commentary performs for Spenser's poem a function roughly similar to that of *Our Exagmination* for *Finnegans Wake*—that is, supplying the reader with interpretative vectors having the author's probable sanction—the material appended to *The Shadow of Night* more precisely resembles the annotations to *The Waste Land*: in both instances the glosses, because they are from the author's own hand, directly affect response to the poems and become part of their fictive contexts. Within the glosses, in the marginal notations, and even in the body of the two poems Chapman cites the names of a dozen-and-a-half authorities for scholarly and poetic precedent; most of these authorities are named once, a few twice, only three more frequently than that. Frequency of reference is, of course, no reliable index to Chapman's use of source material; ever since Schoell's study it has been known that, despite the fact Chapman names him only once, better than three-fourths of the glosses were lifted from Natalis Comes' *Mythologiae*.[1] The more important question is what impression did Chapman wish to create by using the particular authorities he selected from the welter of material in Comes' sourcebook? When considered from this standpoint the names repeatedly mentioned gain significance, and it becomes possible to sort out dominant reactions to the presence of the glosses: first, Chapman wanted to invest his work with the spirit and weight of the oldest Greek philosopher-poets; second, more particularly, he wished to call attention to his two hymns as profound mysteries in the tradition of the Greek hymns—as they were understood in the Renaissance.

The triad of poets whose names occur most importantly in the glosses are Homer, Hesiod, and Orpheus. We know well of Chapman's lifelong devotion to Homer, of the loving labor he expended upon translating the *Whole Works*, and of his unquestioning acceptance of the commonplace belief that Homer read allegorically is a repository of moral wisdom; the

[1] Franck L. Schoell, *Études sur l'humanisme continental en Angleterre* (Paris, 1926), pp. 181–85, 193.

inclusion of the other two names requires more explanation. Having completed his translations of the Homeric epics, Chapman must have been seized with the desire to enlarge his achievement by making available in English more of the earliest Greek poetry; even before issuing *The Crowne of all Homer's Workes* Chapman published his versions of *The Georgicks of Hesiod* (1618) and *The Divine Poem of Musaeus* (1616). His biographical note on Hesiod, who "lived in the latter time of Homer," indicates the regard in which the Greek poet was held:

> His authority was such amongst the ancients, that his verses were commonly learned as *axioms* or *oracles*, all teaching good life and humanity; which though never so profitable for men's now readings, yet had they rather (saith Isocrates) consume their times still in their own follies, than be any time conversant in these precepts of wisdom; of which (with Homer) he was first father, whose interpreters were all the succeeding philosophers—not Aristotle himself excepted:—who before Thales, Solon, Pittacus, Socrates, Plato, &c. writ of life, of manners, of God, of nature, of the stars, and general state of the universe. Nor are his writings the less worthy, that Poesy informed them, but of so much the more dignity and eternity.[2]

In a complimentary poem Drayton exclaims, "What wealth thou dost upon this land confer, / Th' old Grecian prophets hither that hast brought, / Of their full words the true interpreter," and pictures the gratitude of Musaeus, "that ILIAD SINGER," and "noble HESIOD" as they sit in Elysium. It may be difficult to imagine Musaeus in such exalted company; however, we need to remember that in the Renaissance *Hero and Leander* was attributed, not to Musaeus the Grammarian, but to the legendary pupil of Orpheus, the prophet-poet-civilizer.[3] For Chapman Musaeus was, like his mentor, a semimythical personage, conversant with the mysteries of the gods and of the creation; like Homer and Hesiod, he was a prime source of philosophic truth and moral precept, as Chapman's continuation of Marlowe's *Hero and Leander* would suggest. The translations made over twenty years later attest that the importance with which Chapman invests the milieu of these "old Grecian prophets" in *The Shadow of Night* is not simply window dressing.

Of Chapman's hellenic trinity the figure to whom he devotes most attention is Orpheus. In the *Hymnvs in Noctem* he is referred to twice by name; his mother Calliope is described in a marginal note; his musical powers and his descent to Hell provide the substance for a twenty-line passage; indeed, as will be seen, the references to "Orphean Musicke" and the account of Orpheus's career serve as a key to understanding the function of the numerous references to music and poetry in both hymns.

---

[2]Chapman, *Homer's Batrachomyomachia*, ed. Richard Hooper, 2d. ed. (London, 1888), pp. 144–45; for Drayton's poem, see ibid., pp. 146–47.

[3]The ramifications of this confusion will be discussed further in chapter 5.

In the glosses Orpheus is quoted five times: one of these quotations is from the *Argonautica*; two others are identified as being from the *Orphic Hymns*, thus particularly emphasizing the hymnodic context; that context is further supplemented by one quotation from a Homeric hymn and two from a hymn of Callimachus. Two factors which emerge, the role of Orpheus in Renaissance thought and the contribution of the Orphic hymns to it, need individual consideration.

Orpheus enjoyed an exceptional popularity well into the late Renaissance; for centuries commentators had observed that, like Hercules, he was a pagan type of Christ.[4] Recently, however, the studies of Chastel, Walker, and Wind have done much to explain the presence of an Orphic cult emanating from the platonic nexus of Ficino's academy at Careggi.[5] Ficino retained a lifelong enthusiasm for Orpheus, sprinkling his own works with Orphic sayings, to the dismay of a modern scholar who laments: "I am afraid the quotations from Orpheus alone far exceed the sum total of his references to scholastic philosophers."[6] Poliziano, who contributed his verse drama *Orfeo* to the movement, praised Ficino for bringing back to life the true Eurydice, platonic wisdom; and it is true that Ficino, performing on his Orphic lyre, consciously adopted the role of a new Orpheus.[7] Others of the circle equally were involved in the revival: Cristoforo Landino was recognized as "the most accomplished Orphic and Platonic poet of our times" and Pico della Mirandola attempted to unveil the mysteries of Orphic theology.[8] As Chastel per-

---

[4]The best concise account is by D. C. Allen, "Milton and the Descent to Light," *Journal of English and Germanic Philology*, 60 (1961): 614–30. See also John Block Friedman, *Orpheus in the Middle Ages* (Cambridge, Mass., 1970), especially pp. 38–85; Kirsty Cochrane, "Orpheus Applied: Some Instances of his Importance in the Humanist View of Language," *Review of English Studies*, 19 (1968): 1–13; K. R. R. Gros Louis, "The Triumph and Death of Orpheus in the English Renaissance," *Studies in English Literature*, 9 (1969): 63–80; and Thomas H. Cain, "Spenser and the Renaissance Orpheus," *University of Toronto Quarterly*, 41 (1971): 24–47.

[5]André Chastel, *Marsile Ficin et l'Art* (Geneva, 1954), pp. 175–76; D. P. Walker, "Orpheus the Theologian and Renaissance Platonists," *Journal of the Warburg and Courtauld Institutes*, 16 (1953): 100–120; "The *Prisca Theologia* in France," *JWCI*, 17 (1954): 204–59, Walker's essays are now reprinted in his book, *The Ancient Theology: Studies in Christian Platonism from the Fifteenth to the Eighteenth Century* (London, 1972). See also his *Spiritual and Demonic Magic from Ficino to Campanella* (London, 1958), pp. 19–24 especially; and Edgar Wind, *Pagan Mysteries in the Renaissance* (New Haven, 1958).

[6]P. O. Kristeller, "The Scholastic Background of Marsilio Ficino," *Traditio*, 2 (1944): 271–72. Kristeller reprints a letter (ca. 1494–98) illustrating Ficino's undimmed interest in Orphica late in his life, pp. 317–18.

[7]Kristeller, *The Philosophy of Marsilio Ficino*, trans. Virginia Conant (1943; reprint ed., Gloucester, Mass., 1964), p. 22. Walker, *Spiritual and Demonic Magic*, relates Ficino's performances to the astrological music theories in *De vita coelitus comparanda*; see pp. 1–24, especially 19–23. Ficino's lyre was "Orphic" not only because it was ornamented with a picture of Orpheus, but because it accompanied the singing of Orphic hymns.

[8]Landino is so described in *Marsilio Ficino's Commentary on Plato's Symposium*, trans. Sears R. Jayne, Univ. of Missouri Studies, 19 (Columbia, 1944), 4.1. On Pico's poetic theology, see Wind, pp. 24–30.

ceived, Orpheus "obsédait et comblait l'imagination de l'Académie."[9] A good part of this obsession can be attributed to Orpheus's status as a *priscus theologus*; according to one of Ficino's genealogies of wisdom Orpheus was second in the line of descent from Hermes Trismegistus.[10] Moreover, Orpheus was for the academy a symbol of all that could be achieved through a life given to music, poetry, eloquence: "Orphée signifie la pacification des instincts, le bon gouvernement, l'ordre harmonieux, imposés par la 'magie de l'art': la tradition antique est unanime, et l'humanisme florentin avec elle."[11]

The writings attributed to Orpheus consist of fragments of verse which survive through Proclus and the Greek Fathers, of the *Argonautica*, and, most important, the hymns, now believed to date from the second or third century A.D. The *Orphic Hymns* are similar in general form to the *Homeric Hymns* translated by Chapman and, in fact, were frequently considered with them, their association established through the common transmission of hymns by Homer, Orpheus, Callimachus, and Proclus in manuscript collections.[12] Pausanias remarked, "For poetic beauty they may be said to come next to the hymns of Homer, while they have been even more honoured by the gods" (9.30.12).[13] Frances Yates has argued that Ficino's translating the Hermetic writings before the works of Plato is testimony to the extraordinary reputation of Hermes Trismegistus; yet, if Kristeller's surmise is correct, Ficino had translated the *Orphica* prior to that: the Hermes translation was undertaken in 1463, but in 1462 Ficino had enclosed his translation of one of the hymns in a letter to Cosimo de Medici.[14]

The appeal of the hymns, beyond their having been written by the father of poets and employed in actual religious rites, apparently lay in the belief that, concealed beneath their limpid surface, one could detect profound philosophic and religious truths—"ses hymnes médités et vénérés par les Platoniciens célèbrant les principes mystérieux du monde et montrent comment le chaos a été dominé par l'Amour."[15] Pico explains the method of the hymns:

---

[9]Chastel, p. 175.

[10]See Frances A. Yates, *Giordano Bruno and the Hermetic Tradition* (Chicago, 1964), p. 14. Elsewhere Ficino ranks Orpheus third, behind Hermes and Zoroaster (Yates, p. 15, n. 1).

[11]Chastel, p. 176.

[12]See A. W. Mair, *Callimachus: Hymns and Epigrams; Lycophron; Aratus*, rev. ed., Loeb Classical Library (Cambridge, Mass., 1955), pp. 13–15. See also "Hymnorvm Codices," *Homeri Opera* ed. Thomas W. Allen (Oxford, 1912), 5: ix–xi; and Philip Rollinson, "The Renaissance of the Literary Hymn," *Renaissance Papers, 1968* (Durham, N. C., 1969), p. 13.

[13]Pausanias, *Description of Greece*, trans. W. H. S. Jones, Loeb Classical Library (London, 1935), 4.307.

[14]Yates, pp. 12–14. Kristeller, "Scholastic Background," p. 271.

[15]Chastel, p. 175.

But as was the practice of the ancient theologians, even so did Orpheus protect the mysteries of his dogmas with the coverings of fables, and conceal them with a poetic veil, so that whoever should read his hymns would suppose there was nothing beneath them beyond idle tales and perfectly unadulterated trifles. I have wished to say this so that it might be known what a task it was for me, how difficult it was to draw out the hidden meaning of the secrets of philosophy from the intentional tangles of riddles and from the obscurity of fables, especially since I have been aided, in a matter so serious, so abstruse, and so little known, by no toil, no application on the part of other interpreters.[16]

Although Pico complains of the lack of help on this project, almost certainly some guidance was provided by Ficino, who concurred with the notion that philosophic secrets were embedded in the hymns and who wrote to Germain de Ganay a letter analyzing the conception of the *Hymn to Nature* in Plotinian terms.[17] Possibly, Pico was annoyed by Ficino's caution in refusing to publish his Orphic translations, evidently because of sensitivity to the charge that he was reviving pagan religion, despite Ficino's constant use of Orpheus in his own writings. In any case Ficino's reluctance meant that a Latin translation of the hymns was delayed over thirty years until an edition finally was published in 1500. In the mid-sixteenth century, D. P. Walker has shown, Orphism flourished particularly amidst the French platonists when, aside from other Orphic texts, the hymns were published in Greek by Henri Estienne, in Latin by René Perdrier, and even in French by Guy Lefévre de la Boderie.[18] The movement begun by the Florentine group a hundred years earlier had rooted and blossomed extravagantly.

The reader may well ask the relevance of this Orphic cult to Chapman. Even granted that the *Shadow of Night* consists of two poems called "hymns" and addressed to "deities" on the order of those in the hellenic hymns, and that he surrounds these poems with references to Orpheus and to ancient hymns, how can one equate Chapman's long, allegorical narratives with the brief, mystical incantations attributed to Orpheus? The answer must be that Chapman imitates not the form but the spirit of the *Orphic Hymns*. Orpheus wrote them employing the language of mysteries, veiling the "meaning of the secrets of philosophy" with "intentional tangles of riddles" and "the obscurity of fables." So Pico read the *Orphica*, and clearly he believes it a virtue that "whoever should read his hymns would suppose there was nothing beneath them beyond idle tales

---

[16]"Oration on the Dignity of Man," trans. Elizabeth Forbes, in *The Renaissance Philosophy of Man*, ed. Ernst Cassirer et al. (Chicago, 1948), pp. 253–54. Here I prefer Forbes's translation to that by Wallis in the Library of Liberal Arts volume cited in chapter 6.

[17]Kristeller, "Scholastic Background," p. 273, and for the text of the letter, pp. 317–18.

[18]"The *Prisca Theologia* in France," pp. 204–59.

and perfectly unadulterated trifles."[19] The platonic adept, of course, will know better. The eighteenth-century platonist Thomas Taylor instructs us,

> the reader will please to observe through the whole of these Hymns, that the Orphic method of instruction consists in signifying divine concerns by symbols alone. And here it will be necessary to speak of philosophical mythology; as an accurate conception of its nature, will throw a general light on the Hymns.[20]

Chapman's poetic strategy is narrative rather than lyric and the structural component of his narratives most frequently is what Taylor calls "philosophical myth." Northrop Frye comments that "The narrative *epos* form corresponding to the psalm or hymn presents a more connected account of the god."[21] It is also true, as far as Chapman is concerned, that it presents a far more complicated account. Because Chapman reads the *Orphic Hymns* with the allegorical viewpoint promoted by the Florentine academy he endows them, as he does other ancient poems, with a weighty conceptual burden which requires him to employ a complex allegorical myth to convey an equivalent meaning in his own poems. Chapman's enormous expansion of the *Hero and Leander* supplies a case in point. In his continuation Chapman has no intention of making a strict translation—his concern is to stress the moral and philosophical implications that he perceived in the original. That Chapman consciously conceived of his hymns in this manner, as imitations of the spirit of *Orphic Hymns* in a suitable English form, may be seen by a simile from the *Hymnvs in Cynthiam*:

> As in our garments, ancient fashions
> Are newlie worne; and as sweet poesie
> Will not be clad in her supremacie
> With those straunge garments (Romes Hexameters)
> As she is English: but in right prefers
> Our natiue robes, put on with skillfull hands
> (English heroicks) to those antick garlands.

> [Cyn. 85–91]

All the hymns to which Chapman refers in the glosses are, of course, written in hexameters; that he would think of them first as "Romes Hexameters" is symptomatic of his customary reliance upon Latin transla-

[19]See Wind, pp. 24–30.

[20]Thomas Taylor, The Hymns of Orpheus, Translated from the original Greek: With a Preliminary Dissertation on THE LIFE AND THEOLOGY OF ORPHEUS (London, 1792), pp. 109–10; Kathleen Raine and George M. Harper, eds., Thomas Taylor, the Platonist: Selected Writings, (Princeton, 1969), p. 209.

[21]Northrop Frye, Anatomy of Criticism (Princeton, 1957), p. 294.

tions. Comes helpfully supplied both Greek and Latin versions of his quotations and Chapman took full advantage of this convenience in preparing the glosses.[22]

Chapman attempts to envelop his *Shadow of Night* with the religious and magical atmosphere of the *Orphic Hymns* by offering explicit hints that his hymns are concerned with mysteries analogous to those the platonists found in the writings of Orpheus, that he wants his hymns read in this spirit. In the only sustained attempt to find intellectual coherence in *The Shadow of Night* Roy Battenhouse has concluded that the poems are "complementary," the first a "hymn of lament" and the second a "hymn of praise."[23] This is accurate as far as it goes; for purposes of a structural analysis, however, it is helpful to see the *Hymnvs in Noctem* as preliminary, rather than complementary, a necessary introduction to the *Hymnvs in Cynthiam*. The central symbol of the moon-goddess Cynthia, who appears in an epiphany at the ending of the first hymn, operates as the structural and thematic keystone of the whole.[24] The moon goddess in her threefold manifestation as Luna, Diana, and Hecate, united as Cynthia, supplies the narrative structure for the corresponding planes of allegorical activity—the philosophic, political, and poetic. Battenhouse regards the moral allegory as the primary concern of the poem, but one must remember that it was customary to view all realms of life in moral terms and Chapman wished to delineate morality in these particular three dimensions. Since a moral view of life is finally a single vision, the dimensions of activity overlap and interrelate to frustrate separation of allegorical levels except in a general way; this is implied by the myth of the moon goddess. She is triune but one: aspects of her total identity or phases of her influence upon humanity are revealed by the division within essential unity of the myth. "And here," as the recondite Taylor warned us, "it will be necessary to speak of philosophical mythology" in the hope that it will throw "a general light on the Hymns."

LUNA

The symbolic paradigm through which Chapman unites the figure of Orpheus, the legendary theologian-civilizer and poet-musician, with that

---

[22]See Comes' chapter, "De hymnis antiquorum," *Mythologiae sive Explicationvm Fabvlarum* (Paris, 1583), 1.16. On the form of the Greek hymns, see the article by A. T. Shaw in *The Encyclopedia of Poetry and Poetics*, ed. Alex Preminger et al. (Princeton, 1965), pp. 356–58; and Rollinson, p. 13.

[23]Battenhouse, "Chapman's *The Shadow of Night*: An Interpretation," *Studies in Philology*, 38 (1941): 607.

[24]The structure of the poems must be emphasized because it has been misunderstood so often. Swinburne's bafflement is less surprising than that of recent commentators who, in defiance of Elizabethan poetics, have described *The Shadow of Night* in these terms: "a dream-fugue"; "a pattern of emotion and association, not of daylight logic"; "symphonic"; "a surrealist painting."

of Cynthia, the paradoxical embodiment of eternal chastity and continual changeability, has been described expertly by Northrop Frye:

> All the arts are employed as regenerative symbols in the romances, but the
> most important one by far is the traditional one, music. Music is traditional
> because all that is now left of this upper world of nature is the ordered revolu-
> tion of the starry spheres, with their inaudible music that symbolizes the
> harmony of the soul. This harmony of the soul, in its turn, is symbolized by
> female chastity, which in all pastoral romance down to Milton's *Comus* is an
> attribute of the higher order of nature, and a containing of spiritual energy.
> The central symbol of this upper world is the moon, the boundary between the
> two orders of nature and the habitation of Cynthia or Diana, the goddess of
> chastity.[25]

The arts of Orpheus symbolize the possible means of attaining the spiritual harmony, lost since the fall, of which Cynthia is the model. In the
Hymnvs in Noctem Chapman discloses the condition of the world and
mankind since the loss of the original harmony to explicate the need
which should lead man to Cynthia. The *Hymnvs in Cynthiam* reveals the
true nature of Cynthia and is designed to alleviate by example the fears
and reservations resulting from an imperfect understanding of her nature and role.

The theme of the *Hymnvs in Noctem* is the one enunciated by Milton's
Satan upon first sight of his expelled followers: "O how fall'n! how
chang'd." Chapman frames the theme particularly in terms of form and
the fall as a violation or loss of form. He begins by contrasting the primal
chaos that existed when Night was sovereign, of course prior to the
existence of form, with that present formlessness which is a debasement
of the existing standard. He represents chaos as the Empedoclean strife
of opposites, the elemental *concordia discors*, which sustained a perfect
harmony between the "fighting parents" of the universe:

> When earth, the ayre, and sea, in fire remaind,
> When fire, the sea, and earth, the ayre containd,
> When ayre, the earth, and fire, the sea enclosde
> When sea, fire, ayre, in earth were indisposde,
> Nothing, as now, remainde so out of kinde,
> All things in grosse, were finer than refinde,
> Substance was sound within, and had no being,
> Now forme giues being; all our essence seeming,
> Chaos had soule without a bodie then,
> Now bodies liue without the soules of men,
> Lumps being digested; monsters, in our pride.

[*Noct.* 39–49]

---

[25]Northrop Frye, *A Natural Perspective* (New York, 1965), pp. 136–37.

Now that essences have been given body and form is the standard, "So all things now (extract out of the prime)/Are turnd to chaos, and confound the time" (*Noct.* 61–62). The condition persists because man's vision is obscured by "blindnesse of the minde." Chapman personifies the mental disorder as a "Gorgon," a technique used repeatedly in later poems—with "Murther" in *The Teares of Peace*, for instance, and with the sea monster of *Andromeda Liberata*. The motif of negative metamorphosis enters upon an explicit level as the poet analyzes the effect of man's turning away from order and law: "All are transformd to Calydonian bores, / That kill our bleeding vines, displow our fields, / Rend groues in peeces; all things nature yeelds / Supplanting" (*Noct.* 84–87). The image functions in two ways; beyond shifting the discussion of man's condition to the more particular concern of fall as metamorphosis, it introduces the presence of Cynthia as a power in man's life. As Chapman knew from Ovid, the Calydonian boar served as the instrument of Diana's vengeance when the people of Calydon neglected to perform the rites due her. In Chapman's vision too "Religious curb, that manadgd men in bounds, / Of publique wellfare" is "cast away, by selfe-lou's paramores," resulting in the transformation; however, to indicate fully man's self-destructiveness Chapman conflates the victims and the instrument of destruction. Just as man's betrayal of form, his descent to monstrosity, is juxtaposed with the harmonious formlessness of chaos, so Chapman counterbalances the Calydonian metamorphosis: Amalthea, "Though but a Goate," lives in the heavens "and rules a liuing signe / In humane bodies"; even an inanimate object, such as the "sencelesse Argiue ship" by fulfilling its nature can achieve the reward of translation to the stars that are Cynthia's satellites.

The contrast renders man's failure the more reprehensible, as does the central place man holds in creation: "In him the world is to a lump reuerst, / That shruncke from forme, that was by forme disperst" (*Noct.* 101–2). It is man's mind that "frame[s] mans figure," and accordingly his external image can only be that of beast or monster. For this reason the Promethean poet holds a mirror up to fallen nature, creating in verse men "With shapes of Centaurs, Harpies, Lapithes," in the hope that the shock of recognition might generate reform. Thus the story of Orpheus's musical power "bewrayes the force / His wisedome had, to draw men growne so rude / To ciuill loue of Art, and Fortitude" (*Noct.* 142–44) to reeffect the harmony of man's spirit by calming "the perturbations of his minde." Chapman finds in the Orpheus myth both components of the Christian myth, for, if the art of Orpheus symbolizes the possibility of redemption, so his journey to the underworld in search of Eurydice, "Which Iustice signifies," suggests by contrast the opposite phase of Adamic man:[26]

[26]On the "descent to light" motif see D. C. Allen. For the etymological interpretation of Eurydice's name, see Friedman, p. 89.

But if in rights obseruance any man
Looke backe, with boldnesse lesse then Orphean,
Soone falls he to the hell from whence he rose.

[*Noct.* 153–55]

As Chapman permits the reverberations of the Christian fall to enter the poem through this typological variant, the pattern of man's offenses and the abuses of his nature take on a more familiar color: self-love, pride, presumption form the complex. The truly virtuous man particularly abominates "manlesse changes" by those who attempt to rise above their proper station; Chapman thinks of them as "Typhons" that fight "Against their Maker" and, following Comes, uses the golden chain of Homer to signify ambition and avarice. The Orphean harmony prevailing "When Saturnes golden scepter stroke the strings / Of Ciuill gouernment" (*Noct.* 195–96) has yielded to the cacophony of the antimasque "That like loose froes at Bacchanalean feasts, / Makes them seeme franticke" (*Noct.* 189–90). Chapman's antithesis to the Orphic vision is subtle but effective; as he wrote later, "The Ladies of this land would teare him peece-meal / (As did the drunken Froes, the Thratian Harper)" (*M. D'Olive* 2.2.178–79). It is because man has "so much abusd" his "first excellence," that "to the chaos of our first descent,/ . . . / We basely make retrait, and are no lesse / Then huge impolisht heapes of filthinesse" (*Noct.* 221–24). Thus formless, man must make his way in the world in which even the condition of life, to "yeeld Labour his due" (*Noct.* 201–10), is a painful reminder of that lost Golden Age before man sweated to earn his bread. Man seeks the escape to night not only because it shrouds him from "the whoredome of this painted light," concealing from his vision the monstrosity of daily life, but because it restores something of that lost condition. The goddess, "Type, and nurse of death," releases her "sweet seas of golden humor forth," drives the fowls and beasts to "Somnus lodgings," and proclaims "scilence, studie, ease, and sleepe." Day's deceitful malice "From the silke vapors of her Iueryport" sends endlessly variable, treacherous dreams; "But from Nights port of horne she greets our eyes / With grauer dreames inspir'd with prophesies" (*Noct.* 352–53). And for all of this the poet consecrates himself to sacred night and to that glittering goddess who is the heart or soul of night.

In sum, the first hymn is primarily concerned with change as loss of essential form and, thus, change as an entirely negative process. Examples of positive change are given, but these are confined to the two nonhuman metamorphoses and the anonymous star cluster of "All the choise worthies that did euer raigne / In eldest age" (*Noct.* 232–33). These offer little comfort for the present; the praise of unchanging virtue and the hope that time might be stopped (*Noct.* 380–84) to prolong the escape of night even suggest that a static condition may be more desirable than the risk of positive change.

The *Hymnvs in Cynthiam* takes the problem that *Noctem* has postulated implicitly and explores it with more urgency. The perfection of Cynthia's nature is imaged in her form and that form is virtue's pattern: "In perfect circle of whose sacred state, / The circles of our hopes are compassed: / All wisedome, beautie, maiestie and dread, / Wrought in the speaking pourtrait of thy face" (*Cyn.* 6–9). Man's greatest fear can only be that the pattern might change. Accordingly, Chapman employs the two types of lunar eclipse—by the sun and by interposition of the earth between moon and sun—to symbolize the potential dangers. Like all uncommon celestial phenomena, eclipses had long been considered as portents of evil and impending disaster. Kester Svendsen comments, "The encyclopedists limited themselves pretty much to explaining eclipses by natural means; but demonologists and writers on witchcraft considered Satanic intervention long and heavily, from medieval times forward."[27] Milton reflects commonplace superstitions when he attributes lunar eclipse to the agency of witches (*PL* 2.662–66) and describes solar eclipse as perplexing monarchs "with fear of change" (*PL* 1.594–600). More philosophically, Leone Ebreo expounded the movements of sun and moon in a moral sense; and the French platonist Jamyn borrowed his explanation that a lunar eclipse by the earth signified the domination of man's rational soul by the animal passions of his corporeal nature.[28]

Although in the hymns Chapman consistently associates change with passion and lust as a synecdoche for the inharmonious falling away from the temperate ideal, he primarily uses the earthly eclipse to show what might occur if Cynthia, who spans both orders of nature, were to prove susceptible to the lower one: "For if the enuious forehead of the earth / Lowre on thy age, and claime thee as her birth," he speculates that no charms or rituals "We know can nothing further thy recall, / When Nights darke robes (whose obiects blind vs all) / Shall celebrate thy changes funerall" (*Cyn.* 31–32, 37–39). He uses a long battle simile to convey the state of disorder, terror, passion that would overtake man upon the fall "When interposed earth takes thee away." (*Cyn.* 59). Developing the contrast between Romans and Macedonians through the battle simile, the description of eclipse rites, and funeral ceremonies, he concludes that the Macedonian response "With skillesse horrour of thy changes dread" is the only possible one to the prospect of Cynthia's mortality. Throughout *Noctem* the light of day explicitly had been associated with "whoredome," "rape," and indulgence of the passions generally; at one point this train of associations was epitomized in the image of the sun. Chapman appealed to Hercules to "bend thy brasen bow

[27]Kester Svendsen, *Milton and Science* (Cambridge, Mass., 1956), p. 75.

[28]Frances A. Yates, *The French Academies in the Sixteenth Century* (London, 1947), p. 143; and Leone Ebreo, *The Philosophy of Love*, trans. F. Friedeberg-Seeley and J. H. Barnes (London, 1937), p. 218 ff.

against the Sunne," to shoot and "Suffer no more his lustfull rayes to get / The Earth with issue" (*Noct.* 255–65). The unbridled lust of the sun is thus the symbolic antithesis to Cynthia's chastity; and eclipse by the sun connotes loss of that chastity, the threat of which makes man tremble, "lest thy souveraigne parts / (The whole preseruers of our happinesse) / Should yeeld to change, Eclips, or heauinesse" (*Cyn.* 107–9). The pun on *heauinesse* as pregnancy is no doubt intentional; as will be discussed later, the primary allegorical level in this section is the political, and the theme avoidance of marriage. The similar treatment in *Hero and Leander* of the marriage-as-change motif is noteworthy:

> In this conceited skarfe she wrought beside
> A moone in change, and shooting stars did glide
> In number after her with bloodie beames,
> Which figur'd her affects in their extreames,
> Pursuing Nature in her Cynthian bodie,
> And did her thoughts running on change implie.
>
> [*Hero* 4.76–81]

But it must be remembered that still operative is the more general opposition of spiritual harmony to brutish passion, Cynthia's chastity versus the sun's lust, and Chapman is careful to reestablish the mythic context as he describes Cynthia's followers daring "the Sunne, like Thebane Hercules / To calme the furies, and to quench the fire" (*Cyn.* 127–28).

The narrator explains that, since Cynthia's force figures "the forces of the mind," her disciples attain their powers because the "vertue-tempered mind" is "A perfect type" of her state; and he promises "An argument to rauish and refine / An earthly soule, and make it meere diuine" (*Cyn.* 154–55). At this point the mythic narrative commences. During the day Cynthia descends to earth and, acting as "Forme her selfe," creates a temple; afterwards for her pleasure she creates a nymph, an avatar of herself, as well as hunters and hounds. The nymph, transformed into a panther, is pursued into a tormenting thicket, which imprisons the souls of men who have offended Cynthia. The hounds are repulsed, but the hunters press forward until terrifying sights cause them to retreat. The hounds pick up the scent, however, following the panther to a fruitful island, whereupon the panther transforms herself into a boar; the pursuit continues until day ends and the goddess blows retreat. The poet describes the ancient temple of Cynthia, which should be reconstructed in the mind, allowing virtuous men to become Ganymedes. The hymn ends with a thematic recapitulation, the poet's consecration to Cynthia, and celebration of her magic powers.

Obviously, the narrative unit framed by the building of the temples, which encompasses roughly 300 of the hymn's 528 lines, is crucial to understanding the pair of hymns. Somehow the poet's fears of change and eclipse are answered before the concluding couplet, "So shall the wonders of thy power be seene, / And thou for euer liue the Planets Queene," and the answer must lie in the implications of the narrative. Schoell discovered that the catalogue of the hounds' names derives from Comes' De Actaeone,[29] but even this information is not necessary for awareness that the basic narrative component is the Actaeon myth. Chapman carefully prepares for the transition to narrative earlier in the hymn while describing Cynthia's "neuer-tainted" purity:

Thy bodie not composed in thy birth,
Of such condensed matter as the earth,
Thy shunning faithlesse mens societie,
Betaking thee to hounds, and Archerie
To deserts, and inaccessible hills,
Abhorring pleasure in earths common ills,
Commit most willing rapes on all our harts.

[Cyn. 100–06]

Here, in the context of the sun's threat to Cynthia's chastity, the familiar resonances of Ovid's tale come alive—the chaste goddess of archery, the hounds, the inaccessible retreat; and, not least, the witty inversion of Actaeon's "rape," for which he was metamorphosed to a hart, here transformed to Cynthia's rape of men's hearts.

Chapman is able to foreshadow his narrative structure just this much, confident that his readers will anticipate his intentions because the Actaeon myth was one of the allegorists' staples: for Apuleius the story was a warning against impertinent curiosity; Fulgentius, in what became the standard reading, related the curiosity to lust.[30] Tharsalio, in The Widow's Tears, is fully orthodox: "Did you never hear of Actaeon? Curiosity was his death. He could not be content to adore Diana in her temple, but he must needs dog her to her retired pleasures, and see her in her nakedness" (1.3.67, 69–71). Chapman's busy contemporary, Abraham Fraunce, supplies a handy compendium of interpretations: euhemeristically, Actaeon was a man eaten up by the expense of the entourage he foolishly kept; the story warns against curiosity in matters beyond our concern, such as prying in the affairs of state; it warns against falling prey to the lure of physical beauty and so being devoured by one's own passions. This last treatment was one of the stock properties of the sonneteers; Shakespeare's Orsino scrupulously observes convention when he describes his desire as pursuing "like fell and cruell hounds."

---

[29]Schoell, pp. 189–90.

[30]The allegorical development is traced by Walter R. Davis, "Actaeon in Arcadia," Studies in English Literature, 2 (1962): 100–04, who supplies citations for the examples used here. See also T. P. Roche, Jr., The Kindly Flame: A Study of the Third and Fourth Books of Spenser's Faerie Queene (Princeton, 1964), pp. 111–13, and C. W. Lemmi, The Classic Deities in Bacon (Baltimore, 1933), pp. 187–88.

In a poem which sets Cynthia's "Christall, and Imperiall throne" against the lustful sun, this standard allegorization certainly remains relevant.[31] If the hounds and hunters represent men tormented by their own base passions, Cynthia is no Circe, transforming men to swine through her sorcery; *Noctem* makes it clear that man's shape-changing is his own doing, reflecting alterations in his spiritual nature. The hunt that Cynthia creates must illustrate the self-inflicted punishments of men whom Chapman compares to a "flocke of schoole-boys" given leave to sport:

> All as they list to seuerall pastimes fall,
> To feede their famisht wantonnesse with all.
> When strait, within the woods some wolfe or beare,
> The heedlesse lyms of one doth peecemeale teare.

> [*Cyn.* 261–64]

But the Actaeon myth was put to other uses, as well, in Chapman's time. Spenser adapts it to create the episode of Faunus and Molanna in his *Mutabilitie* cantos. Faunus's assault upon Diana functions as a parallel to Mutabilitie's attack against Nature, shadowing the conflict of fallen nature with that higher nature which follows an immutable order. Sherman Hawkins suggests that Spenser uses the myths of Phaeton and Actaeon "to hint at the primary myth of the fall"—employing Phaeton as a type of pride and Actaeon as animal concupiscence to convey the two aspects of the fall—and concludes that "the fall is essential to an account of mutability."[32] As the earlier thematic analysis indicates, in Chapman's hymns the themes of the fall, symbolized by lust, and mutability, or form and change, are inextricably involved, and so they would seem to be in the Actaeon myth.

If the Actaeon myth is mutability, we need to remember that in Chapman's hands, as in Spenser's, it is also mutable. The most important change from the basic source is the omission of Actaeon himself, and the goddess's assumption of Actaeon's part as quarry of the hunt. That Euthimya is simply an avatar of Cynthia in her role as form-giver seems beyond dispute. Cynthia descends to earth during the day and as Form, constructs an allegorical palace, which, like Spenser's Castle of Alma, is the temple of the body:

> Forme then, twixt two superior pillers framd
> This tender building, Pax Imperij nam'd,

---

[31]See Douglas Bush, *Mythology and the Renaissance Tradition in English Poetry*, rev. ed. (New York, 1963), pp. 209–10, and Battenhouse, pp. 602–4.

[32]Sherman Hawkins, "Mutabilitie and the Cycle of the Months," in *Form and Convention in the Poetry of Edmund Spenser*, ed. William Nelson, English Institute Essays (New York, 1961), p. 85.

Which cast a shadow, like a Pyramis
Whose basis, in the plaine or back part is
Of that queint worke: the top so high extended,
That it the region of the Moone transcended:
Without, within it, euerie corner fild
By bewtious Forme, as her great mistresse wild.

[Cyn. 188-95]

Sir Kenelm Digby first explained that Spenser's triangle and circle (FQ 2.9.22) represent the body and soul; Chapman may have studied Spenser's allegory and adapted the structure to suit his purposes. He adds the pillars of the legs and omits the circle as redundant since the palace is occupied by Cynthia who is the world soul and whose image is the perfect circle.[33] Cynthia then creates from a "bright, and daseling meteor" the nymph, Euthimya; she is a nymph because, as Battenhouse noted, in Comes "nymphs symbolize matter in natural phenomena; they receive and preserve the imprint of form."[34] This is why Euthimya "could turne her selfe to euerie shape / Of swiftest beasts, and at her pleasure scape" (Cyn. 226-27). Chapman assigns to her the part played by Actaeon in the original, allowing the Actaeons of the world to become the hounds and hunters.

He would seem to have several reasons for the inversion, the effect of which he anticipates to be striking: "And maruaile not a Nimphe so rich in grace / To hounds rude pursutes should be giuen in chase" (Cyn. 224-25). Since the common allegorical reading treats the hounds as projections of Actaeon's own passions, the shift is not so radical as it might appear at first; moreover, as with his treatment of the Calydonian boar motif in Noctem, by making the pains and confusions suffered by the pursuers the result of their own aggression, it is undeniable that "they brought it on themselves." Chapman thus eliminates the ambiguity in Ovid's account in which the poet finds Actaeon unlucky rather than guilty and records the mixed reaction of the populace, some praising Diana, others finding her too merciless. As Golding translates, "Much muttring was upon this fact" (3.305). This factor is important because, despite the amusement Cynthia extracts from the predicament of the pursuers, Chapman takes pains to indicate that her motives are benevolent. Euthimya's name signifies "contentment or joy of the mind"[35] and pursuit of this goal certainly in itself is not wrong; rather, in their de-

[33]The similarity and the correct interpretation of Chapman's passage was first pointed out by R. H. Perkinson, "The Body as a Triangular Structure in Spenser and Chapman," Modern Language Notes, 64 (1949): 520-22. See the additional remarks of Alastair Fowler, Spenser and the Numbers of Time (London, 1964), pp. 87, 264 n., 278 n.

[34]Battenhouse, p. 603, n. 42; he quotes the translation of C. W. Lemmi, "Classical Episodes in the Faerie Queene," Philological Quarterly, 8 (1929): 276.

[35]Bartlett, Poems, p. 426 n.

based condition the Actaeons are incapable of understanding how this goal properly should be attained. The hunt serves to instruct them: "Euthimya is her sacred name, / Since she the cares and toyles of earth must tame" (*Cyn.* 218–19).

Cynthia creates a body in which to house the soul and an embodiment of form to be pursued by those men who are formless or deformed. Chapman in effect has taken the implications of an Ovidian metamorphosis and rewritten it to make those implications more prominent. Walter Davis writes of the Actaeon story, "The myth itself, like so many of Ovid's myths, describes the soul seeing itself reflected in the process of bodily transformation, and the new awareness resulting therefrom."[36] This was the essential matter which the interpreters and handbook writers extracted from metamorphosis and, whereas such tales themselves were deliberately and deceptively frivolous, there was nothing frivolous about the lessons. *The Golden Ass* was identified upon the title page of the first edition as a compendium of platonic philosophy, and Apuleius's commentator Beroaldus later explained the master's method: "And it appears that under that mystical cover, being deeply versed in Pythagorean and Platonic philosophy, he set forth the dogmas of both these masters, and conveyed the lessons of palingenesis and metempsychosis, that is, of regeneration and transmutation, through the disguise of that ludicrous story."[37] When Adlington translated Apuleius he explained for his Elizabethan audience:

> Verily under the wrap of this transformation is taxed the life of mortal men, when as we suffer our minds so to be drowned in the sensual lusts of the flesh and the beastly pleasure thereof (which aptly may be called the violent confection of witches) that we lose wholly the use of reason and virtue, which properly should be in a man, and play the parts of brute and savage beasts. . . .[38]

This kind of reading accords with that given to Ariosto; in the commentary, which Harington borrowed from Simon Fornari, we read:

> In Astolfo's metamorphosis into a myrtle tree (which tree is said to be dedicated to Venus) we may note, how men given over to sensuality, leese in the end the very forme of man (which is reason) and so become beastes or stockes.[39]

---

[36]Davis, "Actaeon in Arcadia," p. 102.

[37]Quoted by Wind, pp. 189–90.

[38]William Adlington, trans., *Apuleius: The Golden Ass*, Loeb Classical Library (London, 1915), pp. xvi–xvii.

[39]Sir John Harington, trans., *Orlando Furioso in English Heroical Verse* (London, 1591), p. 47.

Harington displays his knowledge of mythic typology by very properly relating the episode "to Cyrces witchcraft in Homer" as does Adlington with Lucius's story. Shakespeare, in *A Midsummer Night's Dream*, undoubtedly was parodying the transformations of Lucian when he changed the ass Nick Bottom into an ass; but parody may well connote serious respect and even Bottom has a bottomless dream: "The eye of man hath not heard, the ear of man hath not seen, man's hand is not able to taste, his tongue to conceive, nor his heart to report, what my dream was" (*MND* 4.1.216–19). Frank Kermode, arguing for the relevance to the play of Pico, Agrippa, Bruno, and the whole context of platonic mysteries, asserts, "Bottom is there to tell us that the blindness of love, the dominance of the mind over the eye, can be interpreted as a means to grace as well as to irrational animalism; that the two aspects are, perhaps inseparable."[40]

If it remains arguable that the notion of symbolic metamorphosis carried this weight for Shakespeare, a far stronger case can be made for Chapman. His most distinctly Ovidian poem is *Hero and Leander* in which he invents two bird metamorphoses: in the tale of Teras a gossipy Athenian girl, Adolesche, is transformed to a parrot; at the end of the poem the lovers are changed into "Thistle-warps," birds who always fly in pairs, never approaching the sea, and whose colors "as we construe colours paint / Their states to life" (6.288–89). D. J. Gordon comments:

> Now the point about metamorphosis is that the subject is changed into a creature that expresses its essence, that most fully expresses its fate: Philomela becomes the lamenting nightingale. Adolesche's essence is her talkativeness. The essence of Hero and Leander is their love and their suffering. In death they finally achieve the form that is perfectly expressive of their being.[41]

In *Cynthiam* Chapman takes a familiar tale of Ovidian metamorphosis, alters it to emphasize more directly the theme of man's quest for true form, and then further emphasizes the idea of transformation by twice changing the form of the nymph Euthimya in the course of the chase. First, she is a panther, then she becomes a boar. We can recreate something of the transformations endemic to poetic process by examining Chapman's sources. Schoell and, more recently, W. Schrickx, have ransacked the text of Comes' *Mythologiae* to document Chapman's very extensive borrowings in *The Shadow of Night*;[42] yet, as Gordon has

[40]Frank Kermode, "The Mature Comedies," in his *Shakespeare, Spenser, Donne: Renaissance Essays* (London, 1971), p. 209.

[41]Gordon, "Chapman's *Hero and Leander*," *English Miscellany*, 5 (1954): 85.

[42]Schrickx, "George Chapman's Borrowings from Natali Conti: Some Hitherto Unnoted Passages," *English Studies*, 32 (1951): 107–12.

shown in connection with Cartari, one also should look at the handbook illustrations to understand how Chapman formulated his images.[43] The first illustrated *Mythologiae* was not published until after *The Shadow of Night*; but, if he saw it later, Chapman surely would have approved the picture selected to accompany *De Luna* and *De Diana*, the chapters he used so heavily in the glosses and in the hymns themselves.[44] He would have recognized it from his edition of Cartari. The illustration shows Diana—"Imagine di Diana Cinthia o Luna" Cartari calls it—winged and horned, holding in one hand a lion and in the other, a panther. To the left of the goddess's head is an inset profile of her attired as a huntress; at the lower left is another inset of a charging boar pursued by a hound. Whether Chapman remembered the Cartari illustration here or sorted significant detail from Comes' prose the hard way does not matter. The illustration permits instant visualization of the animals associated with the moon goddess, which Chapman drew upon for the nymph's changes

[43]Gordon, pp. 45–46.

[44]In the 1616 Padua edition the illustration appears on pp. 132 and 140. Professor Richard Knowles informs me that three seventeenth-century editions of Comes were issued with illustrations, the first being Jean de Montlyard's translation, *Mythologie, c'est a dire explication des fables* (Lyon, 1612). It was followed by the illustrated Latin editions from Padua in 1616 and 1637. Knowles estimates that over half of the Comes woodcuts are copied from Cartari or the translation by Antonio Verderius, *Imagines Deorum* (Lyon, 1581).

"Imagine di Diana Cinthia o Luna," from Cartari, *Imagini delli Dei de gl'Antichi*. Reproduced by permission of the owner.

of form in his mythic narrative. The boar is associated with Diana through Ovid's story of the Calydonian boar, symbol of her divine wrath. Also Chapman could have known from studying Cartari that, when the goddess's triform identity is represented pictorially by giving her three heads, the one appropriate for the hunting goddess is that of the boar.[45]

Just why Diana should be holding a panther and a lion is somewhat more obscure. Comes and Cartari attribute the representation to Pausanias;[46] but Pausanias himself cannot explain the image: "On which account Artemis has wings on her shoulders I do not know; in her right hand she grips a leopard, in her left a lion."[47] Pausanias is at a loss unnecessarily; it would seem likely that the wings signify the swiftness of the moon's flight and the beasts of prey serve to emphasize her prowess in the hunt. The indefatigable Alexander Ross interprets all of Diana's attributes with ease:

> because she hath dominion over the fiercest Beasts, in tempering their raging heat by her moysture, she holds a Lion and Leopard in her hand, whose heat is excessive, but tempered by the Moon; her silver chariot shewes her brightnesse; the stagges and wings do shew her swiftnesse; and because her light increasing and decreasing appeareth like horns, therefore the Bul was sacrificed to her . . . her hunting is to shew how in her motion shee pursues and overtakes the Sun.[48]

Ross's explanation still sheds little light on why Chapman found this complex of hunting animals appropriate to his purposes in the *Hymnvs in Cynthiam*. Following Muriel Bradbrook's analysis, Battenhouse identifies the panther with pride and the boar with lust, thus representing together sin of the spirit and of the flesh: "The story, then, is that the debased forms of joy masqueraded by Euthimya quickly draw men's base affections (the dogs) in hot pursuit; while men's rational souls (the hunters) quickly follow, urging on their steeds (the spirited passions)."[49] Although excessively rigid, this reading may well have some validity for a strictly moral allegory. Certainly in some contexts the panther and boar traditionally represent pride and lust; it is important, however, to consider as many aspects of the poem as possible. Associated with Diana, the animals do not carry these particular connotations. Battenhouse's conception of the goddess luring men to sin, then punishing them for it,

---

[45]Cartari, *Imagini delli Dei de gl'Antichi* (Venice, 1647), ed. Walter Koschatzky (Graz, 1963), p. 64; and p. 60 for the first illustration.

[46]Comes, 3.18; Cartari, p. 61.

[47]Pausanias, *Description of Greece*, trans. W. H. S. Jones and H. A. Ormerod, Loeb Classical Library (Cambridge, Mass., 1926), 5.19.5.

[48]Alexander Ross, *Mystagogus Poeticus, or The Muses Interpreter* (London, 1653), pp. 96–99 (faulty pagination omits 97–98). Cf. Milton's *Comus*, 438–44.

[49]Battenhouse, p. 604.

does not account for all the circumstances of the hunt. Quoting the line "Wisedome conformes her selfe to all earths guises" to argue that Euthimya impersonates the "debased forms of joy," he omits mention of the preceding line "vertues are meate for vices," which more aptly conveys the gist of the passage (*Cyn.* 224–31).

If we recall that the general theme in the hymns is the problem of mutability, we become aware that Chapman's Homeric enthusiasm, focused as always by the mythic allegorizers, may have seen a particular relevance in the animal triad of boar, panther, lion. In the fourth book of the *Odyssey* Menelaus recounts how, when his progress homeward was impeded, he sought the aid of Proteus, "An old Sea-farer in these seas, that gives / A true solution of all secrets here" (4.517–18).[50] Idothea, the god's daughter, instructed Menelaus in the evasions her father would take and explained how he might be forced to talk:

He then will turne himselfe to every one
Of all things that in earth creepe and respire,
In water swim, or shine in heavenly fire.
Yet still hold you him firme, and much the more
Presse him from passing. But when as before
(When sleepe first bound his powres) his forme ye see,
Then ceasse your force and th'old Heroe free.

[*Odyssey* 4.559–65]

Following her advice, Menelaus and his men disguised themselves with seals' skins and crept into the foul-smelling cave to seek the ineluctable modality of the visible. They threw themselves upon Proteus:

And then th'old Forger all his formes began.
First was a Lion, with a mightie mane;
Then next a Dragon; a pide Panther then;
A vast Boare next; and sodainly did straine
All into water. Last, he was a tree,
Curld all at top, and shot up to the skie.

[*Odyssey* 4.609–14]

Now for Plato, Proteus was merely a sophist and Lucian thought he could only be a dancer,[51] but in the Renaissance, by and large it was agreed that he represented prime matter.[52] Milton thus describes alche-

---

[50]Allardyce Nicoll, ed., *Chapman's Homer* (New York, 1956), 2:72 (quoted hereafter).

[51]Plato, *Euthyphro*, 15D; *Euthydemus*, 288B, C; *Ion*, 541C. "The Dance," *Lucian*, trans. A. M. Harmon, Loeb Classical Library (Cambridge, Mass., 1936), 5: 231–33.

[52]Some of the references cited here and many others are compiled by A. B. Chambers, "Milton's Proteus and Satan's Visit to the Sun," *Journal of English and Germanic Philology*, 62 (1963): 280–87; Roche, *The Kindly Flame*, pp. 159–60; W. O. Scott, "Proteus in Spenser and Shakespeare: The Lover's Identity," *Shakespeare Studies*, 1 (1965): 283–84;

mists who "call up unbound / In various shapes old *Proteus* from the Sea, / Drain'd through a Limbec to his native form" (*PL* 3.603–5). Heraclitus had sought to demonstrate this reading on etymological grounds;[53] but more important to Chapman and his contemporaries would have been the authority of Orpheus's *Hymn to Proteus*:

> First-born, by whose illustrious pow'r alone
> All Nature's principles are clearly shewn:
> Matter to change with various forms is thine,
> Matter unform'd, capacious, and divine.[54]

If Chapman actually read the hymns or even read the appropriate excerpts in Ficino and Comes, here again he would have been impressed with the thematic relevance of Proteus to the moon goddess. In *Proteus* he could learn of "thy essence omniform," and then in *Diana* find that "a various form, Cydonian pow'r, is thine." Comes enumerates most of the possible interpretations: on the authority of Orpheus, Proteus is the oldest of gods; he is a natural philosopher, a prophet, a prudent man; he can represent air or matter; in the broadest sense the story relates "ad vniuersam humanae vitae rationem."[55] Bacon, as habitual a user of the *Mythologiae* as Chapman, plundered this section, including the exposition of matter: "The sense of this fable relates, it would seem, to the secrets of nature and the conditions of matter. For under the person of Proteus, matter–the most ancient of all things next to God–is meant to be represented."[56] Out of the welter of commentary come two dominant impressions: the association of Proteus with mutable matter, and with mutable man; the changeability is the thing and, since man is matter, the two strains inevitably converge. Thomas Roche concludes that in *The Faerie Queene* "Proteus represents the whole world of mutable nature and man insofar as man's body is independent of but not opposed to his soul."[57] And Pico della Mirandola triumphantly proclaims:

> Who would not admire this our chameleon? Or who could more greatly admire aught else whatever? It is man who Asclepius of Athens, arguing from his mutability of character and from his self-transforming nature, on

---

A. B. Giamatti, "Proteus Unbound: Some Versions of the Sea God in the Renaissance," in *The Disciplines of Criticism: Essays in Literary Theory, Interpretation, and History*, ed. Peter Demetz et al. (New Haven, 1968), pp. 437–75.

[53]See Chambers, p. 282.

[54]Taylor, *Hymns of Orpheus*, p. 149; *Selected Writings*, p. 238.

[55]Comes, 8.8.

[56]Lemmi, *Classic Deities in Bacon*, p. 92.

[57]Roche, *The Kindly Flame*, p. 160.

just grounds says was symbolized by Proteus in the mysteries. Hence those metamorphoses renowned among the Hebrews and the Pythagoreans.[58]

Knowing the allegorical nexus connected with the metamorphoses of Proteus, Chapman could rely upon his thematic treatment of the Diana myth to bring to the surface the Protean connotations of her animal associates. Although the image of Diana which was disseminated from Pausanias permitted him to employ half of Proteus's six changes and all of the ones appropriate to a hunt context, he chose not to use the lion. The reason for the omission, one supposes, is that simply too many conflicting connotations were attached to the figure of lion.[59] These motives will become more explicable in the exposition of the political allegory. In the immediate context of chastity and lust, form and change, Chapman would have been sensitive to Ovid's tale of Hippomenes and Atalanta.[60] Moreover, the picture of Diana places the panther in the favored right hand, and Chapman might have enjoyed the paradoxical notion of the panther as, like its mistress, a type of constancy in mutability. From the biblical adage he knew that the leopard (the two animals often were confused) could never change its spots.

Looking at Cynthia's hunt as a projection of mutability, symbolized in the narrative by Ovidian and Homeric metamorphosis, the thematic and structural coherence begins to emerge more obviously. Change entered the world with the fall and this change, conventionally represented in *Noctem* by lust and deformity, was countered by positive change, the attainment of true form, imaged as the stellification of virtuous individuals. *Cynthiam* expresses this positive change by the creation of the body and through the allegorical hunt enacting man's quest for form in the fallen world. Body alone is mere matter and, just as the lustful eye of Phoebus cannot penetrate the palace of the body to detect Cynthia's shining court (*Cyn.* 185–87), without instruction man is incapable of knowing that form cannot be found in matter alone. So Euthimya will 'bid the base, to all affection" (with a probable pun on

---

[58]"Oration," *Renaissance Philosophy*, pp. 225–26.

[59]The political and religious associations involving the lion are so profuse and diverse that they cancel out each other: the lion was the emblem of Brabant; R. C. Strong and J. A. Van Dorsten, *Leicester's Triumph* (London, 1964), pp. 69–70, describe an allegorical banquet at which an absent Elizabeth is offered the Dutch lion. Frances Yates, "Queen Elizabeth as Astraea," *Journal of the Warburg and Courtauld Institutes*, 10 (1947): 80–81 n., argues that political allegory is present in Bruno's treatment of the Astraea myth in *Spaccio della bestia trionfante*. Astraea between Leo and Scorpio represents Elizabeth between France and Spain. Yates cites other apparent instances of the King of France figured as a lion. In the *Orlando Furioso* Ariosto personified Pope Leo X as a hunting lion (26.32). And so it goes.

[60]Aided by Venus, Hippomenes won the famous race with Atalanta, slayer of the Calydonian boar, by distracting her with the golden balls; but he neglected to express his gratitude to the goddess. In revenge Venus incited Hippomenes with lust and he made love to Atalanta in the temple of Cybele. The impatient lovers were punished for the desecration by being transformed into lions (*Met.* 10.560 ff.).

base) to "tame" affection, to restore that mental order which produces form. The simile of mistress and school boys (*Cyn.* 256–66) appositely evokes an educational process which seems to encompass two stages: first, the sensual bias of men is used against them; the panther lures the hunters to the thicket imprisoning the formless souls of men destroyed "After [Cynthia] had transformed them into beasts" (*Cyn.* 279). The experience gives them a Dantesque vision of the fate to come:

Eyes should guide bodies, and our soules our eyes,
But now the world consistes on contraries:
So sence brought terror; where the mindes presight
Had saft that feare, and done but pittie right,
But seruile feare, now forgd a wood of darts
Within their eyes, and cast them through their harts.

[*Cyn.* 320–25]

The chase next leads to a "fruitfull Iland," endlessly fertile, delightful, and pleasing to the eye. The brief description suggests qualities similar to those of Phaedria's island and Acrasia's Bower of Bliss, episodes which Spenser uses to teach the tempering of the affections. Chapman's feelings are made plain; the island represents the delusory banquet of senses:

Bewtie strikes fancie blind; pyed show deceau's vs,
Sweet banquets tempt our healths, when temper leaues vs,
Inchastitie, is euer prostitute,
Whose trees we loth, when we haue pluckt their fruite.

[*Cyn.* 374–77]

Euthimya now transforms herself into a boar, clearly the avenging Calydonian boar, and devastates the corrupt island. With this incident the day's hunt, like the life of man, draws to a close; Cynthia sounds retreat, her creations vanish, and she mounts to the skies to complete her ordained cycle.

The narrator, at least, profits from this tale of the futility of attempted fulfillment through matter. Man must act not as an Orion or an Alpheus; rather, complementing Cynthia's creation of the body, he must "reexstruct" the glorious temple of Diana at Ephesus. This reconstruction will take place in the mind's eye; in effect, man will accept Cynthia's image as pattern for his soul and thereby attain the form he seeks:

In-sight illustrates; outward brauerie blinds,
The minde hath in her selfe a Deitie,
And in the stretching circle of her eye
All things are compast, all things present still,
Will framd to powre, doth make vs what we will.

[*Cyn.* 443–47]

Thus the poet entreats "Elisian Ladies" to "Build Cynthiaes Temple in your vertuous parts" (*Cyn.* 451), because "The minde in that we like, rules euery limme / Giues hands to bodies, makes them make them trimme" (*Cyn.* 456–57).

The conception Chapman has worked out here can be illuminated by reference to his *Hero and Leander.* In Chapman's version of the story the consummation of the love without benefit of marriage rites is a violation of ceremony. As Gordon has explained, the idea of ceremony is related to those of form and order, ceremony constituting something like form in action, and the poem is very much concerned with form in a philosophic sense:

> Form is not only the informing principle: the formal is also the efficient and the final cause; form is also *entelechy*, which is *perfectio*; and it is of the nature of each thing—natural or artificial—that it must seek to achieve its form, which is its perfection.[61]

In the fifth sestiad, as an example of ceremony fulfilled, the nymph Teras tells the story of "*Hymen* that now is god of Nuptial rites," and his courtship of Eucharis. Teras offers a myth within the myth of Hymen and Eucharis; she tells how Love came to Hymen's aid:

> And now came *Loue* with *Proteus*, who had long
> Inggl'd the little god with prayers and gifts,
> Ran through all shapes, and varied all his shifts,
> To win *Loues* stay with him, and make him loue him:
> And when he saw no strength of sleight could moue him
> To make him loue, or stay, he nimbly turnd
> Into *Loues* selfe, he so extreamely burnd.
> And thus came *Loue* with *Proteus* and his powre,
> T'encounter *Eucharis*.

[*Hero* 5.206–14]

Love's form attaches itself to the image of Hymen; "She viewd it, and her view the forme bestowes / Amongst her spirits" (5.223–24). The entire procedure is explained thus: "And where *Loues* forme is, loue is, loue is forme."

Chapman comments in *Cynthiam* that love is "the soule of vertue" (315); in this way Cynthia, "Nights faire soule" and pattern of the "vertue-temperd mind," images her perfect virtue and her love for man in the perfection of her form: "In perfect circle of whose sacred state, / The circles of our hopes are compassed" (6–7). Orpheus was honored by Ficino for celebrating the power of love to impose form on chaos,[62] and

---

[61]Gordon, p. 68.
[62]*Marsilio Ficino's Commentary on Plato's Symposium*, 1.3.

Cynthia similarly offers a means of imposing form on the chaos of fallen nature. According to Ficino, love is the desire for beauty and the supreme beauty is the splendor of the divine countenance.[63] The beauty of Cynthia's form should inspire love on the part of the beholder, and this love leads man to imitate, as far as possible, that perfect form to be more like it. This platonic conception of love and imitation of ideal form is the point of Chapman's metamorphoses and the love, of course, is the solution to the quest for form: "loue is forme." Cynthia offers spiritual love as antidote to the lust of the sun (the debased variety to which the poet refers when he says, "loue she hates"). Those poets "That fainde thee fiftie children by Endimion" greviously wrong Cynthia: "Thou neuer any hadst, but didst affect, / Endimion for his studious intellect. / Thy soule-chast kisses were for vertues sake" (Cyn. 493–95).

By building Cynthia's temple in his mind man can model his form upon the lines of her own supreme virtue; the positive transformation thus within man's grasp, the shape which Chapman chooses to symbolize man's regeneration returns us yet again to the legend of Orpheus. Shattered with grief after the second loss of Eurydice, the poet refused to have anything to do with other women. Ovid is not certain whether Orpheus made a vow of constancy or whether he simply could not bring himself to risk the misfortune of loving another woman; but because he rejected all women the Maenads finally tore the poet to bits. Before this violent end, Ovid records that Orpheus gave his love only to young boys and, not having lost his magical power over nature, frequently sat upon a hill among the trees singing his marvelous songs. One song, which drew the grove and all the birds and beasts around him, was about Ganymede, the only mortal admitted among the gods. Xenophon considered this story to conceal an allegory of the mind's superiority to the body, proving it with an etymological explanation of the name;[64] the Florentine platonist Christoforo Landino elaborated this basic conception in his commentary on Dante. For Landino the myth of Ganymede shadowed the superiority of mind to the lower faculties, and the abduction by Jove the achievement of a state of enraptured contemplation:

> Ganymede, then, would signify the mens humana, beloved by Jupiter, that is: the Supreme Being. His companions would stand for the other faculties of the soul, to wit the vegetal and sensorial. Jupiter, realizing that the Mind is in the forest—that is, remote from mortal things, transports it to heaven by means of the eagle. Thus it leaves behind its companions—that is, the vegetative and sensitive soul; and being removed, or, as Plato says, divorced from the body,

---

[63]Ibid., 2.2–3.

[64]Symposium, 8.30. See Erwin Panofsky, Studies in Iconology (1939; reprint ed., New York, 1962), pp. 214–16, for an account of the allegorical development; also Penelope C. Mayo, "Amor Spiritualis et Carnalis: The Myth of Ganymede in Art," unpublished Ph.D. dissertation, summarized in Marsyas, 13 (1966): 48–49.

and forgetting corporeal things, it concentrates entirely on contemplating the secrets of Heaven.[65]

This interpretation gained wide acceptance in the Renaissance; it turns up in Michelangelo's paintings, in Alciati's emblems, and in Comes' *Mythologiae*, whence Chapman found it.[66] Wisdom, Chapman argues, is "the mindes true bewtie" and by means of such beauty all virtuous men can become Ganymedes:

> He is the Ganemede, the birde of Joue,
> Rapt to his soueraignes bosome for his loue,
> His bewtie was it, not the bodies pride,
> That made him great Aquarius stellified:
> And that minde most is bewtifull and hye,
> And nearest comes to a Diuinitie,
> That furthest is from spot of earths delight,
> Pleasures that lose their substance with their sight,
> Such one, Saturnius rauisheth to loue,
> And fills the cup of all content to Joue.
>
> [Cyn. 462–71]

This is the song of Orpheus and this is Chapman's vision of redemption, man transformed not to beast, but to the bird of Jove.

In *The Shadow of Night* the poet always accepts Cynthia as the pattern of virtue and form; the lesson of the hunt is necessary because he does not understand that the pattern is constant, her nature unchanging. According to the tenets of Orphic theology, each god contains in his nature the potentiality to become his own opposite; Pico states in one of his Orphic *Conclusiones*: "He who cannot attract Pan, approaches Proteus in vain."[67] Edgar Wind comments, "All the particular gods, in the Orphic theology as outlined by Pico, seem animated by a law of self-contrariety, which is also a law of self-transcendence. The chaste Diana, despite her coldness, is a mad huntress and changeable as the moon."[68] The poet does not at first understand that there is a constancy, an orderliness in Cynthia's changeability, so he mistakenly fears that her changes will overcome her true nature. Thus he pleads for total constancy:

> Ascend thy chariot, and make earth admire
> Thy old swift changes, made a yong fixt prime,

---

[65]Translated by Panofsky in *Studies in Iconology*, p. 215. See also Henry Reynolds, *Mythomystes*, in *Critical Essays of the Seventeenth Century*, ed. Joel E. Spingarn (1908; reprint ed., Bloomington, 1957), 1: 152.

[66]Schoell, pp. 191–92.

[67]See Wind, "Pan and Proteus," pp. 158–75; quotation, p. 158.

[68]Wind, p. 161.

O let thy beautie scorch the wings of time,
That fluttering he may fall before thine eyes,
And beate him selfe to death before he rise.

[*Cyn.* 16–20]

The poet—not to mention the modern reader—would profit by a reading of Spenser's *Mutabilitie* cantos for, just as fully as Spenser, Chapman
is here concerned with "eterne in mutabilitie." In much more than theme
the two works reveal interesting similarities. Spenser shapes his cantos
out of the matter of Ovid, the tales of Phaeton and Actaeon; the reign of
Cynthia is challenged and her power opposed to the sun's; Diana's chastity is assailed by the lustful Actaeon-figure, Faunus. Mutabilitie and Jove
submit their dispute to the judgment of Nature; claiming dominance
over heaven and earth, Mutabilitie argues that all things are subject to
change. But she fails to understand the difference between aimless
change, for the love of changing, and purposeful change, as Nature explains in her decision:

I well consider all that ye haue sayd,
And find that all things stedfastnes doe hate
And changed be: yet being rightly wayd
They are not changed from their first estate;
But by their change their being doe dilate:
And turning to themselues at length againe,
Doe worke their owne perfection so by fate:
Then ouer them Change doth not rule and raigne;
But they raigne ouer change, and doe their states maintaine.

[*Faerie Queene* 7.7.58]

Sherman Hawkins remarks, "In other words, all things conquer change
by achieving a perfection implicit in their origin; they finally become
what they were first created to be."[69] This is the lesson, too, that the
platonists found in the *Orphic Hymns*: "Fair lamp of Night, its ornament
and friend, / Who giv'st to Nature's works their destin'd end" reads the
Hymn to the Moon, upon which Proclus noted that Diana "finishes or
perfects the essential perfection of matter."[70] Chapman's narrator does
not learn to like the cycle of days, "Thus nights, faire days: thus griefs do
ioyes supplant" (*Cyn.* 400). But he does learn to accept them; he learns
there is a constancy in the cycle of man's days that he can transcend only
by accepting the pattern of unchanging virtue. Chapman's conclusion
compresses the themes of the mutability of lower nature, of the cycle of

---

[69]Hawkins, p. 79. Hawkins's reading of the Mutability cantos has been widely accepted;
but see the caveat by Douglas Bush, *Pagan Myth and Christian Tradition in English Poetry*
(Philadelphia, 1968), p. 28 n.

[70]Taylor, p. 126 and n.; *Selected Writings*, p. 221, n. 18.

months, and of the constancy of the virtue that restores the harmony with higher nature:

> This bewtie hath a fire vpon her brow,
> That dimmes the Sunne of base desires in you,
> And as the cloudie bosome of the tree,
> Whose branches will not let the summer see,
> His solemne shadows; but do entertaine,
> Eternall winter: so thy sacred traine,
> Thrise mightie Cynthia should be frozen dead,
> To all the lawlesse flames of Cupids Godhead.

[Cyn. 477–84]

All this precedes the consecration of "Wise Poets" to serve Cynthia's power "in most religious feare." This "Deare precident for vs to imitate" shall "for euer liue the Planets Queene."

DIANA

That The Shadow of Night contains a dimension of political allegory is not a new observation; Bradbrook, Battenhouse, and Jacquot have commented suggestively on aspects of Cynthiam in this light. No attempt, however, has been made to view the political allegory as a sustained and coherent aspect of the poem. Because the political meaning becomes explicit at certain points in Cynthiam, the tendency has been to conclude that elsewhere this level disappears from the poem, rather than merely becoming implicit. Battenhouse agrees with Bradbrook that "the political allegory is of subsidiary importance, obtruding for a few lines only, than [sic] vanishing."[71] Yet, if one accepts the explicit political allusions, not as random inclusions of incidental relevance but as clues to a general design, a consistency can be perceived.

Chapman, of course, consciously employs the conventional mythological identification of Elizabeth with Cynthia: "truely figuring, (As she is Heccate) her soueraigne kinde, / And in her force, the forces of the mind" (Cyn. 152–53). Fear of the day "When interposed earth takes thee away" may well, as Battenhouse suggests,[72] allude to the national calamity that will ensue at Elizabeth's death; but the warning against marital eclipse is unmistakable:

> No otherwise (O Queene celestiall)
> Can we beleeue Ephesias state wilbe

---

[71]Battenhouse, "The Shadow of Night," p. 603, n. 40; he refers to M. C. Bradbrook, The School of Night (Cambridge, 1936), p. 141. Jacquot briefly discusses political implications, George Chapman, sa vie, sa poésie, son théâtre, sa pensée (Paris, 1951), p. 63.

[72]Battenhouse, p. 600, following Bradbrook, p. 137.

> But spoile with forreine grace, and change with thee
> The purenesse of thy neuer-tainted life,
> Scorning the subiect title of a wife.
>
> [Cyn. 95-99]

With two other references Chapman places the hymn in the context of Elizabeth's military excursions against the might of Spain. A long simile (Cyn. 328-48) describes a skirmish in which the duke of Parma's forces are routed by English troops under Sir Francis Vere (Nijmegen, 1591); and near the end of the poem Chapman celebrates the power of Elizabeth in frustrating the attack of the Armada: "Keeping our peacefull households safe from sack, / And free'st our ships, when others suffer wracke" (Cyn. 507-8).

It is possible to understand precisely the poet's appeal to Elizabeth against marriage. Chapman expressly alludes to Elizabeth's last serious courtship, that of Francois Hercule Valois, duke of Alençon and later of Anjou, when he bids her

> Then set thy Christall, and Imperiall throne,
> (Girt in thy chast, and neuer-loosing zone)
> Gainst Europs Sunne directly opposit,
> And giue him darknesse, that doth threat thy light.
>
> [Cyn. 116-19]

Younger brother of Henri III, Alençon was first advanced as a prospective suitor of Elizabeth in 1571 when the courtship of his brother had foundered on the rock of religion. For some years the match, though intermittently proposed, was not regarded seriously by any party. In 1578 and again in 1580, however, Elizabeth found it expedient to reopen the marriage negotiations as a means of bringing pressure to maintain the balance of power in the Netherlands. Joel Hurstfield observes that "the Alençon marriage project assumed the pattern of all its predecessors, the now classical shape of a diplomatic courtship."[73] The annexation of Portugal in 1580 considerably increased Spain's wealth and military potential, and thereby the threat of her dominance in the Low Countries. Elizabeth then encouraged Alençon's acceptance of a dominant role in the Netherlands, using the marriage negotiations to impress

---

[73]Hurstfield, Elizabeth I and the Unity of England (New York, 1960), p. 120. For Elizabeth's policy motives, see R. B. Wernham, Before the Armada: the Growth of English Foreign Policy 1485-1588 (London, 1966), p. 336. J. A. Bossy, "English Catholics and the French Marriage, 1577-81," Recusant History, 5 (1959): 2-16, emphasizes the fact that on the parts of the principals—Catherine de Medici, who conceived the scheme, Henri III, Elizabeth, and Alençon—the marriage proposal was totally political, not religious, in implication. Also useful on the negotiations and courtship are Conyers Read, Mr. Secretary Walsingham and the Policy of Queen Elizabeth (Oxford, 1925), 2: 1-117; J. E. Neale, Queen Elizabeth (London, 1934), pp. 237-56; Martin A. S. Hume, The Courtships of Queen Elizabeth (London, 1896), pp. 172-333.

Spain with the solidarity of an English-French alliance. To this end (in August 1581) she provided Alencon with £10,000 to help finance his army and, after his lengthy winter visit, sent him off in February 1582 to be invested with the sovereignty of the Netherlands, accompanied by Leicester and with a full show of English backing.[74] Unfortunately, Alençon proved to be traitorous to the trust invested in him by the States, and his early death in 1584 only concluded a political career that already was effectually finished.

If the potentiality of the Alençon marriage was generated dispassionately by coupling Anglo-French aims for political expediency, few Englishmen were able to contemplate the match in such logical terms. The very possibility of a Roman Catholic, foreign consort for Elizabeth was innately repugnant to many of her subjects, and this instinct was only reinforced by Alençon's unsavory career and reputation.[75] John Stubbs detected the encroachment of Antichrist: "they haue sent vs hither not Satan in body of a serpent, but the old serpent in shape of a man, whos sting is in his mouth, and who doth his endeuour to seduce our Eue, that shee and we may lose this Englishe Paradise."[76] Stubbs's vehemence cost him his right hand, but not his loyalty.[77] The attitude articulated by Stubbs provides a context for the likelihood that the portrayal of Alençon in *Bussy D'Ambois* reflects, if not the playwright's own view, at least a climate of opinion extending beyond the needs of dramatic conflict:

> That y' are for perjuries the very Prince
> Of all intelligencers; and your voice
> Is like an eastern wind, that where it flies,
> Knits nets of caterpillars, with which you catch
> The prime of all the fruits the Kingdom yields.
> That your political head is the curs'd fount

---

[74]See Wernham, pp. 361–62; also J. B. Black, *The Reign of Elizabeth, 1558–1603*, 2d ed. (Oxford, 1959), pp. 352–55.

[75]"Francis, Duke of Alençon, . . . was, upon the whole, the most despicable personage who had ever entered the Netherlands. His previous career at home had been so flagrantly false that he had forfeited the esteem of every honest man in Europe, Catholic or Lutheran, Huguenot or Malcontent. . . . History will always retain him as an example, to show mankind the amount of mischief which may be perpetrated by a prince, ferocious without courage, ambitious without talent, and bigoted without opinions. Incapable of religious convictions himself, he had alternately aspired to be a commander of Catholic and Huguenot zealots, and he had acquired nothing by his vacillating course, save the entire contempt of all parties and of both religions." John Lothrop Motley, *The Rise of the Dutch Republic* (New York, 1856), 3: 339.

[76]Stubbs, *The Discoverie of A Gaping Gvlf Whereinto England is Like to be Swallowed by an other French mariage* . . . (1579), A2. Lloyd E. Berry has edited a modern-spelling text: *John Stubbs's Gaping Gulf with Letters and Other Relevant Documents*, Folger Documents of Tudor and Stuart Civilization (Charlottesville, 1968); quotation, pp. 3–4.

[77]J. B. Black, p. 350.

Of all the violence, rapine, cruelty,
Tyranny and atheism flowing through the realm.[78]

When Monsieur makes his initial appearance in the tragedy and commands Bussy, "Up man, the sun shines on thee" (1.1.55), Chapman does more than set into play the complex pattern of light imagery; he identifies the speaker by alluding to Alençon's widely known personal emblem—a rising sun accompanied with the motto, "Fovet et Discutit."
Because the Netherlanders were anxious to exploit the maximum propaganda value from the man they had asked to serve as their figurehead, the symbolic potentiality of Alençon was thoroughly utilized;[79] consequently, we can document substantially both the association of the sun emblem with him and the widespread knowledge of this symbolic identification. After an intensive, three-month courtship visit to England, Alençon finally was prevailed upon in February 1582 to return to his duties in the Low Countries and undergo the formal investiture of his position. On 19 February he entered Antwerp for his inauguration as duke of Brabant; in July he departed from Antwerp for Zeeland where he was received formally in Brussels, and the next month, in Ghent, he was invested as earl of Flanders.[80] All these receptions were accompanied by a full panoply of triumphal arches, pageants, processions, tableaux, and other ornamentation drawing out the political import of the events. The first, and most significant, of the entrances is described minutely and illustrated with detailed plates in La IOYEVSE & magnifique Entrée de Monseigneur Francoys Fils de France, et Frere Vnique dv Roy, par la grace de Dieu Dvc de Brabant . . . (Antwerp, 1582), an account which was immediately translated into English by Arthur Golding.[81] This treatise makes it abundantly clear that the symbolism attendant upon the ceremonies was designed to center upon Alençon's sun image.[82]

---

[78]Bussy 3.2.387–94; I quote from Nicholas Brooke's Revels Plays edition (Cambridge, Mass., 1964).

[79]For an analysis of this symbolic projection based on graphic representation, see Frances A. Yates, The Valois Tapestries (London, 1959), especially pp. 102–6.

[80]Edward Grimestone, A Generall Historie of the Netherlands (London, 1627), pp. 673–82.

[81]Arthur Golding, trans., The Ioyful and royal entertainment of the ryght high and mightie Prince, Frauncis . . . (London, 1582). This translation is reprinted by John Nichols, The Progresses and Public Processions of Queen Elizabeth (London, 1823), 2: 354–85; for the reader's convenience I shall quote from this edition.

[82]The keynote to the entire occasion was sounded in the salutatory oration, proclaiming that God has chosen Alençon so that "the stormes of all troubles, and of all other things that annoied their estate, might, by the beames of his princelie majestie, wisdom, and prowesse, be chased awaie; and the brightnesse of their former prosperitie, heretofore knowne to all nations, be made to spring up and shine foorth againe" (Nichols, 2: 359). After the welcoming speeches, heralds sounding trumpets and crying "God save the Duke of Brabant," threw into the crowd coins bearing "a devise of the sunne, with the Monsieur's

Given such attention, it is not surprising to find Elizabeth belaboring Alençon's emblem to wring out a suitable conceit for a poetic leavetaking at Canterbury—"My care is like my shaddowe in the sunne"[83]—but the manner in which the man and his device are alluded to in the popular histories does establish the general familiarity of the association.[84] Against this background of commonplace knowledge it becomes easier to understand how years after Monsieur's eclipse and death Chapman can incorporate emblem as image in his hymn and, later still, in his tragedy, not as recondite private lore but as public symbol to which he could not u reasonably expect his audience to respond.

The specific identification of Monsieur as "Europs Sunne directly opposit" who threatens to despoil Cynthia with "forreine grace, and change" by imposing the "subiect title of a wife," is not in itself important; our comprehension of it, however, sharpens the focus of political activity within the allegorical structure of the hymn. Since the Alençon marriage project cannot be extricated from its origin in Elizabeth's foreign policy, the reader must see that this passage in the poem is not another gratuitous compliment to the Virgin Queen under the guise of a pretended alarm at the threat to her chastity. Rather, the passage interconnects neatly with the two other explicit topical allusions, the Nijmegen battle simile and the Armada reference, forming a nexus through which one may follow the scheme of the political allegory. We should notice that these three allusions are distributed in the three major sections of *Cynthiam*: the reference to Monsieur's courtship appears in the opening part of the hymn in which the poet reveals his

---

owne inscription, *cherisheth and chaseth*, which is the Monsieur's ordinarie posie" (Nichols, 2: 365–66; Grimestone, p. 673). Proceeding into the town of Antwerp itself, Alençon was treated to an elaborate show of arches, columns, pageants, and allegorical displays: Apollo, "apparelled like the sun," banishing discord, violence, and tyranny (Nichols, 2: 378; *Joyeuse Entrée*, pl. XX); "an egle feeding hir yoong, and turning hirselfe towards the shining of the sunne, as taking hir force of the Prince" (Nichols, 2: 379; *Joyeuse Entrée*, pl. XII); an extraordinarily encumbered elephant with a large sun crest affixed to its head and written on its belly a verse explaining that it now gratefully follows Alençon (Nichols, 2: 371; *Joyeuse Entrée*, pl. VIII); a theatrical company, rather opportunely called "The Follow Sun, after the name of a floure which followeth the sun," representing a Davidic Alençon defeating the Goliath of Spain beneath his emblem and motto (Nichols, 2: 369–70; *Joyeuse Entrée*, pl. VI); a company of rhetoricians depicting the alliance of David and Jonathan, signifying the oath between Monsieur and Brabant, beneath the image of the sun rising over Dutch waters (Nichols, 2: 370; *Joyeuse Entrée*, p. VII). One triumphal arch was devoted entirely to an exposition of Alençon's motto through the sun symbolism; see fig. on page 77 below, and, for a detailed description, see Nichols, 2: 374.

While the reception accorded to Alençon by Antwerp was much the most splendid, the other host cities indulged themselves in very similar civic mythmaking. For Brussels, see Motley, 3: 558; and for Ghent, see Yates, *Valois Tapestries*, p. 35.

[83]Nichols, 2: 346.

[84]See the wordplays by, e.g., William Camden, *Annales: The True and Royall History of Elizabeth Queene of England* (London, 1625), 2: 393–94; and Churchyard and Robinson, in their translation of van Meteren, *A Trve Discovrse Historicall, of the Svcceeding Governovrs in the Netherlands* (London, 1602), p. 49.

Triumphal arch, from *La IOYEVSE & magnifique Entrée de Monseigneur Francoys.* Reproduced by permission of the Milton S. Eisenhower Library of The Johns Hopkins University.

dependency upon Cynthia and his fear of her being eclipsed or changed; the central narrative unit of the allegorical hunt, designed to invalidate the poet's fears, includes the reference to English military opposition to Spain in the Low Countries; finally, the conclusion celebrating Cynthia's immutability offers as example of her prowess against enemies the destruction of the Armada, the climax to the war which resulted from Elizabeth's intervention in the Netherlands.[85]

[85]R. B. Wernham regards Elizabeth's interventionist policy in the Netherlands as the primary cause of Spain's attack upon England. See his "Elizabethan War Aims and Strategy," in *Elizabethan Government and Society: Essays Presented to Sir John Neale,* ed. S. T. Bindoff et al. (London, 1961), pp. 340–68; see especially 344–46.

Chapman's interest in the Netherlands and, more particularly, in the English military intervention therein is evident at many places in his writings.[86] His persistent loyalty to Norris and the Veres—even in *Cynthiam* he can interject a comment that Sir Francis won "More fame than guerdon" (*Cyn.* 336)—and, particularly, his detailed familiarity with the Ghent and Nijmegen battles have been used plausibly to reinforce the conjecture that some of the shadowy years of his preliterary life were spent fighting in the Low Countries.[87] Yet biographical relevance need not blind us—and it certainly did not blind Chapman—to the larger, political importance of English intervention in the Netherlands. In *Eugenia* he writes of Belgia "where, our great Queene / That with her little Kingdome, curb'd the spleene / Of *Spaine*, and *France*; And with her mightie hand / Made even that most diuided Kingdom stand" (340–43). The *Hymnvs in Cynthiam* is political mythography in the manner of the still-to-be-published Book 5 of *The Faerie Queene*, in which the appeal for aid to Lady Belge is answered by Arthur—a historically maladroit tribute to the disastrous governorship of Leicester in 1585–87.[88] In one instance, at least, Chapman handles allegory more skillfully than his greater contemporary.

By the time of Monsieur's courtship, Elizabeth's mythic role as Cynthia, like those of Diana and Astraea, was well established. E. C. Wilson traces origins of the Cynthian cult as far back as the water pageantry at Kenilworth Castle in 1575; but undoubtedly it begins even

---

[86]Chapman's *The Conspiracy of Byron* is historically accurate in having Henri IV utter praise for the heroic leadership of Sir John Norris and Colonel Williams (2.2.214–16); *Pro Vere* lauds Norris, Sir Francis Vere, and Sir Horatio Vere as the three greatest figures "in the Rule of Warre" during "ELIZA'S blessed Raigne"; a simile in the dedicatory epistle to *The Hymns of Homer* describes the extraordinarily skillful retreat executed by Norris when his group was cut off by Parma's greater force. This last feat was performed before the eyes of Orange and Alençon, who observed the retreat from the wall of Ghent: "The *Gallick* Monsiour standing on the wall, / And wondring at [Norris'] dreadful Discipline" (*Poems*, p. 415). Jacquot, pp. 14–16, correctly identifies the historical occasion. See *A Trve Discovrse*, pp. 44–48; Camden, 3: 20–21. Chapman's admiration for Norris was not unique; see, for example, William Blandy, *The Castle or picture of pollicy shewing forth most liuely, the face, body and partes of a commonwealth, the duety, quality, profession of a perfect and absolute Souldiar, the martiall feates, encounters, and skirmishes lately done by our English nation, vnder the conduct of the most noble and famous Gentleman M. Iohn Noris . . .* (London, 1581). Still valuable is Sir Clements R. Markham, *The Fighting Veres* (Boston, 1888).

[87]Jacquot (p. 16) considers it probable that Chapman fought with Vere in 1591, but does not think the Ghent simile justifies placing him with Norris in 1582. Mark Eccles, "Chapman's Early Years," *Studies in Philology*, 43 (1946): 176–93, has produced contemporary testimony to the fact that Chapman spent some years abroad.

[88]For a discussion of prophetic imperialism in *The Faerie Queene*, bk. 5, see Angus Fletcher, *The Prophetic Moment: An Essay on Spenser* (Chicago, 1971), pp. 108–21; and on Lady Belge, pp. 202–4, 211–12. In *Leicester's Triumph* R. C. Strong and J. A. Van Dorsten study the political symbolism of the festivals with which Leicester was greeted on his progresses through the Netherlands in 1585–86.

earlier.[89] Thus, firmly associated with the chaste moon goddess in the guises of both Cynthia and Diana, Elizabeth could be imaged quite obviously as a moon threatened with eclipse by Alençon's sun, and Chapman was not the first to exploit this complex. Stubbs, the loyal but tactless pamphleteer, postulated the danger of a married Elizabeth forced to accompany her husband to his own land:

> eyther must our Elizabeth goe with him out of her owne natiue country and swete soyle of England . . . into a forrain kingdome where her writt doth not runn and shalbe but in a borowed Maiestie as the moone to the sonn, shining by night as other kings wyues . . . or els must she tary here without comfort of her husband, seing herselfe despised or not wifelike esteemed and as an eclipsed son diminished in souereinty. . . .[90]

Stubbs's images of sun, moon, and eclipse prefigure Chapman's particular application of the dominant images in the hymns; from the English point of view the public personalities of Elizabeth and her Monsieur dovetailed neatly with the chaste moon-lustful sun complex broadly established in *Noctem*. Yet Chapman has in mind a traditional political symbolism that transcends the narrow equivalence of Elizabeth and Alençon as personalities and considers them in their roles as national and religious figureheads, as indeed symbols of England and Europe in dynastic conflict.

Frances Yates has elucidated the mythic role of Elizabeth as Astraea in relation to the development of mystical imperialism in her reign, calling attention to the seminal importance for imperialist theory of Dante's *De Monarchia*.[91] The entire third book of the *Monarchia* is devoted to the problem of the confusion of ecclesiastical and civil power, and 3.4 refutes the analogy that, as the moon derives its light from the sun, so the empire derives its temporal authority from the ultimate spiritual authority of the church. Dante argues, rather, that both sun and moon receive their light from God and, of course, he maintains that a similar autonomy should prevail in the realms of imperial and papal

---

[89]It seems unlikely that at Elizabeth's 1566 Oxford visit the choice of topic, whether the moon controls the ebb and flow of the sea—on which Edmund Campion delivered the affirmative position—was purely accidental (see Nichols, 1: 213). And, when Alençon's party inspected the fleet at Rochester, they confessed "that of good right the Queene of England was reported to be Ladie of the seas" (Nichols, 2: 345–46); the last phrase has the ring of a commonplace tag a full ten years before Spenser and Ralegh's "Cynthia, the Ladie of the Sea." For the Kenilworth festivities, see Wilson, *England's Eliza*, Harvard Studies in English, 20 (Cambridge, Mass., 1939): 273–78. His entire chapters on Cynthia, pp. 273–320, and Diana, pp. 167–229, are relevant here.

[90]Stubbs, *Discoverie*, C4; *John Stubbs's Gaping Gulf*, p. 49.

[91]Yates, "Astraea," pp. 27–82. The following discussion of the background is greatly indebted to this study.

authority.[92] Relating this to Dante's earlier discussion of Astraea, Miss Yates comments:

> Dante's treatment, therefore, tends very strongly to sanctify and Christianize the imperial idea. The just virgin is the sacred empire, justified in its own right because it produced the Augustan golden age when the world was most one, and justified by God because it was the fullness of time in which Christ chose to be born. The moon of empire borrows its light direct from the sun of God's approval. The just virgin becomes an imperial virgin, sacred and divine.[93]

The doctrine of the divine right of kings originated from medieval disputes in a period of declining imperialism as the increasingly omnivorous papacy threatened to devour temporal authority entirely. The adherents of the imperial virgin who was the daughter of Henry VIII welcomed the ammunition provided by the Ghibelline partisan, and used it effectively in arguing that Elizabeth represented an imperial Christianity, taking her sanction directly from God instead of from a papal intermediary.[94]

The contest of moon and sun is, then, chastity and lust personified by Elizabeth and Alençon, which itself represents not the simple struggle of Protestant and Catholic—Christ and Antichrist, as Stubbs saw it—but a much broader conflict. In it religious issues are delimited by the political, nationalistic, governmental issues implicit in the challenge to Elizabeth's authority presented by the papacy, whether its instrument is the "politique" Catholicism of France (and the danger of alliance with Henri, marriage with Monsieur) or the militant Catholicism of Spain (culminating in the "enterprise of England" and the defeat of the Armada). A well-known Dutch engraving depicts Diana's discovery of Callisto's breach of chastity. Elizabeth expells a Callisto-Pope, crown defeats tiara, to the applause of the Netherlands.[95] This engraving is similar to the graphic material associated with Leicester's governorship and, crude though it be, it differs more in quality of execution than in kind from the political mythography of Mercilla's court or from *Cynthiam*. Chapman's poem causes Yates to remark, "Here, under the image of an eclipse, the imperial moon is set up against the sun of Europe, in the kind of antithesis

---

[92]See ibid., pp. 34–36; U. Limentani, "Dante's Political Thought," *The Mind of Dante* (Cambridge, 1965), pp. 122–28; H. F. Dunbar, *Symbolism in Medieval Thought and its Consummation in the Divine Comedy* (New Haven, 1929), pp. 41–42; and Ernst H. Kantorowicz, "Dante's 'Two Suns'," *Selected Studies* (New York, 1965), pp. 325–38.

[93]Yates, "Astraea," p. 35.

[94]Scotching the notion that Dante was little known in Tudor England, Yates shows the use made of Dantesque monarchism in John Jewel's *Apology for the Church of England* and in John Foxe's *Acts and Monuments*. Ficino translated *De Monarchia* into Italian and Foxe cites Plutarch, Pico della Mirandola, Ficino, and Angelo Poliziano among those authorities he considers allied with his position. See "Astraea," pp. 38–46.

[95]Yates, "Astraea," p. 76. The engraving is by Pieter van der Heydon.

which we are accustomed to see visualized in the crown versus the tiara."[96]

The imperial theme is first adumbrated as, threading together bits of lunar lore drawn from Comes, Chapman alludes to the ancient practices of attempting to forestall an eclipse with torches, music, and mourning (Cyn. 31–39). Such efforts are vain; nothing can recall Cynthia when she departs. As in the battle of Cannae when the Romans were annihilated by Hannibal's forces after the death of their chief, the destruction of the English will follow upon the fall of "Our sacred chiefe and soueraigne generall" (Cyn. 60). Returning to the description of eclipse superstitions, Chapman versifies Plutarch's account of the eclipse on the eve of Aemilius Paulus's victory over Perseus's Macedonian army (Cyn. 64–75).[97] Rather confusingly here, Chapman conflates two unrelated military events, the Roman defeat by Hannibal and the Roman victory over Perseus. In so doing he wishes his reader to associate Roman (and its inescapable connotations of empire) with English (Roman-kind by virtue of Tudor myth and common Trojan ancestry; imperial, as the hymn will develop). Roman defeat comes with the leader's death; Roman victory comes because they respond religiously to the augury and turn its effects against the Macedonians. Utterly dependent upon their "soueraigne generall" the English can only fear her loss, since the eclipse cannot be prevented, and since it means death of a monarch— within the overall figure, the symbol becomes literal event—eclipse of their moon goddess *is* her death and their fall: "Nor shall our wisedomes be more arrogant / (O sacred Cynthia) but beleeue thy want / Hath cause to make vs now as much affraid" (Cyn. 76–78).

The problem is simply that, in his awareness of the total dependency of the English nation upon Elizabeth personally, the narrator lacks faith in her powers and policies: inevitably she will change, she will be eclipsed. Hence the intensity of the appeal to "set thy Christall, and Imperiall throne . . . / Gainst Europs Sunne." Those faithful and virtuous souls, however, who model themselves upon Cynthia need have no fear. The poem here slips into the familiar macrocosmic equivalence between monarch and country, the harmonious extension of the ruler's well-ordered mind to his well-ordered government. The "vertue-temperd mind" is a "perfect type of thy [i.e., Cynthia's] Almightie state," which refers primarily to Cynthia's role as world soul, the great exemplar for individual spirits; but the use of "state" here demands the political sense as well and extends the analogy to another plane: as Cynthia's state is the mirror of her mind writ large, so the virtuous mind is microcosm of both Cynthia and her state, Elizabeth and England. The object lesson for the

[96]Ibid., p. 73.

[97]"Life of Aemilius Paulus," *Plutarch's Lives*, trans. Bernadette Perrin, Loeb Classical Library (London, 1918), 17.3–4.

doubter commences when Cynthia descends to earth and, acting as pure form, constructs her "rare Elisian Pallace." In the realm of general meaning, as we have seen, the episode signifies the creation of the body, the temple of the soul. By the microcosm-macrocosm analogy, however, the body of the prince or empress becomes the body politic. The "eye of Phebus," having a base disposition, cannot truly appreciate the accomplishment of this great architect: "Forme then, twixt two superior pillers framd / This tender building, Pax Imperij nam'd" (Cyn. 188–89).

The "Pax Imperij" symbolized by the moon is obvious enough. The "superior pillers," as Yates observes, are reminiscent of the pillars of Hercules, the famous device of Charles V by which he sought to emphasize "the vast extension into the new world of his sacred empire, the intensification of the imperial idea through maritime discovery and adventure."[98] The combination of the columns symbolizing the limits of the ancient world and of the *plus ultra* motto conveyed the boast that Charles's empire would far transcend the traditional boundaries of empire. Ariosto incorporated the vision of dynastic imperialism in his epic, explaining that Charles V would be an emperor comparable to Trajan or Augustus. Sir John Harington, the muses' Ajax and Elizabeth's godson, responded more skeptically to the account than Astolfo, explaining marginally the "vaine conceit of some idle head" that Charles meant "to conquer al the world, and then to enter into religion and become Pope & Emperor both, to which this verse seemes to tend." But Harington was not above altering the account of imperial expansion to suit the circumnavigational exploits of Drake, tacitly transferring the maritime imperialism from Charles to Elizabeth.[99] At this point in Chapman's hymn the theme of conquest by sea may only be implicit in the symbol of the Herculean pillars, but the expansionist motif is overt:

> the top so high extended,
> That it the region of the Moone transcended:
> Without, within it, euerie corner fild
> By bewtious Forme, as her great mistresse wild.
> Here as she sits, the thunder-louing Ioue
> In honors past all others showes his loue,
> Proclaiming her in compleat Emperie,
> Of what soeuer the Olympick skie
> With tender circumuecture doth embrace.

[Cyn. 192–200]

---

[98]Yates, "Astraea," p. 52; see pp. 49–56 and pl. 17 a–g for the entire discussion of Carolingian imperialism. See p. 73 for the comment on the Chapman passage.

[99]*Orlando Furioso*, 15.14 and marginal note; the quoted comment annotates 15.18–19. See Yates, pp. 51–53.

Charles's campaign for spiritual and temporal independence from the authority of the Pope—which led to his sacking Rome in 1527—may have seemed a vain conceit to Harington, but Chapman treats his mistress as receiving total and independent sanction directly from Jove, in accord with Dantesque political theory.

Having established her "compleat Emperie" in the form of the palace, Cynthia at this point constructs Euthimya, her pursuers, and the whole allegorical hunt based upon the Actaeon myth. That certain topical events underlie the general theme of this curious hunt has not been overlooked; Bradbrook, perceptively connecting the Nijmegen simile with the hunting activity, suggests that the allegory glances at Elizabeth's war with Spain; Battenhouse thinks that more generally "the hunt could be construed as a flattering tribute to the whole course of the English Queen's shrewd sporting with Europe's passion-driven potentates."[100]

Both suggestions are correct. The treatment of the chastity-lust polarity in this fashion is, like that of moon and sun as Elizabeth and Alençon, only a natural, local extension of the main theme in the hymns, and as such takes advantage of the most familiar reading of the Actaeon myth, that of the man devoured by his own passions. Chapman does not so localize the allegory that he expects us to recognize such individuals as Philip II, Eric of Sweden, or Anjou (later Henri III); he does mount his anonymous hunters upon such heraldic steeds as lions, boars, and unicorns, "being the Princeliest, and hardiest beasts" (Cyn. 295). Again, describing their retreat as comparable to the defeat suffered by the duke of Parma at the hands of Sir Francis Vere certainly connects the action of the hunt with the course of the Spanish war. The Actaeon story presents the moon goddess as Diana the huntress, who with her weapons, her attendant foresters, and her militancy is the most suitable of the moon avatars to symbolize such warfare.

More specifically than this, however, the Actaeon myth persistently from the time of Ovid had been associated with the affairs of princes. Fraunce's second reading of the story warned that "we ought not to be over curious and inquisitive in spying and prying into those matters, which be above our reache, least we be rewarded as *Actaeon* was" and quoted the famous allusion from the *Tristia*, "Inscius Actaeon vidit sine veste dianam" (2.105).[101] In *Ovids Banquet* Chapman found it convenient to adapt the legend that Ovid was banished for making love to Julia, but he must have known the alternate interpretation that Ovid was put away for knowing too much about affairs of state. This is the basis of a passage he read in Comes and from which Bacon borrowed:

[100]Battenhouse, p. 603, n.40 and Bradbrook, p. 141.
[101]Quoted by Davis, p. 103.

For whoever becomes acquainted with a prince's secrets without leave and against his will, is sure to incur his hatred; and then, knowing that he is marked and occasions are sought against him, he lives the life of a stag; a life full of fears and suspicions.[102]

And the now venerable interpretation is solemnly repeated as late as Sandys's *Ovid*: "But this fable was invented to shew vs how dangerous a curiosity it is to search into the secrets of Princes."[103]

Chapman allegorizes the political apostasy of English Catholics who could not bring themselves to pay primary allegiance to Elizabeth—perhaps such pro-Marian and Spanish plotters as Norfolk, Throckmorton, and Babington—and their just punishments in the episode of the thicket (*Cyn.* 251–353) which imprisons

> The soules of such as liu'd implausible,
> In happie Empire of this Goddesse glories,
> And scornd to crowne hir Phanes with sacrifice
> And ceaselesse walke; exspiring fearefull grones,
> Curses, and threats for their confusions.
> Her darts, and arrowes, some of them had slaine,
> Others hir doggs eate, painting hir disdaine,
> After she had transformd them into beasts:
> Others her monsters carried to their nests,
> Rent them in peeces, and their spirits sent
> To this blind shade, to waile their banishment.

[*Cyn.* 272–82]

While the would-be assassins and rebels undoubtedly deserved their fates, this may seem a somewhat high-handed way of writing off the suffering of more innocent recusants; the hymn by no means presents an objective analysis of recent English history. Euthimya leads her pursuers into the thicket in the guise of a panther, appropriately, because she acts as merciless huntress at this point; but the incident anticipates her transformation to avenging boar. It was for a similar neglect of her altars that Diana unleashed the boar on the people of Calydon.

Perhaps Chapman even meant his readers to detect a relevance in the euhemeristic interpretation of Actaeon. If the myth warns against wanton extravagance, the unnecessary maintenance of servants, and undue generosity to favorites, it inevitably was regarded as a cautionary tale for princes. Thus Sandys:

> And some imagine how he was said to be devoured by his hounds, in that he impoverished his estate in sustaining them. But what was that expence to a

---

[102]Quoted by Lemmi, *The Classic Deities in Bacon*, p. 187; Comes, 6.24.

[103]Sandys, *Ovid's Metamorphosis Englished* (Oxford, 1632), p. 100.

Prince? I rather agree with those, who thinke it to bee meant by his main-taining of ravenous and riotous sycophants: who haue often exhausted the Exchequors of opulent Princes, and reduced them to extreame necessity. Bountie therefore is to be limited according to the ability of the giuer, and merit of the receauer: else it not onely ruinates it selfe, but looseth the name of a vertue, & converts into folly.[104]

Elizabeth's famous frugality has been put down by many historians to a compulsive stinginess bordering on the neurotic; recently R. B. Wernham has argued that the queen exhibited uncommon acumen in meeting financial crises and in keeping an always marginal economy solvent dur-ing wartime.[105] Either view contrasts vividly with the turmoil of France or the New-World silver profligacy of Spain; in this sense Chapman may be striving to turn into a virtue the parsimoniousness which many of his contemporaries regarded as a vice.[106]

The preceding argument has attempted to suggest the complex of connotations preestablished in the allegorical vehicle that Chapman selected and adapted, as well as their relevance to the political theme with which he is concerned. In reaction to the multiple application of the Actaeon myth, it might be objected that the reading assumes on Chap-man's part a knowledge of Elizabethan politics transcending the realm of general information. It would not do, however, to scant the possibility that Chapman had access to such knowledge. In the early 1580s he was in the service of Sir Ralph Sadler, a confederate of Burghley and a minis-ter of no little experience.[107] Sadler was one of the commissioners who

[104]*Ovid's Metamorphosis*, p. 100.

[105]Wernham, "Elizabethan War Aims and Strategy," pp. 349–57, 357–68. For an explicit opposition to Wernham's revisionist interpretation of Elizabeth's diplomatic and financial policies in the Netherlands, see Charles Wilson, *Queen Elizabeth and the Revolt of the Netherlands* (Berkeley and Los Angeles, 1970), especially pp. 123–36, who indicts the queen for "conservatism, parsimony, snobbery, distrust" (p. 128).

[106]It might be objected that Chapman should not want to raise the question of excessive generosity to favorites since, on such infrequent occasions, Leicester and Ralegh were notable recipients. But the poem tries to put the best possible face on such inconsistency, presenting it as prudent, far-sighted planning. Similarly it does not matter which inter-pretation of Elizabeth's policies, Wernham's or Wilson's, is more nearly right; Wernham's melioristic evaluation clearly serves as the better gloss upon the political hagiography of *Cynthiam*.

[107]Chapman's relationship with Sadler has been studied most extensively by Jean Robert-son, "The Early Life of George Chapman," *Modern Language Review*, 40 (1945): 157–65. Robertson believes Chapman was in Sadler's service at least by 1583, possibly as early as 1578. Eccles, more cautiously, refrains from speculating on the basis of the documentary evidence that Chapman was so employed in 1585. Thus it is possible that Chapman was attached to the Sadler household during Mary's enforced stays, probable that he re-mained in the household until Sadler's death in 1587, through the time at which Mary was executed. Such experience could have helped instill the Protestant and loyalist attitudes of *Cynthiam*, as well as having provided a more than passing acquaintance with some affairs of state. For Sadler's career, see the summary of Robertson or the (somewhat inaccurate) *Dictionary of National Biography* article.

investigated Mary's part in the Darnley murder; he arrested Norfolk and helped quell the abortive rebellion; from August 1580 until April 1581 he served as Mary's guardian, and again for a period in 1584–85.

But more important than the possibility of the hymn glancing at Elizabethan economics or counterintelligence is our grasp of the central theme and direction of the political allegory. In this sense the hymn is "about" the emergence of Elizabethan imperialism, the forging of a sense of national destiny to implement the awkward, but increasingly evident, power which the country could exert in foreign affairs under Elizabeth's direction. In part, the attitude fostered by Elizabeth and her propagandists toward her public role was a quasi-religious one, in which worship of a virgin queen, via a mythological ambiance with religious overtones, acted as a surrogate for worship of a now-forbidden Blessed Virgin.[108] The suggestion of this adoration in Chapman's poem (holy women worship at Cynthia's altars, 129–31) designedly renders more repulsive the sun's threat to her chastity or the canard that she had physical relations with Endymion (490–94).

Cynthia creates her imperial palace, then sends her avatar Euthimya forth with hounds and hunters in Actaeon-like pursuit. The two transformations of Euthimya mark the two actions of the hunt: as panther she leads the hunters into the thicket to experience a terrifying vision of the punishment of her enemies. The hunters probably are contrived to suggest both suitors and military opponents (both, from the narrator's standpoint, are political enemies); as Elizabeth's policy progressed from courtships to warfare, so the chase progresses, and the Nijmegen simile describing the confused rout of the hunters puts final emphasis on the Spanish war. The second stage of the hunt presents "a fruitfull Iland sited by, / Full of all wealth, delight, and Emperie" (366–67), surely England, and—as the first part is an object lesson for foreign opponents—this one would seem to be a stern admonition to Cynthia's own people. If Cynthia's bounty is abused, if the gift of fertility is not husbanded temperately, lust will supplant chastity and Cynthia, acting as boar, must wreak vengeance upon her own retrograde followers. The mythic prototype, expressly that of the Calydonian boar ("Aetolian," twice mentioned, simply means "Calydonian"), represents punishment for neglect

[108]See Yates, "Astraea," pp. 74–75; also "The Political Petrarchism of the Virgin Queen," in Leonard Forster, The Icy Fire: Five Studies in European Petrarchism (Cambridge, 1969), pp. 122–47. The religious attitude toward Elizabeth is crudely adumbrated in such productions as Stubbs's Gaping Gulf and the Dutch Callisto engraving in which the Pope figures as Antichrist. The symbolism becomes more pointed after the miraculous victory of the Armada. For instance Greene's The Spanish Masquerado (1589) presents the Pope as the Beast of the Apocalypse which ravaged Europe until tracked down by Protestant bloodhounds: "The English victory in the channel . . . was also a victory of Christ over Anti-Christ, of Good over Evil in the most literal of senses." Anthony Esler, "Robert Greene and the Spanish Armada," ELH, 32 (1965): 324. The imagery is a cliché by this date. Cf. Leicester's Triumph, pl. 3c, "Queen Elizabeth I attended by Leicester and the five Provinces vanquishes the Beast of the Apocalypse, 1587."

of worship, not a personification of lust, as Bradbrook and Battenhouse argue. "Bewtie strikes fancie blind; pyed show deceau's vs" suggests an oblique hit at the Circean charms of Mary Queen of Scots, while the destruction of noblest mansions warns that not even the highest families (e.g., Norfolk, Lennox, Lady Shrewsbury) will be immune from punishment for turning away from Cynthia. That the pursuers themselves inflict the havoc on the island and its estates reiterates the self-destructive nature of this behavior, the blameless conduct of Cynthia. Thus the day ends and the life-hunt vanishes. The torch of day falls into the ocean stream as Cynthia

> Guide and great soueraigne of the marble seas,
> With milkwhite Heiffers, mounts into her Sphere,
> And leaues vs miserable creatures here.[109]

The allegorical hunt, intended to justify Cynthia's claim to be the creator of imperial peace and to demonstrate the soundness of Elizabeth's statecraft by a compressed and selective rehearsal of events in the decade preceding the Armada, thus progresses from Diana's province of the forest thicket to Cynthia's sovereignty over the marble seas. Indeed, the theme of England's destiny of emerging imperialism in this hymn might be presented as the transformation from Diana to Cynthia, the Lady of the Sea. Historically it represents the development of England from a land-based, second-rank military power to a bold, innovative nation whose first line of defense was its fleet and who thought it best to place that line in its opponents' territorial waters. The remarkable story of Elizabeth's gamble on the sea—her appointment of Hawkins as treasurer of the Navy, and her encouragement of his efforts to modernize and enlarge the fleet; the license she gave to merchant commerce, privateering, exploration—and the way in which the gamble paid off in the feats of Hawkins, Drake, the defeat of the Armada, is well known.[110] The part it plays in the *Hymnvs in Cynthiam* demands our attention.

One scholar remarks that "our poet seems fond of scattering . . . references or allusions to maritime exploits over his two hymns," unfortunately connecting the perception with authorial whimsy rather than with theme and meaning.[111] *Noctem* opens with the poet lamenting

[109] *Cyn.* 397–99. Since the heifer was one of the animals conventionally associated with Diana, it may be overingenious to suggest that Chapman includes it here as allusion to Elizabeth's protection of the Netherlands. See *Leicester's Triumph*, pl. 4: "Queen Elizabeth I feeds the Dutch Cow. William of Orange steadies it by the horns, Philip II draws blood with his spurs, Anjou pulls it backwards by the tail, and Alva milks it"; and fig. 2, an anti-Leicester adaptation.

[110] Wernham, *Before the Armada*, pp. 342–54; Garrett Mattingly, *The Armada* (Boston, 1959); and A. L. Rowse, *The Expansion of Elizabethan England* (London, 1955) offer detailed accounts of the developments.

[111] Schrickx, "Chapman's Borrowings," p. 109.

the "shipwracke of the world" and *Cynthiam* concludes with homage to the goddess who "free'st our ships, when others suffer wracke." Between these poles we find other significant references. The vocations of labor selectively are enumerated as "the souldier to the field, / States-men to counsell, Iudges to their pleas, / Merchants to commerce, mariners to seas" (*Noct.* 208–10), all professions thematically relevant to Cynthia's sphere of activities. Within the fallen world of *Noctem* two examples of positive metamorphosis are enumerated: the Argive ship was translated to the stars for "Bearing to Colchos, and for bringing backe, / The hardie Argonauts, secure of wracke" (*Noct.* 113–14), and the stars generally symbolize the "choise worthies," patterns of conduct, "not to seamen guides alone, / But sacred presidents to euerie one" (*Noct.* 235–36). In *Cynthiam* it becomes evident that peace is to be effected through imperial expansion via sea power; toward the end of *Noctem* the theme is anticipated: "Sweete Peaces richest crowne is made of starres, / Most certaine guides of honord Marinars" (*Noct.* 374–75). Within *Cynthiam* the poet insists upon the goddess's dominion over the seas in local description throughout (3, 11, 83, 139, 172, 391, 397); not only does she free our ships while others wreck, her followers, with peace in their hearts, have strength to subdue the seas (125–26), and the worst loss of favor could mean the withdrawal of this strength: "Cast hills into the sea, and make the starrs, / Drop out of heauen, and lose thy Mariners" (525–26).

In an earlier section I maintained that Chapman's primary concern with the theme of mutability led him to construct a hybrid in which the Actaeon myth is reshaped and combined with certain aspects of the Proteus myth. Within the political dimension of the allegory, the presence of the god of the sea again is apposite. Reading Comes, Chapman would have been pleased to find that Proteus was considered a philosopher for his understanding of nature, a prophet through his observations of the stars and resultant predictions, a magician for his changes of form. But, most important in Comes' summary, he is a politician.[112] As Sandys put it,

> But Proteus rather was a wise and politique prince; who could temper his passions, and shape his actions according to the variety of times and occasions, in the administration of gouerment: now vsing clemency, and againe severity; said therfore to convert into water, into fire; somtimes a fruitfull tree, then a terrible beast; of his rewarding virtue and punishing offences: now proceeding by force like a Lyon; and now like a Fox with subtilty and stratagems.[113]

---

[112]Comes, 8.8. See also Chambers, pp. 284–85, who notes the similar interpretation of Cartari.

[113]Sandys, p. 297.

An apt description of that protean politician who, after having rung all her changes, could be seen to be, like the mutable Cynthia of our hymn, "semper eadem."[114] The allegorical hunt is about political events. As Chapman blends the prototypic Actaeon story with that of the Caly-donian boar, grafting religious issues to political, and that to the oceanic Proteus story, the events figured combine to become an image of the great Proteus-figure, Cynthia, who herself created all personages in the hunt through her control of matter by imposition of form.[115]

By traditional analogy the end of the hunt and the end of the day imply the ending of the life span, and so seem to admit finally that the mortal Cynthia will be eclipsed. In a graceful compliment the poet addresses her as "thou great Elixer of all treasures." Cynthia, as he described her, certainly is like the fabled Philosopher's Stone in her ability to trans-form the base metal of men to gold by means of her example; Chapman's gloss, however, specifically mentions the *Philosophica Medicina*, thus implying that the old queen has the power to sustain life endlessly. Cynthia will confer this immortality not on her own mortal avatar, but on the empire she has created. Although the poet appeals to her to "discend againe," promising that now all will worship Cynthia properly, the monarch's immortality will be attained in another way. Diana's temple will not literally be "reexstruct" in England as it was in Ephesus; rather, Cynthia's subjects are urged to "Build Cynthia's Temple in your vertuous parts" (*Cyn.* 451). The imperial palace which was constructed on the pattern of Cynthia's mind will survive through the aggregate of indi-

---

[114]Elizabeth's motto, of course, could not escape the attention of her eager poets. For a late example of the *semper eadem* motif, see John Dowland's 1603 madrigal, which proclaims, "See the moon / That ever in one change doth grow, / Yet still the same and she is so." *Lyrics from the Song-Books of the Elizabethan Age*, ed. A. H. Bullen (London, 1897), p. 127.

[115]Perhaps Chapman's hymn was studied by Francis Davison, who wrote *The Mask of Proteus and the Adamantine Rock*, performed by Gray's Inn, March 1595. The power of Proteus is surpassed by Cynthia:

> Yet even that [Pole] Star gives place to Cynthia's rays,
> Whose drawing virtues govern and direct
> The flots and re-flots of the ocean.
> But Cynthia, praised by your wat'ry reign,
> Your influence in Spirits have no place.

The ebb and flow of the tide is equated with Cynthia's influence in foreign lands, and the Armada makes its inevitable appearance:

> In the Protection of this mighty Rock,
> In Britain land, whilst tempests beat abroad,
> The lordly and the lowly shepherd both,
> In plenteous peace have fed their happy flocks.
> Upon the force of this inviolate Rock,
> The giant-like attempts of Power unjust
> Have suffer'd wreck.

A text of the mask is reprinted in Nichols, 3: 309–19; quotations, p. 317; and some discus-sion of it occurs in Stephen Orgel, *The Jonsonian Masque* (Cambridge, Mass., 1965), pp. 8–18.

viduals who make up the English nation and attain the "Pax Imperij" because they have modeled the individual temples of their souls on Cynthia's temple. In this way, through the diminutions and exfoliations of the microcosm-macrocosm principle, Cynthia, the macrocosm as world soul of England, provides the form for the microcosm of individual souls, who then join into the governmental macrocosm of the Elizabethan Empire.

The nature of the political allegory leads to the tempting conjecture that identifiable historical personages besides Elizabeth and Alençon lurk beneath its surface. Battenhouse tentatively offers a guess that Seymour and Leicester might be equated with Orion and Alpheus.[116] Seymour seems too remote from the rather carefully defined context of foreign affairs and emergent imperialism; certainly Leicester should be present, although within this political ambiance in a somewhat more positive guise. One remembers Prince Arthur hastening to Lady Belge's relief; perhaps here Leicester enters incongruously as the Endymion whom Cynthia did affect only for his "studious intellect." It would only be fitting if Ganymede should unmask as, say, Sir Philip Sidney—Orphean poet, Protestant politician, eloquent protestor against the Alençon marriage, and gallant casualty of Leicester's Netherlands campaign.[117] But, as Battenhouse rightly reminds us, specific identifications are both perilous and unnecessary. A more patient sifting of state papers and contemporary gossip may clarify such details as the identities of Salmacis, Cydippe, or Ganymede, although such topical clarification probably will not alter our comprehension of the hymn's meaning as political allegory. The important point about Ganymede is his function within the framework of the mythic narrative. For Dante the resemblance

---

[116]Battenhouse, p. 605, n. 45.

[117]Matthew Roydon, to whom the hymns are dedicated, commemorated the death of Sidney with "An Elegie, or friends passion, for his Astrophill," first published in the 1593 miscellany The Phoenix Nest. In the poem Astrophil immortalizes Stella through his verse before being slain by an envious Mars. A chorus of emblematic birds (similar to those in The Phoenix and Turtle), turtledove, swan, eagle, and phoenix mourn. "The skie bred Egle roiall bird" (6), despite the phoenix motif of the volume, is given the climatic position:

> The egle markt with pearcing sight,
> The mournfull habite of the place,
> And parted thence with mounting flight,
> To signifie to Loue the case,
>   What sorow nature doth sustaine,
>   For Astrophill by enuie slaine.
> And while I followed with mine eie,
> The flight the Egle vpward tooke,
> All things did vanish by and by . . . .

Publicly, of course, as cup-bearer to the queen, Sidney played Ganymede to Elizabeth's Cynthia; more privately he alluded to the myth to designate the relationship of Astrophil to Stella. See sonnet 70.1–4.

between the form of the letter *M* ("omo," man) and the shape of the eagle's body suggested a general relationship: the eagle symbolizes human nature or humanity. But in specifically political terms Dante recalled the ancient beast-lore which held the eagle to be the only living creature able to gaze at the sun with open eyes,[118] prompting him to relate the eagle to the sun-moon symbolism of church and state. Therefore, the eagle comes to symbolize not only "the work of all righteous governors" in the *Monarchia*, but further, "The Eagle is the symbol of empire, *l'uccel di Dio*—the sole bird which can look upon the sun, governing mankind 'sotto l'ombra delle sacre penne,' that is, tempering to them the light of God and sheltering on occasion even the church beneath those wings."[119] Chapman so uses the image in *De Guiana* as he argues that Ralegh's colonial projects will "seat the Monarchie of earth, / Like to *Ioues* Eagle, on *Elizas* hand." Similarly, Chapman's Ganymede is the loyal subject who accepts his monarch's will, making it the pattern of his mind, for which he is finally rewarded by metamorphosis to that greater empire:

> The bit, and spurre that Monarcke ruleth still,
> To further good things, and to curb the ill,
> He is the Ganemede, the birde of Ioue,
> Rapt to his soueraignes bosome for his loue,
> His bewtie was it, not the bodies pride,
> That made him great Aquarius stellified.

[Cyn. 460–65]

This beauty of mind causes Ganymede to be the only mortal elevated to the status of divinity; the imperial eagle thus becomes great Aquarius and the poet can only wish that all virtuous men would model themselves on Ganymede as Ganymede had modeled himself on Cynthia.

HECATE

It would be difficult to dissociate strictly political from poetic implications in Chapman's hymns; both activities have for him moral and ethical centers in which his stance is the same. By the logic of correspondences, a man whose taste in poetry is faulty will also be suspect politically. Bad politics and bad poetry amount to the same thing. Accordingly, while Chapman's dedication to *The Shadow of Night* always

---

[118]J. M. Steadman summarizes traditional eagle lore in "Chaucer's Eagle: A Contemplative Symbol," *PMLA*, 75 (1960): 153–56.

[119]Dunbar, p. 45; preceding quotation, p. 71. See the entire discussion pp. 69–74. See also the account of eagle as portent of kingdom or kingship in Agrippa, *Three Books of Occult Philosophy*, trans. J[ohn] F.[rench] (London, 1651), 1.54.

has been recognized as a tantalizing clue to literary schisms in the 1590s, it should be kept in mind that the ultimate basis of the factionalism is political.[120]

Following the death of Leicester, a power struggle to seize the favorite's mantle and gain ascendancy over the old generation of councillors, now represented almost solely by Burghley, polarized the younger courtiers around the figures of Essex and Ralegh. Essex, as Leicester's stepson and heir to both Sidney's widow and best sword, directly maintained the continuity of the Leicester-Sidney group; his principal ally soon proved to be Southampton, a friend from the days when both had been wards in Burghley's household. The two young men consciously emulated the Sidney role of Renaissance man, courtier-poet and soldier-statesman; indeed, for the year or two immediately before his coming of age, to the eyes of writers needing patrons and of court hangers-on assessing favor, Southampton's star seemed to glitter more brightly than Essex's.[121] Meanwhile, owing to an unwise marriage and mixed success as a privateer, Ralegh was suffering an eclipse. Just why Chapman should oppose himself to the Essex-Southampton faction must remain obscure. Since the thrust in *Cynthiam* seems to be against Southampton in particular, the answer may lie in Southampton's then-Catholicism,[122] his literary taste, or some affront to the championed Ralegh. Unquestionably the dedication to *The Shadow of Night* attempts to ingratiate Chapman with a group of men in the Ralegh camp.

Chapman's dedication to Matthew Roydon claims an intellectual affinity with Roydon and obviously seeks an introduction to his associates, Derby, Northumberland, and George Carey, "heire of Hunsdon," to whom he attributes similar scholarly and literary inclinations. Roydon, Sidney's elegist; Northumberland, a student of mathematics, alchemy, and Chapmanesque author of an essay, *On the entertainment of a Mistress being inconsistent with the pursuit of Learning*; Derby, minor

---

[120]I do not propose to consider here the perennially intriguing but unprovable "School of Night" hypothesis; although my argument does not conflict with this theory, the argument itself does not depend on the existence of such a school. The most energetic proponent of the "School of Night" is Frances A. Yates in her *A Study of Love's Labour's Lost* (Cambridge, 1936); however, one should consult the temperate review of evidence and conjecture in Richard David's introduction to the New Arden *Love's Labour's Lost*, rev. ed. (London, 1951). See "The Topical Context," pp. xxxvii–1.

[121]On Essex's leadership of the former Sidney faction and on Essex and Southampton as imitators of the Sidney ideal, see, e.g., F. J. Levy, "Philip Sidney Reconsidered," *English Literary Renaissance*, 2 (1972): 16–17; and G. P. V. Akrigg, *Shakespeare and the Earl of Southampton* (Cambridge, Mass., 1968), pp. 184–88; also, pp. 36–40 for the literary attention Southampton received prior to reaching his majority on 6 October 1594.

[122]On Southampton's Catholicism see Akrigg, pp. 176–81. His conversion to the Church of England is usually dated after 1603, although Akrigg would place it as early as his marriage to Elizabeth Vernon (Essex's cousin) in 1598. Certainly he was an ardent Catholic as a boy and his position as head of a great Catholic family meant that his public image was unaltered until well after *The Shadow of Night*.

versifier, Spenser's "Amyntas," sponsor of Leicester's old dramatic company which later came under the patronage of Hunsdon—all are figures intellectually compatible with Chapman. At the same time, how-ever, they are men with whom Chapman could feel a political com-patibility: Roydon, to whom Chapman also dedicated *Ovids Banquet*, was Ralegh's man; Northumberland, who when later unjustly im-prisoned read Chapman's *Homer* in the Tower, was a staunch friend of Ralegh; and Chapman could only have admired the loyal way in which Derby had resisted and exposed the Catholic plot in 1593.[123]

Chapman writes his explicitly learned and moral poetry in self-conscious opposition to the triviality of then-popular modes of erotic poetry and—it is fairly safe to assume—to Shakespeare's *Venus and Adonis* in particular:

Presume not then ye flesh confounded soules,
That cannot beare the full Castalian bowles,
Which seuer mounting spirits from the sences,
To looke in this deepe fount for thy pretenses.

[Cyn. 162–65]

As many readers have observed, this seems an unmistakable allusion to the Ovidian tag which Shakespeare prefixed to his poem; as such, Chapman's hymns would also reflect unfavorably upon Southampton to whom the Shakespeare poem was dedicated. Southampton's hedonistic tastes were known to his contemporaries and a good possibility exists that he encouraged the writing of erotic poetry far more lascivious than *Venus and Adonis*, in which case Chapman's warning would indicate more than a purely personal rivalry.[124] Chapman's *Shadow* implicitly and

---

[123]See the *DNB* articles on these men. Northumberland's very interesting essay on learning is printed by Yates as Appendix 3 to her *Study of LLL*; see also her discussion, pp. 137–51.

[124]Thomas Nashe's "The Choice of Valentines or The Merie Ballad Of Nash his Dildo" circu-lated in manuscript and was well enough known to earn him Gabriel Harvey's attack for "emulating Aretino's licentiousness." In one ms. a dedicatory sonnet is addressed "To the Right honorable the Lord S." J. S. Farmer, *The Choise of Valentines* (London, 1899), viii–ix, concludes that this is Southampton; R. B. McKerrow, *The Works of Thomas Nashe* (1910; reprint ed., Oxford, 1958), 5: 141, argues that Strange is a more likely candidate. I would suggest that the phrase, "sweet flower of Matchless poetrie," could describe someone who is the subject of poetry (Southampton) as well as someone who is a poet (Strange), and that the poem is more in keeping with the character of Southampton.

In 1592 Nashe's *Pierce Penilesse* bafflingly commended that "matchlesse image of Honor, and magnificent rewarder of vertue, *Joves Eagle-borne Ganimed*, thrice-noble *Amyntas*" (*Works*, 1: 243). This Ganymede has been identified with Southampton (see Akrigg, pp. 181–82), the fourth Earl of Derby (see J. B. Hunter, *Notes and Queries*, 196 [1951]: 75–76), and Ferdinando Stanley, then Lord Strange and later fifth Earl of Derby (see F. P. Wilson, "supplementary notes" to Nashe, *Works*, vol. 5). All three nominations raise the possibility of further resonances to Chapman's use of the Ganymede myth in *Cynthiam*: he may have wished to praise the person of the living or the memory of the dead Derby. But, in the context of Chapman's assault on erotic mythological poetry, Southamp-ton, possibly associated with homosexuality by Nashe's Ganymede allusion (see Akrigg),

explicitly draws as distinct a line between kinds of patrons and their attitudes as it does between kinds of poetry, and, for understanding the hymns, Ralegh-versus-Southampton is more important than Chapman-versus-Shakespeare. As we have seen, the chastity-lust polarity signifies a moral opposition that works out primarily in political terms. The same opposition applies to the factionalism behind the poems: Southampton, who commissions poems approving of lust, naturally would be an adherent of Essex with his lust for power; Roydon and Northumberland, the last with his preference for Arabian mathematicians to Arcadian romance, just as naturally would be adherents of chaste poetry and the imperialist politics of Ralegh, in support of which Chapman later wrote De Guiana. Thus, in the fashion of interlocking Chinese boxes, the themes of the hymns constantly interrelate; and in the following discussion of them as a poetic manifesto, the implicit political correlation must be taken for granted.

This discussion of The Shadow of Night began with an explanation of the poems as Orphic hymns and with a reminder of the function of Orphic music. The true harmony of the soul is symbolized by chastity or by the moon, which marks the boundary between the orders of nature, and the symbols coalesce in the figure of the chaste moon goddess, Cynthia, Diana, Luna. The poet or musician reproduces in audible form that cosmic harmony which Pythagoras once heard and so through art becomes an instrument of reform or regeneration, providing fallen man with a pattern of that larger lost harmony.[125] This explains the myth of Orpheus's fabled power over nature:

So when ye heare, the sweetest Muses sonne,
With heauenly rapture of his Musicke, wonne
Rockes, forrests, floods, and winds to leaue their course
In his attendance: it bewrayes the force
His wisedome had, to draw men growne so rude
To ciuill loue of Art, and Fortitude.

[Noct. 139–44]

---

remains the most fascinating possibility. It would be like Chapman to wish to restore the debased myth to its proper dignity. Unquestionably Nashe dedicated The Unfortunate Traveller to Southampton in 1593; and in 1597 William Burton dedicated The Most Delectable History of Clitophon and Leucippe to Southampton. Akrigg remarks the episodes involving homosexuality and erotic sadism, concluding: "What is interesting is that Burton chose Southampton as the dedicatee for his work. Presumably he thought the Earl would like it" (p. 55).

[125]Since they are both based on "numbers," the arts of poetry and music were believed to be essentially similar. Poetry is closer to "true" music, i.e., a combination of singing and playing on a stringed instrument, than wholly instrumental music because it employs the human voice. See John Hollander, The Untuning of the Sky: Ideas of Music in English Poetry 1500–1700 (Princeton, 1961), p. 34.

Orpheus the musician is Orpheus the civilizer or the savior; but it is in still another role that Orpheus and his art should be perceived in Chapman's poems. Orpheus for the Renaissance not only was a *priscus theologus* but a *priscus magus,* and his hymns were believed to be magical incantations actually used in religious rites.[126]

The Orphic magic which Ficino practiced in an effort to cure his own constitutional melancholy was astrological, based on the conception that planets have the moral characteristics of their mythological namesakes and that by properly invoking a planet one can establish a sympathetic spirit-bond, drawing down the planet's "virtues." By power of empathy the magus obtains for himself the qualities associated with or symbolized by the planet he addresses. In his popular magical handbook *De occulta philosophia* (written by 1510, published in 1533), Agrippa gives the earliest full exposition of Ficino's astrological magic, complete with details of the planetary music:

> This exposition is taken, often *verbatim,* from the *De Triplici Vita,* and is combined with an Orphic *Conclusio* of Pico and an interpretation of the Orphic Hymns as astrological invocations; but it is dispersed and embedded in Agrippa's vast survey of magic, and therefore closely associated, one might say contaminated, with quite different kinds of magic.[127]

It is in this dominantly platonic, but highly eclectic, manual that one finds the most detailed account of how actually to perform the astrological magic which Ficino and Pico recommended in far less mundane terms.

The Shadow of Night consists of two hymns, Orphic hymns as Chapman understood them, which adapt the procedures for invoking the virtues of a planet; *Noctem* should be considered as providing a context for the invocation in *Cynthiam,* which expresses the character of the moon goddess. The "magic" which the poet attempts to invoke is both subjective, medically curative as it was for Ficino, and transitive, an effort to work a quasi-religious, wholly political "influence" upon his audience.[128] An analysis with the astrological magic formulas found in Ficino and Agrippa should reveal the techniques by which Chapman seeks to impart to his hymns both the ritual magic associated with the

---

[126]A number of recent studies have emphasized the central importance of magic and occultism in the main currents of Renaissance thought. The most valuable of these remain Walker's *Spiritual and Demonic Magic from Ficino to Campanella* and Yates's *Giordano Bruno and the Hermetic Tradition.* I am much indebted to Walker's study as background for my analysis.

[127]Walker, *Magic,* p. 91; see the entire section, pp. 90–96, and Yates's useful summary of Agrippa's book, *Bruno,* pp. 130–43.

[128]Walker, *Magic,* p. 82, helpfully distinguishes the two kinds.

Orphic Hymns and the particular symbolic characters of night and the moon.

Obviously any attempt to use the procedure for astrological magic as the vehicle of an aesthetic construct requires some adaptation and re-shaping of the formulas. Chapman's approach to his mythological sources invariably is syncretic—cutting, trimming, conflating, developing to suit his needs. With *The Shadow of Night* the most noticeable divergence from the conventions of Orphic magic is necessitated by the public symbols of the political mythology, Elizabeth's moon image, and symbolic polarity of imperial moon and papal sun. In Orphic magic and in other forms of astrological magic, as well, the predominant emphasis is solar;[129] Chapman, accordingly, was forced to eliminate solar imagery and influences from his poetic magic. Since Orpheus did address hymns to night, to the moon, to Diana (which Chapman knew in the passages excerpted by Comes, if not firsthand), the problem of re-emphasis did not involve any shortage of material.

Noctem commences with an invocation of the goddess that establishes both the cermonial religious quality of the hymns and the important astrological emphasis. Drawing directly upon the material supplied in Comes' "De Nocte" chapter, Chapman presents earth as an altar with Night the presiding goddess; from this altar "endlesse fumes exspires, / Therefore, in fumes of sighes and fires of griefe," an image which distinguishes between kinds of exhalations with technical precision.[130] The poet's appeal to the goddess, following the first invocation, also anticipates the two states of mind that correspond to the opposition between two kinds of night developed through the first hymn. He asks:

> now let humor giue
> Seas to mine eyes, that I may quicklie weepe
> The shipwracke of the world: or let soft sleepe
> (Binding my sences) lose my working soule,
> That in her highest pitch, she may controule
> The court of skill, compact of misterie,
> Wanting but franchisement and memorie
> To reach all secrets.
>
> [*Noct.* 8–15]

The "shipwracke of the world" for which he would weep is caused by "A stepdame Night of minde" or "blindnesse of the minde" and therefore is symptomatic of the crippling "black" melancholy. The true night should be associated with both the religious contemplation of the One that is the Orphic *nox* and the creative, intellectual Saturnian mel-

---

[129]See Yates, *Bruno*, index entry for "sun".

[130]See S. K. Heninger, Jr., *A Handbook of Renaissance Meteorology* (Durham, N.C., 1960), p. 184.

ancholy.[131] Night can in this way cause the poet to lose his "working soule" in religious contemplation, and this implies a poetic based upon the platonic doctrine of reminiscence: all secrets can be reached through memory which allows the soul to control the mysterious court of skill. Chapman's conception of the contemplative *nox* blotting out the delusory sensations of the day echoes Agrippa's account of the conditions requisite for prophetic dreaming—"for the most usuall time for dreams is the night, when the senses are freed from wandring objects, and meridian errours, and vain affections; neither doth fear strike the minde, nor the thoughts tremble, and the minde being most quiet, doth stedfastly adhere to the Deity" (Agrippa 3.51). So illusory daydreams, as phantasmal as day itself, are inspired by the gate of ivory, while Night's gate of horn "greets our eyes / With grauer dreames inspir'd with prophesies" (*Noct.* 352–53). For the Renaissance, attainment of the creative state of melancholy depended upon occult study of the *prisca theologia*. In *Il Penseroso* this means mastering the recondite lore of Plato and "Thrice-Great Hermes"; Chapman's poem is, as Millar MacLure remarks,[132] his version of *Il Penseroso* and the guiding magi are Plato and Orpheus (arrived at, of course, through the willing intermediaries of Ficino, Agrippa, and Comes). The presentation of poetry and prophecy as platonic reminiscence reminds us that one function of astrological magic is to be a memory device and that Chapman's contemporary Giordano Bruno made Hermetic magic into an elaborate art of memory:

> By using magical or talismanic images as memory-images, the Magus hoped to acquire universal knowledge, and also powers, obtaining through the magical organisation of the imagination a magically powerful personality, tuned in, as it were, to the powers of the cosmos.[133]

With Chapman the art of memory becomes the art of poetry as the Orphic artist remembers the lost harmony of soul and recreates it in his own art.

The desired Saturnian melancholy and the Orpheus myth are linked by the myth of the Golden Age; when Astraea lived among men the now-lost harmony of society and nature existed—"When Saturnes golden scepter stroke the strings / Of Ciuill gouernment"—which the Orphic music emulates. By understanding what is lost, the poet can make corrective and didactic verse, bringing man to an awareness of his condition by showing him the forsaken standard (*Noct.* 21–28, 131–38). The Orpheus story implies two processes: the poet calms "the perturbations

---

[131]For creative melancholy see Chastel, *Marsile Ficin et l'Art*, pp. 163–71; and Raymond Klibansky et al., *Saturn and Melancholy* (London, 1964).

[132]MacLure, p. 35.

[133]Yates, *Bruno*, p. 192; and her full account in *The Art of Memory* (Chicago, 1966).

of his minde"; then, having gained this harmony of spirit, uses his art "to draw men growne so rude / To ciuill loue of Art, and Fortitude." The Orphic art thus is both subjectively therapeutic and transitive magic. Therefore the poet consecrates his life to the Orphic *nox* (*Noct.* 271), and seeks the support of others in his dedication to corrective art; they should compress "all the powre of Art," "fiction, and hyperboles" into their visions of man's corruption:

> But paint, or else create in serious truth,
> A bodie figur'd to your vertues ruth,
> That to the sence may shew what damned sinne,
> For your extreames this Chaos tumbles in.
>
> [*Noct.* 316–19]

All worthwhile poets must "Come consecrate with me, to sacred Night" for "No pen can any thing eternall wright, / That is not steept in humor of the Night" (*Noct.* 376–77); only then can they attain to prophetic vision and be rewarded with the inmost vision. The poet describes the goddess Night as "blacke in face, and glitterst in thy heart" (*Noct.* 227). The heart of darkness is "Nights faire soule," Cynthia, who appears to the initiate in the vision of the triumphal procession at the end of *Noctem*. Chapman seems to combine the Plotinian image of moon as world-soul with Ficino's conception that the soul of the world infuses the occult virtues into all things through a quintessential medium of spirit.[134] MacLure suggests that the first of Chapman's hymns "is concerned with art, the second with nature";[135] but this Spenserian scheme is too neat. Both hymns abound with Orphean references to poetry, art, music, and both are concerned with what it might be more proper to call the super-natural. The first hymn penetrates the darkness with which Cynthia, like all Orphic mysteries, is enveloped; the second invokes her directly. Just as *L'Allegro's* conclusion creates a bridge by suggesting the thematic issues of *Il Penseroso*, however, the ending of *Noctem* adumbrates the political issues of *Cynthiam* with its references to "imperiall Night," the delusive Protean dreams "taking formes of Princes," focusing finally on the "dreadfull presence of our Empresse."

The theme of astrological invocation had been maintained in *Noctem* through images of the zodiac—Amalthaea, the Argive ship (which also brings to mind Orpheus's Argonautic career) and the images of the guiding stars, which point to the major political ramification of spiritual harmony: "Sweete Peaces richest crowne is made of starres, / Most certaine guides of honord Marinars" (*Noct.* 373–74). *Noctem* describes the state of mind which afflicts both poet and world, and the contempla-

---

[134]Battenhouse, p. 598, for the moon image; for his adaptation of Ficino see Agrippa, 1.11 and 1.14, discussed by Yates, *Bruno*, p. 132.

[135]MacLure, p. 36.

tive *nox* to which man must attain before envisioning Cynthia; nonetheless, the relationship between night and Cynthia as soul of night makes it difficult to distinguish sharply between the two. Why then does Chapman treat his subject in two hymns? One might conjecture that he was influenced by the precedent of separate hymns "to Night" and "to the Moon" from Orpheus; even by Chapman's somewhat elastic conception of the form, one poem including all of this material would have been improbably long to call a hymn. It is possible, too, that Chapman's pair of hymns reflects awareness of numerology: "The number two is ascribed to the Moon, which is the second great light, and figures out the soul of the world" (Agrippa 2.21).

Cynthiam, like *Noctem*, commences with a direct invocation of the goddess, but the means by which one establishes the sympathetic bond with a planet to partake of its "virtues" go far beyond mere direct address. Agrippa's treatise is rich particularly in the formulas of lunary magic, devoting chapters to "What things are Lunary or under the power of the Moon," "Of the Images of the Moon," "Of the images of the head & tayle of the dragon of the moon," "Of the Images of the Mansions of the Moon," in addition to the secondary discussions of the moon within chapters on planetary names, places, colors, incense, music, and the like. Agrippa serves as a useful guide to the lunary magic of Chapman's poems in two ways: often a correspondence between the procedures recommended by Agrippa and those in the hymns indicates the thematic function of a passage or line of imagery; at other times an exact parallel in the imagery will show Chapman's strict reliance on the tradition of astrological magic. Agrippa was one of Comes' authorities and Chapman without doubt read of Agrippa's opinions there; whether he then sought out the treatise directly, got his lore firsthand from Ficino, or third-hand from another disseminator, is immaterial. A comparison with Agrippa reveals how closely Chapman works with the standard procedures.

The names of the planets and their epithets are many and diverse, and the magus who wishes to establish the bond of *spiritus* must correctly invoke these names. Agrippa's short list of names for the moon fills half a page, after which he concludes with the advice: "he that will know more, and make more curious enquiry, must betake himself to the hymns of *Orpheus*, which he that truely understands, hath attained to a great understanding of naturall Magick" (2.59). There is some direct correlation between Agrippa's list and the names employed by Chapman, since many of them are conventional to lunary myth generally as well as to lunary magic specifically; more interestingly, the profusion of the names and epithets and the importance of the ritual procedure explain punctiliousness in this area as something more functional than elegant variation. In the poems he uses *Hyperions horned daughter*, *Natures bright eye-sight*, *Nights faire soule*, *Great Cynthia*, *gracious*

Cynthia, sacred chiefe, soueraigne generall, sacred Cynthia, Queene celestiall, mightie Cynthia, Heccate, Goddesse, Titanides, Elixer of all treasures, great Lucifera, Thrise mightie Cynthia, Planets Queene. The glosses contribute *daughter of the sun, moon, Lucina, Ilythia, Prothyrea, Diana, Luna, Ignifera,* in addition to explanations of many names used in the hymns. Some, of course, are repeated several times.

The elements associated with the moon are earth and water; hence the places particularly under her influence are: "wildernesses, woods, rocks, hils, mountaines, forrests, fountaines, waters, rivers, seas, seashores, ships, groves, high-waies, and granaries for Corn, and such like" (Agrippa 1.48). Of the elementary combination water predominates; therefore, while in the Diana-like allegorical hunt Chapman develops imagery of wilderness, wood, forest and thicket, the dominant patterns in both hymns relate to water: tears, seas, streams, ocean, ship and shipwreck, maritime activity. The moon controls not only ocean tides but fresh waters and "all moist things." Chapman does not trouble to individualize the vegetable life under her influence, but moisture predominates in the matter from which the hunt is constructed: "Then straight the flowrs, the shadowes and the mists, / (Fit matter for most pliant humorists) / She hunters makes" (*Cyn.* 220–22). According to Ficino's list of celestial influences, stones and metals particularly pertain to the moon.[136] Chapman includes steel, adamant, marble, crystal, and Cynthia herself becomes the philosopher's stone (*Cyn.* 404, and gloss). Especially appropriate to the moon, Agrippa notes (1.24), are those stones, metals, gems, and creatures which are white or silver, for these are the moon's colors. Marble and crystal therefore are doubly appropriate; and the color symbolism explains, too, why Cynthia is drawn by "a brase of siluer Hynds / In Iuorie chariot" (*Noct.* 392–93) at her first appearance and by "milkwhite Heiffers" (*Cyn.* 398) at her last.

Animals especially subject to lunary influence "are such as delight to be in mans company, and such as do naturally excell in love, or hatred, as all kinds of Dogs"; also "Swine, Hinds, Goats, and all Animals whatsoever, that observe, and imitate the motion of the Moon. . . ." Thus we have silver hind, milk-white heifers, the "rabid mastiffs" which love Cynthia and hate her enemies, the celebration of Amalthaea, and the metamorphosis of the boar. Significantly, magical lore explains why Chapman should select the panther from the lion-panther combination of Diana iconography: "Panther . . . is said to have a spot upon her shoulder like the Moon, increasing into a roundness, and having horns that bend inwards" (Agrippa 1.24).[137] Chapman has the complicating factor in *Cynthiam* of translating the static invocations of the Orphic

---

[136]Walker, *Magic*, p. 15.

[137]The lore is repeated by la Primaudaye, *The French Academie: Fvlly Discovrsed and finished in foure Bookes* (London, 1618), 3.85.

magus to function within a narrative scheme. The use of incense is important in the Orphic rituals and Walker speculates that Ficino dutifully employed fumigations.[138] Agrippa offers a barbarically medieval formula: "For the *Moon* we make a suffumigation of the head of a Frog dryed, the eyes of a Bull, the seed of white Poppy, Frankincense, and Camphir, which must be incorporated with Menstruous blood, or the blood of a Goose" (1.44). But how is this sort of thing to be integrated with a narrative? Chapman solves the problem of getting scent into the hymn by taking advantage of a staple of panther-lore—all other creatures are infatuated with her scent and when hunting she uses this odor to entrap them.[139] Chapman's panther is Euthimya, an avatar of Cynthia herself; the panther sprinkling about her scent to lure on the hounds thus infatuates them with a fumigation of Cynthia (*Cyn.* 354-65).

Reserving direct description of Cynthia for points of narrative climax where they will have greatest effectiveness, Chapman borrows from the images of the moon only at the end of each hymn. In *Noctem* Cynthia appears in an ivory chariot, accompanied by meteors, comets, and lightning:

> swifter then the winds,
> Is great Hyperions horned daughter drawne
> Enchantresse-like, deckt in disparent lawne,
> Circled with charmes, and incantations,
> That ride huge spirits, and outragious passions.

> [*Noct.* 393-97]

At the conclusion of *Cynthiam*, the poet beseeches,

> Looke with thy fierce aspect, be terror-strong;
> Assume thy wondrous shape of halfe a furlong:
> Put on thy feete of Serpents, viperous hayres,
> And act the fearefulst part of thy affaires.

> [*Cyn.* 519-22]

The second of these passages is based on the Gorgonian description in Comes' *De Hecate*.[140] Both the versions here and those in Comes are in keeping with the image presented by Ficino: "Luna puella cornuto capite super draconem vel taurum, serpentes supra caput & sub pedibus habens."[141] Chapman relies heavily upon Comes' Hecate chapter in the second hymn because, as Hecate, the moon goddess is most directly associated with witchcraft and the "artes magicae." And it is the magical

[138]Walker, *Magic*, pp. 23 and 30.

[139]See, e.g., *The French Academie,* 3.85.

[140]See Schrickx, "Chapman's Borrowings," p. 108.

[141]Ficino, *Opera* (Basil, 1576), p. 557.

attributes of Hecate that are stressed in these descriptions. She is "enchantresse-like," wears her "fierce aspect," "wondrous shape," and acts "the fearefulst part" of her protean role. The *Noctem* passage pictures her "Circled with charmes, and incantations," and *Cynthiam* exhorts her: "Then in thy cleare, and Isie Pentacle, / Now execute a Magicke miracle." The perfect circle is, of course, the form of the moon and the inevitable image of Cynthia's perfection, but circle and pentangle also happen to be the two geometrical forms most closely associated with magic: "they who adjure evil spirits, are wont to environ themselves about with a circle. A Pentangle also, as with the vertue of the number five hath a very great command over evil spirits" (Agrippa 2.23).

This emphasis on charms, incantations, and magic at the climax of each hymn only exaggerates what has been evident throughout—the thematic concentration upon magic and, particularly, astrological magic. The eclipse is the most awesome feat of astrological magic,[142] as the long account of the terrified Romans and Macedonians attests, and the poet's problem in *Cynthiam* is that, while he has attained a vision of the goddess, he still cannot accept on faith the necessity of and—for her true followers—the goodness of Cynthia's magical changes. At this stage he cannot fully project the Orphic vision of magic art, so the Roman use of "Soul-winging musicke" to echo the "charmes" of the moon seems a failure because it does not forestall eclipse. The poet's knowledge of astrological magic is incomplete and he needs the lesson of the allegorical hunt to become like Endymion: "And since his eyes were euermore awake, / To search for knowledge of [her] excellence, / And all Astrologie: no negligence, / Or female softnesse fede his learned trance" (*Cyn.* 496–99).

Before leaving the subject of invocational formulas in the planetary magic, we must consider one other aspect of the handbook lore and its presence in the poems. Chapman writes of Cynthia "Musicke, and moode, she loues," and further he describes her "heauenly Magicke mood" and liking for the "change of Musick." The spelling and pronunciation practices of Renaissance England did not distinguish between *mood* and *mode*, homophonic coincidence thus reinforcing the ancient conception that musical modes were affective emotionally and that the emotional response simultaneously triggered a moral response, that each mode produced its own ethos.[143] Now the way in which Chapman

---

[142]Walker, *Magic*, pp. 206–10, has an interesting account of Campanella's attempts to prevent eclipses.

[143]See Hollander on "Ethos", pp. 31–36, and "Mode & Mood", pp. 206–20. Gretchen L. Finney, *Musical Backgrounds for English Literature: 1580–1650* (New Brunswick, n.d. [1962]), emphasizes the neoplatonic bias of Renaissance music theory, pp. 76–125; discusses the affective power of modes, pp. 50–56; and, summarizing Walker, planetary music, pp. 106–12. Edward E. Lowinsky, *Tonality and Atonality in Sixteenth-Century Music* (Berkeley and Los Angeles, 1962), pp. 33–37, provides a technical discussion of the

connects *Musicke* and *mood* in the one instance and *Magicke* and *mood* in the other (the phonic similarity of *musicke* and *magicke* is itself suggestive in the context of Orphic magic) indicates his consciousness of the effect that mode can elicit in the rituals of Orphic incantation.

Agrippa has a number of things to say about astrological music; following Ficino, he reports that *"Saturn, Mars,* and the *Moon* have more of the voice then of the Harmony. *Saturn* hath sad, hoarse, heavy, and slow words, and sounds, as it were pressed to the Center; but *Mars,* rough, sharp, threatning, great and wrathful words: the *Moon* observeth a mean betwixt these two"* (Agrippa 2.26).[144] Relating the four most common modes of music to the humors and elements, Agrippa contrives these associations: Dorian, water and phlegm; Phrygian, choler and fire; Lydian, blood and air; Mixolydian, melancholy and earth. Finally, Agrippa designates the modes appropriate to the respective planets, and we learn that the Hypodorian (i.e., the mode a distinct interval below the ordinary Dorian) is assigned to the moon. This hierarchy is supplemented with one pairing the nine muses to the planets, *"Clio* with the *Moon* move after the *Hypodorian* manner,"* and with some doggerel to serve as a mnemonic aid: *"After the Hypodorian Clio sings, / Persephone* likewise doth strike the Base strings"* (Agrippa 2.26). A considerable body of lore accrues to the four basic modes; and one finds a fair degree of consistency in descriptions of their moral effects, primarily originating from Plato's refusal to allow within his republic any modes except the Phrygian and the Dorian. This platonic sanction undoubtedly contributed to the exceptional popularity which the Dorian enjoyed in the Renaissance. The moral character of the Dorian was taken to be temperate, grave, ceremonial, manly, sometimes warlike but never frenzied. John Hollander notes that Dorian becomes "almost a synonym for 'solemn'" and that in association with Protestant church music it comes to stand for a grave, pious style in the early Puritan opposition to the elaborate polyphony of some liturgical music.[145] Although much less material is available on such a relatively recherché mode as Hypodorian, it seems reasonable to suppose that a "deepening" of the Dorian would result in an intensification of the effects ordinarily attributed to it. Thus, one may assume, the Hypodorian will be even more grave and solemn

---

theory of modality. Hollander, pp. 162–76, and Finney, pp. 210–19, consider the Orpheus myth as it relates to music and musical lore.

[144]See Walker, *Magic,* pp. 17–18.

[145]See Hollander, pp. 33, 213, 254–56. M. Y. Hughes, *Ten Perspectives on Milton* (New Haven, 1965), "Lydian Airs," pp. 1–11, documents the dominance of the ethical, platonic Dorian mode in the Renaissance. The characteristics of the primary modes become so conventionalized that Comes knows he does not have to name Phyrgian, Lydian, and Dorian—only their effects: "Alius fuit musicae modus, cum per numeros animi in bellum essent incitandi, alius modulus fuit in conuiuiis, alius inter Deorum sacrificia." *De Apollo* 4.10.

than its antecedent, temperate and manly, but with ceremonial associations lending a quasi-religious tone.[146] All these qualities obviously are
most relevant to the thematic issues of Chapman's hymns.

When Ficino or Agrippa tells us that the mood has more of the "voice"
than of "harmony" in her music, he tells us something about the "radical
of presentation" which is, to borrow Northrop Frye's terminology, *epos*
rather than *melos*. That is, he suggests another reason why Chapman
thought it fit to translate a lyric form, the Orphic hymn, into mythic
narrative. As Frye has remarked, myth expresses itself mainly in *epos*,
with poet reciting to audience,[147] and—despite the convention of address
to the two deities—Chapman is very conscious of the audience overhear-
ing the prayers: "Ye living spirits then" (*Noct.* 288), "Kneele then with
me" (*Noct.* 324), "Presume not then ye flesh confounded soules" (*Cyn.*
162), "Build Cynthiaes Temple in your vertuous parts" (*Cyn.* 451). The
poet is primarily concerned with addressing his audience, with the
transitive rather than the subjective magic. Thus his exchange of the
black melancholy for the creative melancholy is an object lesson for the
audience, a conventional problem in the same manner as the threat of a
political marriage now eleven years past is a conventional problem.

Although Chapman knows that music is a "charm" or "enchanting"
and that the Orphic hymns are incantatory, he remains consistent to the
conventional rhythmic principles of verse *epos* and to the allocation of
"voice" to lunar music. There is little effort in *The Shadow of Night*
to employ a musical diction or the tempo and dominant accents which
contribute to a musical pattern of sound. Instead, Chapman's metrical
unit is the rimed iambic-pentameter couplet in which the stresses are
regular and all syllables usually given their full value. This regular,
stately, rather slow line results in a recurrent pattern which is emphasized by the sound repetitions of the couplet structure. Although Chapman uses the colon frequently to indicate an intermediate sound pause
(often these could be repunctuated as sentences), his full stops are not
frequent; except at points of narrative climax sentences tend to run from
ten to twenty lines, often extending the length of the verse paragraph
that constitutes the thought unit. The length of the sentence and paragraph units, in conjunction with syntactic complexity (largely responsible for the obscurity and density), the slow metrical tempo, and delib-

---

[146]Aristoxenus remarks that "some of the Harmonists hold that the Hypodorian is the
lowest of the keys. . . ." *The Harmonics of Aristoxenus*, ed. and trans. Henry S. Macran
(Oxford, 1902), p. 192. Athenaeus, *The Deipnosophists*, trans. C. B. Gulick, Loeb Classical
Library (Cambridge, Mass., 1950), 6: 369, equates the Hypodorian with the Aeolian mode
and comments on "the turgid quality" and "pretense of nobleness," a description which
some critics would happily apply to *The Shadow of Night*. See Athenaeus's entire discussion, 14.624.C-625.A. R. P. Winnington-Ingram, *Mode in Ancient Greek Music* (Cambridge,
1936), explains the difficulties in understanding what *Hypodorian* might have meant. See
pp. 12–14, 36–38.

[147]*Anatomy*, pp. 251–62, 270–81, 293–96.

erate syllabic articulation, creates a tone of measured solemnity, gravity, and regularity—a dignified, ceremonial tone. In genre, style, and tone, therefore, Chapman selected the direct poetic equivalents of the voice and mode proper to musical invocations of the moon.

The poet, by discipline of mind and through knowledge of occult philosophy, had attained an epiphany of Cynthia in *Noctem*; *Cynthiam* represents an attempt to put his dedication into practice by modeling himself upon Cynthia and so becoming an instrument of her will. The astrological magic represents the means by which the poet can become infused with her spirit or virtues, thereby attaining the state of the Orphic prophet and reformer. First, however, the lingering doubts of Cynthia's constancy, the residue of the pessimistic melancholy must be dispensed with before he becomes the Saturnian creative intellectual. He appeals for inspiration, then promises an argument "to rauish and refine / An earthly [i.e., sublunary, melancholic] soule, and make it meere diuine" (*Cyn.* 154–55). Purest eyes will penetrate "With ease, the bowells of these misteries." The allegorical hunt and the construction of the two temples, with their already manifold implications, thus yield a poetic lesson as well. As I have argued, the allegory exhibits Cynthia as "Forme her selfe," acting as the primal creator, imposing the shape of life upon the chaos of raw matter. The temple of the body, or, on the macrocosmic level, the "Pax Imperij" vanishes at the end of the day; material things are ultimately as mutable as the hunt of life itself. It is love of intellectual beauty, perception of the form of Cynthia's mind, that—as is implied in the Orphic account of Love imposing form on Chaos—produces the true immutability, the order that is the imposition of spiritual harmony upon the flux of life.

The commonplace analogy regards the poet as godlike creator; the account of Cynthia creating the palace and actors for the hunt presents goddess as poet. The goddess creates order and life by giving form to matter; the poet recreates life and order in his verse, which is, for Chapman, form. By the Pythagorean conception form is number; since poetry is based on number, it must embody form. Millar MacLure writes: "Chapman's use of the term 'form' is obsessive rather than philosophically definitive—a fair enough practice for a poet. He applies it indifferently to the worlds of art, politics, physiology and ethics."[148] I would argue, rather, that Chapman's conception of *form* is philosophically definitive, in the Renaissance conception of moral philosophy which of course makes it the supreme good, the crown of all learning, and that he applies it "indifferently" to all spheres of activity precisely because moral philosophy still is the governing monarch of all the other arts and sciences. Chapman is scrupulous in his concern for poetic form because,

---

[148]MacLure, p. 64. Gordon, "Chapman's *Hero and Leander*," pp. 65–73, analyzes the philosophic bases of Chapman's conception of form.

like the arts of Orpheus, it supplies a pattern for that lost harmony of the soul. The function of poetry is to dispose temperately "all the tender motiues of the mind, / To make man worthie his hel-danting kinde" (*Noct.* 157–58), that is, like Orpheus, to calm the hellish perturbations of his mind. The allegory of creative form in *Cynthiam* teaches the narrator this and he learns both to frame the temple of the mind and to sing for others Orpheus's own song, the metamorphosis of Ganymede.

The transitive magic of the hymns cuts two ways, working on the sexual feelings of the audience, which Walker notes is typical of such magical practices.[149] For those who are converted to Cynthia's ways the magic is a purification rite, a banishment of "all the lawlesse flames of Cupids Godhead," the whoredom of daylight, the sun's lust, and affections' storm. When the "Sunne of base desires" is dimmed, one can be transposed to the stellar realm of pure intellect, become a Ganymede whom "Saturnius rauisheth to loue," or an Endymion who received "soule-chast" kisses from Cynthia herself. But no reformer is so sanguine as to expect complete success and the narrator is aware of the plenitude of bad poets so sunken in lust and vice that they are incapable of heeding his plea; hence, the terrible visage of Hecate, the admonitory tone throughout, and, finally, the anathema of the direct curse which the poet invokes upon Cynthia's enemies. *Noctem* carefully spells out the difference between good and bad poets in terms of analogies with painting and music. Whereas "Promethean Poets" create images of man's deformity to measure against the ideal in order to shame him (*Noct.* 131–38), "rude painters," having no notion of true form, make images so misshapen that they can be recognized only by their titles (*Noct.* 171–80). Similarly, now that the Orphic harmony extant when "Saturnes golden scepter stroke the strings" is gone, we have instead the debased pastoral:

A flocke of shepherds to the bagpipe treads
Rude rurall dances with their countrey loues
. . . .
Now hearing musicke, thinke it is a charme,
That like loose froes at Bacchanalean feasts,
Makes them seeme franticke in their barraine iestes.

[*Noct.* 182–83, 188–90]

The black enchantment of this lustful music effects a grotesque dance of passion like that of the maddened bacchantes who murdered Orpheus.

The opposition here between stringed instrument and wind instrument is not casual; mythologically, its antecedents can be traced as far back as the Apollo-Marsyas and the Apollo-Midas stories, in which the preference for the tuned string instrument rests upon the mathematical

---

[149]Walker, *Magic*, p. 82.

conception of musical intervals and, ultimately, on Pythagorean theories of harmony. John Hollander concludes, "The polarity of string and wind, then, bore a long tradition of association with the antitheses of reason and uncontrolled passion."[150] Moreover, as we know from *Othello*, from Chaucer's Miller, and from the paintings of Bruegel and Bosch, the bagpipe is a standard symbol of sexual lust.[151] The more general passion-reason antithesis thus narrows into the lust-chastity symbolism of the hymns, with the Orphic poet as the voice of chaste reason and his opponents that of irrational passion, epitomized as sexual appetite, which supplies music for the formless sensual dance. These poets are the "flesh confounded soules" unable to bear the Castalian bowls which separate spirits from the senses. Their impurity prevents them from understanding the "argument" of the revealed mysteries; spiritually blinded, they cannot perceive the philosophical sense of the myths, and thus they grossly misread the Endymion story to slander Cynthia herself. "Wise Poetes faine [her] Godhead properlie," but the narrator calls down the wrath of Hecate upon the lust-driven idolaters. Paradoxically, chastity brings the blessing of prosperity and fertility; the curse of lust is barrenness, intellectual and spiritual. On the subject of possible harmful influences, Agrippa attributes to the Moon "the inconstant progress of all things, and whatsoever is contrary to mans nature: and by this means man himself by reason of his unlikeness with the heavenly things receiveth hurt" (3.39). But for those who correctly attune their own souls with the *spiritus* of the moon the rewards are great indeed: "a peace-making consonancy, fecundity, the power of generating and of growing greater, of increasing and decreasing, and a moderate temperance, and faith which being conversant in manifest and occult things, yeeldeth direction to all" (Agrippa 3.38).

Despite the many ways in which Chapman rigorously adheres to the procedures of lunary magic, there seems to be no suggestion that the hymns are magically potent in any literal way. Indeed, Chapman's decision to eschew the lyric hymn mode and to translate hymn into mythic narrative would seem to presuppose the philosophical interpretation of myth, toward which Chapman does continually direct us, especially in his comments on Orpheus, Ganymede, and Endymion, rather than the intuitive apprehension of essences implicit in the magic incantations. Magic becomes what Walker calls "a metaphysical metaphor" for a pro-

---

[150]Hollander, p. 35.

[151]See Lawrence J. Ross, "Shakespeare's 'Dull Clowns' and Symbolic Music," *Shakespeare Quarterly*, 17 (1966): 107–28; especially pp. 117–24; E. A. Block, "Chaucer's Millers and their Bagpipes," *Speculum*, 29 (1954): 239–43; and D. W. Robertson, Jr., *A Preface to Chaucer: Studies in Medieval Perspectives* (Princeton, 1963), pp. 128–33, 482, and the relevant figures. Fig. 33 contrasts a lascivious bagpiper to David with his harp. G. F. Jones, "Wittenwiler's *Becki* and the Medieval Bagpipe," *Journal of English and Germanic Philology*, 48 (1949): 209–28, gives more background.

gram of religious philosophy and learning designed to unite the English people behind Elizabeth in a vision of peaceful, imperialistic nationalism.[152] That the magical virtues of the moon and of Orphic wisdom are embodied in a living monarch gives an especially concrete appeal to the program, but does not materially alter its identity as a symbolic religious projection of manifest destiny. Chapman frames the whole conception upon the myth of the Orphic poet and the correlative tradition of the *Orphic Hymns*. The magus who recommended to his friend "the deepe search of knowledge" and the "vitall warmth of freezing science" as preparation for reading *The Shadow of Night* would not have been displeased to read in later years Bacon's interpretation of the myth:

> The story of Orpheus, which though so well known has not yet been in all points perfectly well interpreted, seems meant for a representation of universal Philosophy. For Orpheus himself,—a man admirable and truly divine who being master of all harmony subdued and drew all things after him by sweet and gentle measures,—may pass by an easy metaphor for philosophy personified.[153]

DE GUIANA

I have argued that Chapman took advantage of the triform identity of the moon goddess to erect in *The Shadow of Night* an elaborate thematic structure—allocating to Luna the "natural" or "philosophic" meaning, to Diana the political and military, to Hecate the poetic, metamorphosing each and subsuming all within the controlling image of Cynthia. The division of issues itself is a familiar one, stemming from Varro's three-part anatomy of theology as mythical, natural or physical, and political. Augustine devoted Book 6 of his *De civitate Dei* to a scathing attack upon Varro's system; Ficino, reading Augustine, rather typically ignored the denunciation and picked up the division for his own use, translating the terms to "philosophical, civil, and poetic," and commending Varro for giving dominance to the first of these.[154] Chapman presumably found Ficino's exposition apposite for his own purposes. The originality of his conception lies in correlating the thematic complex to the three phases of lunar mythology and implementing them through the persona of Orphic poet.

---

[152]See Walker's discussion of Guy Lefévre de la Boderie, whose *Galliade* (1578) already had directed Orphic magic to political ends (*Magic*, pp. 119–26). Since La Boderie was employed as Alençon's secretary and his poetry served a Catholic monarchy, he stands as a mirror image to Chapman.

[153]Lemmi, *Classic Deities in Bacon*, p. 152.

[154]See Augustine, *The City of God*, bks. 1–7, trans. D. B. Zema and G. G. Walsh, in *The Fathers of the Church*, (New York, 1950), 8:303–37; especially pp. 314–17. Walker, *Magic*, translates the relevant passage from Ficino and comments upon it, pp. 50–51.

As if anticipating Keats's admonition to Shelley, Chapman in these hymns is very much the artist, loading every rift of his subject with ore. It is just for this reason that the hymns do break down. Chapman imparts an immensely complex conceptual burden to them, and the narrative line of the mythological structure is not sufficiently developed to sustain it.[155] Moreover, although the themes and central symbols all are at least introduced in Noctem, their development, particularly with the political allegory, occurs mainly in the second hymn. Muriel Bradbrook has conjectured that the poem was satirized while still in manuscript and that Chapman hastily revised the first hymn to eliminate the obvious political references. By her account Noctem describes "Ralegh's dejected state"; Ralegh would have been subject to satire whereas Elizabeth in Cynthiam would not.[156] This is an interesting and not implausible guess; but in the absence of such manuscripts we can only evaluate the hymns as they were printed in 1594. Accordingly, a disproportion is evident between the hymns, both in the allocation of thematic materials and in the mode of narrative development; the first focuses upon abdication from the world and religious consecration, and the second upon allegorical narrative. The two stages follow the conventional procedure for describing the worship of a goddess in narrative epos:

> This myth has two main parts: legend, recounting the god's biography or his former dealings with his people; and the description of the ritual he requires. Often the first leads up to, and provides an explanation for, the second.[157]

This is just the relationship we have in The Shadow of Night: Noctem explains what the world was before the goddess's withdrawal, how man precipitated her withdrawal, and his resultant condition; Cynthiam describes the nature of the goddess and the "ritual" necessary to reestablish harmonious relations with her. Nonetheless, the division of this material into two hymns with differing modes of presentation, symbolic and allegorical, creates an imbalance. This and the far too elaborate conceptual scheme—rather than stylistic obscurity, private symbolism, and the vagaries of Chapman's syntax—are responsible for the partial failure of Chapman's extremely interesting, first poetic venture. He never again attempted anything so complicated.

---

[155]Commenting on the tendency toward symbolic overload characteristic of neoplatonic syncretism, C. S. Lewis has stated: "The aim is to load every inch of the canvas or every stanza of the poem with the greatest possible weight of 'wisdom,' learning, edification, suggestion, solemnity, and ideal beauty. Symbols that are on different levels or come from very different sources are not logically harmonized in the pictorial design or the narrative flow." "Neoplatonism in Spenser's Poetry," Studies in Medieval and Renaissance Literature (Cambridge, 1966), p. 160.

[156]Bradbrook, The School of Night, pp. 127–28.

[157]Frye, Anatomy, p. 294.

The thematic and imagistic complex with which Chapman worked in the hymns stayed in his mind, however, and two years later when he found occasion once again to pursue the muse of Clio, he achieved a remarkable fusion of this material in *De Guiana, Carmen Epicum*. D. J. Gordon and, more recently, Millar MacLure have stressed the close connection of subject in this poem with the procolonial *Masque of the Middle Temple*, celebrating the marriage of Princess Elizabeth and Frederick V in 1613.[158] Undoubtedly such a connection should be emphasized; but the particular themes and the images in which Chapman embodies them are much closer in *De Guiana* to the vision of *The Shadow of Night* than to the later masque. Because the poem is an overt appeal for support of Ralegh's colonial expeditions, not simply a theoretical affirmation of the policy of imperialist expansion for which Ralegh's circle stood, the spirit which lingered in the shadows of the hymns can enter the poem directly and Ralegh takes the symbolic role that was Elizabeth's in *Cynthiam*, "the soule of this exploit." Given this difference in concern with personages, *De Guiana* is, nonetheless, striking in its compression and synthesis of the symbols that proved recalcitrant in the hymns.

Once again Chapman addresses "you *Patrician* Spirites that reine Your flesh to fire," and "skorne to let your bodies chooke your soules." These men "lift [their] eies for guidance to the starres," living not for self-interest "but to possesse / Your honour'd countrey of a generall store" (110–11). Elizabeth again is the "most sacred Maide: whose barrennesse / Is the true fruite of vertue" whom he urges to act as creator of form: "Let your breath / Goe foorth vpon the waters, and create / A golden worlde in this our yron age" (30–32). The poet describes Ralegh, "heroike Author of this Act," and his "*Eliza*-consecrated sworde," imagining in his prophetic "furie" that the queen will come finally to the aid of Ralegh's colony:

And now she blesseth with her woonted Graces
Th' industrious Knight, the soule of this exploit,
Dismissing him to conuoy of his starres.

[*De Guiana* 152–54]

Ralegh will be a bridegroom symbolizing the marriage of England and Guiana, where each English settler "were an *Orpheus*," civilizing the tame savages and making the ideal of the Golden Age an actuality. All this Chapman envisions as the end result justifying his theme of imperial expansion.[159] "So let thy soueraigne Empire be encreast," he

---

[158]Gordon, "*Le Masque Memorable* de Chapman," *Les Fêtes de la Renaissance*, ed. Jean Jacquot (Paris, 1956), 1:305–15; and MacLure, pp. 13–15, 232–33.

[159]On Ralegh's conscious imperialist motives, see David B. Quinn, *Raleigh and the British Empire* (New York, 1949); for Chapman another link to Ralegh's American voyages was his

argues to Elizabeth; in the world that Ralegh has discovered all things are possible, all paradoxes resolved:

> *Riches*, and *Conquest*, and *Renowme* I sing,
> *Riches* with honour, *Conquest* without bloud,
> Enough to seat the Monarchie of earth,
> Like to *Ioues* Eagle, on *Elizas* hand.
>
> [*De Guiana* 14–17]

The final image of harmonious civilization emerging from the wilderness through the agency of Ralegh's imperial program is not merely Renaissance Utopianism, if only because Chapman believes that the dream can be realized through Elizabeth:

> And there do Pallaces and temples rise
> Out of the earth, and kisse th'enamored skies,
> Where new *Britania*, humblie kneeles to heauen,
> The world to her, and both at her blest feete,
> In whom the Circles of all Empire meet.
>
> [*De Guiana* 180–84]

Whereas in *The Shadow of Night* the backbone of the two hymns is essentially a framework of mythological allusions too fragile not to be crushed by the flesh it should support, the immediate and tangible motive of *De Guiana*, the appeal for support of Ralegh, gives Chapman a foundation upon which he can build his mythology of Elizabethan empire into an effective poem. His choice of blank verse as the metrical vehicle for this *Carmen Epicum* shows an acute sensitivity to the requisite modulation of poetic form. Although the central icon remains the same, the image of Elizabeth "In whom the Circles of all Empire meet" (the poet employing his habitual symbol of formal perfection), the occasion of the appeal here is very different from that which produced the "magic" religious hymns and demands a corresponding change in the form of prophetic utterance. Finally, the song introduces the theme of social ceremony, epitomized here and elsewhere as marriage:

---

friendship with Thomas Harriot, about whom see my discussion in chapter 4, pp. 126–29; and Quinn, "Thomas Hariot and the Virginia Voyages of 1602," *William and Mary Quarterly*, 27 (1970): 268–81.

The apparent incongruity of supporting Ralegh's colonial projects with Orphic magic is lessened when we reflect that Ralegh himself knew Ficino's *Pimander* and used it in his *History of the World*; and that for Dr. John Dee, an early advocate of an Elizabethan maritime empire, both overseas exploration and occult studies were partial and compatible aspects of a quest for ultimate knowledge. For Ralegh, see Yates, *Bruno*, p. 403 n.; and P. M. Rattansi, "Alchemy and Natural Magic in Raleigh's *History of the World*," *Ambix*, 13 (1966): 122–38; and, for Dee, see Walter I. Trattner, "God and Expansion in Elizabethan England: John Dee, 1527–83," *Journal of the History of Ideas*, 25 (1964): 17–34.

But all our Youth take *Hymens* lightes in hand,
And fill each roofe with honor'd progenie.
There makes *Societie* Adamantine chaines,
And ioins their harts with wealth, whom wealth disioyn'd.

[*DeGuiana* 173–76]

While encompassing the imperial theme of the hymns, *De Guiana*, by dispelling the shadows of night with Hymen's torches, looks forward to the more positive and human societal concerns of *Hero and Leander* and *Andromeda Liberata*.

FOUR
AN
UNNATURAL
PERSPECTIVE:
OVIDS
BANQUET
OF
SENCE

If in *The Shadow of Night* Chapman publicly takes sides against the vogue for the erotic Ovidian poem, seemingly epitomized for him by *Venus and Adonis,* and darkly proclaims his allegiance to the Ovid of the allegorized *Metamorphoses,* his next major poetic ventures extend the argument. He presents his position in depth with, first, an exposure of the opposition through a mock-erotic Ovidian poem and, then, with an example of the "true" Ovidian poem in his continuation of *Hero and Leander. Ovids Banquet of Sence* confronts the reader, in the very design of the volume, with the choice of Hercules; as Frank Kermode has argued,[1] the juxtaposition of *Ovids Banquet* with *The Coronet for his Mistress Philosophy* poses the alternatives of the two traditional Banquets, sensual and philosophic, as well as those of the two mistresses who provide the fare of these feasts, Corinna and Philosophy. The possessive of the latter title leaves no doubt about Chapman's own choice, no matter how erroneously his readers may take sides.

By making the poet Ovid protagonist in the kind of poem popularly associated with him,[2] Chapman both registers his own protest against the misappropriation of a favorite author and illustrates the procedure by which, exploiting the body of legend that has accrued over a period of time, it is possible for a writer to mythologize an historical personage. The personal attributes and notable episodes in the lives of such figures as Socrates, Alexander the Great, or Julius Caesar become as fixed and well known as those of Hercules, Adonis, or Orpheus. Moreover, in the

---

[1]Frank Kermode, "The Banquet of Sense," *Bulletin of the John Rylands Library,* 44 (1961): 68–99; also in his *Shakespeare, Spenser, Donne: Renaissance Essays* (London, 1971).

[2]Kermode suggests that the writers of Elizabethan epyllia established Ovid as a "sort of counter-Plato" (p. 74). Hallett Smith, *Elizabethan Poetry: A Study in Conventions, Meanings and Expression* (Cambridge, Mass., 1952), pp. 64–101, surveys the range of "Ovidian poetry."

centuries before the modern awareness of historicity and historical methodology had been formulated, distinctions between the two orders of being were less sharply drawn. Like Homer and Virgil, Ovid, too, inevitably "underwent the medieval metamorphosis of ancient worthies. It was not merely among the peasants of his own Sulmo . . . that he was magician, necromancer, merchant, philosopher, paladin, prophet, or saint."[3]

The question of Ovid's Elizabethan reputation cannot easily be settled. Following Kermode's lead, others have asserted that this reputation was simply bad;[4] however, the contemporary examples which Kermode adduces postdate Chapman's poem and may well reflect its strong influence rather than a dominant tradition. The several theories which developed to explain the cause of Ovid's exile ranged from consideration of the poet as the innocent victim of court politics or circumstances to the guilty corrupter both of public morals and the emperor's daughter.[5] It would seem more accurate to conclude that tradition supplied no uniformly pejorative image of Ovid, but that the conception of the poet could vary according to the frame of reference established by particular poems. The moralist and philosopher associated with the *Metamorphoses* literally was a different person from the *praeceptor amoris* associated with the *Ars Amatoria* and the *Amores*.[6]

The fictional Ovid's offer to Corinna, "For thy sake will I write the Art of loue," reminds us that this is another octavo in an Elizabethan battle of the books. To mount his oblique attack on the erotic-Ovidian fashion, Chapman chose from among the several theories for Ovid's banishment: (1) his infatuation with Julia, (2) his inadvertent sight of Julia naked in her bath, (3) his affront to morality with his erotic writings—components which he combined in an incident of his own fabrication, just as he al-

---

[3]L. P. Wilkinson, *Ovid Recalled* (Cambridge, 1955), p. 386. For Chapman's mythic use of an ancient historical personage elsewhere, cf. Homer in *The Teares of Peace* or the Alexander allusions in the Byron plays. For a discussion of the last, see Peter Ure, "The Main Outline of Chapman's Byron," *Studies in Philology*, 47 (1950): 571–82.

[4]See N. J. C. Andreasen, *John Donne: Conservative Revolutionary* (Princeton, 1967), pp. 31–53, and James P. Meyers, Jr., "'This Curious Frame: Chapman's *Ovid's Banquet of Sense*," *Studies in Philology*, 45 (1968): 201. The often-cited C. B. Cooper, *Some Elizabethan Opinions of the Poetry and Character of Ovid* (Menasha, Wis., 1914), is a brief monograph of 34 pp.

[5]The fullest consideration of the matter is by John C. Thibault, *The Mystery of Ovid's Exile* (Berkeley and Los Angeles, 1964). See also Wilkinson, *Ovid Recalled*; E. K. Rand, *Ovid and his Influence* (New York, 1928); Giovanni Pansa, *Ovidio nel medioeva e nella tradizione populare* (Sulmo, 1924), pp. 18–19; and G. Ghisalberti, "Medieval Biographies of Ovid," *Journal of the Warburg and Courtauld Institutes*, 9 (1946): 10–59.

[6]Ovid's erotic poems gained public consciousness relatively late in the sixteenth century. See C. M. Scollen, *The Birth of the Elegy in France, 1500–1550* (Geneva, 1967). Petrarch, whose penitential psalms Chapman translated and whose *Secretum* he read, considered the *Ars* to be a work of insanity and denounced its author, "lascivissimus poetarum Naso." See Rand, pp. 150–51.

ways adapted, reshaped, and combined myths to suit his own purposes while still exploiting established connotations.[7]

By explicating the banquet *topos* and by showing how Chapman combines the platonic hierarchy of the senses with the sensory banquet and the convention of the *quinque lineae amoris*, Kermode has clarified greatly both the tradition in which the poem should be examined and the general structure of action within it. He has, in effect, provided a context for reading the poem. That subsequent readers have acknowledged the pertinence of Kermode's study in tradition but have continued to arrive at diametrically opposed interpretations of the poem serves to confirm his evaluation of it as "one of the most difficult poems in the language."[8] The critics divide endlessly, like Ramist dichotomies, over the question of whether Ovid rises to a spiritual epiphany or sinks in sensual debauch, with the "ascent" advocates having greater numbers but the "descent" group gaining in strength recently. In this poem, especially, Chapman has the facility for exacerbating critical sensibilities in such a way as to provoke pungent abuse, the better examples of which have been much savored by connoisseurs.[9]

Even though I have opted for the "descent" reading, I would like to pause over the issue raised by the sharply divergent responses, since some critics of considerable reputation have arrived at the "wrong" reading, and since nearly all readers have felt impelled to score the conceptual perversity, or the faulty execution, or both, a reaction suggesting a pervasive uneasiness with the mental set of the poem. The questions to consider are these: if the poem permits opposed readings which are themselves consistent within a given inverse range, can a large portion of these reader responses be dismissed as self-evidently wrong? If not, then how can we make sense out of these polarized responses? And how does the poem manage to accommodate, or even encourage, these dichotomous reactions? In an effort to answer these questions, I shall focus upon a well-known puzzle in the intellectual structure of *Ovids Banquet* to illuminate the poetics which Chapman postulates in the dedicatory epistle, and its relation to the dominant metaphor—what Sidney in appropriately platonic terms called the "fore conceit"—of the entire poem.

One of the difficulties in determining whether Ovid ascends to the spiritual or descends to the material by means of the sensory ladder

---

[7]The originality of Chapman's imaginative blending of conventions is suggested by Phyllis Bartlett's failure, not surprisingly, to find a source for the banquet *topos* in Ovid; see "Ovid's 'Banquet of Sense'?" *Notes & Queries*, 197 (1952): 46–47.

[8]Kermode, p. 68.

[9]For surveys of critical reaction, see Kermode, p. 85; Millar MacLure, *George Chapman: A Critical Study* (Toronto, 1966), p. 50; Meyers, pp. 192–93. I borrow the "ascent" and "descent" labels from Meyers, p. 194.

originates in his arrangement of the hierarchy. Although seemingly everyone agrees that Chapman employs the senses in a hierarchial scheme, his placement of vision, in particular, does not correspond to any of the traditional ones. The sensory scales of Ficino, Plato, Aristotle, and Lucretius have been cited in an effort to explain Chapman's ordering—*auditus, olfactus, visus, gustus, tactus*—but none of these arrangements offers a precedent for placing the sense of smell higher in the order than that of vision. The question of whether hearing or vision was the most "rational" of the senses and thus which belonged at the top of the hierarchy was recognized as a philosophically arguable matter. As James Meyers remarks, "The prominence given Hearing by Chapman thus has authoritative precedent; but why he should place Smell second, thus relegating Sight to third position on the scale, is a moot point." Facing this dead end with sources and analogues, Meyers began to look for an explanation of Chapman's sensory hierarchy by considering its function within the action of the poem. "But if it is true that Sight is thus made to assume a less esteemed or prestigious rung on the ladder, it is also true that it attains greater thematic value from this medial placement, for Sight comes at the poem's climax—indeed, its indulgence provides the poem's climax—and Chapman takes pains to underscore its thematic importance."[10] With a poet less devoted to conceptual superstructure one might feel that vision would be moved from its normal placement in the hierarchy simply to avoid the possibility of anticlimax in a dramatic presentation (which almost demands an early visual encounter).[11] But the poet surely could have found more than one solution to the requirements of dramatic mode, and Meyers certainly seems correct in suggesting that thematic considerations primarily govern Chapman's course here.

The dedication to *Ovids Banquet* contains Chapman's famous defense of poetic obscurity: "Obscuritie in affection of words, & indigested concets, is pedanticall and childish; but where it shroudeth it selfe in the hart of his subiect, vtterd with fitnes of figure, and expressiue Epethites; with that darknes wil J still labour to be shaddowed." Obscurity in short must be functional, not merely ornamental, to be justified; style, as always, should be appropriate to subject matter:

[10]For the sensory hierarchies, see Meyers, pp. 198–200; the quotations are from pp. 200, 200–201. For the traditional primacy of sight, see D. J. Gordon, "Chapman's *Hero and Leander*," *English Miscellany*, 5 (1954): 65 and n. It may be that the search for sources and analogues has been too strictly limited to philosophic contexts. Representations of the five senses were a very popular subject in the visual arts. Jan Brueghel, for instance, painted two versions of an *Allegory of the Senses*, one series of five separate paintings and one pair deploying an unorthodox grouping of three (hearing, taste, touch) and two (sight and smell); see the descriptive monograph by Fabrizio Clerici, *Allegorie dei sensi di Jan Brueghel* (Florence, 1946).

[11]The argument from dramatic necessity has been made by Rhoda M. Ribner, "The Compasse of This Curious Frame: Chapman's *Ovids Banquet of Sence* and the Emblematic Tradition," *Studies in the Renaissance*, 17 (1970): 243.

> That, *Enargia*, or cleernes of representation, requird in absolute Poems is not
> the perspicuous deliuery of a lowe inuention; but high, and harty inuention
> exprest in most significant, and vnaffected phrase; it serues not a skilfull
> Painters turne, to drawe the figure of a face onely to make knowne who it
> represents; but hee must lymn, giue luster, shaddow, and heightening; which
> though ignorants will esteeme spic'd, and too curious, yet such as haue the
> iudiciall perspectiue, will see it hath, motion, spirit and life. [*Poems* p. 49]

Doubtless Rosemond Tuve is correct in noting that Chapman's distinction here is traditional, probably deriving from Quintilian.[12] But Chapman's choice of a rhetorical concept associated with *visual perception*
and developed through an analogy, again commonplace but nonetheless
significant here, that poetry should be a "speaking picture," establishes
a concern with visual epistemology which obtains through the preface
and into the poem.[13] The contrast of "ignorants" with "such as haue the
iudiciall perspectiue" transposes into a figure with direct application to
the poem: "I know, that empty, and dark spirits, wil complaine of pal-
pable night: but those that before-hand, haue a radiant, and light-
bearing intellect, will say they can passe through *Corynnas* Garden
without the helpe of a Lanterne" (*Poems* p. 50). I would argue that the
"actual meanes to sound the philosophical conceits" should be related to
this emphasis upon vision prefacing a poem in which vision has been
wrenched from its standard position in the sensory orders and given the
central place in the poetic action. Millar MacLure has seen the connection
between the analogy of the speaking picture, the appeal to an audience
with a special vision, and the Elizabethan vogue for perspective devices.[14] I would extend this insight to its logical conclusion by maintaining that, more than enunciating a general poetics, the dedication is designed to establish a working metaphor for the entire poem as a
"speaking picture." Jean Jacquot remarked that in *Ovids Banquet* "Les
problèmes de la physiologie et de la psychologie de la perception les
préoccupent."[15] These problems of perception are presented, with an
insistence remarkable in a poem which must cover the entire sensory
range, most importantly in visual terms.

Within the framework of Renaissance art theory, one can see that
Ovids Banquet is contrived as a perspective poem. The signal achievement of Renaissance art was the theoretical mastery of vanishing-point
perspective, permitting the two-dimensional pictorial surface to be

[12]Rosemond Tuve, *Elizabethan and Metaphysical Imagery* (Chicago, 1946), p. 32. She
also cites Richard Sherry's identification of *enargia* with visual perception.

[13]On the *ut pictura poesis* concept, see Tuve, pp. 50–60; also the articles by W. G. Howard,
"Ut pictura poesis," *PMLA*, 24 (1909): 40–123, and R. W. Lee, "*Ut Pictura Poesis*: The
Humanistic Theory of Painting," *Art Bulletin*, 22 (1940): 197–269.

[14]MacLure, pp. 46–47.

[15]Jean Jacquot, *George Chapman (1559–1634), sa vie, sa poésie, son théâtre, sa pensée*
(Paris, 1951), p. 65.

treated as a window through which a three-dimensional scene is revealed.[16] With the Renaissance writers upon and practitioners of perspectivism we find, as well, the theoretical origins of pictorial illusionism, its largely unexplored by-product.[17] We have become accustomed to the idea that theoretical and technical breakthroughs tend to occur not in isolation but when a cultural climate formulates a need or provides a receptive context for them. They are, in this sense, the exterior manifestations of the psychological drives of a given people in a given time. The differences between the dominant tendencies in medieval and Renaissance art should be seen as products of their respective intellectual milieus: medieval, in its preoccupation with universals, tends toward the iconic and conceptual; Renaissance, in seeking the universal through the particular, tries to capture the individual reality through illusionist techniques.[18]

Ernst Cassirer has explained how Nicholas of Cusa, dissatisfied with the failure of the Scholastics to solve the problem of the One and the Many by appeals to authority and to the hierarchy of logical causation, arrived at his own solution, one which provided a model for the entire Renaissance. Cusanus reasoned that if no one authority brings us closer to the truth of the infinite, then any one authority, individual experience, or point of view is just as valid as any other, since none takes precedence and all possess a partial but valid symbolic perception of the One. Cassirer's brilliant formulation of Cusanus's solution to the problem of the One and the Many remains essential for understanding the fascination with exploring modes of subjective experience in Renaissance literature.[19] The very direct relationship between Cusanus's concept of the One and the Many and the artists' need to rediscover techniques for representing convincingly a subjective point of view may be seen his *De visione Dei*; in it Cusanus describes as a symbol of his argument the self-portrait of Rogier van der Weyden, a trick perspective portrait in which the eyes of the subject appear to look directly at the viewer wherever he stands.[20]

---

[16]See, e.g., Joan Gadol, *Leon Battista Alberti: Universal Man of the Early Renaissance* (Chicago, 1969), p. 21. Gadol provides an up-to-date bibliography on perspective scholarship; also her sections, "The Optical Theory of Natural Perspective," pp. 22–32, and "Rational Seeing and the Renaissance," pp. 70–81, are of some relevance here.

[17]E. H. Gombrich, *Art and Illusion*, rev. ed. (Princeton, 1961), who casts a long shadow in this chapter, is exceptional in the attention he gives to this issue. See also J. Baltrusaitis, *Anamorphoses ou Perspectives Curieuses* (Paris, n.d.); and the fine selection of illustrations in Fabrizio Clerici, "The Grand Illusion: Some Considerations of Perspective, Illusionism, and Trompe-l'oeil," *Art News Annual*, 23 (1954): 98–180.

[18]My version of the thesis, as well as the characterizations of medieval and Renaissance art, I borrow from Gombrich, *Art and Illusion*.

[19]Ernst Cassirer, *The Individual and the Cosmos in Renaissance Philosophy*, trans. Mario Domandi (Oxford, 1963), p. 11. I summarize the argument developed in chap. 1, pp. 7–45.

[20]Cassirer in *The Individual and the Cosmos*, pp. 31–32, comments: "This represents for us, in a sensible parable, the nature of the basic relationship between God, the all-encompass-

Art historians understandably have concentrated upon the ramifications of perspective theory and technique for the development of legitimate art. As artistic developments were extrapolated beyond artistic circles, however, the extreme application of perspective techniques in optical illusion—trompe l'oeil and anamorphosis, as we see with Nicholas of Cusa—most fascinated philosopher, poet, and layman, simply because the radical extension of perspective principles makes their perceptual consequences more explicit.

In Renaissance literary contexts the term *perspective* persistently implies more than just the appearance of relative positions, magnitudes, and distances between objects when viewed from a fixed point; it carries strong connotations of outright deception, distortion, visual trickery.[21] Such references can be sorted roughly into two groups. The first pertains to the science of optics proper, *perspectiva naturalis*, and includes references to optical devices used for viewing objects—distorting mirrors, telescopes, spyglasses, the *camera obscura*, and perspective machines.[22]

---

ing being, and the being of the finite, the ultimate particular. Each particular and individual being has an immediate relationship to God; it stands, as it were, face to face with Him. But the true sense of the divine first discloses itself when the mind no longer remains standing at *one* of these relationships, nor even at their simple total, but rather collects them all in the unity of a vision, a *visio intellectualis*. Then we can understand that it is absurd for us even to want to think the absolute in itself without such a determination through an individual point of view." On pictures in which the eyes follow the viewer, see Gombrich, *Art and Illusion*, p. 276 and n.

[21]Claudio Guillen, "On the Concept and Metaphor of Perspective," in *Comparatists at Work*, ed. S. G. Nichols, Jr. and R. B. Vowles (Waltham, Mass., 1968), pp. 41–42, comments on the pejorative connotations.

[22]For George Puttenham perspectives are "false glasses": "There be againe of these glasses that shew thinges exceeding faire and comely; others that shew figures very monstrous & illfauored. Euen so is the phantasticall part of man . . . " (*The Arte of English Poesie*, ed. Gladys D. Willcock and Alice Walker [Cambridge, 1936], p. 19). Della Porta, in a technical account "Of Strange Glasses," pauses for a laconic anecdote of sensory titillation: "Seneca reports that Hostius made such Concave-Glasses, that they might make things shew greater: He was a great provoker to lust; so ordering his Glasses, that when he was abused by Sodomy, he might see all the motions of the Sodomite behind him, And delight himself with a false representation of his privy parts that shewed so great" (*Natural Magick*, ed. D. J. Price [New York, 1951], 17.4). Jack Donne would have enjoyed this tale of private self-aggrandizement, but the more somber Dr. Donne used optical distortion to explain the parable of talents: "God's perspective glass, his spectacle, is the whole world . . . and through that spectacle the faults of princes, in God's eye, are multiplied far above those of private men" (*Sermon Preached in the Evening of Christmas-Day, 1624*, as quoted by Marjorie Nicolson, *Science and Imagination* [Ithaca, New York, 1956], p. 56). Shakespeare, too, stressed the selective focus of the spyglass: "Contempt his scornfull Perspective did lend me, / Which warpt the line of euerie other fauour" (*All's Well that Ends Well* 5.3.48–49). An attractive feature of such optic devices is the possibility of infinitely expanded perspective. Robert Burton speaks of "some rare perspective glass, or Otacousticon, which would so multiply appearances, that a man might hear and see all at once" (*Anatomy of Melancholy*, ed. Floyd Dell and Paul Jordan-Smith [1929; reprint ed. New York, 1948] p. 56). In *Paradise Regained* Milton warns, "By what strange Parallax or Optic skill / Of Telescope, were curious to inquire" (4.40–42); but when Satan so well disposes his "Airy Microscope"

The second category encompassed a technical application far more appealing to English writers, if one may judge by frequency of occurrence—the trick perspective picture which appears to have no coherent form until viewed through a special optical device or from a particular angle. Hobbes likened Davenant's *Gondibert* to such a construct:

I beleeve, Sir, you have seen a curious kind of perspective, where he that looks through a short hollow pipe upon a picture containing divers figures sees none of those that are there painted, but some one person made up of their parts, conveyed to the eie by the artificial cutting of a glass. I finde in my imagination an effect not unlike it from your Poem.[23]

In *Richard II* Bushy tries to console the queen by assuring her that grief has given her the wrong perspective on events:

For sorrow's eye, glazed with blinding tears,
Divides one thing entire to many objects;
Like perspectives, which rightly gazed upon
Show nothing but confusion, eyed awry
Distinguish form. . . .

[*Rich. II* 2.1.16–20]

Ironically, in this instance the queen's forebodings prove sound and Bushy's meliorism is "awry."

Very frequently, as if to heighten the perceptual dilemma, the paradox of form versus formlessness in a single image may be reshaped as a question of true versus false form by means of an image which presents two coherent and intelligible, but logically contradictory, forms when viewed from two different perspectives. Burton calls these "turning pictures," using the idea to illustrate human inconstancy:

I will determine of them all, they are like these double or turning pictures; stand before which, you see a fair maid on the one side, an ape on the other, an owl; look upon them at the first sight, all is well; but farther examine, you shall find them wise on the one side, and fools on the other; in some few things praiseworthy, in the rest incomparably faulty.[24]

---

that Christ "mayst behold / Outside and inside both" in viewing the splendors of Rome, it is evident that the diabolic inventor of cannon has achieved something very like Burton's magic glass. On outside-inside architectural illusions, see E. H. Gombrich, "Illusion and Visual Deadlock," in *Meditations on a Hobby Horse* (London, 1965), pp. 151–59, and figs. 132–34.

[23]Thomas Hobbes, "The Answer to Davenant's Preface to Gondibert," in *Critical Essays of the Seventeenth Century*, ed. Joel E. Spingarn (1908; reprinted, Bloomington, 1957), 2: 66–67.

[24]Burton, "Democritus Junior to the Reader," *Anatomy of Melancholy*, pp. 97–98. And again: "One take upon him temperance, holiness, another austerity, a third an affected

Drayton, in a relatively crude way, employs the turning-picture metaphor to reinforce the psychic transformation of metamorphosis, but achieves only bathos:

> The milk-white Heifor, *Io, Joves* faire rape,
> Viewing her new-ta'en figure in a Brooke,
> The water seeming to retayne the shape,
> Which lookes on her, as shee on it doth looke,
> That gazing eyes oft-times them selves mistooke:
> By prospective divis'd that looking nowe,
> She seem'd a Mayden, then againe a cowe.
>
> [*Mortimeriados* 11.2332–38]

Shakespeare's Cleopatra uses it to convey her conflicting reactions to Antony's behavior: "Though he be painted one way like a Gorgon, / The other way's a Mars" (*Antony and Cleopatra* 2.5. 116–17). Duke Orsino, groping to express a reaction to the physical doubling of identities he has discovered, can only think of such a trick portrait: "One face, one voice, one habit, and two persons, / A natural perspective, that is and is not!" (*Twelfth Night* 5.1.223–24).

The vogue for perspective metaphors and analogies struck English writers hard in the 1590s and did not exhaust their interest until well into the Restoration, when attention was shifting from optical illusion to landscape perspective. Chapman uses them more heavily than most of his contemporaries, over various stages of his career, and in a more complex way oftentimes. He likes the turning-picture device:

---

kind of simplicity, when as indeed he, and he, and he, and the rest are hypocrites, ambo-dexters, out-sides, so many turning pictures, a lion on the one side, a lamb on the other" (p. 53). Jonson describes society as a turning picture (*Alchemist* 3.4.87–93). William Drummond refers to such devices as "double pictures": "Here were many double Pictures, the first view shew old men and young Misers gathering carefully, the second view shew young men and prodigals spending riotously with *stultitiam partiuntur opes*" (quoted by Rosemary Freeman, *English Emblem Books* [London, 1948], p. 16). Freeman describes this as one image superimposed upon the other, but there is no reason to suppose Drummond means anything other than the turning picture. For a genuine description of superimposed images, a picture painted on a mirror, see *Upon Appleton House* in which cattle "seem within the polisht Grass / A Landskip drawn in Looking-Glass" (stanza 58) and the comment by Rosalie L. Colie, "*My Ecchoing Song.*" *Andrew Marvell's Poetry of Criticism* (Princeton, 1970), pp. 208–9.

As the writers whom I quote themselves blurred distinctions between several kinds of optical-illusion pictures, so I shall treat the turning picture, the anamorphotic picture, and the puzzle picture on the order of Gombrich's "rabbit or duck?" drawing as members of a paradigm. The sequence describes a progression from, as it were, literal to psychological anamorphosis. Strictly speaking, there is no problem of interpretative ambiguity with turning pictures; quite simply they are double pictures which the viewer sees one at a time. But the pairing of subjects which are moral or aesthetic opposites leads almost irresistably to regarding the dual perceptions as positive and negative, "right" and "wrong," and thence to choice between the two. For the "rabbit or duck?" problem, see Gombrich, *Art and Illusion*, p. 5 and fig. 2.

And what is Beauty? a mere quintessence,
Whose life is not in being, but in seeming.
And therefore is not to all eyes the same,
But like a cozening picture, which one way
Shows like a crow, another like a swan.

[*All Fools* 1.1.44–48]

He is, however, more fond of representing the perspective picture as one
in which it is possible to see any image subjectively appropriate and miss
the one true image, unless the viewer employs the right angle of vision.
So Allegre tries to describe the true nature of his master Chabot:

As of a picture wrought to optic reason,
That to all passers-by seems, as they move,
Now woman, now a monster, now a devil,
And, till you stand, and in a right line view it,
You cannot well judge what the main form is;
So men, that view him but in vulgar passes,
Casting but lateral, or partial glances
At what he is, suppose him weak, unjust,
Bloody, and monstrous; but stand free and fast,
And judge him by no more than what you know
Ingenuously, and by the right laid line
Of truth, he truly will all styles deserve
Of wise, just, good; a man, both soul and nerve.

[*Chabot* 1.1.68–80]

Chabot, like Bussy D'Ambois, is a figure with such extraordinary qualities and energies that assessments by lesser men tend to be partial and
distorted; the simile, therefore, is apt. Chapman also finds the perspective analogy suitable for characterizing the subjectivity of individual
responses to large social institutions and concepts, such as religion:

Her lookes were like the pictures that are made,
To th'optike reason; one way like a shade,
Another monster like, and euery way
To passers by, and such as made no stay,
To view her in a right line, face to face,
She seem'd a serious trifle; all her grace
Show'd in her fixt inspection. . . .

[*Eugenia*, 173–79]

Or ceremony:

Her face was changeable to euerie eie;
One way lookt ill, another graciouslie;
Which while men viewd, they cheerfull were & holy:
But looking off, vicious and melancholy. . . .

[*Hero and Leander* 3.125–28]

In each instance Chapman goes beyond the simple notion of the turning picture to elaborate imaginatively upon the implications that he saw in the perspective picture. For him the interest lies not primarily in the perspective device itself or in its artist constructor, but in the response of the beholder; and the potential for human error is infinite.

Some distinctions about the usage of perspective would be in order. Although the poets might naturally be expected to take a pejorative view of the artists and craftsmen, who, after all, abuse their knowledge and powers of creativity by taking advantage of man's credulity, there is very little emphasis on that. Of the instances I have cited here only Milton takes a clearly negative attitude toward the perpetrator of the illusion (in both *Comus* and *Paradise Regained*), and his habitual distrust of science and of the inventions of postlapsarian civilization make him a special case. The others tend to ignore the intentions behind the device, lens, or picture to concentrate on the metaphoric potential in the thing itself—for Burton, the contradictions and deceits of human nature; for Drayton, Io's loss of identity and altered state of mind; for Cleopatra, Antony's inconstancy when he elects a Roman, rather than an Egyptian, course of behavior. Receding to another plane of generality, William Drummond finds the shifting of perspective a suitable figure for his varying estimates of life itself: "All, that we can set our eyes on in these intricate mazes of Life, is but Alchimie, vain Perspective and deceiving Shadows, appearing far otherwise afar off, than when enjoyed and looked upon at a near Distance."[25]

Chapman tends to ignore the figurative identification of the "perspective" with human behavior, characteristics, and individuals. The emphasis, as I have remarked, usually is upon the human propensity to misinterpret the picture, not upon the duplicity of the picture itself. Rinaldo of *All Fools* does describe Beauty as "like a cozening picture," but the speech characterizes Rinaldo, whose professed ambition is to cozen all the "gulls" in the play; on the other hand Allegre, much closer to being a *raisonneur*, points to the central problem of interpreting Chabot's character ("judge what the main form is"). The fallibility of human judgment, Chapman's most persistent concern in all his perspective allusions arises from man's excessive dependence on sensory impressions, inadequately checked by his rational faculty.

Both Allegre and the narrator of *Eugenia* specify a comparison with pictures "wrought to optic reason." The phrase "optic reason" first occurs in Chapman's writings with the description of Niobe's statue in *Ovids Banquet*, which usage Schoell has traced to Comes' *Mythologiae*: "quae quasi ad opticam rationem excisa."[26] Since the phrase does not come from Comes' classical source, one does not know whether he

[25]William Drummond, *The Cypress Grove*, in *The Poetical Works*, ed. L. E. Kastner (Edinburgh, 1913), 2: 80.

[26]Franck L. Schoell, *Études sur l'humanisme continental en Angleterre* (Paris, 1926), p. 39.

picked it up somewhere else or whether it is his own embellishment. In either event, optic reason, as Chapman employs it, denotes the rules of perspective upon which these illusionist pictures were constructed, which means upon mathematical formulas—i.e., their foundations were in abstract, "rational" knowledge. Because of his own platonic disposition toward mathematics, Chapman could easily make the association between "optic reason" and "right reason," which seems implicit in his constant directions to correctly apply this reason: "view her in a right line," "in her fixt inspection," "by the right laid line / Of truth." Obtaining the correct angle of vision requires gaining some distance on the problem, putting the sensory data into perspective with the properly dominant power of reason, and being constant, gazing steadily from a fixed point.[27] All these describe accurately enough the techniques of viewing perspective; but, as he must readily have grasped, they also describe neatly the particulars of Chapman's own moral stance—the allegiance to reason, the demand for constancy in behavior, the drive to disengage from a too immediate involvement in order to arrive at a dispassionate decision.

This moralistic construction was, of course, not the only one that could be placed upon the perspective metaphor. To compare Chapman with Shakespeare, who also was particularly fond of perspective allusions, is illuminating. Shakespeare frequently will use the references, with no connotation of trickery, deception, or misuse of judgmental faculty, to suggest the enlargement of experience or knowledge, or an expanded concept of identity; and it is toward both realms that Orsino's bewildered "natural perspective" gropes.[28] Consider, for example, the Induction to *Taming of the Shrew*. When Christopher Sly does not immediately succumb to the illusion that he is not a drunken tinker but a wealthy lord, the jokers press the deception by offering Sly all the accoutrements of his new social position:

> *Sec. Serv.* Dost thou love pictures? we will fetch thee straight
> Adonis painted by a running brook,
> And Cytherea all in sedges hid,
> Which seem to move and wanton with her breath,

---

[27]Guillen summarizes the principal assumptions of perspective, pp. 33–34. For the importance of distance, see pp. 34, 42, 48; he also discusses the transference of the concept from spatial to temporal terms, as in "historical perspective," pp. 48–49. As Guillen suggests, the platonic affinity for perspectivism enters via Pythagorean mathematics and the pervasiveness of the aesthetic predicated on harmony. Interestingly, an anonymous biographer of Ficino credits him with a ms. treatise dealing with vision, perspective, and mirrors. P. O. Kristeller believes this may be the surviving ms., *Questions de luce et alie multe Marsilii*. See Kristeller, "The Scholastic Background of Marsilio Ficino," in *Studies in Renaissance Thought and Letters* (Rome, 1956), pp. 45–46; the ms. is printed on pp. 77–79.

[28]A similar conclusion is reached by Guillen, p. 47: "There is ultimately an important concentration not on the content of a given theme but on how it can be *known*."

Even as the waving sedges play with the wind.
Lord. We'll show thee Io as she was a maid,
And how she was beguiled and surprised,
As lively painted as the deed was done.
Third Serv. Or Daphne roaming through a thorny wood,
Scratching her legs that one shall swear she bleeds,
And at that sight shall sad Apollo weep,
So workmanly the blood and tears are drawn.
Lord. Thou art a lord and nothing but a lord.

[*Taming of the Shrew* Ind. 2.51–63]

The obvious point about the three pictures offered is that they all depict Ovidian myths which suggest psychic transformation; however, the strong emphasis upon pictorial illusionism in all three implies that, if Sly's visual perception of reality can be altered, his concept of self will alter accordingly. Whereas the Io and Daphne descriptions seem to suggest nothing more than a bravura simulation of three-dimensional realism, the Cytherea picture, with its sedges "Which seem to move and wanton with her breath," moves distinctly into the realm of trick perspectivism.

Whether the deception of Sly has negative consequences remains, of course, an open question. Without a conclusion to the frame-story Shakespeare's intentions cannot be guessed; within our dramatic experience of the play Sly's transformation to a lord is as enduring as the transformation of Kate's personality. *A Midsummer Night's Dream* gives us a less equivocal example. After the misadventures of the night, the lovers are awakened by Theseus's party to discover that all misdirected romantic impulses have vanished, although they know not how, as in a dream; and their natural loves have coalesced into something of great constancy. Not understanding what has taken place but, nonetheless, not doubting its reality, the lovers struggle to explain their experience, primarily through the dream metaphor of the play's title and, secondarily—but not insignificantly, I think—by recourse to perspective analogies:

Demetrius. These things seem small and undistinguishable,
Like far-off mountains turned into clouds.
Hermia. Methinks I see these things with parted eye,
When every thing seems double.

[*Midsummer Night's Dream* 4.1.191–94]

The doubling of Hermia's vision, as plainly as Orsino's "natural perspective," underscores the expanded consciousness which the action of the play has forced upon its participants. Shakespeare here uses perspective to gloss the radical dream metaphor of the comedy in a fashion that could be approved by Kenneth Burke, who has argued: "Metaphor is a device for seeing something in terms of something else. . . . A metaphor tells us something about one character considered from the point of view of another character. And to consider A from the point of view of B is, of course, to use B as a *perspective* upon A."[29]

If Shakespeare can convince us that in dreams begin realities, then Chapman would probably have been profoundly distrustful of any dream or illusion not ticketed by the divine afflatus. It is not news, however, that Chapman's imaginative range was more restricted than Shakespeare's; and, while narrower, Chapman's moralistic response to perspective and illusion seems more typical of his time and, certainly, not without interest in its own right.

Why the perspective picture should have taken so strong a hold on the imaginations of these poets at this particular time in the 1590s can only be a matter of conjecture. One factor could be the inevitable time-lag in the dissemination of continental developments in art theory and technique, especially at a popular level.[30] One notes, however, that trick perspective paintings had been known in England at least as early as Holbein's *The Ambassadors* (1533) and William Scrots's *Edward VI* (1546). Of the latter Roy Strong informs us that "throughout the late sixteenth and early seventeenth century this portrait or anamorphosis, to use the proper technical term, was shown to every official tourist visiting Whitehall Palace."[31]

Circumstances permit an equally speculative but considerably more specific line of inference about Chapman. In 1598 he published *Achilles Shield* with a prefatory poem "To my Admired and Sovle-Loved Friend, Mayster of all essentiall and true knowledge, M. Harriots." The poet offers his translation to Harriot "for censure":

> O had your perfect eye Organs to pierce
> Into that Chaos whence this stiffled verse
> By violence breakes: where Gloweworme like doth shine
> In nights of sorrow, this hid soule of mine:
> And how her genuine formes struggle for birth,

[29]Kenneth Burke, *A Grammar of Motives* (New York, 1945), pp. 503–4. This conception of metaphor, of course, was not alien to Shakespeare's century. See Emmanuele Tesauro's important treatise, *Il cannocchiale aristotelico*. Eugenio Donato concludes that "the concept of visual perception is fundamental" in Tesauro's thought. See Donato, "Tesauro's Poetics: Through the Looking Glass," *Modern Language Notes*, 78 (1963): 15–30; esp. pp. 23–30.

[30]Guillen, p. 41, finds that "Metaphors based on perspective in painting—*perspectiva artificialis*—do not take hold, outside of Italy, until the early 17th century. Previous usage proceeds from the medieval *perspectiva* or optical science and designates instruments that improve or modify vision, like magnifying lenses or spyglasses."

[31]Roy Strong, *The Elizabethan Image* (London, 1969), p. 19. Baltrusaitis devotes chap. 2, pp. 15–32, to "Anamorphoses: XVI et XVII siecles," and chap. 6, pp. 58–70, to "'Les Ambassadeurs' de Holbein."

Vnder the clawes of this fowle Panther earth;
Then vnder all those formes you should discerne
My loue to you, in my desire to learne.

["To Harriot," *Achilles Shield* 41–48]

This passage is well known, having persistently been interpreted in pathetic terms as Chapman's confession of his inability to achieve a level of poetic execution commensurate to his inspiration, a reading which, unfortunately, ignores the Plotinian idea of creativity.[32] For the present, however, I wish to focus upon the synecdoche of Harriot's "perfect eye," apparently alluding to a perspective glass or telescope.[33]

Thomas Harriot, that shadowy figure who was almost exactly Chapman's contemporary, emerged from Oxford in 1580 to become Ralegh's tutor in mathematics. Five years later Ralegh sent him as a surveyor to accompany Grenville's voyage to Virginia; Harriot's *Briefe and True Report of the New Found Land of Virginia* (1588) describes, among the other scientific instruments with which he astounded the Indians, "a perspective glass whereby was showed many strange sights."[34] Around 1590, probably through the offices of Ralegh, Harriot became acquainted with "the wizard Earl" Northumberland, who granted him a comfortable annual pension which sustained Harriot's scientific investigations for the remainder of his life, although it would now appear that when Northumberland resided in the Tower, with Chapman's *Homer* for solace, Harriot remained at Sion House.[35] The nineteenth century dismissed Harriot's scientific achievement as minor, regarding him as a careful, accurate observer whose significant findings were anticipated by continental virtuosi, but recent scientific historians, looking more carefully at the bulk of unpublished papers, have paid him greater homage. He is now credited with an important role in the revival of atomism, with significant discoveries in mathematics, astronomy, me-

---

[32]See Bartlett, *Poems*, pp. 3–4. MacLure, pp. 9–10, 68, knows the convention from Plotinus (*Enneads* 1.6.9, 5.8.1–2), but still reads the image as confessional.

[33]I would discount the possibility that Chapman refers to Harriot as possessing, figuratively, the Adamic perfect vision which penetrates to essences. The description of this "eye" as lacking "Organs" implies that it is not natural but a mechanical contrivance. Chapman praises his friend for fabricating scientific instruments which are "perfect" in the sense of being the very best of their kind.

[34]The phrase is quoted in the *Dictionary of National Biography*, s.v. "Harriot." For his life, see also Jean Jacquot, "Thomas Harriot's Reputation for Impiety," *Notes and Records of the Royal Society*, 9 (1952): 164–87; Robert Kargon, *Atomism in England from Harriot to Newton* (Oxford, 1966), pp. 18–30; Muriel Rukeyser, *The Traces of Thomas Hariot* (New York, 1970); and D. B. Quinn and J. W. Shirley, "A Contemporary List of Hariot References," *Renaissance Quarterly*, 22 (1969): 9–26. This list was compiled by Harriot himself, and includes, "Master Chapman's Achilles."

[35]See Kargon; and also J. W. Shirley, "The Scientific Experiments of Sir Walter Ralegh, the Wizard Earl, and the three Magi in the Tower, 1603–1617," *Ambix*, 4 (1949): 52–66.

chanics, and optics.[36] According to Johannes Lohne, Harriot was the first scientist to make systematic and accurate observations of refractions: he knew the sine law of refraction before Descartes; was the first to compute the radius of the rainbow from a correct theory; measured the dispersion of white light with a prism; and found that green and red rays have differing refrangibilities. Robert Kargon concludes that "these optical discoveries alone would be enough to establish Harriot as the peer of Galileo and one of the greatest English scientists before Newton."[37]

The points of contact between Chapman's literary circle and Harriot's scientific one are too numerous to dismiss as inconsequential. Chapman's first two volumes of poetry are dedicated to Ralegh's associate Matthew Roydon; The Shadow of Night pays tribute to "the deep searching Northumberland" in 1594; in 1596 Chapman's De Guiana, supporting Ralegh's colonial ventures, is published with A Relation of the second Voyage to Guiana, which its author, Lawrence Keymis, dedicated to Harriot.[38] In 1598, Chapman publicly offers his Homer translations for Harriot's criticism and alludes familiarly to Harriot's own unpublished writings; evidently the criticism was forthcoming, since he gratefully acknowledges Harriot's assistance in his preface to the 1616 Homer. Clearly, Chapman knew Harriot very well by 1598 and could easily have been acquainted with him several years earlier, possibly before the publication in 1594 of The Shadow of Night. Although Harriot did not master the law of sines until the summer of 1602, he is known to have done scientific observations of refractions as early as 1597;[39] the interest in perspective glasses demonstrably goes back as early as the Virginia voyage in the mid-1580s, and was well enough associated with Harriot's name for Chapman to make the play upon it in Achilles Shield. I think it is legitimate to speculate that this interest in optical theory and visual phenomena was sufficiently current in the Ralegh-Northumberland intellectual sphere by the mid-1590s to have given impetus to Ovids Banquet of Sence;[40] and that Harriot himself may well have been one of

[36]On the varying reputation, see Johannes Lohne, "The Fair Fame of Thomas Harriott," Centaurus, 8 (1963): 69–83. For modern scientific estimates of Harriot's work, see Kargon, Atomism; Lohne, "Thomas Harriott, the Tycho Brahe of Optics," Centaurus, 6 (1959): 113–21; Rosalind C. H. Tanner, "Thomas Harriot as Mathematician: A Legacy of Hearsay," Physis, 9 (1967): 235–47, 257–92; and Jon V. Pepper, "Harriot's Calculation of the Meridional Parts as Logarithmic Tangents," Archives of the History of Exact Science, 4 (1968): 359–413. Marjorie Nicolson was a pioneer in calling attention to Harriot's possible literary impact; see Science and Imagination, pp. 32–37.

[37]Kargon, Atomism, p. 23; Lohne, "Optics."

[38]Rukeyser, Traces, p. 140.

[39]Lohne, "Optics," p. 117.

[40]On Northumberland's interest in optics and allied subjects, see Kargon, Atomism, pp. 12–14.

those readers of "light-bearing intellect" and "iudiciall perspectiue" who were expected to appreciate the poem.

After the prefatory matter, the extraordinary emphasis upon vision in the poem itself commences with the second stanza, which describes, first, the sun "fill[ing] his eyes with fire," and then the setting of the round bower with a spring at the center. As Chapman notes, "By *Prosopopaeia*, he makes ye fountaine ye eye of the round Arbor, as a Diamant seems to be the eye of a Ring; and therefore sayes, the Arbor sees with the Fountaine." He is, in fact, establishing a microcosm / macrocosm relationship between the local setting and action of the poem and the universe at large, relying implicitly upon the conventional image of the sun as the eye of the world.[41] The analogy becomes explicit at points: in the description of Corinna's emblematic jewels, two overtly involving the sun and the third being "an Eye in Saphire set" (71.1); and in the image of Corinna as a phoenix "burning gainst *Apollos* eye" (31.7). Mythological references persistently invoke fables of visual powers—Argus (67), the Basiliske (81), the eagle who is able to gaze at the sun (Corinna's song)—or, yet more pointedly, of the unfortunate consequences of vision—Actaeon, whose sight of Diana bathing proves his destruction (41).

In stanza 2, Corinna's sympathetic attraction to the sun anticipates two major associations, her solar affinity and her responsiveness to physical passion. Presenting the sun as the eye of the world turns the setting for the entire action into an emblem of vision, with the concomitant suggestion that the world will be watching this microcosm of itself; further, it effects a rhetorical bridge to the perspective statuary, since it is the fountain "Into which eye, most pittifully stood / Niobe, shedding teares, that were her blood." The stanza describing Niobe bears quoting:

> Stone *Niobe*, whose statue to this Fountaine,
> In great *Augustus Caesars* grace was brought
> From *Sypilus*, the steepe *Mygdonian* Mountaine:
> That statue tis, still weepes for former thought,
>   Into thys spring *Corynnas* bathing place;
> So cunningly to optick reason wrought,
>   That a farre of, it shewd a womans face,
> Heauie, and weeping; but more neerely viewed,
> Nor weeping, heauy, nor a woman shewed.
>
> [*Ovids Banq.* stanza 3]

Chapman adapts to his Roman context the description which Comes, in turn, found in Pausanias and embellished slightly with Ovidian reminis-

---

[41]For Ovid's use of the image, see *Metamorphoses* 4.226–28.

cences and the *ad opticam rationem* phrase.[42] The perspectival feature is unchanged from Pausanias, who was describing a cave in the rocks under the Acropolis:

> This also has a tripod over it, wherein are Apollo and Artemis slaying the children of Niobe. This Niobe I myself saw when I had gone up to Mount Sipylus. When you are near it is a beetling craig, with not the slightest resemblance to a woman, mourning or otherwise; but if you go further away, you will think you see a woman in tears, with head bowed down.[43]

Chapman has imaginatively conflated the two separate components of Pausanias's anecdote, moving the stone Niobe from her mountain and incorporating the Acropolean images of Apollo and Artemis slaying her children into one fictitious group of statuary:

> Behind theyr Mother two Pyramides
> Of freckled Marble, through the Arbor viewed,
> On whose sharp brows, *Sol*, and *Tytanides*
> In purple and transparent glasse were hewed,
>   Through which the Sun-beames on the statues staying,
> Made theyr pale bosoms seeme with blood imbrewed,
>   Those two sterne Plannets rigors still bewraying
> To these dead forms, came liuing beauties essence
> Able to make them startle with her presence.
>
> [*Ovids Banq.* stanza 6]

The "curious imagrie" of the Niobe group becomes functional only seasonally: "In Sommer onely wrought her exstasie" (4.1). Apparently, the two optical tricks, the illusion that the statue presents a weeping woman and the suggestion that the ivory carvings of Niobe's children are bleeding, caused by prismatic refraction of light rays through the colored glass of the twins, can only be effected when the sun is close to earth and its rays direct and intense. The connection of the sun with visual process once again is studied. The glass images of Apollo and Artemis are affixed to bases described as "Pyramides of freckled marble." The choice of geometrical form has its significance; the pyramid recurs later in Ovid's thoughts about the transmission of visual impressions: "Betwixt mine Eye and obiect, certayne lynes, / Moue in the figure of a Pyramis, / Whose chapter in mine eyes gray apple shines, / The base within my sacred obiect is" (64.1–4), a passage which caused Schoell to wonder why Chapman diverged from his presumed

---

[42]Comes, *Mythologiae*, (Paris, 1583), 6.13; and Schoell, p. 39. For the full Niobe story, see *Metamorphoses* 6.165–312; Ovid alludes to the weeping rock in *Heroides*, 20.103–6, "Acontius to Cydippe," a passage, interestingly, which juxtaposes Niobe and Actaeon. Jonson also linked them as figures of presumption and self-love (see *Cynthia's Revels*, 1.2.82–87).

[43]Pausanias, *Descriptions of Greece*, trans. W. H. S. Jones, Loeb Classical Library (Cambridge, Mass., 1918), 1.21.3.

source to translate *conos* as *pyramis*.[44] Actually, the terms seem to have been interchangeable in optical theory from ancient times on,[45] and Chapman could have gotten his information about the visual pyramid (which theoretically limits the field of vision through which rays pass from object to base) from any number of sources, not excluding conversation in the Northumberland circle. The pyramidal obelisks, therefore, suggest the visual pyramids that frame the very act of seeing, in which case the locus of vision emanates from Latona's twins, fixed at the points where the pyramidal lines converge. Here, as elsewhere in the poem, the connotations of the sun are twofold: if, on the one hand, the sun represents vision, on the other, the solar element is fire, which the form of the pyramid symbolizes.[46] The fire of the sun provides the source for the dense cluster of imagery involving heat, flame, and burning, persistently associating the motivations of Ovid and Corinna with passion and lust. Because the illusion of the statuary can be projected only in the proximity of the sun, this group, with its necessary interaction of sun myth and the real sun, initiates the theme of nature manipulated through art: and in the context of the garden or bower setting this theme was associated by Ariosto and Spenser with illicit sexuality.[47]

The reader enters the garden and is forced by the poet to share Ovid's initial perceptual dilemma, a limiting of viewpoint similar to that by which Milton makes his reader see paradise through Satan's eyes. What is the reader to make of these perspective tricks? The Niobe illusion takes priority, since, if the viewer does not identify the statue with her form, the subsidiary illusion of Apollo and Diana murdering her children becomes meaningless. Kermode reads the entire group as a warning against presumption, certainly a standard interpretation of the story in Chapman's time.[48] Elizabeth Donno has inverted Kermode's interpretation, arguing that "'more nearly viewed,' the statue does not even appear to be the figure of a woman. Thus Ovid's nearer view becomes a symbol of what 'searching wits' apprehend rather than what the 'profane multitude' sees from afar."[49] Her reasoning fails to convince because, not only does it disregard Chapman's customary moral stance, it violates a

---

[44]Schoell, p. 244 n.

[45]So I am informed by David C. Lindberg, *contra* Joan Gadol, pp. 29–30, who credits Alberti with introducing the term "pyramid" of sight.

[46]See Plato, *Timaeus* 56B; Diogenes Laertius, *Lives of Eminent Philosophers*, 3.70; Plutarch, *Moralia*, 427D, 428D.

[47]The interaction of art and nature is a major concern in the study by Rhoda Ribner (esp. pp. 241–51), although she interprets it as wholly positive. The most comprehensive study of the general theme is Edward W. Tayler, *Nature and Art in Renaissance Literature* (New York, 1965); on Spenser, see also A. B. Giamatti, *The Earthly Paradise and the Renaissance Epic* (Princeton, 1966), pp. 254–90.

[48]Kermode, pp. 88–89; see also the Niobe emblem, "Superbia vltio" in Whitney's *A Choice of Emblemes* (1586), p. 13.

[49]Elizabeth Donno, ed., *Elizabethan Minor Epics* (New York, 1963), p. 13 n.

convention of viewing perspective pictures, well established by the end
of the sixteenth century, that the sense of such constructions is perceived
by viewing them from a distance.[50] The statuary makes sense from a
distance, which is to say that Ovid's rational faculty controls his senses
and interprets the data supplied by them. If he gets too close, commits
his presumptuous act, he then loses perspective, the sensory data over-
whelm his intelligence, and he perceives only non-sense.

Like Phaeton and Icarus (cf. stanzas 15 and 28), Ovid wanders too near
the sun and suffers for it. First, he is overcome by sound as Corinna's
Apollonian song proclaims that "soules are rulde by eyes," and sets
Ovid's senses on fire (17.1). Corinna's perfume, likened to the spices of
the phoenix, a solar creature (31), incites Ovid with desire to see the
object of his passion (40–41). His audacity impells the narrator to rebuke:

> Stay therefore *Ouid*, venter not, a sight
> May proue thy rudenes, more then show thee louing.
> . . ..
> Thou would'st be prickt with other sences stings,
> To tast, and feele, and yet not there be staide.

> [*Ovids Banq.* 42.1–2; 43.6–7]

The warning, of course, has no effect. Ovid prays to Juno, who can aid
"Such as in Cyprian sports theyr pleasures fix" (47.7), for her assistance,
and

> This sayde, he charg'd the Arbor with his eye,
> Which pierst it through, and at her brests reflected,
> Striking him to the hart with exstasie:
> As doe the sun-beames gainst the earth prorected,
> With their reuerberate vigor mount in flames,
> And burne much more then where they were directed,
> He saw th' extraction of all fayrest Dames:
> The fayre of Beauty, as whole Countries come
> And shew theyr riches in a little Roome.

> [*Ovids Banq.* stanza 49]

The Marlovian tag epitomizes the conception of the banquet of sense as
exposure to a microcosm of all possible sensory delights.

---

[50]On distance as a principal assumption of perspective, see Guillen, pp. 34, 42, 48. Gombrich, *Art and Illusion*, pp. 191–202, discusses paintings and statues designed to be viewed
from a distance; see also Rosalie Colie, *Paradoxia Epidemica: The Renaissance Tradition
of Paradox* (Princeton, 1966), pp. 287–88. My interpretation is in accord with Meyers, p. 203,
who more tentatively remarks, "I would suggest that the 'perspective statue' stands as a
reminder of the unreliability and imperfection of visual (and, in general, of sensual) perceptions, and perhaps even of the dangers with which the thematically important sense Sight
is fraught in the poem."

At this midpoint in the narrative and in the scheme of sensory fulfillment, the narrator explicitly enters the poem with a "digression" (consisting of nine stanzas; 48 stanzas precede the digression and 60 follow
it), which, as the term itself implies, breaks the continuity of the narrative illusion to supply an external perspective upon the action. "Heere
Ouid sold his freedome for a looke" (50.1), the poet instructs us, and
distinguishes carefully between proper and improper use of sight, the
visual attraction which leads to apprehension of ideal beauty and that
which ends with sensory infatuation, enthrallment to the world of appearances. "For sacred beautie, is the fruite of sight, / The curtesie that
speakes before the tongue, / The feast of soules, the glory of the light"
(52.1–3); it is "The summe and court of all proportion," and, returning
explicitly to the poetic of *ut pictura poesis*, soundless music or "All
Rethoricks flowers in lesse then in a worde" (52.9). But the kind of beauty
with which Ovid has just been bedazzled in his "powrefull sight" of
Corinna, unless the beholder has the strength of character and per-
specuity to withstand its effects (51.5–9), leads elsewhere:

> This beauties fayre is an enchantment made
> By natures witchcraft, tempting men to buy
> With endles showes, what endlessly will fade,
> Yet promise chapmen all eternitie.
>
> [*Ovids Banq.* 51.1–4]

The nice pun upon the poet's own name calls attention, as a private joke
for his audience of cognoscenti, to the way in which Ovid's "misreading"
of Corinna functions as a metaphor for the predicament of those unwary
readers who are deceived, in precisely the same manner, by the surface
of the entire poem.[51] The unpleasantness suggested by this apparently
contemptuous attitude toward the untutored audience is mediated by the
acknowledgement of his poetic imperfections, which closes the digression. In explaining man's propensity to prefer the vision of the lesser
beauty to the greater, Chapman, unoriginally enough, points to innate
human imperfection, and alludes to his dissatisfaction with his own
efforts to capture poetically (52–54) the vision of "sacred beauty," and
to the necessary accommodation to human limitation:

> But as weake colour alwayes is allowed
> The proper obiect of a humaine eye,
> Though light be with a farre more force endowde
> In stirring vp the visuale facultie,

---

[51]Colie, "My Ecchoing Song," p. 152, and Angus Fletcher, *The Prophetic Moment: An Essay
on Spenser* (Chicago, 1971), p. 102, both suggest that puns serve as the verbal equivalent of
anamorphosis.

> This colour being but of vertuous light
> A feeble Image; and the cause dooth lye
> In th' imperfection of a humaine sight,
> So this for loue, and beautie, loues cold fire
> May serue for my praise, though it merit higher.
>
> [*Ovids Banq.* stanza 55]

The digression, then, occurs at the pivotal point in both the schematic and dramatic actions of the poem. Immediately after Ovid receives visual gratification, the narrator stops to interpret his behavior as an abuse of sight, to supply an account of the correct use of sight, to rationalize such abuses. To this point in the poem references to vision and sight have been understandably frequent; crucial to an appreciation of the visual analogy underlying the entire poem, however, is an awareness that such references do not stop with Ovid's visual fulfillment. His eye continues to "carue him on that feast of feasts" (58.2); he dilates upon the function of sense to excite the mind with a technical description of visual process (63–64); and compares the attraction of Corinna's beauty to that which a candle burning in darkness has for the eye (66). The narrator interjects a description of Corinna's emblematic jewels with their visual warning (70–71) preliminary to her visual discovery of Ovid:

> With this, as she was looking in her Glasse,
> She saw therein a mans face looking on her:
> Whereat she started from the frighted Grasse,
> As if some monstrous Serpent had been shown her:
> Rising as when (the sunne in *Leos* signe)
> *Auriga* with the heauenly Goate vpon her,
> Shows her horn'd forehead with her Kids diuine,
> Whose rise, kils Vines, Heauens face with storms disguising;
> No man is safe at sea, the Haedy rising.
>
> [*Ovids Banq.* stanza 74]

The device of showing Ovid's face in the mirror is, of course, itself a perspective trick, analogous to the insets used in Renaissance paintings—self-portraits on the wall as in Pintoricchio's *The Annunciation*, the *memento mori* of Holbein's *The Ambassadors*, or reflections in mirrors as in Titian's *Vanitas* and *Young Woman Doing Her Hair*—to call attention to the larger perspective scheme of the paintings. The mirror, more-over, is the most standard iconographic attribute of vision,[52] serving to suggest, as had the eye-of-the-world metaphor earlier, that Corinna's

---

[52]See S. C. Chew, *The Pilgrimage of Life* (New Haven, 1962), p. 193; also Ribner, pp. 247–48. For other meanings of mirrors, see Guy de Tervarent, *Attributs et Symbols dans l'art pro-fane, 1450–1600* (Geneva, 1958–59), 2: 273; and Erwin Panofsky, *Problems in Titian, Mostly Iconographic* (New York, 1969), p. 93. Jan Brueghel's allegory of vision (see n.10 above) deserves mention as a remarkable anthology of vision iconography as well as illusion and perspective *topoi*.

abstract role in the poem may be to symbolize the faculty of vision. But the face in the mirror, seen presumably by both Ovid and Corinna, is his own, stirring the reader's awareness that the traditional image for self-knowledge, that of a man viewing himself in a mirror,[53] presents itself to Ovid's glance only to be ignored. *Teipsum et orbem* was the motto, also ignored, of the third jewel in Corinna's hair.

Even Richard II found his mirrored visage vexing enough to make him shatter the glass, but Ovid does not pause over the glass or Corinna's rebuke that sight "attainteth" her honor, "for Thought Sights childe / Begetteth sinne" (78.7–8). Ovid delivers another dissertation on optics to maintain "All excellence of shape is made for sight" (80.5), and protests, with ironic accuracy, that "Tis I (alas) and my hart-burning Eye / Doe all the harme, and feels the harme wee doo: / I am no Basiliske, yet harmles I / Poyson with sight, and mine owne bosome too" (81.1–4). Even the gratification of the other senses is cast in visual terms. When Corinna accedes to Ovid's request for a kiss, "Her moouing towards him, made *Ouids* eye / Beleeue the Firmament was comming downe" (97.1–2); and when she agrees to satisfy his sense of touch, she again exposes the beauty of her body to his vision: "Close to her nauill shee her Mantle wrests, / Slacking it vpwards, and the foulds vnwound, /Showing *Latonas* Twinns, her plenteous brests" (105.5–7).

The poem ends abruptly with a trick, a cheat, the pornographer's conspiratorial wink designed to convey to the gullible the illusion that, were it not for the need to outwit the vigilant censor, he would be getting something really titillating and not merely this tame stuff. Ovid is "interrupted with the view / Of other Dames," and forced to flee the garden, like Alexander the Great, grieving "that no greater action could be doone" (116. 1–2, 7). The final impression permitted the reader, however, is not that of coitus interruptus:

> But as when expert Painters haue displaid,
> To quickest life a Monarchs royall hand
> Holding a Scepter, there is yet bewraide
> But halfe his fingers; when we vnderstand
> The rest not to be seene; and neuer blame
> The Painters Art, in nicest censures skand:
> So in the compasse of this curious frame,
> *Ouid* well knew there was much more intended,
> With whose omition none must be offended.

> *Intentio, animi actio.*
> Explicit conuiuium.
> [*Ovids Banq.* stanza 117]

---

[53]See, *inter alia*, Alciati, *Emblemata* (Padua, 1621), no. 187, "Dicta Septem Sapientum," and commentary, p. 787; Ripa's emblem of knowledge holding a mirror (*Iconologia* [Rome, 1603], p. 444); or the mirror in which Spenser's Britomart first sees Artegall (*Faerie*

Even without the terminal comment the reader understands that he is to take the seduction as successfully consummated. The perspective analogy makes that evident: just as we accept the illusion of the portrait for the reality of the whole man, so we are to take the poem as representational of its completed action. Beneath the simile resonates a famous classical locus for pictorial illusionism, the allusion here at the end of the poem matching the adaptation of Pausanias's description of Niobe at the beginning. Among the bits of artistic technique and theory preserved by Pliny is the following observation:

> For the contour ought to round itself off and so terminate as to suggest the presence of other parts behind it also, and disclose even what it hides. This is the distinction conceded to Parrhasius by Antigonus and Xenocrates who have written on the art of painting.[54]

This description of the particular skill of Parrhasius immediately follows Pliny's account of what was perhaps the most celebrated feat of classical art, the contest in representational illusionism between Parrhasius and Zeuxis.[55] Whereas the latter created a picture of grapes so convincing that birds pecked at them, Parrhasius won the palm by producing a picture of a curtain realistic enough that Zeuxis tried to lift the curtain to see the painting which he assumed was behind it. Thus the concluding stanza of *Ovids Banquet* firmly anchors the poem in the *ut pictura poesis* conception. More than this, however, it cryptically signals the method of the poem, "suggest[ing] the presence of other parts behind it also, and disclos[ing] even what it hides," to the "serching spirits" addressed in the preface, and at the same time it calls attention to the illusionistic skill of its artificer, a Parrhasius among poets, calmly anticipating misapprehension of his work. For those who do grasp the "fore conceit" of the poem correctly, the poetic illusion of complete sensory fulfillment supplies its own implicit moral. The principle is the same as that which E. H. Gombrich has formulated for trompe l'oeil paintings:

> For every painted still life has the *vanitas* motif "built in" as it were, for those who want to look for it. The pleasures it stimulates are not real, they are mere illusion. Try and grasp the luscious fruit or the tempting beaker and you will hit against a hard cold panel. The more cunning the illusion the more impressive, in a way, is this sermon on semblance and reality. Any painted still life is *ipso facto* also a *vanitas*.[56]

Queene 3.2.18–19). For a discussion of knowledge and mirror symbolism, see G. W. O'Brien, *Renaissance Poetics and the Problem of Power* (Chicago, 1956), pp. 20–30.

[54]Pliny, *Natural History*, trans. H. Rackham, Loeb Classical Library (Cambridge, Mass., 1952), 36.68.

[55]Ibid., 36.65–66. See Gombrich, *Art and Illusion*, pp. 206–7.

[56]Gombrich, *Meditations on a Hobby Horse*, p. 104.

The general lesson about falling prey to sensory delusion, here epitomized as visual seduction, becomes evident through the presentation of
the poem as a speaking picture (and that picture as an optical illusion),
reinforced by the shifts of perspective, from Ovid's viewpoint to the
narrator's, in digression and narrative intrusion, as well as in the admonitory allusions. To trace more particularly the consequences of such
abuse of the senses and so, from the narrator's perspective, the issue of
what goes wrong in the relationship of Ovid and Corinna after he has
surrendered reason to sensory impulse, requires recapitulating the
structure of language and imagery involving fire, the sun, and alchemical process.

The poem opens with a description of natural generative process, of
the masculine sun with its generative heat fertilizing earth to create life:
"The Earth, from heauenly light conceiued heat, / Which mixed all her
moyst parts with her dry, / When with right beames the Sun her bosome
beat, / And with fit foode her Plants did nutrifie" (1.1–4). It is a pattern
for natural masculine and feminine relationships, unfortunately to be
ignored by Ovid; also, for alchemical process, constituting, as MacLure
observes, a still, a natural limbeck.[57] The scene then shifts to the artificial,
the sterile, the nonliving in the garden with its fountain and statuary, all
focusing upon "liuing beauties essence," Corinna herself.

Drawn to the "eye" of the garden by the sun's heat, Corinna, as we
have remarked, persistently is associated with the sun. The first description of Corinna has been admired as a specimen of Chapman's metaphysical style: "The downward-burning flame, / Of her rich hayre did
threaten new accesse, / Of ventrous *Phaeton* to scorch the fields" (7.3–
5), although it might be more to the point to consider the function of the
image. A "downward burning" flame, while vividly evoking the sensuous
immediacy of Corinna's hair, also suggests that attraction to the source
of this flame leads to a descent. Like the even more explicit allusion to
Phaeton, the initial image is admonitory. Again and again in the fire
imagery, Corinna appears as the source of the flame, as in fact the sun:

---

[57]MacLure, p. 53. Henry Peacham, *Minerva Britanna, 1612*, English Emblem Books No. 5
(Menston, Yorkshire, 1969), p. 142, has an emblem which strikingly illustrates Chapman's
conception here. Beneath the motto "hei mihi quod vidi," the picture shows a giant eye in
the heavens, weeping down upon the earth:

Looke how the Limbeck gentlie downe distil's
In pearlie drops, his heartes cleare quintescence:
So I, poore Eie, while coldest sorrow fills
My brest by flames, enforce this moisture thence,
In Christall floods, that thus their limits breake,
Drowning the heart, before the tongue can speake.

> Then cast she off her robe, and stood vpright,
> As lightning breakes out of a laboring cloude;
> Or as the Morning heauen casts off the Night.
> . . . .
> Her sight, his sunne so wrought in his desires,
> His sauor vanisht in his visuale fires.
> . . . .
> Shee lifts her lightning arms aboue her head,
> And stretcheth a Meridian from her blood.
>
> [*Ovids Banq.* 8.1–3; 40.8–9; 69.5–6]

While Corinna acts as the sun goddess, Ovid is cast as a Niobe—that is, as the presumptuous but weak, defenseless, and therefore endangered, mortal: Phaeton, Icarus, Prometheus (here not portrayed as the artist-creator, but as the thief punished for stealing fire from the sun [38.5–7, 41.1–2]), Actaeon (41.9). The Actaeon role, definitively, is Ovid's by virtue of his self-identification, alluding to the cause of his exile (*Tristia* 2.105), and it suits Chapman's purposes to draw upon the standard connotations of lust, passion, and presumption. But does not the identification of Corinna with Diana, and therefore with the moon, confuse the sun goddess role? Rather, I think, Chapman uses the solar imagery to undercut the prototypic role of Diana. If Ovid should not act like Actaeon, certainly Corinna does not act like Diana, the goddess of chastity. Corinna, in a sense, has a choice of role models posed by the Niobe statuary; she can be like Tytanides/Diana or Sol/Apollo. Chapman does not forbear to remind us of what she should be and is not: thus the "Romaine *Phoebe*" epithet (11.3) and the anatomical microcosmism of "*Latonas* Twinns, her plenteous brests / The Sunne and *Cynthia*" (105.7–8).

Although Corinna remains the sun, Ovid's role, even in nonmythological terms, can be seen as inferior and subservient to hers; in meteorological imagery he is a falling star to her planet (50, and Gloss) or follows the sun "like a fiery exhalation" (13.5–6).[58] Conversely, the more indirect of Corinna's associations still strengthen the solar part which she has assumed: the "Iewels of deuise" which she arranges in her hair, the Phoenix simile, her rising up like "the sunne in *Leos* signe" (74.5); even her kiss creates endless music "Like *Phoebus* Lute, on *Nisus* Towrs imposed" (98.9), reminding us of the Apollonian nature of her earlier singing and lute-playing (12 ff.).

Starting from the natural limbeck of stanza two, there extends through the poem a running parallel to alchemical process and a fairly extensive use of alchemical symbolism,[59] reinforcing on yet another

---

[58]This imagery is considered by S. K. Heninger, Jr., *A Handbook of Renaissance Meteorology* (Durham, N.C., 1960), pp. 185, 195–96.

[59]For brief mention of the alchemical symbolism, see Jacquot, *George Chapman*, p. 64; MacLure, pp. 49, 51, 53–54. Chapman takes for granted (as does Drummond in the passage

plane, the frame of reference established by solar myth and by natural process (from which, undoubtedly, much of alchemical process derives). Delimited by the suggestive settings of fountain and garden, the alchemical context operates most often at a subsurface level with the primary language referents explicable in other terms. The alchemical analogy seems to be present in Ovid's mind as he, for instance, describes the notes of Corinna's song as "Not vapord in her voyces stillerie" (26.7). More significant is his insistence upon the metaphor when he reaches the final stage of his sensory progression:

> The minde then cleere, the body may be vsde,
> Which perfectly your touch can spritualize;
> As by the great elixer is trans-fusde
> Copper to Golde, then grant that deede of prise.

> [Ovids Banq. 104.1–4]

Beyond such explicit occurrences, the reader encounters a barrage of terms and concepts susceptible to an alchemical interpretation—purgation, essence, purification, distillation, death, restoration, rarification, rebirth, excitation, refinement, extraction, flood, infusion, chaos, vapor, spirit, digestion, propagation, generation, sulphur, gold, balm, phoenix, eagle, sun, moon—which convey the impression, albeit rather obscurely, that the stages of the sensory progression correspond loosely to those of the alchemist's experiment.[60]

Chapman apparently has in mind the basic metaphor of the alchemical "marriage." F. Sherwood Taylor explains: "The combination of Sol and Luna, 'our gold' and 'our silver,' is symbolized in these terms, often with a frankness of sexual symbolism unacceptable in a modern published work. Sol is to impregnate Luna in order to generate the stone."[61] The radical metaphor shaped the alchemist's view of the entire experiment: "The combination of two bodies he saw as *marriage*, the loss of their characteristic activity as *death*, the production of something new as a *birth*, the rising up of vapors, as a *spirit leaving the corpse*, the formation of a volitile solid, as the making of a *spiritual body*."[62] Chapman's literalization of the alchemist's sexual metaphor here is very similar to

---

quoted on p. 123 above) our knowledge that alchemy and optics or perspective were sister arts. For Della Porta the "instruction of a Magician" includes the study of alchemy and optics both (*Natural Magick*, p. 3); Campanella's *De sensu rerum et magia* (1620) has a chapter on optical illusions; and the title of Jean Francois Nicèron's *Perspective curieuse ou Magie artificielle des effects merveilleux de l'optique* (Paris, 1638) makes plain the continuing association.

[60]For such terminology, consult Martin Ruland, *A Lexicon of Alchemy* (1612), trans. A. E. Waite (London, 1964).

[61]F. Sherwood Taylor, *The Alchemists: Founders of Modern Chemistry* (1949; reprint ed., New York, 1962), p. 119.

[62]Taylor, p. 116.

Donne's poetic strategy in *The Dissolution*, which could have been written before *Ovids Banquet*. Jay Levine has demonstrated how Donne's poem punningly functions as a twofold elegy, ostensibly a funeral elegy but actually an Ovidian erotic elegy figuring the "death" of sexual consummation as an unsuccessful alchemical process.[63] For both poets the association of Ovid with alchemy probably depended on his reputation as an eroticist and as a spiritual mythographer. The end of alchemy and metamorphosis both is transformation, a coincidence not missed by the alchemical commentators on the *Metamorphoses*.[64]

If Chapman did indeed expect his select audience to read *Ovids Banquet* against an awareness of the alchemical "marriage," Ovid's self-serving persuasion conspicuously misuses the concept. Whereas the marriage of Sol and Luna was designed to generate an hermaphroditic spiritual body, the stone or elixir, Ovid's appeal in stanza 104 casts Corinna, not as Luna (which properly she should be) or even Sol (which she has been throughout the poem), but as herself the "great elixer" who can spiritualize by her touch and "trans-fuse" Ovid's copper to gold—a false marriage even in the court of Venus.

The alchemical analogy offers in microcosm a model of the proper relationship of the sexes figured in stanza 1 with the description of the Sun impregnating Mother Earth. Renaissance alchemy was, in large part, the technological arm of Hermeticism and derived much of its essential theory from the Hermetic tradition, which ascribed a special position in the universe to the sun, conceiving it as the source of life-giving energy.[65] This generative energy was transmitted as fire; the entire natural world was envisioned dialectically as an interaction of active and passive, masculine and feminine, with all substances or beings possessing the generative fire classified as masculine.[66]

Ovid's offense, similar to the Petrarchan lover's (but differing, of course, in the Ovidian physicality of his passion), originates from surrendering the distancing perspective of his reason to the mindless dominance of his senses. The short-circuiting of sexual attraction from its proper purpose of generation to the sterile satisfaction of lust causes Ovid to abrogate his rightful masculine position, perversely making

[63]Jay Arnold Levine, "'The Dissolution': Donne's Twofold Elegy," *ELH*, 28 (1961): 301–15.

[64]On the alchemical allegorizations of Ovid, see D. C. Allen, *Mysteriously Meant: The Rediscovery of Pagan Symbolism and Allegorical Interpretation in the Renaissance* (Baltimore, 1970), pp. 178–79 and n.

[65]For the relationship of alchemy to Hermeticism, see Taylor, pp. 161–81; and Frances A. Yates, *Giordano Bruno and the Hermetic Tradition* (Chicago, 1964), pp. 44 ff., 150–51.

[66]See J. A. Mazzeo, "Notes on John Donne's Alchemical Imagery," in *Renaissance and Seventeenth-Century Studies* (New York, 1964), p. 73; and a pair of articles by William B. Hunter, Jr., "Milton's Materialistic Life Principle," *Journal of English and Germanic Philology*, 45 (1946): 68–76, and "Milton and Thrice Great Hermes," ibid., 327–36; also Yates, *Giordano Bruno*, pp. 151–56.

Corinna his sun and the source of fire, while assuming for himself the passive, feminine, nonetheless presumptuous part of a Niobe, mere exhalation to Corinna's sun. Judged from all the perspectives which Chapman builds into the poem counter to Ovid's own, the relationship is unnatural, the marriage demands annulment, and the experience can be interpreted as spiritual only by shutting out every viewpoint except that of Ovid's sophistic rhetoric.

To sum up: the dedication to the poem addresses itself to a learned, select audience who will have the interpretative resources to understand correctly the poem and without which the poet knows it will be misunderstood. As a radical metaphor or interpretative key to the work he offers the analogy of the speaking picture, which relinquishes its meaning only to those who possess the proper judicial perspective. This reading perspective coordinates the perspectival elements within the body of the poem—the disproportionate and reordered emphasis on the faculty of vision, the inclusion of optical theory and of the optical-illusion sculpture, the reliance on illusionistic conceptions of painting— to arrive at an important qualification to the critical commonplace, *ut pictura perspectivans poesis*. As a "perspective poem," then, *Ovids Banquet* can be interpreted in more than one way; the problem for the reader is to find the vantage point determining the right perspective.[67] Most simply the problem reduces to the old one of interpreting narrative method: does Chapman present Ovid as a dramatic character within a narrative framework, thereby requiring a sharp distinction between the views of narrator and character, or is Ovid no more complex than a fictional embodiment of Chapman's viewpoint or philosophy, and the narrator's comments merely supplementary, not corrective?

I have argued that Chapman's "understander" was expected to bring to the poem external perspective in the form of knowledge of the conventions of perspective and illusionistic representation, of optical theory, of alchemical symbolism and Hermetic doctrine, of solar myth and lore, of philosophic consideration of the senses. This knowledge surely would have divorced yet more distinctly the narrator's point of view from Ovid's than have the "perspective shifts" generally acknowledged—the narrative intrusions and digressions, the warnings imparted in mythological allusions, the statuary and the emblematic jewels, the

---

[67] I have suggested elsewhere that *Antony and Cleopatra*—which employs spectacle and visual symbolism to an unusual degree, is preoccupied with the correct interpretation of appearances, and alludes to perspective devices—functions similarly as a "perspective play." See R. B. Waddington, "*Antony and Cleopatra*: 'What Venus Did with Mars,'" *Shakespeare Studies*, 2 (1966): 210–27. Perspectivism may provide a helpful interpretative context for other problematic literary works in this period.

satiric epigraph, the arrangement of the volume with the implicit comparison to the *Coronet*.[68] Such a perspective does indeed require a recondite audience, exactly like the one Chapman describes in his dedication to Roydon; that he reached a few such readers may perhaps be indicated by the commendatory poems in the volume. Richard Stapleton writes of Chapman's muse singing 'Sweet philosophick strains," and John Davies, while warning that for some wits the poem is "too misticall and deepe," concludes, "Ouids soule, now growne more old and wise, / Poures foorth it selfe in deeper misteries."

The separation of speakers to which this reading leads, however, is more stringent than nearly all Chapman's twentieth-century critics have cared to maintain. Even those critics who have been relatively careful in following the narrative technique of the poem take, for instance, stanza 114 with its complaint about the difficulty of finding patronage to be Chapman directly voicing his own concerns.[69] But the stanza is spoken by Ovid, not by the narrator. It comes after Ovid's ultimate perversion of platonic theory to gain tactile satisfaction, between his promise to write the *Ars Amatoria* for Corinna's sake (113.5) and his pledge to make her the patron of his art (115). If the foregoing reconstruction of intellectual and literary context means anything, if indeed the conventions of narrative technique mean anything, this can *not* be Chapman's complaint about his own hard luck in landing a patron. Corinna, as the muse re-

---

[68]For mythological warnings, in addition to those commented upon earlier, one should not miss the description of Corinna's "bright Pelopian shoulders" (*Ovids Banquet* 59.4). Tantalus, father of Niobe and Pelops, when invited to feast with the gods, arrogantly tested their knowledge by serving up his own son as the banquet fare. When Ceres absent-mindedly ate Pelops's shoulder, the gods replaced it with one fashioned from ivory. A standard of beauty, yes, but also a deceptive and unwholesome banquet, indeed. (see *Metamorphoses* 6.404 ff.). Chapman may be mocking Marlowe's use of the epithet (*Hero* 1.65).

On the epigraph, see R. B. Waddington, "Chapman and Persius: The Epigraph to *Ovids Banquet of Sence*," *Review of English Studies*, 19 (1968): 158–62. While it has become commonplace to recognize that the *Coronet* of linked sonnets describes the form of a circle, the crown awarded to Philosophy, the full significance of the form still escapes notice. Donne's linked sequence, *La Corona*, requires a total of seven sonnets because that number symbolizes perfection and infinity in the Christian tradition postulated by the subject of the group. Chapman's circle suggests much the same qualities, but because he turns to Pythagorean traditions of numerology, the total number of sonnets must be ten. On the meaning of ten, see F. M. Cornford, "Mysticism and Science in the Pythagorian Tradition," *Classical Quarterly*, 17 (1923): 1 ff; Christopher Butler, *Number Symbolism* (London, 1970), pp. 5–6, 34. Further, according to Agrippa, the number has solar connotations, which is suggestive in view of the extensive sun symbolism in *Ovids Banquet*: "The number ten is *Circular*, and belongs to the *Sun*, after the same manner as unity," *Three Books Of Occult Philosophy*, trans. J.[ohn] F.[rench] (1651), 2.21. The imagistic and thematic relationships of the *Coronet* to *Ovids Banquet* are complex. For instance, the refraction image of the seemingly bleeding statues is itself refracted positively: "And as a purple tincture gyuen to Glasse / By cleere transmission of the Sunne doth taint / Opposed subiects: so my Mistresse face / Doth reuerence in her viewers browes depaint" (*Coronet* 8.5–8).

[69]See, e.g., MacLure, pp. 58–59, "The poet is now speaking in his own person, voicing his usual complaint against the 'outward' world of gold-seekers—and incidentally fishing for a noble patron."

sponsible for the art of love, embodies the side of Ovid's work with which Chapman has the least sympathy and which had generated the contemporary vogue for erotic elegiac and mythological verse. Chapman seems to be mimicking the complaints of such fashionable poets and, as he had in *The Shadow of Night*, exhibiting his own scorn for their—to him—unprincipled mendacity.

Both Chapman's productions are, in this sense, poems about poetry. The dogmatic stance had been assumed in the preface to *Ovids Banquet*:

> charms made of vnlerned characters are not consecrate by the Muses which are diuine artists, but by *Euippes* daughters, that challengd them with meere nature, whose brests J doubt not had beene well worthy commendation, if their comparison had not turned them into Pyes. [*Poems*, p. 49]

Chapman resorts to the true Ovid with a fable of metamorphosis to express his contempt for such unlettered, merely natural poets. The story of Evippe's daughters challenging the muses to a singing contest and being transformed to magpies for their presumption neatly parallels the competition between the children of Niobe and Latona, while making the terms of the offense yet more precise. George Sandys supplies an instructive seventeenth-century gloss on the singing contest:

> The Pye is the hieroglyphick of vnseasonable loquacity: deciphering those illiterate Poetasters (by the Satyre called the Pye-poets) who boast of their owne composures, and detract from the glory of the learned. Iustly therefore are the Pierides changed into those siluan scoulds, for their arrogancy and impudence: but aboue all for extolling the flagitious Gyants, and vilifying the Gods, since Poesy in regard of her originall, inspired into the mind from aboue, should chiefly, if not onely, be exercised in celebrating their praises, as here exemplified by the Muses.[70]

In other words, hymns are sung to Cynthia not Corinna, sonnets are sacrificed not on the altar of erotic love (*Ovids Banq.* 21.5) but to his mistress Philosophy.

Although *Ovids Banquet* is constructed to permit two differing perspectives on the action and interpretations of the meaning, I do not believe there can be any possibility that Chapman considered the perspectives equally valid. First, such latitude is entirely contrary to the conventions of the turning picture, which always presents a positive and a negative image—swan and crow, maiden and ape, lion and lamb, Gorgon and Mars—never two positive or neutral images. Second, it is contrary to the expectations created by Chapman's narrative strategy and by the total presentation of the poem itself. While Donne can observe of the Paracelsian controversy that "one soule thinkes one, and another

---

[70]*Ovid's Metamorphosis Englished*, trans. George Sandys (Oxford, 1632), p. 199.

way / Another thinkes, and 'tis an even lay," Chapman relies upon a dense context of traditional assumptions which do not permit such judgmental neutrality.

In a recent study Rhoda M. Ribner examines the technique and meaning of *Ovids Banquet* in the light of Renaissance emblem books, an approach certainly valid and pertinent for the technique of the poem, and which complements the above emphasis on illusion and perspective. Perhaps because she relies on secondhand studies of emblem books, however, Ribner penetrates no further than "a thematic concern with art and nature," and falls into the trap of failing to distinguish Chapman from Ovid.[71] Had Ribner not depended upon a modern-anthology edition of the poem, she might have perceived the care with which the original volume itself was designed as an entity and so noticed the actual

[71]Ribner, "The Compasse of This Curious Frame," pp. 233–58; quotation, p. 233.

Ouids Banquet of
SENCE.

A Coronet for his Miſtreſſe Phi-
loſophie, and his amorous
Zodiacke.

VVith a tranſlation of a Latine coppie, written
by a Fryer, Anno Dom. 1400.

*Quis leget hæc ? Nemo Hercule Nemo,
vel duo vel nemo : Perſius.*

*CONSCIA
SIBI RECTI*

AT LONDON,
Printed by I. R. for Richard Smith.
Anno Dom. 1595.

Title page, from Chapman, *Ovids Banquet of Sence.* Reproduced by permission of the Folger Library, Washington, D.C.

emblem apparently chosen for the volume by Chapman himself, which appears on the title page directly beneath the epigraph from Persius.[72]

The emblem depicts a straight stick half in water and half out, casting a bent reflection on the surface of the water, headed by the motto *sibi conscia recti*. MacLure has reminded us of McKerrow's conclusion that the emblem represents the author and cannot be explained as a printer's device. In calling attention to the emblem, MacLure connects it to the speaking-picture analogy but focuses upon the motto, which he uses as an epitome of Chapman's thought, rather than pursuing the visual relationship with *Ovids Banquet of Sence*.[73]

Chapman's emblem technically stands incomplete without verse to elucidate the lesson of picture and motto (as Chapman has designed it, of course, the entire poem acts as the explanatory verse); but the lack may be supplied by consulting Henry Peacham's *Minerva Britanna* (1612), which offers a version of the emblem corresponding closely to

---

[72]The volume is now readily available in the excellent Scolar Press facsimile, *Ovids Banquet of Sence, 1595* (Menston, Yorkshire, 1970). The question of the extent to which the entire volume was designed by Chapman as a single conception is raised anew by Alastair Fowler's numerological reading of *The Amorous Zodiac*. Fowler asserts: "In Chapman's 'The Amorous Zodiac,' a verbal narrative of the sun's course round the eleptic is so repeatedly and so closely related to the poet's progress through the poem that few sympathetic readers could miss his broad hints at a spatial organization," *Triumphal forms: Structural patterns in Elizabethan Poetry* (Cambridge, 1970), pp. 5, 140–46. Such a reading certainly is consonant with the one of *Ovids Banquet* which I have presented. Fowler passes too quickly, however, over the problem of authorship and the relationship with its source, Gilles Durant's *Le zodiac amoureux* (see Bartlett, *Poems*, p. 434).

Another emblem appears on the last page of the book, the familiar one of Time rescuing his daughter Truth from a cave. Here, although the initials *R.S.* make it virtually certain that the emblem is a device of the printer, Richard Smith, it might be noted that they are also the initials of Richard Stapleton, author of the first commendatory poem, and the man accepted as the author of *The Amorous Contention of Phillis and Flora*, sometime candidate for the authorship of *The Amorous Zodiac*.

[73]MacLure, p. 49. He uses the motto for the title of his concluding chapter, pp. 225–30.

"Nec te quaesiveris extra," from Henry Peacham, *Minerva Britanna or a Garden of Heroical Diuises*. Reproduced from the Scolar Press facsimile edition by permission of the Glasgow University Library.

Chapman's.[74] Again the picture represents the stick bent in water, and, as in Chapman's, blazoned across the upper part of the picture, a Latin motto *mihi conscia recti*. Beneath the picture, the verse:

> Although the staffe, within the river cleere
> Be straight as Arrow, in the *Persian* bow:
> Yet to the view, it crooked doth appeare,
> And one would sweare, that it indeed were so:
> So Soone the Sence deceiu'd, doth iudge amisse,
> And fooles will blame, whereas none error is.
> This staffe doth shew, how oft the honest mind,
> That meaneth well, and is of life vpright,
> Is rashly censur'd, by the vulgar blind,
> Through vaine *Opinion*: or vile envious spite:
> But if thou know'st, thy conscience cleere within,
> What others say, it matters not a pinne.[75]

The points of emphasis are exactly those which, more laboriously, we have inferred from *Ovid's Banquet*—the deceptiveness of knowledge based on sensory impressions, the erroneousness of the judgment which relies on such knowledge. The scorn exhibited for the rash censures of "the vulgar blind" even conveys the same tonal quality as Chapman's dismissal of the "empty, and dark spirits" of the "profane multitude," who are neatly tricked into exposing their failures of discernment as they cast aside reason to judge Chapman's poem on deceptive impressions.

The history of the stick bent in water goes back much further than the Renaissance emblem books. Since the beginnings of Greek philosophy it has recurred as one of the inevitable *topoi* in discussions of epistemology and of the reliability of sense impressions.[76] Plato mentions it in *The Republic*: "And the same things appear bent and straight to those who view them in water and out".[77] Lucretius particularizes it

---

[74]On Peacham and his emblem book, see Freeman, *English Emblem Books*, pp. 68–82.

[75]Peacham, *Minerva Britanna*, 1612, p. 67. MacLure, p. 225 n., identifies *Aeneid* 1.604 as the source of Chapman's motto. Peacham's glosses offer analogues from Persius, Ovid, and St. Paul, suggesting that versions of this tag may be as commonplace as the image it illustrates. Julius Wilhelm Zincgreff acknowledges *The Aeneid* for the motto, although his emblem employs the variant image of an oar bent in water; see *Emblematum Ethico-Politicorum Centuria* (Frankfort, 1619), no. 59. Zacharias Heyns, *Emblemata, Emblemes Chrestienes et Morales* (Rotterdam, 1625), 3: 13, has the bent-stick emblem with the motto, "Fallit imago."

[76]The durability of the image can be substantiated by its frequent appearance in Colin M. Turbayne, *The Myth of Metaphor* (New Haven, 1962); see pp. 103, 114–15, 204, 207–8. Turbayne, a contemporary philosopher, attempts to divest metaphysics of mechanical metaphor and substitute the metaphor of visual language.

[77]Plato, *The Republic*, trans. Paul Shorey, Loeb Classical Library (Cambridge, Mass., 1935), 10.602C. Cf. the Cornford translation, which, tending to make figurative implications explicit, renders the passage, "a straight stick looks bent when part of it is under water." *The Republic of Plato*, trans. F. M. Cornford (New York, 1945), 10.602.

as an oar broken below the waterline (*De Rerum Natura* 4.438 ff.). In this guise it is best known through Pyrrhonic skepticism as a stock visual-illusion problem, along with the changing colors of a pigeon's neck and the square tower which appears round from a distance.[78] Since many of these classical loci occur in the writings of authors revered by the humanists, we are not surprised to find a considerable currency given to the image in the Renaissance. Like Chapman and Peacham, Montaigne had connected it with opinion and judgment: "To judge of high and great matters, a high and great minde is required; otherwise we attribute that vice vnto them, which indeed is ours. A straight oare being vnder water, seemeth to be crooked. It is no matter to see a thing, but the matter is how a man dooth see the same."[79]

We should remember that the bent stick is no philosopher's invention but a real problem of perception and, therefore, of moment to both artists and optical theorists. It is instructive to learn from Diogenes Laertius that Pyrrho, the founder of academic skepticism, began his career as "a poor and unknown painter" by whom some "indifferent" works survive (*Lives* 4.62), and to reflect that the third trope of Aenesidemus is based on differences in the senses. "That the senses differ from one another is obvious. Thus, to the eye paintings seem to have recesses and projections, but not so to the touch."[80] In optics both John Pecham, author of *Perspectiva communis*, and Roger Bacon offer explanations for

[78]In the first century B.C. Aenesidemus formulated these traditional problems into his famous ten tropes or modes, loose categories of sensory-data problems designed to marshal support for a relativistic conception of knowledge. Sextus Empiricus presents the bent oar in the fifth trope (*Outlines of Pyrrhonism* 1.119); for Diogenes Laertius it illustrates the seventh, which includes problems of appearance involving distance, position, and place (*Lives* 9.85–86). It is evident from the dialogue in Cicero's *Academica* that the pigeon's neck and the bent oar are old chestnuts in such discussions (2.7.19; 2.25.79); see also the note in the edition of the *Academica* by J. S. Reid (1885; reprint ed., Hildesheim, 1966), p. 269. To find the bent oar in Philo's allegorical commentary on Noah's drunkenness seems an oddity; however, Philo discusses drunkenness as illustrating the inconstancy of impressions, borrowing from the ten tropes for data (*De Ebrietate* 181–82). Seneca lists the bent oar as one of his *Quaestiones Naturales* (1.3.9); and Macrobius finds the problem to be a mandate for the use of reason (*Saturnalia* 7.14.19).

[79]Montaigne, *The Essayes*, trans. John Florio (1603), 1.40, "That the taste of goods or evilles doth greatly depend on the opinion we have of them." The standard authority on scepticism in the Renaissance is Richard H. Popkin, *The History of Scepticism from Erasmus to Descartes* (1960; reprint ed., New York, 1964); for Montaigne, see chap. 3. Also useful are the studies by D. C. Allen, *Doubt's Boundless Sea: Scepticism and Faith in the Renaissance* (Baltimore, 1964), and Eugene F. Rice, Jr., *The Renaissance Idea of Wisdom* (Cambridge, Mass., 1958).

For a few later examples of the bent-stick *topos*, see Thomas Fuller, *Collected Sermons*, ed. J. E. Bailey and W. E. A. Axon (London, 1891), 1: 546; *The Philosophical Works of Descartes*, trans. E. S. Haldane and G. R. T. Ross (Cambridge, 1912), 2: 193–94; Bishop Berkeley, *Three Dialogues between Hylas and Philonous*, ed. C. M. Turbayne, Library of Liberal Arts, no. 39 (New York, 1954), p. 85; Tennyson, *The Higher Pantheism*. This poem was read, appropriately, at the first meeting of the Metaphysical Society; see Christopher Ricks, ed., *The Poems of Tennyson* (London, 1969), pp. 1204–5.

[80]Sextus Empiricus, *Outlines of Pyrrhonism*, trans. R. G. Bury, Loeb Classical Library (Cambridge, Mass., 1933) 1.92.

the appearance of the object partly in water and partly in air; and, on the evidence of Thomas Harriot's unpublished papers, we know that Chapman's friend studied the angles of refraction of *baculus in aqua*.[81]

Aside from the practical experiments of these scientists, it is possible to discern a fairly consistent intellectual bent in the sticks here bundled together. The philosophic contexts tend to be skeptical or idealistic, strains, of course, which are interwoven in the dialogues of Plato; thus the first example from *The Republic* assumes more than a chronological priority in the survey. Let us return again to the passage:

> And the same things appear bent and straight to those who view them in water and out, or concave and convex, owing to similar errors of vision about colours, and there is obviously every confusion of this sort in our own souls. And so scene-painting in its exploitation of this weakness of our nature falls nothing short of witchcraft, and so do jugglery and many other contrivances.[82]

The paragraph occurs in a context of which no serious Renaissance poet could have been ignorant, the attack on dramatic poetry.[83] Earlier in the dialogue Plato distinguished three kinds of poetry—pure dramatic poetry, pure narrative poetry, and a mixed type with narrative and dramatic passages interspersed, e.g., epic—and seemed to exclude all dramatic poetry from the republic (3.392C–398B). In this later section, he returns to the point and elaborates upon his reasons for his dislike: dramatic poetry appeals to the emotions, not to reason, and thus encourages the indulgence of baser emotions which serve to undermine the character. The analogy of the bent stick is used to explain the effect of such poetry upon human nature. Like other illusionistic skills, magic, scene-painting, sleight-of-hand, which deceive the senses, dramatic poetry appeals to the emotions. Just as sensory illusions can be corrected by the reasoning faculty, so illusory exaggeration of the emotions should be checked by reason; but the whole purpose of the dramatic poet is to encourage sympathetic identification with, rather than detached judgment of, emotions portrayed.

E. H. Gombrich has argued cogently that Plato's diatribe against mimetic art reflects his dissatisfaction with changes of artistic representation occurring in his own culture, the movement away from the conceptual, iconic style of Egyptian art to the illusionistic, mimetic technique of Zeuxis and Apelles, a movement paralleled in poetry by the narrative techniques of Homer or the mimetic realism of Euripides.[84]

[81]On Bacon, see Turbayne, *Myth of Metaphor*, p. 152; on Pecham, see *John Pecham and the Science of Optics: Perspectiva cummunis*, ed. and trans. David C. Lindberg (Madison, Wis., 1970), pp. 216–17; on Harriot, see Rukeyser, *Traces*, p. 181.

[82]*The Republic* (trans. Shorey) 10.602C.

[83]See, e.g., Bernard Weinberg, *A History of Literary Criticism in the Italian Renaissance* (Chicago, 1961), 1: 251–52.

[84]Gombrich, *Art and Illusion*, pp. 116–45.

A similar artistic cycle may be observed during Chapman's own lifetime. Roy Strong has described the shift in the artistic style of portraiture from the Tudor, which is primarily iconic and heraldic, emphasizing the social position and status of the subject rather than his individual personality, to the Jacobean, which is psychological,[85] stressing precisely the qualities Plato would regard as accidental and transitory. A related movement in poetic modes may be discerned, away from the conceptual, iconic, narratives of Spenser and Chapman to the dramatic, psychologically mimetic mode of Donne and the other metaphysicals.

Pursuing Plato's discrimination of the three kinds of poetry and his analogy about sensory deception, one could say that the use of a controlling narrator or authorial presence corresponds to the presence of the rational faculty which interprets the impressions received by the senses. From this viewpoint, dramatic poetry, with no intrusive controlling intelligence, would be the most pernicious form, which presumably explains its banishment; the mixed form and the straight narrative would, by successive degrees, be less subject to this criticism in inverse proportion to the presence of the narrator's controlling intelligence. The point is worth reflecting upon, since it allows us to perceive the relative eccentricity of Chapman's narrative method in *Ovids Banquet of Sence*. Most of Chapman's long poems fall into the middle category of the mixed mode, with dramatic speeches interspersed in the narration; but typically the narrator is a strong, controlling presence, with any dramatic speakers carefully designated and subordinated to the overall design.[86] The narrator of *Ovids Banquet* is extraordinarily self-effacing by comparison with the other poems. This is literally true in the allocation of lines; Ovid's dialogue totals half again as many stanzas as the number assigned to the narrator, creating in the reader by sheer bulk, as well as didactic tenor, the impression that Ovid should receive a corresponding amount of attention. It is the mixture of media, one recalls, the thrusting of the stick halfway in water, which produces in the beholder the illusion of crookedness, an illusion which can be dispelled only by reason and knowledge.

[85]Roy Strong, *The English Icon: Elizabethan and Jacobean Portraiture* (New York, 1969).

[86]The hymns in *The Shadow of Night* are entirely in the poet's voice; the sestiads of *Hero and Leander* have increasingly more narration and less dialogue, although throughout Chapman employs dialogue more sparingly than does Marlowe in the first two sestiads. In the *Teares of Peace*, the poet, Homer, and Peace all have dialogue, and the body of the poem is entirely dialogue. But with the poet as one of the speakers, the point of view differs considerably from the handling in *Ovids Banquet*; also the central dialogue is framed and controlled by the induction, invocation, and conclusion. *An Epicede or Funerall Song* for Prince Henry is almost wholly narrated. There are speeches by Fever and Henry, and a supposed narrative shift to "Muses lachrimae," but the last results in little discernible difference in mode. The frame story of *Eugenia* is narrated, but the vigils are spoken by Eugenia, Fame, and the last sung by Poesie and the chorus of muses; as with *The Teares of Peace*, the personifications are so transparently nonrepresentational that the problems of dramatic dialogue do not arise. With *Andromeda Liberata* narration again dominates over dialogue.

If, as I argue, Chapman brings to his skirmish with the erotic Ovidians the heavy artillery of Plato's condemnation of dramatic poetry, what are we to make of sonnet 10 in *The Coronet*, which praises the greatness of classical drama and urges its revival while condemning the contemporary theatrical abuses? First, there is nothing new about the probability that Chapman, like any other humanist, used his classical proof-texts selectively, either not noticing inconvenient and contradictory materials or simply ignoring them for tactical purposes. Which is to say, he found it convenient to apply the weight of Plato's censure to erotic poetry of the mixed mode; he intended to extend it no further. Certainly he would have disavowed the attack on Homer. Second, Plato talks about the *abuse* of the dramatic mode, permitting the inference that it could be employed unobjectionably. Chapman believed that the great classical dramatists achieved this, and that he could emulate their achievement.

Continuing his argument that drama panders to the undesirable side of human nature, Plato defines the rational and the irrational characteristics of the mind, impulses which are mixed in most men, charging that, because such imitation is easier and more assured of success, dramatists represent only the irrational:

> "And does not the fretful part of us present many and varied occasions for imitation, while the intelligent and temperate disposition, always remaining approximately the same, is neither easy to imitate nor to be understood when imitated, especially by a nondescript mob assembled in the theatre? For the representation imitates a type that is alien to them." "By all means."
> "And is it not obvious that the nature of the mimetic poet is not related to this better part of the soul and his cunning is not framed to please it, if he is to win favor with the multitude, but is devoted to the fretful and complicated type of character because it is easy to imitate?"[87]

Surely Chapman's condemnation of servile dramatists "That liue by soothing moods, and seruing tymes" (*Coronet* 10.12) echoes Plato's contempt for those who earn the applause of the ignorant mob. Critics of Chapman's own tragedies have amply documented, indeed sometimes exaggerated, the Stoic element which becomes prominent with the passive protagonists, Clermont, Cato, Chabot, of the post-Bussy dramas. But while the particulars of ethical code may be derived from Stoic contexts, the aesthetic problem of presenting dramatically the character of a temperate and rational man had been formulated for Chapman by Plato.

In *Ovids Banquet of Sence* Chapman imitates "the fretful part" of man in dramatic narrative, writing with the full expectation that many of his readers will misapprehend the imitation. Although he firmly locates the poem in an interpretative context—by the abuse of vision both in action

---

[87]*The Republic* (trans. Shorey) 10.604E–605A.

and intellectual hierarchy, by Ovid's abuse of relational and mental hierarchy, by the perspective metaphor, by the bent-stick emblem, and by his entire manipulation of point of view—he expects that many will lack the "meanes to sound the philosophical conceits." To a modern audience this readiness to permit the deception of the unwary for illustrative purposes, making them unwitting exempla of the poem's thesis about sensory deception, perhaps will smack of coterie verse, written only to gratify an attitude of superiority assumed by the poet and his friends. Such a response would be mistaken, for the only admission requirements to this inner circle are learning and reason. Chapman's poem implies a definition of poetry that evolves from the humanist tradition of *ut pictura poesis* and that is still consonant with the general vision of Horace's *Ars poetica* from which the catch phrase is lifted. The "*Enargia*, or cleerenes of representation," required in "absolute" poems and paintings alike is a matter of viewing experience with mind and body together, intelligently and with a moral responsibility—to paraphrase Arnold, of seeing life steadily and seeing it whole. By projecting such a definition and upholding it as a standard, Chapman lays fair claim to having written an "absolute" poem.

FIVE
AN
OVIDIAN
EPIC:
HERO
AND
LEANDER

Chapman's continuation of the Marlowe *Hero and Leander* has had two eloquent champions: C. S. Lewis put his considerable reputation behind a defense of the poem as poetry by declaring it a "great, neglected work," and—paraphrasing Chapman's own estimation of his *Homer*—"the work that he was born to do."[1] In an impressive examination of the intellectual content D. J. Gordon has demonstrated the density, the complexity, and coherence of the ideas underlying the poem.[2] Nevertheless Chapman's continuation remains undervalued, disliked, and inappropriately compared to Marlowe's portion. Some of this reaction, I believe, is the result of inattention to the kind of poem Chapman shaped. Generic choice always was a significant matter for Chapman; and attentiveness to the implications of genre frequently can direct our responses into the most rewarding interpretative channels.

Neither Marlowe nor Chapman intended his work to be received as a translation of the Musaeus *Hero and Leander*. Whereas Musaeus was the primary source for their versions, the story of Hero and Leander, like that of Troilus and Cressida, had attained mythic status and was immensely popular in sixteenth- and seventeenth-century poetry;[3] consequently, when Marlowe took up the story, he had no compunctions about adding to or subtracting from the original. Much later, when Chapman published an actual translation of Musaeus, he addressed the question of its relationship to "that partly excellent Poem of Maister Marloe's. For your all one, the Works are in nothing alike; a different character being held through both the style, matter, and invention."[4] The distinction holds as

---

[1] C. S. Lewis, *English Literature in the Sixteenth Century* (Oxford, 1954), pp. 488, 513.

[2] D. J. Gordon, "Chapman's *Hero and Leander*," *English Miscellany*, 5 (1954): 41–92.

[3] See Douglas Bush, *Mythology and the Renaissance Tradition*, rev. ed. (New York, 1963), pp. 123–24.

[4] I quote throughout chap. 5 from the edition by Richard Hooper, *Homer's Batrachomyomachia*, 2d ed. (London, 1888), p. 213 (hereafter referred to as Hooper). The Hesiod was published in 1616. Elizabeth Donno, *Elizabethan Minor Epics* (New York, 1963), p. 16, speculates that it was translated before Chapman completed *Hero and Leander*.

true for his continuation as for Marlowe's beginning; and, by assaying the differences among the three versions, we can perhaps better appreciate their respective individuality.

The story of Hero and Leander is not a product of Greek classicism but comes from the Alexandrian period. Musaeus, called "the Grammarian," composed his *Hero and Leander* in the late fifth century A.D., five centuries after Ovid included their imaginary love letters in the *Heroides*. But, in a historical accident similar to the misdating of the *Hermetica*, the naïveté of the Renaissance humanists permitted a false identification of this Musaeus with the legendary Musaeus from the dawn of civilization, moving the composition of the poem back a millenium in time.[5] For this reason Chapman titles his translation *The Divine Poem of Musaeus. First of all Bookes*, and supplies a fabulous biographical note: "He lived in the time of Orpheus, and is said to be one of them that went the Famous Voyage to Colchos for the Golden Fleece. He wrote of the Gods' Genealogy before any other; and invented the Sphere" (Hooper, p. 215).

The *Hero and Leander*, as its hexameters, invocation, and style indicate, is a small epic; this, combined with the spurious mantle of antiquity which invested its supposed author with quasi-religious authority, caused it to receive an unwarranted reverence from Renaissance humanists. Scaliger notoriously preferred it to Homer; Chapman notes that "all the most learned" judge it the "incomparable Love-Poem of the world"; Puttenham balances Homer and Musaeus in the same breath, finding "both of them *Heroick*, and to none ill edification." Drayton, in a commendatory poem on Chapman's translations, imagines: "In blest Elysium, (in a place most fit) / Under that tree due to the Delphian God, / MUSAEUS and that ILIAD SINGER sit, / And near to them that noble Hesiod."[6] The positioning suggests that Homer and Musaeus are the same kind of poet, while Hesiod is not. In the eyes of the Renaissance, then, Musaeus had written an epic or heroic poem.

---

[5]The great scholar Isaac Casaubon was the first man to recognize both errors. See *The Poems: Christopher Marlowe*, ed. Millar MacLure, The Revels Edition (London, 1968), p. xxvi, n.; and Frances A. Yates, *Giordano Bruno and the Hermetic Tradition* (Chicago, 1964), pp. 398–403.

[6]*Select Translations from Scaliger's Poetics*, trans. F. M. Padelford, Yale Studies in English, no. 26 (New York, 1905), pp. 15–16; Chapman, "To the Commune Reader," in Hooper, p. 213; Puttenham, *The Arte of English Poesie*, ed. G. D. Willcock and A. Walker (Cambridge, 1936), p. 41; Drayton, "To My Worthy Friend Mr. George Chapman, and his Translated Hesiod," in Hooper, p. 146. Harry Levin, *The Overreacher* (1952; reprint ed., Boston, 1964), p. 139, observed that the Renaissance poets must have thought Musaeus brought them into communion with the elemental source of poetry.

Marlowe consciously detaches his poem from this high mimetic mode.[7] In referring to Leander, "Whose tragedie diuine *Musaeus* soong" (52), he makes it evident that his retelling is not intended to strike a tragic note by omitting an invocation and apologizing comfortably for his earthbound muse:

> my rude pen
> Can hardly blazon foorth the loues of men,
> Much lesse of powerfull gods; let it suffise,
> That my slacke muse sings of *Leanders* eies.
>
> [Marlowe *Hero* 1.69–72]

Marlowe further muted the tragic tone by conflating sources other than Musaeus, although he was undoubtedly the primary source. A number of details and phrasings indicate that Marlowe relied to a considerable extent on *Heroides* 18 and 19, as well.[8] The vastly altered tone and emphasis of his narrative, however, reveal that his vision of the nobly suffering heroines was colored by the *Amores*, which he had already translated.[9] Thus, in his hands, *Hero and Leander* becomes a tale of Ovidian eroticism crossbred with Italianate romance; and the aggressively masculine sexual attitude in Ovid's erotic poems may account for shifting the focus from Hero to Leander.

Marlowe makes his antiheroic attitude integral to the conception of the story by systematically eliminating serious elements. The context of social responsibility is minimized. Musaeus's Hero twice stated her sense of obligation to her parents; Marlowe omits both passages. Leander is provided with a father unmentioned by Musaeus, but an acquiescent one who only mildly rebukes his son. It is symptomatic that Marlowe eliminates the famous torch by which Hero guides Leander on his swim to Sestos, since the torch has been a central component in all serious treatments of the story: for Musaeus it emphasized the pathos of a love unsanctioned by the proper marriage torches; Fulgentius allegorized it as sexual passion; and, as in Donne's epigram on the lovers, the

---

[7]Harry Levin, p. 140, calls Marlowe's tone "mock-heroic." His view has been extended by Erich Segal, "Hero and Leander: Gongora and Marlowe," *Comparative Literature*, 15 (1963): 338–56.

[8]See Donno, p. 8 and n. Douglas Bush enumerates some of the borrowings from *Heroides* in "Notes on Marlowe's *Hero and Leander*," *PMLA*, 44 (1929): 760–64. For the Musaeus text used by Marlowe, see T. W. Baldwin, "Marlowe's Musaeus," *Journal of English and Germanic Philology*, 54 (1955): 478–85.

[9]Although *Hero and Leander* was not published until 1598, it was entered in the Stationer's Register on 28 September 1593, four months after Marlowe's death; literary allusions establish that it was circulated extensively in ms. from 1593 to 1598. See MacLure, *Marlowe*, pp. xxiii–xxiv; and Bush, *Mythology*, pp. 122–23. There is general agreement that Ovid's *Elegies* date from Marlowe's Cambridge period (ca. 1580–87).

flaming torch is necessary for a schematic treatment of the four elements.[10]

Marlowe's poem is not devoid of a moral perspective, of course. He tags Leander as "a bold, sharpe Sophister," dwells on the offensiveness of his publicly wearing the sacred ring with which Hero vowed religious chastity; and, using the platonic myth so popular in the Renaissance, describes the impassioned Leander as "a hote prowd horse" who "breakes the raines / Spits foorth the ringled bit."[11] But the societal viewpoint is invoked more for an ironic than for a censorious effect; like the impudently amoral protagonists in Donne's *Elegies*, which evolve in large part from Marlowe's translations of Ovid, Leander here seems set against conventional behavior for shock effect.

Chapman responds to the uncompleted Marlowe poem by seeking to restore the high seriousness. His dedication to Lady Walsingham takes pains to distinguish this from any ordinary love story, urging her to accept it as "a serious argument": "being drawne by strange instigation to employ some of my serious time in so trifeling a subject, which yet made the first Author, diuine Musaeus, eternall" (*Poems*, p. 132). All Chapman's major poems preceding *Hero and Leander* record his reaction against the current fashion of the Ovidian erotic, mythological narrative: the two hymns in *The Shadow of Night* cryptically attack Shakespeare's *Venus and Adonis*, while asserting Chapman's preference for the philosophic Ovid of the allegorized metamorphoses; in *Ovids Banquet of Sence*, Chapman satirizes the fad and ridicules the image of the erotic Ovid by making him protagonist of a seduction poem. With the opportunity to change the direction of Marlowe's fortuitously unfinished poem, the most famous and influential of the kind, Chapman must have seen the possibility, not only of restoring appropriate dignity to Musaeus, but also of presenting the "correct" kind of Ovidian love story by modulating from the *Amores* to the *Metamorphoses*.

As a result Chapman gives his poem an epic treatment far exceeding the suggestions in Musaeus. There is, first of all, the matter of length. Chapman devoted 1,600 lines to the portion of the narrative which Musaeus had done in 40. To conclude simply that Chapman was incompetent at narration would miss the point. When Chapman published, nearly two decades later, his own translation of Musaeus, it extended to only 480 lines, a quite moderate rate of expansion considering the Renaissance taste for copious invention. Elizabeth Donno suggests that the size of the poem results from the tender-hearted author's reluctance

---

[10]See Musaeus, ll. 292–305; Fulgentius's interpretation was given contemporary currency by Abraham Fraunce, for which see Bush, *Mythology*, pp. 123–24. Donne's epigram, "Both rob'd of aire, we both lye in one ground, / Both whom one fire had burnt, one water drownd," is placed by John Shawcross in the period ca. 1587–95; see *The Complete Poetry of John Donne*, (Garden City, New York: Anchor, 1967), p. 411.

[11]Marlowe, *Hero and Leander* 1.197; 2.108–16, 141–45. For the platonic myth, as used by Shakespeare, see R. P. Miller, "Venus, Adonis, and the Horses," *ELH*, 19 (1952): 249–64.

to reach the tragic conclusion;[12] but, Dickensian theories of creativity to the contrary, the length obviously lays a claim to epic stature, as does the division of the poem into six books with arguments preceding each book. The divisions of the poem are called "sestiads," implying the epic of Sestos, just as Chapman would insist later on the plural in the title of his Homer translation, *Illiads*.

Modern editions permit us to forget that Marlowe's beginning was split by Chapman into two sestiads with prefatory arguments; if we read the Marlowe as it was printed in the first edition of 1598, as a continuous and unadorned narrative, the contrast between their differing conceptions would be even more apparent.[13] The deliberate shifting of tone at the beginning of the third sestiad underscores Chapman's epic aspiration: "More harsh (at lest more hard) more graue and hie / Our subiect runs and our *sterne Muse* must flie." C. S. Lewis has remarked the similarity to *Paradise Lost*, Book 9; and, as we know Chapman's verse had some influence on Milton, the resemblance may not be accidental.[14] Marlowe's beginning may have precluded the possibility of a formal invocation, but the passage describing the effect of Marlowe's spirit upon Chapman's imagination plainly serves as a surrogate: "thou most strangely-intellectuall fire, / That proper to my soule hast power t'inspire / Her burning faculties." With these and other conventions— most notably the use of epic similes, the descents of goddesses in the third and fourth sestiads, the extended allegorical description of Hero's scarf with details which suggest the shield of Achilles—the invention and amplification constantly assert an epic stature.[15]

The invention which does not serve the generic function largely amplifies Chapman's thematic conception, building upon small suggestions in Marlowe's portion to restore the societal context with materials derived, as Gordon has shown, from Cartari's handbook of mythology.[16] The most unexpected invention in the poem occurs as the denoue-

---

[12]Donno, p. 16.

[13]The first edition was published by Edward Blunt; the Marlowe-Chapman ed. followed later in the same year, published by Paul Lynley. All modern editions of the Marlowe that I have seen follow the form imposed by Chapman. A facsimile of the first, edited by Louis L. Martz, has been published in the Folger Facsimile series (New York, 1972). Martz and Richard Neuse, "Atheism and Some Functions of Myth in Marlowe's *Hero and Leander*," *Modern Language Quarterly*, 31 (1970): 424–39, take the extreme view of regarding the Marlowe as a complete poem.

[14]Lewis, *English Literature*, p. 515. In a forthcoming study of Milton's prosody, Edward Weismiller details the influence of Chapman's Homer translations upon Milton's epic; see *The Prosody of the English Poems*, vol. 6 of *A Variorum Commentary on the Poems of John Milton* (New York, 1970—).

[15]MacLure, *Marlowe*, p. xxvii, comments briefly on the epic invention. For the scarf, see Bush, *Mythology*, p. 215, n. 22. Chapman's translation of *Achilles Shield* was published in 1598.

[16]D. J. Gordon, "Chapman's use of Cartari in the Fifth Sestiad of *Hero and Leander*," *Modern Language Review*, 39 (1944): 280–85; and "Chapman's *Hero and Leander*," pp. 43–54.

ment after the deaths of both lovers. Chapman creates the original myth of Neptune, motivated by pity, transforming the pair into goldfinches or, as Chapman calls them, "Thistle-warps." Even though the mode of the poem is epic, the ending comes from Ovidian metamorphosis.

All Chapman's critics, of course, have noticed these factors, although not all have taken the epic pretensions seriously enough to wonder why Chapman's conclusion is Ovidian rather than Homeric. Millar MacLure, who has thought about the apparent incongruity of elements, speculates that Chapman may have consciously sought an effect of bathos.[17] I believe, rather, that any dissonance between epic and metamorphosis exists only in the mind of the modern reader. Some implicit support for this position has been lent by recent Ovidian scholarship, most particularly by that of Brooks Otis, who has reexamined assumptions about the form of the *Metamorphoses*. Otis concludes that the poem is not simply a concatenation of tales with a mechanical and superficial relationship, but an epic with a coherent structure and a unified succession of episodes, motifs, and ideas.[18]

Chapman's tendency to overread Ovid and to overvalue his writings as a repository of "philosophy" would have worked to exaggerate and even distort the inherent epic qualities the poem does possess. The *Metamorphoses* does not figure largely in the voluminous sixteenth-century critical discussions of epic, but enough circumstantial evidence exists to allow us a reasonable inference about the generic status of the poem in Chapman's time. The epic was supposed to contain all the wisdom, learning, and science of its age; and the allegorical interpretations of Ovid's tales, moral, philosophic, even alchemical, certainly accustomed Renaissance readers to find that kind of depth.[19] The length and scope of the poem, from creation to a dynastic prophecy of Rome's future, wholly accorded with the vision of the religious, encyclopedic, and nationalistic elements which the Renaissance saw as united in epic. Arthur Golding's "Epistle to Leicester," accompanying his 1567 translation of the *Metamorphoses*, expounds upon Ovid's consonance with Christian morality and history alike. Agreeing with Ovid's own claims to prophetic stature, Golding compares him extensively to Moses, who was for Christians the first and greatest of literary creators:

> What man is he but would suppose the author of this booke
> The first foundation of his woorke from Moyses wryghtings tooke?

[17]MacLure, *Marlowe*, p. xxvii.

[18]Brooks Otis, *Ovid as an Epic Poet* (Cambridge, 1966); see also, e.g., T. F. Brunner, "The Function of the Simile in Ovid's *Metamorphoses*," *Classical Journal*, 61 (1966): 354–63.

[19]For a concise summary of Renaissance concepts of epic, see Northrop Frye, *Five Essays on Milton's Epics* (London, 1966), pp. 1–15; for "Undermeanings in Ovid," see D. C. Allen, *Mysteriously Meant* (Baltimore, 1970), pp. 163–99.

Not only in effect he dooth with Genesis agree,
But also in the order of creation, save that hee
Makes no distinction of the days.[20]

Golding undertakes to show further "How Ovids scantlings with the
whole true patterne doo agree" ("Epistle," line 379), maintaining that
"partly in the outward phrase, but more in verie deede, / He seemes according too the sense of scripture too proceede" ("Epistle," lines 415–
16). Beyond the creation of the world, Golding doggedly surveys the
familiar correspondences in the stories of man's creation, comparing the
Golden Age and Eden, the falls into sinfulness, the punishments by flood,
and the subsequent restorations of order in the postdeluvian world.

If Ovid can be seen as a Roman Moses whose vision of history penetrated the "whole true patterne," it is also evident that the critical con-
troversies generated by the need to justify the Italian romance epics
against the strictures of Aristotelean theory served to evolve a flexible
conception of the epic which easily encompasses the *Metamorphoses*.
The key issue turned on the unities, especially on the question of single
action or multiple action with digressive technique; and, in addition to
the obvious appeal Ovid would have to the taste for the marvellous
developed by Ariosto, it is suggestive that Geraldi Cinthio could cite the
Metamorphoses approvingly for the variety of its content.[21]

Classical scholars still disagree as to whether the Pythagorean oration
in Book 15 of the *Metamorphoses* provides a seriously intended philosophic rationale for all Ovid's myths or merely a convenient focal point,
or organizational center.[22] Renaissance readers had no such doubts.[23]
Golding believes that the interpretative key to the entire poem may be
found in Book 15: "The oration of Pithagoras implyes / A sum of all the
former woorke" ("Epistle," lines 288–89). For Golding "this same dark
Philosophie of turned shapes" is consistent throughout. The transformations are to be understood figuratively: "Not that they lost theyr manly

---

[20]*"Shakespeare's Ovid": Arthur Golding's Translation of the Metamorphoses*, ed. W. H. D.
Rouse (Carbondale, Ill.: Centaur Classics, 1961), ll. 342–46. See also Angus Fletcher, *The Prophetic Moment: An Essay on Spenser* (Chicago, 1971), pp. 90–92, who discusses "The Ovidian
Matrix." For Moses as poet and the implications of Golding's phrase "the whole true pattern," see Maren-Sofie Røstvig, "Structure as Prophecy: the influence of biblical exegesis
upon theories of literary structure," in *Silent Poetry: Essays in Numerological Analysis*, ed.
Alastair Fowler (New York, 1970), pp. 32–72.

[21]E. M. W. Tillyard quotes Cinthio's observation in *The English Epic and its Background*
(1954; reprint ed., New York, 1966), p. 227. For the whole epic controversy, see Bernard
Weinberg, *A History of Literary Criticism in the Italian Renaissance*, 2 vols (Chicago, 1961).

[22]See R. A. Swanson, "Ovid's Pythagorean Essay," and "Ovid's Theme of Change," *Classical Journal*, 53 (1958–59): 21–24, 201–5; and W. C. Stephens, "The Function of Religious
and Philosophical Ideas in Ovid's *Metamorphoses*" (Ph.D. diss., Princeton University,
1957). Otis, pp. 296–302, finds literary art but no philosophic depth in the oration.

[23]See Fletcher, p. 91.

shape as too the outward showe: / But for that in their brutish brestes most beastly lustes did growe." And further:

> But if wee suffer fleshly lustes as lawlesse Lordes too reigne,
> Than are we beastes, wee are no men, wee have our name in vaine.
> And if wee be so drownd in vice that feeling once bee gone,
> Then may it well of us bee sayd, wee are a block or stone.
> This surely did the Poets meene when in such sundry wyse
> The pleasant tales of turned shapes they studyed too devyse.
>
> ["Preface," *Met.* 111–16]

Golding, we may surmise, must have been predisposed to find philosophic profundity in the oration because of the enormous reputation of Pythagoras. Just as Musaeus was considered the first poet, so Pythagoras was acknowledged to be the first of all philosophers. Legend, in fact, credited him with inventing the name *philosopher*.[24] In the Renaissance, although Pythagoras was notorious for his beliefs in the transmigration of souls, in vegetarianism, and in the science of emblems, his system of macro- and microcosmic correspondences always returns to numerology, since number is form.[25]

The problem of the Pythagorean oration and the entire mythology of Pythagoras are germane to the Renaissance understanding of Ovid because, if the *Metamorphoses* is read as hidden philosophy, then the oration does become the conceptual center of the poem. And in writing his own Ovidian epic Chapman creates a formal and thematic analogue to the oration, what we might call a Pythagorean sestiad. He does not present the doctrine directly as Ovid did, although of course Ovid would have seemed direct only to a degree. Insofar as the deeper meanings which were attributed to Ovid could not be found directly in his poem, it was concluded that he presented them by indirection, obscurely and cryptically. Chapman, reading and writing with the perspective of a platonic mystagogue, veils his meaning, simultaneously concealing and revealing.[26]

---

[24]S. K. Heninger, Jr., "Some Renaissance Versions of the Pythagorean Tetrad," *Studies in the Renaissance*, 8 (1961): 13.

[25]See, for instance, the entry for Pythagoras in Sir Thomas Elyot's 1538 *Dictionary* (quoted by Heninger, p. 7): "An excellente Phylosopher, whose Phylosophye was in mysticalle sentences [he refers to the ethical precepts], and alsoo in the Scyence of noumbers." We now have Heninger's full study of Renaissance Pythagoreanism and its literary consequences: *Touches of Sweet Harmony: Pythagorean Cosmology and Renaissance Poetics* (San Marino, California, 1974). Valuable background may be found in W. K. C. Guthrie, *A History of Greek Philosophy*, vol. 1, *The Earlier Presocratics and the Pythagoreans* (Cambridge, 1967); see especially 1: 206–8, on the world as a *kosmos*; 1: 212–15, on numbers and the *kosmos*; 1: 220–26, on musical harmony; 1: 229–51, on all things as number; 1: 295–301, on the harmony of the spheres; 1: 306–19, on the soul as a harmony; 1: 336–40, on the nature of time. For Pythagoras in the tradition of Renaissance occultism, see Yates, *Giordano Bruno*.

[26]On this attitude, see especially Edgar Wind, *Pagan Mysteries in the Renaissance* (New Haven, 1958), and chap. 1 above.

D. J. Gordon has explicated the meaning of form in *Hero and Leander*, commencing with an exposition of the allegorical goddess Ceremony, who appears to Leander in sestiad 3 and who represents "ciuill forms."[27] After Gordon, we may trace this theme through the poem: Hero's loss of identity, when her inner being is at variance with the forms of society, is strikingly imaged by the action of concealing herself with a shapeless, black robe:

No forme was seene, where forme held all her sight:
But like an Embrion that saw neuer light:
Or like a scorched statue made a cole
With three-wingd lightning: or a wretched soule
Muffled with endless darkness, she did sit.

[*Hero* 3.301–5]

We follow Hero through her decision to present a false form and yet to continue in her role as a priestess of Venus, which results in the creation of Dissimulation, a small myth about hypocrisy. We see Hero using the form of Leander's image to delude herself, just as later we find the self-deluded Leander compared to "an emptie Gallant full of forme" (clearly, false form). And we respond to the exemplary myth of how internal and external forms can be harmonized in the story of Hymen's courtship and marriage: "And where Loues forme is, loue is, loue is forme" the poet tells us.

I wish to extend the implications of the theme of form by recalling the Pythagorean thesis that all form is number.[28] Briefly, I shall argue that Chapman's use of numerological symbolism relates integrally to the idea of form; and that the thematic complex upon which form and number center takes its definition from Pythagorean tradition. This thematic complex, an extraordinarily dense and rich one, focuses upon the question of justice in several spheres of experience, principally upon man's relations to his society, to his marital partner, and to himself. Renais-

---

[27]"Chapman's *Hero and Leander*," pp. 55–85; Gordon's subsidiary argument about the importance of ceremony to the Elizabethans has been extended by T. N. Marsh, "Elizabethan Ceremony in Literature and in the Wilderness," *English Miscellany*, 10 (1959): 27–47, and Eileen Z. Cohen, "The Visible Solemnity: Ceremony and Order in Shakespeare and Hooker," *Texas Studies in Literature and Language*, 12 (1970): 181–95.

[28]MacLure, *George Chapman*, p. 64, sees the relevance of this point; but, perhaps because he finds Chapman's use of *form* "obsessive rather than philosophically definitive," he does not develop it.

For the general background, see Guthrie, 1: 212 ff.; F. M. Cornford, "Mysticism and Science in the Pythagorean Tradition," *Classical Quarterly*, 16 (1922): 136–50, and 17 (1923): 1–12; F. E. Robbins, "The Tradition of Greek Arithmology," *Classical Philology*, 16 (1921): 97–123; Christopher Butler, *Number Symbolism* (London, 1970). For help with sources on pp. 163–65, I am indebted to Heninger.

sance poets believed such concerns were fit matter for an epic, as comparisons with Spenser and Milton will indicate. Chapman's conception of *Hero and Leander* both in form and content is epic, the epic of Ovid's *Metamorphoses* imbued with the Pythagorean science of numbers. An examination of these elements will bring us back to a renewed look at the meaning of Ceremony in the poem.

If we consider the presence of overt numerological symbolism, we must again turn to sestiad 5 (and the placement can only be deliberate) with Teras's tale about the marriage of Hymen. There, in the description of Hymen's own marriage rites, we find this long passage:

> Next before her went
> Fiue louely children deckt with ornament
> Of her sweet colours, bearing Torches by,
> For light was held a happie Augurie
> Of generation, whose efficient right
> Is nothing else but to produce to light.
> The od disparent number they did chuse,
> To shew the vnion married loues should vse,
> Since in two equall parts it will not seuer,
> But the midst holds one to reioyne it euer,
> As common to both parts: men therfore deeme,
> That equall number Gods doe not esteeme,
> Being authors of sweet peace and vnitie,
> But pleasing to th'infernall Emperie,
> Vnder whose ensignes Wars and Discords fight,
> Since an euen number you may disunite
> In two parts equall, nought in middle left,
> To reunite each part from other reft:
> And fiue they hold in most especiall prise,
> Since t'is the first of number that doth rise
> From the two formost numbers vnitie
> That od and euen are; which are two, and three,
> For one no number is: but thence doth flow
> The powerful race of number.

[*Hero* 5.317–40]

Chapman selects the fifth sestiad in which to demonstrate how Hero and Leander might have resolved the dilemma of her vow of chastity without breaking it:

> Two louers . . . had long crau'd mariage dues
> At *Heros* hands: but she did still refuse,
> For louely *Mya* was her consort vowd
> In her maids state, and therefore not allowd
> To amorous Nuptials: yet faire *Hero* now
> Intended to dispence with her cold vow.

[*Hero* 5.33–38]

Mya's situation, in other words, is Hero's own exactly; she has taken, and regretted, the same vow of chastity as Hero. But rather than simply violate the vow, as Hero and Leander have done, Mya and her lover appeal to her immediate superior for release and eventually receive it. Hero frees Mya from the vow, marries the couple, and it is at their marriage celebration that Teras appears to tell the story of Hymen. Hymen's ceremony has canonical authority because he *is* the god of married love. Chapman's gloss on the five torches (an implicit contrast to Hero's single, untrustworthy torch)[29] tells us that five is the number of marriage; thus we know that sestiad 5 itself is the marriage sestiad, and perceive the relationship with the goddess Ceremony, who wears a pentad. Chapman got the numerology immediately from Cartari, more remotely from Plutarch, whose *Moralia* he knew well. The second of the *Roman Questions* asks, "Why in the marriage rites do they light five torches?" and the answer, in part, goes: "Now of the odd numbers, five is above all the nuptial number; for three is the first odd number, and two is the first even number, and five is composed of the union of these two, as it were of male and female."[30]

This much Chapman could explain openly and pertinently in the context of Hymen's wedding ceremony; however, it encompasses only half the conventional Pythagorean symbolism for the number five. I believe he also expected his readers to respond to the association of five with justice. In earlier times four, the first square number, had been most frequently identified with justice; but in the Renaissance, it was five. Because justice and marriage almost invariably were conjoined in discussions of five by the commentators and in the poetic adaptations, one suspects that the basically bourgeois Renaissance society found the coincidence of meanings significant and not at all accidental. Chapman might have found the association in Cornelius Agrippa's *Three Books of Occult Philosophy*:

> the number five is of no small perfection, or vertue, which proceeds from the mixtion of [odd and even]: It is also the just midle of the universal number, *viz.* ten. For if you divide the number ten, there will be nine and one, or eight and two, or seven and three, or six and four, and every collection makes the number ten, and the exact midle alwaies is the number five, and its equadis-

[29] As an attribute of Venus and Hymen both, the torch was an ambivalent symbol. See Guy de Tervarent, *Attributs et Symboles dans l'Art Prophane, 1450-1600* (Geneva, 1958-59), 2: 381-82.

[30] Plutarch, *Moralia*, trans. F. C. Babbitt, Loeb Classical Library (Cambridge, Mass., 1936), 263F-264A. Elsewhere in the *Moralia* (388C) Chapman would have found the explicit identification of this symbolism with Pythagorean tradition; and he might have known that Plato thought wedding guests ought to be admitted by fives in accordance with the symbolism (*Laws* 775A). See also Cartari, *Imagini delli Dei de gl'Antichi* (Venice, 1647), ed. Walter Koschatzky (Graz, 1963), p. 103.

tant; and therefore it is called by the *Pythagoreans* the number of Wedlock, as also of justice, because it divides the number ten in an even Scale.[31]

And he could hardly have missed the immediate poetic precedent of the recently published *Faerie Queene*. Book 5 is Spenser's Book of Justice; and at the center of the book is Britomart's dream in Isis Church. The mysterious dream involving Isis and Osiris, who were man and wife before they became symbols of justice and equity, prophesies both the marriage of Britomart and Artegall and the establishment of ideal justice in England.[32]

Just why the quality of justice should have been associated with Pythagoras perhaps requires some explanation. Among the mysterious ethical precepts attributed to Pythagoras was the commandment not to step over the beam of the balance. Diogenes Laertius, in his life of Pythagoras, offers an early interpretation: "This is what they meant. . . . Don't step over the beam of the balance: don't overstep the bounds of equity and justice."[33] In working out the proposition by number, five represents justice as a mean between excess and defect, dividing ten, the perfect number which contains all others, into two equal parts.[34] Thomas Taylor, who popularized traditional numerology for the early nineteenth century, explains that five is the midpoint in any arithmetical arrangement of the decad and allegorizes it as the beam of the balance:

> Hence, it is worse to do than to suffer an injury: and the authors of the injury verge downward as it were to the infernal regions; but the injured tend upwards as it were to the Gods, imploring the divine assistance. Hence the meaning of the Pythagoric symbol is obvious, "Pass not above the beam of the balance." Since however injustice pertains to inequality, in order to cor-

[31]Agrippa, "Of the Number Five, and the Scale thereof," *Three Books of Occult Philosophy*, trans. J.[ohn] F.[rench] (London, 1651), 2.7. See also Nichomachus of Gerasa, *Introduction to Arithmetic*, trans. Martin Luther D'Ooge, with F. E. Robbins and L. C. Karpinski (New York, 1926), p. 106; see also p. 85, n. 4.; Theon of Smyrna, *Expositio rerum mathematicarum ad legendum Platonem utilius*, trans. Ismael Bulli.aldus (Paris, 1644), note to p. 159 on p. 283. Alastair Fowler, *Spenser and the Numbers of Time* (New York, 1964), pp. 34–36, has some information.

[32]The same structural symbolism and the same association of justice with marriage remains evident, more than a half-century later, in Sir Thomas Browne's *Garden of Cyrus*. Browne begins chap. 5 apologetically, "To enlarge this contemplation unto all the mysteries and secrets accomodable unto this number, were inexcusable Pythagorisme, yet cannot we omit the ancient conceit of five surnamed the number of justice . . . ;" and shortly after completes the equation, "Antiquity named this the Conjugall or wedding number, and made it the Embleme of the most remarkable conjunction. . . . " In *The Prose*, ed. N. J. Endicott (Garden City, New York: Anchor, 1967), pp. 338–39. Spenser, Chapman, and Browne of course share platonic tendencies as a context for their interest in the science of numbers.

[33]Diogenes Laertius, *Lives of Eminent Philosophers*, trans. R. D. Hicks, Loeb Classical Library, rev. ed. (Cambridge, Mass., 1931), 8.18. See also Plutarch, *Moralia*, 12D–E.

[34]Agrippa, 2.7; Theon, p. 283. Also see Thomas Stanley, *History of Philosophy*, 2d ed. (London, 1687), p. 527.

rect this, equalization is requisite, that the beam of the balance may remain on both sides without obliquity.[35]

Originating with the precept that makes five the symbol of equitable division, the association of justice with Pythagoras was strengthened by his reputation as a man of probity and by the legend of the austerely religious life he led.[36] This personal reputation must have been responsible for the attribution to him of the allegorical "Pythagorean letter." Servius explains in his commentary on the *Aeneid*:

> As we know, Pythagoras of Samos divided human life according to the form of the letter Y; in the uncertainty of early age men have not yet given themselves to virtues and vices; but the parting of the ways, of the letter Y, begins with adolescence at the time when men follow either the vices, that is the left side, or the virtues, that is the right side.[37]

Cesare Ripa's *Iconologia* pictures free will as a young man in regal habit, wearing a crown of gold and carrying a scepter topped by the Greek letter Y. This letter, Ripa explains, denotes "quella sententia di Pitagora Filosofo famoso."[38] We can also learn the allegory from the pseudo-Virgilian epigram, which Chapman translated: "This letter of Pythagoras, that beares / This forkt distinction, to conceit prefers / The forme mans life beares."[39] The right-hand fork looks steep and difficult but leads to surpassing pleasure; the sinister path starts easily but ends in disaster and perdition. Obviously there is a familial resemblance between this story of the Greek Υ and the better-known one of Hercules at the crossroads; in fact, the Υ or Y becomes almost an emblem or a schematic representation of the Herculean story.[40] The connection, once again, is significant because Hercules was known as a champion of justice; this tradition, as well as his choice of paths, enters prominently into Spenser's Book of Justice. The implication of both stories, of course, is

[35]Thomas Taylor, *Theoretic Arithmetic* (London, 1816), pp. 194–95. Taylor's treatise is a pastiche of Theon, Nicomachus, Iamblichus, and other sources available in the Renaissance.

[36]See Guthrie, 1: 148–53, 166–69, 174–75; also the lives of Pythagoras by Diogenes Laertius and Iamblichus; and the accounts of the Pythagorean schools in Aulus Gellius, *Attic Nights*, 1.9.1–2, and in the life of Apollonius of Tyana by Philostratus.

[37]Trans. T. E. Mommsen in his *Medieval and Renaissance Studies* (Ithaca, 1959), p. 184.

[38]Cesare Ripa, *Iconologia* (Rome, 1603), pp. 295–97, and fig. on p. 296.

[39]Published in 1612 in *Petrarchs Seven Penitentiall Psalms*. The epigram is translated from an edition of Virgil with commentary by Iodocus Badius Ascensius. See Bartlett, *Poems*, p. 447. I have consulted the Paris, 1500, *Opera* in which Ascensius's discussion of the Pythagorean letter extends to six folio pages.

[40]On this, see Mommsen, "Petrarch and the Story of the Choice of Hercules," in *Medieval and Renaissance Studies*, pp. 175–96, esp. 184–90. See also Phillip Damon, "Geryon, Cacciaguida and the Y of Pythagoras," *Dante Studies*, 85 (1967): 15–32.

"Libero Arbitrio," from Ripa, *Iconologia*. Reproduced by permission of the owner.

that a man cannot determine justice for others until he has first, by using his faculties and abilities to a virtuous end, ordered his own life justly, as Hercules and Pythagoras were supposed to have done.[41]

Beyond the specific question of how marriage and justice should have been conjoined in the taxonomy of Pythagorean symbolism, there is an appropriateness in the relationship through the Pythagorean metaphor of harmony. In Chapman's platonic conception of marriage, the essence of the union must be a proportional relationship, an ordering of complementary qualities into a harmonic unity, a *concordia discors*.[42] Chapman may have felt that the *concordia discors* theme existed inherently in the story of Hero and Leander, with its guiding torch and stormy sea. One of the questions about the marriage ceremony, which he took from Plutarch via Cartari, asks "Why do they bid the bride touch fire and water?" Plutarch answered:

---

[41]Two decades ago Hallett Smith pointed out the relevance of Hercules' choice to *The Faerie Queene*; see *Elizabethan Poetry* (Cambridge, Mass., 1952), pp. 290–303. For the present state of Herculean interpretation, see T. K. Dunseath, *Spenser's Allegory of Justice in Book V of the Faerie Queene* (Princeton, 1968); and Jane Aptekar, *Icons of Justice: Iconography and Thematic Imagery in Book V of The Faerie Queene* (New York, 1969).

[42]On *concordia discors*, see the discussion in chap. 2, pp. 35–39, 43–44.

just as fire without moisture is unsustaining and arid, and water without heat is unproductive and inactive, so also male and female apart from each other are inert, but their union in marriage produces the perfection of their life together.[43]

Chapman incorporated this ritual into Hymen's wedding:

Before them on an Altar he presented
Both fire and water: which was first inuented,
Since to ingenerate euery humane creature,
And euery other birth produ'st by Nature,
Moysture and heate must mixe: so man and wife
For humane race must ioyne in Nuptiall life.

[Hero 5.359–64]

The explanation of five as the marriage number exemplifies perfectly the *concordia discors* principle: the masculine three and feminine two, odd and even, unite into a whole which cannot be split into equal parts. The proposition that marriage consists of an inseparable harmonious union of parts was strikingly illustrated by the platonic myth of the Androgyne;[44] and the persistent association of marriage and justice recurs again in Ficino's commentary on Aristophanes' grotesque myth of human bisexuality: "Justice is called Bi-Sexual; feminine inasmuch as because of its inherent innocence it does no one any wrong, but masculine inasmuch as it allows no harm to be brought to others, and with more severe censure frowns upon unjust men."[45] By Ficino's view *concordia discors*, marriage, and true justice are all one.

Pico della Mirandola extended the principle of *concordia discors* into an aesthetic theory: "Beauty in general is a *Harmony resulting from several things proportionably concurring to constitute a third* . . . it being the union of contraries, a friendly enmity, a disagreeing concord."[46] The easy transferal of *concordia discors* from a theory of marriage to one of beauty, both types of harmony, helps us to appreciate the allegorical impulse behind Chapman's emphasis on Hymen's androgynous beauty. "*Hymen* that now is god of Nuptiall rites, / . . . / Of *Athens* was a youth so sweet of face / That many thought him of the femall race" (*Hero* 5.91,

---

[43]*Moralia* (trans. Babbitt), 263E–F.

[44]Plato, *Symposium*, 189C-193D; *Marsilio Ficino's Commentary on Plato's Symposium*, trans. Sears R. Jayne, University of Missouri Studies, 19 (Columbia, 1944), pp. 154–63; also R. V. Merrill with R. J. Clements, "The Androgyne," *Platonism in French Renaissance Poetry* (New York, 1957), pp. 99–117. The emblem of a hermaphroditic tree as "Matrimonii Typus" in Barthelemy Aneau, *Picta Poesis* (Lyon, 1552), p. 14, has been cited in reference to Spenser. See Donald Cheney, "Spenser's Hermaphrodite and the 1590 *Faerie Queene*," *PMLA*, 87 (1972): 192–200.

[45]*Ficino's Commentary*, p. 160.

[46]*A Platonick Discourse Upon Love*, 2.5, in *The Poems and Translations of Thomas Stanley*, ed. G. M. Crump (Oxford, 1962).

93–94). So ideally mixed were the proportions of color and form in Hymen's face that they provided a model for the perfect union of lovers:

> In such pure leagues his beauties were combinde,
> That there your Nuptiall contracts first were signde. . . .
> And such sweete concord was thought worthie then
> Of torches, musick, feasts, and greatest men.
>
> [*Hero* 5.97–98; 111–12]

Chapman's extension of marital harmony, from the actual union of lovers to ceremony ("torches, musick, feasts") and then to law ("Nuptiall contracts"), anticipates the macrocosmic application of this discussion. Law is, after all, the codification of the social relationships mimed by ceremony; and the function of that codification is the implementation of justice. The vision of justice presented in *Hero and Leander* originates with classical tradition. A knowledge of that tradition, of accepted legal distinctions and points within the general code of justice, far from being a scholastically arid gloss, illuminates Chapman's motives and directions in expanding the narrative. Cicero calls justice "the principle by which society and what we may call its 'common bonds' are maintained."[47] According to Aristotle, two kinds of justice exist, distributive and corrective, which operate by geometrical and arithmetical proportion, respectively. Corrective justice pertains to individual transactions, and I will defer discussing it until we consider Leander's case. Distributive justice pertains to the divisible assets of the community which may be allotted to its members. This kind of justice, Artistotle says, "is therefore a sort of proportion; for proportion is not a property of numerical quantity only, but of quantity in general, proportion being equality of ratios."[48] Less abstractly, Sir Ernest Barker offers the following description:

> Justice is thus, in its original notion, the quality or aptitude of joining: it ties together whatever it touches. Primarily it ties men together, by the common bond of a right and "fitting" order of relation, under which each has his position in the order and receives his due place; each has rights as his share of the general Right pervading and constituting the order.[49]

Justice, in this broad sense, constitutes the harmoniously operating social order, and has as its objective, as in the fifth book of *The Faerie Queene*, no more nor less than peace; and the model after which the just

---

[47]Cicero, *De Officiis*, trans. Walter Miller, Loeb Classical Library (Cambridge, Mass., 1913), 1.7.20.

[48]Aristotle, *Nicomachean Ethics*, trans. H. Rackham, Loeb Classical Library, rev. ed. (Cambridge, Mass., 1934), 5.3.8.

[49]Sir Ernest Barker, *Principles of Social and Political Theory* (Oxford, 1951), p. 168; quoted by Fletcher, pp. 284–85.

social order is patterned is the divine order symbolized by the harmony of the spheres. In *Andromeda Liberata*, for instance, the principals in a politically advantageous marriage are presented as a microcosm of the planets Mars and Venus, a pattern of *concordia discors*; Chapman intimates the same pattern can be followed to effect governmental harmony, which is to say, justice. In the Prologue to Book 5 of *The Faerie Queene*, Spenser emphasizes the connection between the two realms of heavenly and earthly activity by telling us that the celestial spheres fell out of harmony after man sinned.[50] With this Pythagorean vision of the correspondences between all levels of the creation and all realms of human activity still pervasive in the Renaissance, the relation between justice and marriage becomes vital. Even that great sceptic John Donne, could console his wife at a leave-taking by telling her "Thy firmness makes my circle just."

Marriage may, in fact, be understood as the original pattern for the kind of communal order we have described as distributive justice. Tribes, cities, nations, and governments were considered to be successive enlargements of the pattern of familial relationships established in the marriage of Adam and Eve. *Paradise Lost* is thoroughly traditional in implying that the natural order of human relations before the fall creates such a model for subsequent societal relations.[51] Milton also would have subscribed to Aristotle's inversion of the pattern, which makes marriage the macrocosm to the microcosm of personal justice. In debating the question "can a man treat himself unjustly," Aristotle argues:

> Metaphorically and in virtue of a certain resemblance there is a justice, not indeed between a man and himself, but between certain parts of him; yet not every kind of justice but that of master and servant or that of husband and wife. For these are the ratios in which the part of the soul that has a rational principle stands to the irrational part; and it is with a view to these parts that people also think a man can be unjust to himself, viz. because these parts are liable to suffer something contrary to their respective desires; there is therefore thought to be a mutual justice between them as between ruler and ruled.[52]

The infolding of the relational pattern here is exactly the same as we have seen with Hymen's beauty: even though Hymen is only one partner

---

[50]This point is made by Dunseath, p. 209.

[51]See, for instance, the narrator's first description of Adam and Eve, *PL* 4.288–324, which emphasizes majesty, nobility, true authority in Adam, free submissiveness in Eve.

[52]*Nicomachean Ethics* 5.11.9; here I have quoted the translation from *Introduction to Aristotle*, ed. Richard McKeon, Modern Library (New York, 1947), p. 423, in preference to Rackham. This passage is cited in reference to Spenser by Judith H. Anderson, "The Knight of Justice in Book V of Spenser's *Faerie Queene*," *PMLA*, 85 (1970): 74. Jane Aptekar, pp. 97–98, finds the question of justice in marriage germane to Book 5, and traces its provenance to *Nicomachean Ethics* 5; see 5.6. 8–9 for further comment on justice between husband and wife.

in the ideal marriage, we find in him the harmonious model for all marriages.

These, then, are the values Chapman invests in his Pythagorean sestiad to create the perspective from which he wishes his reader to judge the actions of the lovers. By successive degrees of expansion from micro- to macrocosm he sets forth the pattern of true justice as a *concordia discors* in the individual's relations with himself, his marriage, his society, all imitated from the original harmonious order established at the creation. To turn from the positive to the negative, let us consider Hero and Leander's violation of that pattern, which moves us from the realm of distributive to corrective justice.

Corrective justice concerns the attempts to remedy inequities conceived in the transactions between individuals.[53] Leander, by the accepted standards of justice, actually offends in three ways—against the social harmony of the community by abrogating its laws; against Hero by persuading her to break her faith; but, before either of these, against himself by failing to maintain a just harmony in his own soul—for, as Aristotle observes, it is not a characteristic of the just man to act unjustly.[54] In that marriage of rational and passionate faculties which constitutes the soul, Leander had permitted the husband Reason to be overmastered by effeminate passion. Chapman knew this from Marlowe's simile comparing "mad Leander" to that uncontrollable horse, originally stabled in the *Phaedrus*.

The paradigm of male reason dominating female passion properly obtains externally as well as internally; hence, the difference in the treatment of the two lovers. By Chapman's ethics, Leander must assume the primary responsibility for their actions. The situation is analogous to Milton's interpretation of the Fall: despite Eve's initiative, the fault is Adam's; when he attempts to shift the responsibility to Eve, he is rebuked for his "effeminate slackness." Weighed by the Pythagorean balance, symbol of equality in personal transactions, Leander, as the person committing rather than suffering the injury, again deserves the censure. The differences between the lovers in roles and responsibilities account for Chapman's variations in a largely parallel process. Both lovers undergo encounters which indicate what they have done wrong; but, whereas Ceremony descends to rebuke Leander directly and explicitly, Hero's lesson is conveyed obliquely in Teras's story of Hymen. The distinction again anticipates one in *Paradise Lost*, whereby Adam learns the consequences of his sin directly from the angel Michael, but Eve learns through a dream.

In Chapman's version of the separate deaths of the lovers, the Fates are responsible for Leander's death, suggesting a punishment; Hero,

[53]*Nicomachean Ethics* 5.4.
[54]Ibid., 5.9.16.

however, simply expires of grief at Leander's death, with no apparent connotation of suprahuman decree. From its entire thrust, the presentation of Leander conveys the impression that Chapman conceives of the young man as someone who, upon reaching that crucial fork in the road of life, chose the wrong path. This is not to suggest that the narrator's attitude toward the lovers is dominantly moralistic. Rather, despite the necessity to "censure the delights, / That being enioyd aske judgement" and the immediate focus upon Leander's guilt (3.23–36), the emphasis remains upon tragic waste, the destruction of valuable human potential. In the Pythagorean conception a loss of virtue means very simply an individual break with the pervasive harmony which encompasses all things.[55]

Conventionally, the discussions of justice make a distinction between absolute justice and equity, which involves recourse to general principles of justice to ensure that the letter of the law does not violate the spirit in any individual case.[56] Equity in civil law thus has a function analogous to the role of casuistry in canon law. In England equity refers to an actual system of law existing beside the common and statute laws, superceding them when they conflict.[57] In *The Faerie Queene* Osiris embodies justice (5.7.2), while Isis personifies "That part of Iustice which is Equity." As sun and moon, man and wife, Artegall and Britomart, "they both like race in equall iustice runne."[58] Under the English legal system, equity particularly concerned itself with conflicting claims of property; injustice in this context would especially be associated with illegal possession of property.[59] If we bear in mind the common-law definition of a wife as her husband's property,[60] it becomes significant that Leander's offense is the illegal possession of Hero. The conflicting claimants for this property would include Venus to whom Hero is wedded already by her vows of chastity, and even those parents eradicated by Marlowe.

The application of legal concepts of justice serve to illuminate those portions of the continuation centering upon Hero, as well. Since the

[55]See, for instance, Diogenes Laertius, *Lives* 8.33.

[56]See James E. Phillips, "Renaissance Concepts of Justice and the Structure of *The Faerie Queene*, Book V," *Huntington Library Quarterly*, 33 (1970): 111–13; W. N. Knight, "The Narrative Unity of Book V of *The Faerie Queene*: 'That Part of Justice Which Is Equity,'" *Review of English Studies*, 21 (1970): 267–94; also *Oxford English Dictionary*, s.v. "Equity," 2.3.

[57]*OED*, s.v. "Equity," 2.4.

[58]On this, in addition to Phillips and Knight, see René Graziani, "Elizabeth at Isis Church," *PMLA*, 79 (1964): 376–89; and Frank Kermode, *Shakespeare, Spenser, Donne: Renaissance Essays* (London, 1971), pp. 49–59.

[59]Knight, pp. 271–72.

[60]See, e.g., *Encyclopedia Britannica*, 11th ed., s.v. "Husband and Wife"; Odgers and Odgers, *The Common Law of England*, rev. by Roland Burrows, 3rd ed. (London, 1927), 2:730–44.

fourth sestiad largely concerns Hero's decision to continue to fulfill the forms of her office illegally, which results in the creation of the monster Dissimulation, we might reflect upon Cicero's belief that hypocrisy is the most flagrant of injustices.[61] Or, to go to the fifth sestiad again, the appeal of the subordinate priestess Mya to be released from her vows to marry presents a direct parallel to Hero's own situation, with the clear object of demonstrating how the laws of equity might have solved her dilemma. That Hero's motives in judging Mya's petition are not disinterested simply mirrors those situations in which Venus judges her or the Fates pursue Leander. The implication would seem to be that law, justice, and the social order have a functional validity beyond their individual human components.[62]

Although Chapman uses conceptions of justice to interpret myth, it would be wrong, nevertheless, to read the poem by the letter of the legal code, with no appeal to equity. Most of the arguments from justice pertinent here are commonplaces, requiring no specialized knowledge. The rhetoric books, for instance, can be illuminating on the subject. The *Ad Herennium* tells us

> We shall be using the topics of Justice if we say that we ought to pity innocent persons and suppliants; . . . if we explain that we ought to punish the guilty; if we urge that faith ought zealously to be kept; if we say that the laws and customs of the state ought especially to be preserved; if we contend that alliances and friendships should scrupulously be honored; if we make it clear that the duty imposed by nature toward parents, gods, and fatherland must be religiously observed. . . .[63]

Here we have virtually the rhetorical essence—as distinct from the mythological amplification—of Chapman's argument: from Leander's abuse of hospitality, to Hero's breach of faith with parents, gods, and fatherland, to Neptune's (and the poet's) pity for the still-innocent lovers. And, in all this, the emphasis remains upon the harmonious social order, on the necessity of ceremony.

Using the context supplied by the traditions of justice, I wish to reexamine the figure of Ceremony, which Chapman created for the poem. Although he calls her only "Ceremony" in the text, Chapman's argument to the third sestiad describes her as "Thesme, the Deitie soueraigne / Of Customes and religious rites." L. C. Martin noted that Chapman created

---

[61]*De Officiis* 1.13.41.

[62]Gordon, "Chapman's *Hero and Leander*," pp. 89–92, on the contrary, detects injustice.

[63]*Ad Herennium* trans. Harry Caplan, Loeb Classical Library (Cambridge, Mass., 1954), 3.3.4.

the name by adding a feminine ending to Thesmos: law, ordinance, rule, or rite.[64] Gordon suggested as a contributing influence Themis, "the usual personification of law."[65] The words come from the same root; but I would claim a somewhat larger share for Themis, who, more than a personification of law, is usually the goddess of justice and prophecy.[66] Chapman's Thesme appears with divine music in a rainbow of light, wearing a crown of all the stars and with "the bench of Deities" hanging from her hair. The last detail, Gordon remarks, is an allegory of the chain of being; as such it suggests that she controls the social order vertically, to its divine origins, as well as horizontally, on the human plane. Music and its visual analogue, light, and stars, all indicate her alliance with the harmony of the spheres. The rainbow reminds us that justice is peace, perhaps additionally suggesting her role here as the messenger of marriage.[67] Such institutions as religion and society, such attitudes as devotion and reverence can exist only in her presence because they are dependent upon vision and hearing, the highest, most "rational" senses, according to the platonic sensory hierarchies.[68]

The traditional identifying attribute of justice is the balance or scales. The "pentackle" Ceremony wears suggests, in the language of Pythagoras, both her advocacy of marriage and that balance. With her virgin purity and piercing sight Ceremony resembles the personification of justice reported by Aulus Gellius:

> she is properly represented too as stern and dignified, with a serious expression and a keen, steadfast glance, in order that she may inspire fear in the wicked and courage in the good; to the latter, as her friends, she presents a friendly aspect, to the former a stern face.[69]

Gellius's account, in fact, seems a probable source for the "perspective" quality Chapman attributes to Ceremony's countenance: "Her face was changeable to euerie eie; / One way lookt ill, another graciouslie; / Which while men viewd, they cheerfull were & holy: / But looking off, vicious and melancholy" (*Hero* 3.125–28). By the "Mathematique Christall," presumably a crystal ball, she distinguishes the "estates of men" (hierarchy, order, degree), eliminates confusion, and establishes social decorum, "*Morallitie* and *Comelinesse*." Perhaps the crystal also suggests Themis's prophetic powers; the Orphic hymns make her a daughter

---

[64]Martin, *Marlowe's Poems* (London, 1931), p. 70.

[65]Gordon, p. 60 n.

[66]See, e.g., *The Oxford Classical Dictionary* and the *EB* entries.

[67]A Cartari illustration (p. 99) shows Iris coming from Juno with a rainbow.

[68]On the superiority of sight and hearing in the sensory hierarchy, see chap. 4, p. 116.

[69]Aulus Gellius, *Attic Nights*, trans. J. C. Rolfe, Loeb Classical Library, rev. ed. (Cambridge, Mass., 1952), 14.4.4.

of the sun, who sees all and penetrates all mysteries.[70] The rod (taken, according to Gordon,[71] from Apollo's laurel) with which she beats back barbarism and avarice, stresses her connection with civilization—arts, science, games, culture. Policy, who draws "snaky" [prudent] paths to "obserued law," does the same. She tells Leander "how poore was substance without rites, / Like bils vnsignd . . . / Not being with ciuill forms confirm'd and bounded, / For humane dignities and comforts founded" (3.147–48, 151–52).

The detail that "The *Howrs* and *Graces* bore her glorious traine" suggestively delimits Chapman's conception. The earliest individualized account of the Hours occurs in Hesiod's *Theogony*, wherein we learn that Themis, as second wife of Zeus, gave birth to the Hours, Eunomia (order), Dike (justice), and Eirene (peace).[72] The same union also produced the Fates (Clotho, Lachesis, and Atropos), and the succeeding passage describes the Graces as Zeus's children by Eurynome. Chapman's pairing of the Graces with the Hours here probably is meant to reinforce the quality of ceremony, since their Hesiodic names mean pageantry, happiness, and festivity.[73]

Hesiod's association of the Hours with Themis intimately links two related kinds of justice. Themis embodies justice of divine origin and Dike that of human origin. Thus Themis becomes the representative of divine justice in all its relations to mortals; Dike figures the custom arising out of usage or precedent.[74] As the mythology of the Hours developed, Dike soon came to overshadow her sisters.[75] Chapman knew this from the first book of Hesiod's *Works and Days*, of which he later published his own translation. Werner Jaeger has concluded, "All the first part of [Hesiod's] poem is inspired by a religious faith which sets the

---

[70]See *EB*, s.v. "Themis;" also Thomas Taylor's translation of the hymn "To Themis," in *Thomas Taylor, the Platonist: Selected Writings*, ed. K. Raine and G. M. Harper (Princeton, 1969), p. 286.

[71]Gordon, p. 61.

[72]*Theogony*, lines 901 ff. See also *Noctem*, lines 381–82, and Chapman's gloss.

[73]Although it is possible that the pairing simply reflects the widespread confusion of the Graces and the Hours in the Renaissance, the internal consistency would indicate that Chapman is using his allusions precisely and knowledgeably.

[74]See *EB*, s.v. "Greek Law." According to Werner Jaeger, *Paideia: The Ideals of Greek Culture*, trans. Gilbert Highet (New York, 1945), 1: 103: "The meaning of themis is confined rather to the *authority* of justice, to its established position and validity, while dike means the legal enforceability of justice."

[75]For a sixteenth-century example, Jean Bodin identifies the three forms of justice, which he calls arithmetical, geometrical, and harmonical, with "les trois filles de Themis;" see *Les six Livres de la Republique* (Paris, 1583), p. 1058. Thus, for Bodin, the Hours all are justice. His three forms would seem to conform to the tripartite division into absolute justice, equity, and clemency or mercy, for which see Phillips, "Renaissance Concepts of Justice," 103–20.

idea of justice at the center of life."[76] This prophetic ideal of "equal Justice" leads Hesiod to implore his idle brother to seek the true path to virtue:

> her path long and steep,
> And at your entry 'tis so sharp and deep,
> But scaling once her height, the joy is more
> Than all the pain she put you to before.
> The pain at first, then, both to love and know
> Justice and Virtue, and those few that go
> Their rugged way, is cause 'tis follow'd lest.

[*Works and Days* 1.457–63]

The image is a familiar one; and Chapman cannot resist annotating it: "this painful passage to Virtue Virgil imitated in his translation of the Pythagorean letter Y."[77]

Chapman's presentation of the Hours is truer to Hesiod than Spenser's. In the description of Mercilla enthroned, Spenser gives her as attendants temperance, reverence, and the "lovely daughters of high Jove" and "righteous Themis." Their function is to "treat for pardon and remission / To suppliants, through frayltie which offend," thereby strengthening the concept of justice as mercy already signified by the queen's name.[78] Chapman, by contrast, wishes to heighten the notion of justice as a proper ordering of human relations through time, a notion inherent in the name of the Hours and in their association with the seasons. He could not have missed the theme from Hesiod's *Works and Days*: beyond the "crooked Justice" of the law courts, Dike is a matter of ordering one's life through labor to the rhythm of nature.[79] In all the Renaissance literary fascination with time, Milton gives us the most brilliant treatments of the impulse to premature action (and the lesson of his Christ, "All things are best fulfill'd in their due time" is pertinent here).[80] But the present poem is a worthy predecessor.

Leander's offense, after all, is an abuse of time; the blame is not in what he does but when he does it: "And who like earth would spend that dower of heauen, / With ranke desire to ioy it all at first?" What simply

---

[76]Jaeger, 1: 68; the entire chapter on Hesiod, pp. 57–76, is pertinent. On Plato's adaptation of Hesiod's *Horai*, particularly Dike, in the *Laws*, see Friedrich Solmsen, "Hesiodic Motifs in Plato," in *Hésiode et son Influence*, Entretiens sur de'antiquité classique, 7 (Geneva, 1960): 191–93.

[77]Hooper, pp. 168–69, and n.

[78]Cf. Phillips, pp. 114–20, and Dunseath, pp. 209–11.

[79]Jaeger, 1: 69–73.

[80]On the theme of time, see Ricardo J. Quinones, *The Renaissance Discovery of Time* (Cambridge, Mass., 1972).

"kils our hunger, quencheth thirst," Chapman tells us, is not civil, not humane; "But what doth plentifully minister / . . . / So orderd that it still excites desire, / And still giues pleasure freenes to aspire"—that is worthy of human love.

> Thus *Time*, and all-states-ordering *Ceremonie*
> Had banisht all offence: *Times* golden Thie
> Vpholds the flowrie bodie of the earth,
> In sacred harmonie, and euery birth
> Of men, and actions makes legitimate,
> Being vsde aright; *The vse of time is Fate*.

> [*Hero* 3.59–64]

The only direct allusion to Pythagoras in the poem (the myth of his golden thigh)[81] equates him with time, bringing together the harmonic nexus of time, number, and form with the argument that justice consists in orderly relations of man with man and of man with nature, on the pattern of that harmony discovered by Pythagoras.

"The use of time is Fate" Chapman says, in deliberately ambiguous prophecy. The proper use of time would have allied Leander with Ceremony and the Hours, and would have legitimatized his actions. By causing only injustice and discord, Leander cast his lot with the cruel sisters, the Fates, introduced into the poem by Marlowe. Both trios of daughters represent particular manifestations of the more abstract character of Themis, for in its primary sense the word *themis* apparently meant "that which had been laid down," an ordained decision, analogous to the Anglo-Saxon *doom*.[82] One authority tells us that the opposite of themis "is Hybris, or insolent encroachment upon the rights of others, on whose track she follows to punish, like Nemesis."[83] In platonism there is a kind of ethical determinism; a man's voluntary acts are determined in proportion to his knowledge of the good he seeks.[84] Rather than obtaining the freedom that would have been his had he chosen the true good, Leander has become enslaved to a false, apparent good. By breaking time with the social harmony, Leander loses the power to order his own time, becoming instead the victim of fate. One recalls Chapman's epigraph to *Caesar and Pompey*, "Only a iust man is a freeman." As Harry Levin perceived, Leander is another version of the Marlovian overreacher;[85] and

[81]See Diogenes Laertius, *Lives*, 8.9.

[82]On this point, see *EB*, s.v. "Greek Law," and Jane E. Harrison, *Themis: A Study of the Social Origins of Greek Religion* (Cambridge, 1927), p. 483.

[83]*EB*, s.v. "Themis." Harrison, pp. 527–28, assigns the nemesis role to Dike. On nemesis and the Fates, see also W. C. Greene, *Moira: Fate, Good, and Evil in Greek Thought* (Cambridge, Mass., 1944).

[84]See, e.g., "Ethical Determinism" in Paul Edwards et al., eds., *Encyclopedia of Philosophy* (New York, 1967), 2: 359.

[85]Levin, pp. 142–45.

his particular brand of hybris seals his doom. From the first, it is only a matter of watching time run out for him.

I have explained, perhaps too elaborately, the way Chapman changed his continuation into an Ovidian epic informed, as is the *Metamorphoses,* by Pythagorean philosophy. Just as he made that Pythagorean doctrine— numbers, harmony, marriage, justice, time—into a coherent thematic center for the poem, so he also made his conclusion, with its invented metamorphosis, an integral part of the whole Ovidian redaction.

Consider the problem as Chapman would have encountered it. Marlowe had invested *Hero and Leander* with the garment of the erotic Ovid, disregarding the approved moral and philosophic Ovid of the *Metamorphoses.* Although the story of Hero and Leander does have authentic stature in the Ovidian corpus, because it occurs in the *Heroides* it lacks the transformation motif which by definition is necessary to identify it with the "dark Philosophie of turned shapes." Accordingly, Chapman must fabricate an appropriate conclusion for the story. He does not, however, have license to create an original ending; the principle of imitation, essential to his poetic,[86] requires that his invention be true to the spirit of Ovid, that the conclusion be one Ovid himself might have devised. Chapman found the solution to his problem in the typological adaptation of myths, a procedure at which he, like other humanist poets, became extremely adept. In *The Teares of Peace* (1609), Chapman conflates the Gallic Hercules, symbol of eloquence, with Harpocrates, the god of silence, to create the new figure of silent eloquence, his image for the intuitive revelation of the Hermetic *gnosis.* And in *Andromeda Liberata* the topical circumstances of the Somerset wedding dictated his use of the Perseus-Andromeda myth, but he adapted that to conform to the Mars-Venus myth with its appropriate connotations of marital harmony. With the present poem Chapman needed to search the *Metamorphoses* for a myth which conformed to the type of the Hero and Leander story and to the meaning he wanted it to convey. Then he could invent a transformation modeled on that in the parallel myth.[87]

I have quoted Golding's assertion that metamorphosis symbolizes the psychic transformations which man undergoes; an animal transformation, for example, represents a state of mind in which lust and appetite

[86]On concepts of imitation, see Rosemond Tuve, *Elizabethan and Metaphysical Imagery* (Chicago, 1947), pp. 27–49.

[87]For a particularly relevant analogue to this kind of typological adaptation, see E. H. Gombrich's *Symbolic Images* (New York, 1972) pp. 7–11, on the principle of decorum which Renaissance authors and artists used in the selection of stories, images, and motifs appropriate to a given subject.

have overthrown the reason that gives man his identity. Such an inter-
pretation is by no means eccentric: Adlington's translation of the
Golden Ass and Harington's of *Orlando Furioso* assert the same theory;[88]
and it retains vitality in original poetry as late as *Comus* or the Satan of
Paradise Lost, Book 10. Mistakenly, we tend to think of metamorphosis
largely in negative terms, the descent into the bestial or the subhuman.
In point of fact, the range of metamorphoses in Ovid is nearly as broad as
Pythagoras's theory of universal change. For the sake of convenience we
may sort them into three rough categories: punishment, reward, and
those motivated by pity. We may think most readily of the punishments—
Actaeon transformed to a stag, Picus to a bird, Niobe to a statue, Midas
given ass's ears—but the rewards are there—Julius Caesar transformed to
a star, Hercules deified, Pygmalion's statue come to life. And there are
acts of pity, too—Io regains human form, Narcissus becomes the flower,
Lotis a tree. Often, Ovid will suggest that the changed form symbolizes
the dominant emotion or personal characteristic, or even a prominent
feature of the myth; thus, Niobe weeps eternally, Midas's ears expose his
musical taste, and the color of the hyacinth reminds us of the spilled
blood. But the symbolic transformation usually conforms to one of the
three general categories I have specified. The categories of reward and
pity will occasionally overlap; more often, however, the transformation
for pity represents a middle ground, a moral or judgmental neutrality,
between the extremes of reward and punishment.

Chapman builds examples of each type into the poem; as if to teach
Hero the possibilities implicit in human free will, he includes both positive and negative changes in sestiad 5, before the pathetic central
change in sestiad 6. The positive metamorphosis, of course, is the story
of Hymen, who, as we are told at the beginning and end of the tale, was
once mortal and earned the right to divinity: "And thus blest *Hymen*
ioyde his gracious Bride, / And for his ioy was after deifide." The
punishment, Chapman's own creation, is the story of Adolesche, the
gossipy Athenian girl who tries to betray Hymen's love and is transformed to a parrot for her efforts. Both, we might note, are symbolic
metamorphoses: the embodiment of perfect love becomes the god of
marriage; the gossip becomes a creature characterized by mindless
speech.[89]

For his central metamorphosis Chapman needed a myth with these
components: a story of devoted lovers who, nonetheless, bring about
their own doom; a cruel or treacherous goddess; the separation of lovers
by sea; the death of the male lover in a storm at sea, possibly an act of
punishment; the death of the woman for grief. I suggest he found it in
the story of Ceyx and Alcyone. Ceyx was king of Trachis, Alcyone his

---

[88]See chap. 3, pp. 60–61.

[89]Gordon, p. 85, discusses this.

devoted wife. Required, despite Alcyone's pleas, to travel by sea to consult the oracle, Ceyx drowns in a terrible storm. At home Alcyone's incessant prayers for her husband's safety irritate Juno, who sends a false image of Ceyx to inform Alcyone of his death. Grief-stricken, she haunts the waterfront where she last saw Ceyx, only to discover his floating body. Through the compassion of the gods, the two are transformed into sea birds, halcyons, and reunited. Folklore tells us that halcyons nest at sea at the time of the winter solstice when the waters are calm and tranquil, and they remain ever faithful to their mates.

Chapman could well have been led to this story by Ovid, who by alluding twice to Ceyx and Alcyone in *Heroides* (18.81–82; 19.191–204) underscores the parallels in the two myths. If so, Chapman found virtually everything he wanted in Ceyx and Alcyone; the anger of Juno and the phantasm of Ceyx may even have provided the suggestion for the angry Venus and for Hero's self-delusion with the image of Leander. In the *Metamorphoses* Ceyx and Alcyone is the second longest of the episodes; it is given epic treatment; and, according to Brooks Otis, it fulfills a central thematic role, representing the achievement of human, conjugal love against the extremes of unnatural or imperfect love in so many of the other myths.[90] Certainly Golding understood the story in this way: "In Ceyx and Alcyone appeares most constant love, / Such as betweene the man and wyfe too be it dooth behove." So did George Sandys, who remarks that the gods "convert them both into birds of her name, which we call Kings-fishers; who still retaine their conjugall affections."[91]

I will speculate further that Chapman was a good enough mythographer to know the variant of the story extant in Ovid's sources, but which Ovid chose not to use in the *Metamorphoses*.[92] In this version Ceyx and Alcyone still exemplify conjugal devotion; but in pride they attribute divine qualities to themselves, and it is for this impiety that Ceyx is drowned in the storm. The later metamorphosis, still, is motivated by pity for Alcyone's grief. This version remains common enough to turn up in Sandys's commentary on Ceyx:

> happy in his faire and affectionat wife, in his peacable gouernment, and other felicities of fortune: which swelled him, as others haue written, so fare aboue the sense of his mortality, that he caused himself to be called Iupiter, and his wife Alcyone, Iuno; for which by the diuine vengeance he was shipwrackt and drowned. . . .[93]

---

[90]Otis, pp. 263–77; and, on the epic qualities of the episode, pp. 231–34.

[91]Golding, "Epistle to Leicester," lines 232–33; Sandys, *Ovid's Metamorphosis Englished* (Oxford, 1632), p. 397.

[92]See Otis, pp. 393–94, for a full discussion of the sources and variants.

[93]Sandys, p. 394.

Here, then, were all the ingredients Chapman required: the appropriate narrative elements almost point for point; and the necessary thematic elements, the hybris, the tragically faithful love, even marriage.

Chapman's decision to follow a two-stage metamorphosis, allowing the heavy change of death by water to expiate the offenses against justice and ending on the compassionate note of the pathetic metamorphosis, suggests his awareness that mercy or clemency is the third and last topic of justice. As James Phillips has shown, Renaissance theorists and commentators did not regard justice as fully analyzed until absolute justice and equity were completed by mercy, which they ordinarily distinguished from "misericordia" or false pity.[94] Chapman satisfies the legitimate demands of absolute justice with Leander's punishment; and, avoiding the sentimentality of misericordia which might have sought to spare the lovers (as did Henry Petowe in his sequel), he illustrates with their metamorphosis the true mercy that "never doth from doome of right depart."[95]

Because the crucial issue is that his lovers did not get married, Chapman rings changes on the bird metamorphosis. Ceyx and Alcyone become sea birds who are given periods of calm sea to atone for the terrible storm; during the halcyon days, they nest in peace and tranquility. Hero and Leander become land birds, always shunning the sea, always flying together. Their colors symbolize qualities—blue for truth, yellow for the jealousy of Venus, black and red for death and pity. The thistles on which they feed signify their earthly sorrows.[96] Their consolation comes in art: "They were the first that euer Poet sung."

[94]See Phillips, pp. 114–20, for mercy as an aspect of justice. As Milton's legalistic God would put it, "Die hee or Justice must" (PL 3.210).

[95]Faerie Queene 5.10.2.7.

[96]See Gordon, p. 85; for the thistles, see George Ferguson, Signs and Symbols in Christian Art (1954; reprint ed., Oxford, 1971), p. 38.

SIX
ARTICULATE CLOCKS AND A SPLENDID RECOVERY

The decade between *Hero and Leander* and *Euthymiae Raptus or The Teares of Peace* (1609) is marked by Chapman's departure from his narrative poetry to a furious absorption in writing for the theater. This period produced a sequence of brilliantly experimental comedies, one great tragedy, and interesting attempts to modify dramatic form to accommodate a platonic aesthetic. Chapman's work in this medium, however, ought to be seen as a natural extension of the interests embodied in the poems of the 1590s. Again and again he uses mythic narrative as the basic structure for ideas and action both; and his generic experimentalism bespeaks his concern that the form of poetic utterance accurately reflects its content. Such time as could be stolen from the theater appears to have been devoted almost exclusively to the Homer translations, which punctuate this time-span with *The Seaven Bookes of the Illiads* and *Achilles Shield* in 1598 and *The Twelue Bookes* in 1609. Curiously, it is this increasing involvement with Homer that motivated the writing of *The Teares of Peace*. Although the ostensible occasion of the poem was the truce between Spain and the Netherlands, which King James helped to effect, it would be more accurate to describe it as a celebration of Prince Henry's promise to sponsor the complete *Illiads* (1207–32). *The Teares of Peace* is—in the best sense of the phrase—a promotional letter.

This poem is the only one in the Chapman canon which seems in any danger of being overrated. Douglas Bush calls it the "most central and lucid exposition" of Chapman's philosophy, and MacLure maintains, "The argument of *The Teares of Peace* is tedious and repetitive, but must be considered at length, for it is the centre of Chapman's thought and the clue to his inner life."[1] The operative terms in these statements are *exposition*, *argument*, and *thought*: the poem, in other words, is regarded as important for its content, not for its poetic merit. The destinc-

---

[1]Douglas Bush, *English Literature in the Earlier Seventeenth Century, 1600–1660*, rev. ed. (Oxford, 1962), pp. 96–97; Millar MacLure, *George Chapman: A Critical Study* (Toronto, 1966), p. 70.

tion needs to be made clearly, because the same prosy discursiveness which gives Chapman's argument lucidity signals its failure, albeit an interesting one, as a poetic construct.

Chapman casts *The Teares of Peace* in the form of a dream vision. The poet, meditating by himself in "least trodden fieldes," suddenly sees "a comfortable light / Brake through the shade; and, after it, the sight / Of a most graue, and goodly person shinde" (33–35). In a trance, the two view each other "soule to soule," and the visitor, identifying himself as Homer, who had previously inspired Chapman to translate him, offers to conduct him to "true Peace." By "rent[ing] a Cloude downe, with his burning hand," Homer permits the poet to view a strange funeral procession. It is presided over by Peace, "A Lady, like a Deitie indew'd," who explains that she mourns the death of human love, which is a consequence of the lack of true learning in mankind. Peace and the poet anatomize this subject for some eight-hundred lines before the procession can resume. Entering a fearsome wood, Peace then rescues the body of human love from the monster "Murther" and completes the funeral ceremony before all but the poet are "rauisht" to heaven.

The entire formal concept of vision projecting the narrator into a consolation-debate with a personification who represents a didactically superior position, originated with Boethius.[2] Here, although Chapman probably knew Boethius, the use of conventions Englished from the *Roman de la Rose* and the entire medieval flavor suggest that Chapman is emulating both Chaucer and the vision of medievalism which Spenser projects in his poetry.[3] The episode of Murther in his cave (1128–65), the simile about "errant Knights, that by enchantments swerue, / From their true Ladyes being; and embrace / An ougly Witch, with her phantastique face" (456–58), the thematic emphasis on temperance, all are particularly Spenserian touches, although probably Chapman is thinking of Spenser's complaints as much as of *The Faerie Queene*.[4]

Within the dream-vision framework of *The Teares of Peace* Chapman pursues the subject of learning in relentless detail. In the Plotinian sculptural analogy, learning gives form to man by cutting away the excesses "Of Humors, perturbations and Affects" to reveal the image of

[2]See Morton W. Bloomfield, *Piers Plowman as a Fourteenth Century Apocalypse* (New Brunswick, N.J., 1962), p. 20; on the popularity of "debate" or "contest" literature, see Erwin Panofsky, *Galileo as a Critic of the Fine Arts* (The Hague, 1954), pp. 1–4.

[3]Robert K. Presson has suggested that Chapman's reading of Boethius inspired *A Coronet for his Mistresse Philosophie*; see "Wrestling with This World: A View of George Chapman," *PMLA*, 84 (1969): 48. For helpful accounts of dream-vision conventions, see Constance B. Hieatt, *The Realism of Dream Visions* (The Hague, 1967), pp. 16–18, 79; and J. V. Cunningham, *Tradition and Poetic Structure* (Denver, 1960), pp. 63–64, 68–69.

[4]The Spenserian quality of Murther was noticed by Elizabeth Holmes, *Aspects of Elizabethan Imagery* (Oxford, 1929), p. 79.

his indwelling soul (366–84). Three kinds of men are the greatest enemies of learning—active men, who consume their lives in ambition; passive men, who are characterized by idle curiosity; and intellective men, who use learning for mere reward and actually attain only the shadow of learning (409–62). True learning is temperance, the informing faculty of the soul (504–23), turns "blood to soule," and makes peace with God (556–66). It teaches the soul how to control her empire; "Then, (like a man in health) the whole consort / Of his tun'd body, sings" (671–72). The poet explains how and why learning is abused, and how to reform the abuses with self-discipline, temperance, harmony. Man's soul, after attaining peace through learning, self-knowledge, and understanding, can then ascend to union with God. The poet closes by consecrating himself to peace in the hope that his verse will inspire Henry, who is to be the form of true peace (1021–80).

MacLure believes that "This poem undoubtedly marks the transition from Chapman's admiration of the Achillean virtues to his glorification of the inward powers in Odysseus, or from Bussy and Byron to Clermont, or from wisdom as the initiation into *mysteria* to wisdom as the *habit* of self-discipline and virtue."[5] Possibly; but MacLure seems to ignore the generic implications of the poem. The convention of the vision poem suggests that the dream is a revelation or that it symbolizes a higher order of truth.[6] Admittedly, the length of the consolation-debate makes it difficult to remember the framework of the vision, but, in fact, the wisdom of the poem is presented exactly as "the initiation into *mysteria*."

Jacquot plausibly suggested that the apparition of Homer is modeled upon the appearance of Pimander to Hermes Trismegistus in Book 1 of *The Pimander* and that the imagery and attributes given to Homer derive from Book 10, "The Key." "*La Clef* nous explique donc toutes les circonstances de cette apparition: la lumière surnaturelle, le corps de feu, la bienveillance de l'esprit qui conseille au poète de le regarder sans timidité, car tout homme a le pouvoir de devenir semblable a lui."[7] Building upon Jacquot's insight, Maren-Sofie Røstvig pointed to the influence of Pico della Mirandola's Hermetic oration:

> *The Teares of Peace* should be compared to sections 13 and 14 of Pico's Oration, and when this has been done, it will be realized that Chapman's introduction of Homer was inspired by Pico. Thus Pico makes the point that only moral

[5]MacLure, p. 75.

[6]Bloomfield, p. 11. Chapman's alternative title, *Euthymiae Raptus*, insists upon the same point.

[7]Jean Jacquot, *George Chapman (1559–1634), sa vie, sa poésie, son théâtre, sa pensée* (Paris, 1951), pp. 74–75. Jacquot believes that Chapman "connaissait bien" the *Corpus Hermetica*; see p. 74, n. 30.

philosophy is capable of checking "the leonine passions of wrath and violence" and in this connection he recalls Homer's definition of nature as strife. And if nature is strife, then only the study of moral philosophy can induce in man "a true quiet and unshaken peace."[8]

The sections of the oration to which Røstvig directs our attention are, in their overt concern with peace, certainly pertinent to *The Teares of Peace*. Even more pervasively than this, however, the poem and the oration exhibit a consonance of ideas. For instance, Pico's discussion of the three Delphic precepts, "nothing too much," "know thyself," and the greeting to God, "Thou art," comes very close to Chapman's lessons. The same is true of his explanation of the Pythagorean precepts as warnings to excise the passions and appetites of the body and to nourish the soul with proper knowledge. Indeed, since one of Pico's major objectives is to defend his study of philosophy, the argument of the oration frequently runs parallel to Chapman's defense of "learning" (for Chapman, virtually identical to what Pico calls "philosophy" or "the liberal arts").[9] This emphasis on learning may seem counter to the Hermetic cultivation of the intuitive faculty, which Yates has described: "Philosophy was to be used, not as a dialectical exercise, but as a way of reaching intuitive knowledge of the divine and of the meaning of the world, as a gnosis, in short, to be prepared for by ascetic discipline and a religious way of life."[10] But for the Renaissance littérateur that preparation was likely to take the form of a disciplined, religious study of revered classical texts. Pico and Chapman both would have approved the course of Milton's poet:

> let my Lamp at midnight hour,
> Be seen in some high lonely Tow'r,
> Where I may oft outwatch the *Bear*,
> With thrice great *Hermes*, or unsphere
> The spirit of *Plato* to unfold
> What Worlds, or what vast Regions hold
> The immortal mind that hath forsook
> Her mansion in this fleshly nook.[11]

[8]Maren-Sofie Røstvig, *The Hidden Sense*, Norwegian Studies in English, no. 9 (Oslo, 1963), p. 78 n. I find this suggestion much more persuasive than the claim for Erasmus's *Querela Pacis* made by Jacquot (pp. 73–74).

[9]I use the translation by C. G. Wallis in Pico della Mirandola, *On The Dignity of Man, On Being and the One, Heptaplus*, Library of Liberal Arts, no. 227 (Indianapolis, 1965), pp. 10–12, 13–18.

[10]Frances A. Yates, *Giordano Bruno and the Hermetic Tradition* (Chicago, 1964), p. 4; see also her discussion of Pico, pp. 84–116.

[11]*Il Penseroso*; quoted from John Milton, *Complete Poems and Major Prose*, ed. Merritt Y. Hughes (New York, 1957), lines 85–92.

There is an essential fitness in the strong possibility that Chapman, who promised a never-written "Poeme of the mysteries / Reueal'd in *Homer*," borrowed the structure and particulars of an argument from Pico, who boasted that Homer was a magician which "we shall prove sometime in our *Poetic Theology* to have disguised this magic too, just as he did all other wisdoms, under the wanderings of Ulysses."[12] Kindred projectors with kindred visions.

Both the form of *The Teares of Peace* and the philosophic context of its ideas, then, proclaim that we remain in the familiar realm of revealed mysteries. Chapman's complaints about manless men, the chaotic world, and the need to create spiritual form in individuals are not any newer than his remedies—harmony to replace the prevailing disorder, temperance to control the passions and appetites. The same complaints could be detailed from the *Hymnvs in Noctem* and *Ovids Banquet of Sence*, just as the values could be inferred from *Cynthiam* and *Hero and Leander*. Chapman himself shows full awareness of the continuity of thought: "and I now must note / The large straine of a verse, I long since wrote. / Which (me thought) much ioy, to men poore presented" (*Teares* 632–34). The difference, rather, is more a shift in focus than a change in concept; here he troubles to spell out the reasons for that arduous learning which previously, in the dedications to his poems, he had taken for granted. The full anatomy of learning would seem to have been dictated by the occasion of the poem; it announces the forthcoming completion of his Homer translation under the patronage of Prince Henry. Since Homer in Chapman's eyes contains all truth, wisdom, philosophy, what better way to promote interest in the translation than by exposing the need for learning which can best be attained by reading Homer?

This may be the time to suggest, without impugning Chapman's sincerity in the least, that Shakespeare's gibe about "that affable familiar ghost / Which nightly gulls him with intelligence" has misled Chapman's critics into taking the claim to direct inspiration from Homer, like the invocation to Marlowe in the *Hero and Leander*, much too literally. Here Chapman makes Homer say,

> I am (sayd hee) that spirit *Elysian*,
> That (in thy natiue ayre; and on the hill
> Next *Hitchins* left hand) did thy bosome fill,
> With such a flood of soule; that thou wert faine
> (With acclamations of her Rapture then)
> To vent it, to the Echoes of the vale;
> When (meditating of me) a sweet gale

[12]Pico, *On the Dignity of Man*, p. 27.

Brought me vpon thee; and thou didst inherit
My true sense (for the time then) in my spirit;
And I, inuisiblie, went prompting thee,
To those fayre Greenes, where thou didst english me.

[*Teares* 75–85]

Integral to Chapman's poetics is the descent of the *divinus furor* during
the creation of any serious poem; but the frequency of such claims in his
prefaces and the poems themselves should alert us to see them, like the
muse which visited Milton's slumbers nightly, as a part of the entire
symbolic projection of vatic persona, not necessarily as biographical
data or psychic phenomena. The assertion of direct inspiration by a
translator or by a poet working in a tradition is not uncommon. In the
prologue to his *Annales* Ennius, the first Roman to write an epic, notoriously claimed a Pythagorean transmigration of souls from Homer to
himself (after his previous incarnation as a peacock). Jasper Heywood,
the Elizabethan translator of Seneca, wrote a twenty-five page verse
preface, describing how, on 24 November in bad weather, he happened
to fall asleep over a book only to have a vision of a figure dressed in
scarlet, crowned with bayes and carrying a book. It is Seneca, of course,
who not only commands Heywood to finish his translation but explains that discriminating readers will not blame Heywood for printer's
errors and obligingly offers to help him with the hard bits.[13]

The problem with the *Teares of Peace*, however, is not that the ideas
are familiar ones amplified or that the vision framework may be more
"conventional" than "personal"; such things never matter in poetry. It
is, rather, that Chapman fails to use the imaginative construct of the
vision form and the mythic narrative to translate the homily on learning
into poetry. George Herbert's defense might be offered: "Who sayes that
fictions onely and false hair / Become a verse? Is there in truth no
beautie? / Is all good structure in a winding stair?" (*Jordan 1*, lines
1–3). But such a defense would be inappropriate because Chapman's
handling of the vision and even of the funeral procession set up sophisti-
cated expectations that are aborted by the simplicity with which he
handles the long consolation-debate section. The effect is analogous to
entering a chrome-and-glass elevator and being handed a rope ladder by
the attendant. To call the instructional center of the poem a "consolation" or a "debate" is itself a misnomer, because Chapman does not
differentiate that much between the two speakers in voice, point of view,
and degree of knowledge. As Jacquot and MacLure have noted, both
Peace and the poet speak with one voice and it is impossible to read this

---

[13]Ennius' *Annales* survives only in fragments but the prologue is mentioned by, e.g.,
Lucretius, *De rerum natura* 1.123–25; Cicero, *Academica* 2.51; and Persius, *Satirae* 6.10–11.
For Heywood's preface, see *The Seconde Tragedie of Seneca entituled Thyestes, faithfully
Englished by Jasper Heywood* (London, 1560).

section as anything other than monologue.[14] Morton Bloomfield has stated that "the weakness of this genre from the point of view of aesthetic considerations . . . is a tendency to bog down in endless talk."[15] A tendency, unfortunately, which Chapman was unable to resist.

The only point of poetic interest in the long desert of didacticism which stretches from lines 266 to 1080 occurs when the narrator digresses to describe the figure of Justice as he once saw her:

> by the Seas shore, she sat giuing lawe
> Euen to the streames, and fish (most loose and wilde)
> And was (to my thoughts) wondrous sweet and milde;
> Yet fire flew from her that dissolued Rocks;
> Her lookes, to Pearle turnd pebble; and her locks,
> The rough, and sandy bankes, to burnisht gould;
> Her white left hand, did goulden bridles holde;
> And, with her right, she wealthy gifts did giue;
> Which with their left hands, men did still receiue;
> Vpon a world in her chaste lappe, did lye,
> A little Iuory Book, that show'd mine eye,
> Where all Arts, were contracted, and explainde;
> But one Page onely; that one verse containde,
> All policies of Princes, all their forces;
> Rules for their feares, cares, dangers, pleasures, purses,
> All the fayre progresse of their happinesse here,
> Iustice conuerted, and composed there.

[Teares 613–29]

This complex, syncretic icon gives us a better sense of Chapman's meaning than do several hundred surrounding lines of exposition. Her macrocosmic identity is fixed by the first detail of giving law, which means order, to nature; at the same time the globe of empire, Astraea's book of law, and her position by the seashore serve to suggest that the earthly embodiment Chapman once saw was Elizabeth, as Astraea and as Cynthia, queen of the ocean.[16] Although she displays some of the conventional attributes of justice—the book of law and a sight which penetrates to essences, for instance—the better-known sword and balance are missing.[17] The combination of attributes here suggests that Chapman

---

[14]Jacquot, p. 76, and MacLure, p. 73.

[15]Bloomfield, p. 21.

[16]For some of the many pictorial representations of Elizabeth with globe and scepter, see the plates to Frances Yates, "Queen Elizabeth as Astraea," *Journal of the Warburg and Courtauld Institutes*, 10 (1947): 27–82. On the book which Astraea left behind see Comes, *Mythologiae Sive Explicationvm Fabvlarum* (Paris, 1583), 2.2.

[17]On the book as attribute, see Guy de Tervarent, *Attributs et Symboles dans l'Art Profane, 1450-1600* (Geneva, 1958–59), 2:251. For Justice with piercing sight, see Aulus Gellius, *Attic Nights* 14.4. According to Erwin Panofsky, the figure of blind Justice "is a humanis-

has conflated Justice with the figures of Doctrina, who also has her book, and Temperance, to whom the golden bridles belong. Henry Peacham's Temperance holds the bridle in her right hand and a cup in her left, establishing the priority of restraint over generosity; Chapman's Justice reverses this order in her own actions, although the men who receive her bounty ought to prefer restraining their appetites.[18] The implicit praise of Elizabeth's generosity a half-dozen years after her death is generous in itself, if more restrained than Sir John Davies's acrostical *Hymnes to Astraea*, wherein Justice-Eliza holds reward in her right hand and clemency in her left.[19] Chapman's description gradually focuses upon the open book with its single verse which contracts all laws to the single form or pattern leading to peace. Proportion, order, harmony, restraint are the gifts given by Chapman's Justice, and which, he adds parenthetically, can be found in "The large straine of a verse, I long since wrote":

It might (for the capacitie it beares)
Be that concealed and expressiue verse,
That Iustice, in her Iuorie Manuell writ;
Since all Lines to mans Peace, are drawne in it.

[*Teares* 636–39]

The qualities and the total symbolic meaning of justice are clear enough; what may be obscure is Chapman's reason—other than nostalgia for the old queen—for making this figure the imagistic key to his disquisition on learning. Evidently here his conception was influenced, as it had been in *Hero and Leander*, by the platonic tradition which assigns to justice an importance exceeding the other cardinal virtues, because justice is the power of the soul which determines the particular functions of the others.[20] This icon of justice at the center of the consolation-debate is one manifestation of an extremely complex mythic form which Chapman conceived for the poem but only fitfully realized. The other tangible clues to this phantom structure are the narrator's vision

---

tic concoction of very recent origin" (*Studies in Iconology* [1939; reprint ed., New York, 1962], p. 109 and n). For sword and balance, see Tervarent, s.v.

[18]For Doctrina and Temperance, see Henry Peacham, *Minerva Britanna 1612*, English Emblem Books no. 5 (Menston, Yorkshire, 1969), pp. 26, 93. Peacham's Doctrina derives from Ripa's "Dottrina." See Ripa, *Iconologia* (Rome, 1603), p. 113. The symbolism of Chapman's Justice was noticed, in passing, by Holmes, p. 78. On the meaning of the bridle, see A. D. S. Fowler, "Emblems of Temperance in *The Faerie Queene*, Book II," *Review of English Studies*, 11 (1960): 143–44.

[19]See Yates, "Queen Elizabeth as Astraea," p. 65.

[20]See Edgar Wind, "Platonic Justice, designed by Raphael," *Journal of the Warburg Institute*, 1 (1937–38): 69–70; the source of the idea is *The Republic* 4.432–34.

"Temperentia," from Henry Peacham, *Minerva Britanna or a Garden of Heroical Diuises*. Reproduced from the Scolar Press facsimile edition by permission of the Glasgow University Library.

"Doctrina," from Henry Peacham, *Minerva Britanna or a Garden of Heroical Diuises*. Reproduced from the Scolar Press facsimile edition by permission of the Glasgow University Library.

of Homer, with its shadowing of Pimander's revelation to Hermes, and an extraordinary passage in the conclusion.

To permit the passage of the funeral procession Peace dispells the conditions and mental attitudes antithetical to her nature:

> But now (made free from them) next her, before;
> Peacefull, and young, Herculean silence bore
> His craggie Club; which vp, aloft, hee hild;
> With which, and his forefingers charme hee stild
> All sounds in ayre; and left so free, mine eares,
> That I might heare, the musique of the Spheres,
> And all the Angels, singing, out of heauen;
> Whose tunes were solemne (as to Passion giuen)
> For now, that Iustice was the Happinesse there
> For all the wrongs to Right, inflicted here.

[*Teares* 1105–14]

The personification of silence as "Herculean" requires considerable explanation; but, since I have ventured a detailed statement elsewhere, I shall only outline the process here.[21] The mystery religions, the Pythagoreans, and the platonists developed a cult of silence, which paradoxically was regarded as a high form of eloquence. When the Greeks sought a personage to represent the idea of silence, they found him ready-made, through a fortuitous misinterpretation of Harpocrates, the child Horus. In Egyptian iconography Harpocrates invariably was pictured holding his finger to his lips, a gesture symbolizing his childishness which the Greeks mistook as meaning silence. Wrong though it was, the idea of Harpocrates as the god of silence with his characteristic gesture was perpetuated by all the Renaissance mythographers. The iconography of silence undergoes a metamorphosis in Achille Bocchi's *Symbolicarvm Qvaestionvm*, which pictures Hermes with his finger at his lips in the Harpocratean gesture. Hermes had long been the god of eloquence and Bocchi, knowing the esoteric tradition of eloquent silence, blends the two gods to make a new figure of silent eloquence. But Bocchi also plays upon the confusion between the Greek Hermes and the Egyptian Hermes Trismegistus, who in the *Hermetica* is associated with the silence of contemplation and mystical illumination.

Chapman gives us the last turn of the screw. Very possibly the whole process began in his mind with a passage in Pico's oration. Just after the reference to Homer commented upon by Røstvig, Pico explains that Theology will be our guide to that lasting peace which natural philosophy cannot reach:

> As we are called so sweetly and are invited with such kindness, let us fly on winged feet like earthly Mercuries into the embrace of our most blessed mother and enjoy the longed-for peace: the most holy peace, the indivisible bond, the friendship which is one soul, the friendship whereby all minds do not merely accord in one intellect that is above every intellect but in some inexpressible fashion become absolutely one. This is that friendship which the Pythagoreans say is the end of all philosophy. This is that peace which God makes on his heights and which the angels descending to earth announced to men of good will, that by this peace the men themselves ascending into heaven might become angels.[22]

Chapman transforms Pico's declamation to poetry. His Peace replaces Pico's Theology; the conjuction of references to Pythagoreans and angels raises the possibility of the enraptured soul hearing the music of the spheres and the angelic choir. But, while the Hermetic context of Pico's

---

[21]R. B. Waddington, "The Iconography of Silence and Chapman's Hercules," *Journal of the Warburg and Courtauld Institutes*, 33 (1970): 248–63; the paragraph here summarizes the argument of pp. 248–59. For a conventional figure of silence, see *Hymnvs in Noctem*, 388–89.

[22]Pico, *On the Dignity of Man*, pp. 11–12.

oration can plausibly suggest transforming the simile of "earthly Mercuries" ("quasi terrestres Mercurii") to the silent, Egyptian Hermes, by what imaginative leap does he become silent Hercules?

Chapman relies upon three phases of his favorite hero's protean career: the association of Hercules with wisdom and learning; the tradition, which Spenser used in Book 5 of The Faerie Queene, of Hercules as god of justice; and the tradition of the "Gallic Hercules," which celebrated the hero for his eloquence rather than for physical strength. Whether Chapman knew directly the precedent of Bocchi's Hermes is unimportant. He may have, but his own grasp of the complex material was so sure and typological adaptation so characteristic of his poetic strategy that he could have just as readily arrived at the analogous conclusion independently. However it was done, to Bocchi's blending of the three figures, Harpocrates and the two Hermes, he adds a fourth, a silently eloquent Hercules.

In Chapman's image the attributes of the gods are delicately balanced to imply a harmonious melding of qualities. "Herculean silence" is represented as "Peacefull, and young." An eloquent and youthful Hercules, of course, violates the dictum of Lucian's Gauls, for whom he is extremely old and bald-headed, revealing the moderating influence of the child-god Harpocrates.[23]

In the Stoic tradition, importantly elaborated for the sixteenth century by Salutati's De Laboribus Herculis, the onetime strong man becomes a type for temperance and moderation while his labors are allegorized as the triumph of reason over the baser passions.[24] The role of learning in conquering passions as man strives to temper his own mind is a dominant theme in Chapman's poem:

> But this is Learning; To haue skill to throwe
> Reignes on your bodies powres, that nothing knowe;
> And fill the soules powers, so with act, and art,
> That she can curbe the bodies angrie part.
>
> [Teares 504–7]

He had characterized "the deepe search of knowledge" as "that Herculean labour" in the dedication to The Shadow of Night; and in The Teares of Peace, as well, the pattern of behavior through which the virtuous man can attain knowledge to transcend the world and "ascend the high-heauen-reaching Skale / Of mans true Peace" (863–64) is again that of Hercules' labors:

---

[23]On the Gallic Hercules, see Waddington, "The Iconography of Silence," pp. 260–61.

[24]See Eugene M. Waith, The Herculean Hero in Marlowe, Chapman, Shakespeare and Dryden (New York, 1962), pp. 39–45; also Marcel Simon, Hercule et le christianisme (Strasbourg, 1955).

> the Ills infinite,
> That (like beheaded *Hydra's* in that Fen
> Of bloud, and flesh, in lewd illiterate men)
> Aunswere their amputations, with supplyes
> That twist their heads, and euer double rise;
> Herculean Learning conquers.

[*Teares* 693–98]

The association of Hercules with peace in the conclusion, therefore, has been anticipated in the debate section. The silence of Hercules is designed to imply the achievement of that state of spiritual dominance and self-control through knowledge which in the Hermetic doctrine must precede regeneration, a theme foreshadowed in the vision by the Pimander-Hermes relationship of Homer and the narrator.[25]

Chapman merges the figures of Hercules and Harpocrates, connoting wisdom and silence, and bridges the conditions by the common attribute of eloquence. The act by which the sounds of the world are stilled projects a balance between the essential identities of the deities. As the iconographic signature of the gesturing forefinger had come to epitomize Harpocrates, so the lion skin and gnarled club proclaimed Hercules. Chapman's description insists upon the ensuing silence as the product of Hercules' composite nature; "his forefingers charme" and "His craggie Club" held aloft together effect the suspension of the barbarous discord. Cesare Ripa explains that the club signifies reason; Spenser calls it "The club of Iustice dread."[26] Either interpretation accords well with the theme of peace attained through "Herculean learning." The paradox that the potential violence of the threatening club enforces peace and harmony itself points toward the nonphysical nature of Hercules' strength, just as the cragginess of the club connotes the strenuous achievement of spiritual discipline. Like the pointing finger, the club directs attention "vp, aloft," indicating the traditional course of the soul's ascent to union with the divine. For the Hermeticist wisdom and silence coalesce to form the state inducive of spiritual regeneration; and the image of Chapman's hybrid god symbolizes the result of the spiritual program urged by his poem: "For now, that Iustice was the Happinesse there / For all the wrongs to Right, inflicted here."

The imaginative conception of this fictive body as a vehicle for his ideas is brilliant. Had Chapman succeeded in wedding the mythic and

[25]Jacquot, too, feels that Chapman transforms the Hermetic elements into an imaginative unity (p. 76). Yates, *Giordano Bruno*, p. 4, states, "The Hermetic treatises, which often take the form of dialogues between master and disciple, usually culminate in a kind of ecstasy in which the adept is satisfied that he has received an illumination and breaks out into hymns of praise"—not a bad description of *The Teares of Peace*.

[26]Ripa, "Virtu Heroica," in *Iconologia*, p. 507; *Faerie Queene* 5.1.2.9.
For Chapman's use of Ripa elsewhere, see D. J. Gordon, "*Le Masque Memorable* de Chapman*," in *Les Fêtes de la Renaissance*, ed. Jean Jacquot (Paris, 1956), 1: 305–15.

generic forms of the poem—indeed, had he been able to use the generic form with ordinary competence—*The Teares of Peace* might legitimately have ranked as one of his greatest accomplishments. But the conception is so imperfectly realized, the flickers of real poetry so infrequent, that we can only admire *The Teares of Peace* platonically, as one might admire an architect's design for a house. Michael Murrin reminds us, "The basic plot of an allegory must always be mythic. Where it is not, the poet has failed—has not succeeded in converting his tale into metaphor."[27] And Chapman has not succeeded here.

Because Chapman's next two narrative poems, *An Epicede or Fvnerall Song* for Prince Henry ("my most deare and Heroicall Patrone") and *Eugenia* for the death of Lord Russell, exhibit the same failings as *The Teares of Peace*, we shall consider them only briefly. The three are alike in their elegiac occasions (if we want to put weight on the fictional mourning in *The Teares of Peace*) and in their author's evident inability to coordinate his generic and mythic inventions effectively.

An Epicede (1612) is cast as a lamentation spoken over the unburied body and culminates with an epitaph to enscribe the prince's hearse.[28] The generic choice dictates a greater emphasis upon grief with correspondingly less attention to the consolation; the immediacy of the event and the poet's grief are underscored by his scorn for the "wits prophane," whose inferior tributes will follow the "sacred rage" of this verse (326–32). For the myth of *An Epicede* Chapman turned to a famous neo-Latin poem, the *Elegia sive Epicedion in Albierae Albitiae immaturum exitum*, by Angelo Poliziano, the grammarian and poet of the Medici circle.[29] Chapman must have felt an affinity for Poliziano, who was a fellow admirer and translator of Homer, friend of Ficino, and mythographer. The deaths of the two subjects, Henry and Albiera, were circumstantially similar, both premature and both by fever. But, most interesting of all, Poliziano invented for his elegy the myth of the goddess Fever, contriving out of various classical components, mainly Ovidian, a new, syncretic myth appropriate to his needs.[30] Poliziano's technique in creating Fever is very similar to Chapman's own invention of Herculean silence; Poliziano may well have been one of Chapman's teachers.

[27]Michael Murrin, *The Veil of Allegory: Some Notes Toward a Theory of Allegorical Rhetoric in the English Renaissance* (Chicago, 1969), p. 99.

[28]Three epitaphs follow Chapman's epicedium. The second appears on the base of Henry's hearse in the engraving which accompanies the volume. For a description, see Bartlett, *Poems*, pp. 451–52. On the types of funeral songs, see O. B. Hardison, *The Enduring Monument* (Chapel Hill, 1962), p. 198.

[29]See Hardison, pp. 131–37, for an analysis of the *Elegia*. Chapman also paraphrased Poliziano in two of his prefaces to Homer; see Bartlett's note, *Poems*, p. 486.

[30]See Alessandro Perosa, "Febris: A Poetic Myth Created by Poliziano," *Journal of the Warburg and Courtauld Institutes*, 9 (1946): 74–95.

Since the "discovery" that the second half of *An Epicede* is an adaptation of the Poliziano elegy, Chapman has been abused for his lack of inventiveness, for padding his poem, and for the disharmony of its parts.[31] No doubt Chapman would have been astonished that anyone could have missed recognizing the adaptation; he even cues its presence with an obvious pun, "aske an Angels tongue" (333). And he did try to unify the parts on the conceptual level with a sustained architectural figure. The underlying conceit is the body as temple of the spirit, which Chapman integrates with the macrocosmic relation between a man and his house. Chapman finds symbolic currency in the names of the prince's houses, Saint James and Richmond:

His house had well his surname from a *Saint*,
All things so sacred, did so liuely paint
Their pious figures in it: And as well
His other house, did in his Name fore-tell
What it should harbour; a rich world of parts
Bonfire-like kindling, the still-feasted Arts.

[*Epicede* 166–71]

The "Heroique formes" of Henry's mind provided a pattern of virtue for all men to emulate in the same way that the form of a great temple impresses its meaning upon the minds of beholders in ages after (277–314). With Henry's premature death the edifice is destroyed: "And as the ruines of some famous Towne, / Show here a Temple stood; a Pallace, here; / A Cytadell, and Amphitheater" (316–18), "So of our Princes state, I nought rehearse / But show his ruines, bleeding in my verse" (323–24). The ancient Romans built temples to Fever (422–25), whose jealousy of Henry is aroused when she learns that "*Temples* rayse/To his *Expectance*, and *Vnbounded Praise*" (434–35). Goaded to a fury by Rhamnusia (Nemesis), Fever enters the darkened palace where sleep ("th'Ominous forme of death") has breathed on Henry's "bright Temples," and she strikes. The last house that Henry will occupy is the "sable Phane" sheltering his tomb. Again, as with *The Teares of Peace*, an idea of a poem may be discerned here, but the execution is another matter. Ruth Wallerstein, who has examined *An Epicede* carefully, comments, "The styles of the two sections differ widely, and even the style of the first section itself is not all of a piece." And, although I do not find her whole argument tenable, her conclusion that Chapman has "destroyed the literary type and tone" of the Poliziano elegy "without achieving any new synthesis" seems just.[32]

---

[31]See, e.g., Franck L. Schoell, "George Chapman and the Italian Neo-Latinists of the Quatrocento," *Modern Philology*, 13 (1915): 220–31; and Bartlett, *Poems*, pp. 7–8.

[32]Ruth Wallerstein, *Studies in Seventeenth-Century Poetic* (Madison, 1950), pp. 88, 90.

Chapman has a facility for driving his critics to hyperbole, but *Eugenia* (1614)—with its anniversary intention, allegory, inductions, four vigils, hymns, multiple speakers, and marginal glosses—probably deserves MacLure's denunciation as "the most cluttered poem in English literature."[33] The organizing concept here calls for the praise of Russell's virtue by focusing upon the idea of heavenly fame,[34] but Chapman's scheme seems far less coherent than in the two preceding poems. The Inductio starts promisingly with the "House of Fame" myth, adapted from Ovid, and the bizarre, iconic figure of Religion.[35] This framework ceases to be functional in the succeeding vigils, however; and only the themes of form and formlessness, and the idea of fame maintain a nominal conceptual unity among the poem's diverse parts. In *The Teares of Peace* (530–33) Chapman argued that true learning will act to inform the body and reveal the soul's image; unless it serves this end, learning is worthless: "And let a Scholler, all earths volumes carrie, / He will be but a walking dictionarie: / A meere articulate Clocke, that doth but speake / By others arts." By Chapman's own poetics, the same proposition holds true for poems. Although *Eugenia* is easily the worst, all three of Chapman's funereal narratives must be adjudged "articulate clocks."

Surfaces deceive endlessly. What acquaintance of Jack Donne, that great frequenter of the theater and favorite of the ladies, could have imagined the preacher of *Death's Duell*, wrapped in his own shroud? Or, conversely, who would expect Chapman, for all his grumbling about the state of the world, to prove so much happier in poems for weddings rather than for funerals? The difference may merely have been a matter of temperament determining personal vision, Chapman's integrative and Donne's disintegrative. But it is tempting to infer that philosophy, more than the accident of temperament, ordains the focal point of that vision. Beneath Donne's veneer of platonism lurks a strong strain of medieval Christianity in the tradition of *contemptus mundi*. Chapman's brand of platonism runs deep in his thought, committing him to a view of life perceived as wholeness and harmony. That odd knack of his for writing popular comedy was not such an anomaly.

[33]MacLure, p. 79. Hardison, pp. 165–66, detects the influence of Donne's first *Anniversary*.

[34]See Edwin B. Benjamin, "Fame, Poetry, and the Order of History in the Literature of the English Renaissance," *Studies in the Renaissance*, 6 (1959): 83.

[35]Religion's metamorphosis to a grasshopper (with a probable pun, *grace-hoper*), deriving from the Tithonus myth, is caused by human neglect (see *Eugenia* 166–68). But the description—"All full of spiders was her homespun weede, / Where soules like flies hung" (*Eugenia* 187–88)—defies conventional associations; see, e.g., George Ferguson, *Signs and Symbols in Christian Art* (1954; reprint ed., New York, 1961), for spider and fly.

With *Andromeda Liberata* (1614) Chapman got another chance to demonstrate his best art. The spectacular aftermath of the Somerset-Howard wedding, which underscores the apparent gross ineptitude and tactlessness of Chapman's epithalamion, has seemed far more interesting than the poem itself. Douglas Bush remarks: "In the first place it is a little disconcerting to find our grave and high-minded moralist celebrating the virtues of that precious pair, the Earl of Somerset and the Countess of Essex, whose marriage, with its train of intrigue and murder and executions, was the scandal of the age."[36] Jean Jacquot finds the interest of the poem to be "surtout biographique." Although he considers the execution praiseworthy in some respects, he finally deems the poem only an example of Chapman's failure of inventiveness: "Mais les aimables lieux communs de la mythologie érotique ne suffisent pas à Chapman et il a recours, une fois encore, aux commentaires de Ficin sur le *Banquet* de Platon."[37]

Yet the simple fact that the poem is an epithalamion might indicate that it offers more than biographical interest, for the genre is particularly accommodating to Chapman's range of poetic interests. As Thomas M. Greene observes, "the typical epithalamion is a ritualistic *public* statement, unconcerned with the actual intimate experience undergone by individuals." The genre, moreover, well suits the vertical, hierarchial vision of the vatic poet: "[The wedding] may be primarily a sexual event, but it may be also a social event, a religious event, or, at the highest level, a political event. It may even in certain poems be related to the natural macrocosmos and thus become a kind of cosmic event."[38]

Marriage especially appealed to Chapman as a microcosmic harmony of opposites. It could be argued that the epithalamion inevitably involves a consideration of harmonic unity; but, in practice, emphasizing such a quality would depend entirely upon the individual writer. To a platonist like Spenser the harmony symbolized by the hymeneal union is of marked importance, as A. Kent Hieatt's exposition of the number symbolism in *Epithalamion* has demonstrated.[39] In *Hero and Leander* the crucial role of the goddess Ceremony, as well as the significance attached to the violation of the marriage rite and to the object lesson of the "Epithalamion Teratos," should suggest that the wedding, and hence the wedding poem, is of comparable importance to Chapman.

The story of the Somerset-Howard wedding and its ramifications is both too well known and too complex to warrant a detailed summary

[36]Douglas Bush, *Mythology and the Renaissance Tradition in English Poetry*, rev. ed. (New York, 1963), p. 221.

[37]Jacquot, p. 72.

[38]Thomas M. Greene, "Spenser and the Epithalamic Convention," *Comparative Literature*, 9 (1957): 221; see also pp. 215–28.

[39]A. Kent Hieatt, *Short Time's Endless Monument* (New York, 1960).

here.[40] It will be enough to recall that for political reasons James had arranged in 1606 a child marriage between Frances Howard, daughter of Thomas Howard, Earl of Suffolk, and the third Earl of Essex. After some years Frances began an intrigue with Robert Carr, James's powerful Scottish favorite, and petitioned for an annulment of her marriage on the pretext that Essex was impotent. With the approval of James, the marriage was annulled on 25 September 1613. Carr's fortunes for a time improved remarkably: on 3 November, he was made Earl of Somerset; on 23 December, treasurer of Scotland; on 26 December, married to Frances; in 1614, appointed Lord Chamberlain and Keeper of the Privy Seal. It was in March of 1614 that Chapman's poem celebrating the wedding was registered.

The mythic form which Chapman selected as the appropriate embodiment of his poetic reaction to this affair was the Perseus-Andromeda story. The kind of myth and the ritual banishment of the many, "Away, vngodly Vulgars, far away," intimate a return to the full-blown allegorical rhetoric and mythic narratives of his earlier poetry. Always an attractive vehicle for allegory, this story has been used by as recent a poet as Hopkins, who saw Andromeda as the human soul and Perseus as Christ. In Chapman's own day the fable was interpreted variously.[41] Comes' *Mythologiae* provides the source of the story as Chapman uses it,[42] but on this occasion Chapman consults the handbook for plot rather than meaning. John Marston, who—perplexed by poetic obscurity—called upon Comes to "ayde me to unrip / These intricate deepe oracles of wit / These dark enigmaes, and strange ridling sence, / Which pass my dullard braines intelligence,"[43] might here have been thwarted if he could not penetrate the surface of the poem itself. An acute reader

---

[40]The most detailed, scholarly account remains that of S. R. Gardiner, *History of England from the Accession of James I to the Outbreak of the Civil War, 1603–1642* (London, 1883), 2: 166–86, 304–63. For more recent studies, see, e.g., Beatrice White, *Cast of Ravens: The Strange Case of Sir Thomas Overbury* (London, 1965); and Edward S. Le Comte, *The Notorious Lady Essex* (New York, 1969).

[41]Christine de Pisan, available to Chapman in Stephen Scrope's translation, interpreted Andromeda as the soul (Bush, *Mythology*, p. 31). Francis Bacon makes no mention of Andromeda, but represents Perseus as "Warre" and interprets the slaying of the gorgon as an allegory of military strategy (*Wisedom of the Ancients*, trans. Sir Arthur Gorges [London, 1619], pp. 38–45). Abraham Fraunce regards the gorgon episode as an allegory of celestial grace and wisdom overcoming mortality (*The Third Part of the Countesse of Pembrokes Yuychurch, entitled, Amintas Dale* [London, 1592], p. 29), while George Sandys reads Andromeda as "innocent virtue" and Perseus as "honour and felicities" (*Ovid's Metamorphosis Englished* [Oxford, 1632], p. 168). Sir John Harington's preface to *Orlando Furioso* presents a three-level exegesis—historical, moral, and theological—of the myth (in C. Gregory Smith, *Elizabethan Critical Essays* [Oxford, 1904], 2: 202–3); Bush, *Mythology*, p. 71, discusses Harington's sources.

[42]See Franck L. Schoell, *Études sur l'humanisme continental en Angleterre a la fin de la renaissance* (Paris, 1926), p. 195.

[43]*The Poems of John Marston*, ed. Arnold Davenport (Liverpool, 1961), pp. 72–73.

would have found it unnecessary to seek the mythographers, for Chapman's concerns in the poem are sufficiently obvious that his whole treatment implements his particular use of the myth.

Briefly, the theme of the poem is order and disorder. Disorder, Chapman explains in the dedicatory epistle, was the condition of things before the formation of the world, "all confus'd, like waues struck with a storme," and "in no set being, staid":

> All comprehension, and connexion fled;
> The greater, and the more compact disturb'd
> With ceaseles warre, and by no order curb'd,
> Till earth receiuing her set magnitude
> Was fixt her selfe, and all her Birth indu'd
> With staie and law: so this small world of ours
> Is but a *Chaos* of corporeall powers,
> Nor yeelds his mixt parts, forms that may become
> A human Nature; But a randome rome
> Past Brutish fashions, and so neuer can
> Be cald the ciuill bodie of a man.
>
> [*Andr.* d.e. 124–34]

This chaotic, disorderly state of human nature, which echoes the primordial condition before God created law, form, and order, is seen as an inbalance of elements, wherein one quality goes to excess: "The more great in command, made seruile more, / Glutted, not satisfied: in plenty, poore" (d.e., 137–38). The poet consciously opposes himself to these unbalanced, lawless spirits; "And therefore, should no knowing spirit be driuen / From fact, nor purpose; for the spleens prophane / Of humours errant, and *Plebeian*" (d.e., 8–10). Within the poem this condition is identified as the property of the "*rauenous Multitude*," the people at large, "Whose poysons all things to your spleenes peruert, / And all streames measure by the Fount your Heart, / That are in nought but misrule regulare" (9–11). The rabble sullies Andromeda's innocence with malicious scandal: "vertues, lighted euen to starres, / All vicious Enuies, and seditious Iars, / Bane-spitting Murmures and detracting Spels, / Bannish with curses to the blackest hels" (29–32). Allied with the mob are the "*Neireides*," who persecute Andromeda because of jealousy. Both are represented in the myth by the sea monster which threatens Andromeda:

> And then came on the prodegie, that bore
> Jn one masse mixt their Image; that still spread
> A thousand bodies vnder one sole head
> *Of one minde still to ill all ill men are*
> *Strange Sights and mischiefes fit the Populare.*
>
> [*Andr.* 166–70]

Set in opposition to the discordant multitude are the temperate soul of Perseus, the harmonious beauty of Andromeda, and their transcendent union in marriage, which supplies the already admirable Perseus with the one moderating quality he needs to produce a seemingly quintessential *concordia discors*. The poet states the causes for Andromeda's intended sacrifice, sets the scene of her ordeal, and provides a lengthy description of her beauty (125–54). As she is threatened by the "whale" Perseus appears, "He that both vertue had, and beauty too / Equall with her" (237–38). The emphasis on this superlative physical beauty is deliberate; Chapman explains the interconnection between the beautiful or divinely attuned soul and its reflection in external form:

The minde a spirit is, and cal'd the glasse
In which we see God; and corporeall grace
The mirror is, in which we see the minde.
Amongst the fairest women you could finde
Then *Perseus*, none more faire; mongst worthiest men,
No one more manly: *This the glasse is then*
To shew where our complexion is combinde:
A womans beauty, and a manly minde:
Such was the halfe-diuine-borne Troian Terror
Where both Sex graces, met as in their Mirror.

[*Andr.* 241–50]

The function of Perseus as a *concordia discors* emblem becomes evident through his depiction as a spiritual hermaphrodite who encompasses the desirable characteristics of each sex. The particular qualities for which Perseus is commended are enumerated in units of three and two; one recalls from *Hero and Leander* that *three* and *two* are the male and female numerical equivalents, while five is the ritual marriage number.

Young was he, yet not youthfull, since mid-yeeres,
The golden meane holds in mens loues and feares:
Aptly composde, and soft (or delicate)
Flexible (or tender) calme (or temperate)
Of these fiue, three, make most exactly knowne,
The Bodies temperate complexion:
The other two, the order doe expresse,
The measure and whole Trim of comelinesse.

[*Andr.* 255–62]

The resultant balance of qualities produces a mean of temperance and moderation, actually a harmony of harmonies, since each of the particular qualities specified is, in itself, a judicious compromise between extremes. As Perseus is young but not too young, he is "pliant" but not excessively so:

> Not flexible, as of inconstant state,
> Nor soft, as if too much effeminate,
> For these to a complexion moderate
> (Which we before affirme in him) imply,
> A most vnequall contrariety.
>
> [*Andr.* 277–81]

It is exactly this same temperate moderation in all things, this personal *concordia discors*, for which Chapman, as if to make his meaning explicit, praises his patron in the dedication. Somerset is young, but already possesses the accumulated wisdom of age—"All fruits, in youth, ripe in you" (d.e., 95). In the same fashion that evening dew preserves the quality of day's beauty, "So you (sweete Earle) stay youth in aged bounds" (d.e., 105). Rhetorically and syntactically Chapman suggests the achieved median state through the balanced antitheses of an *eclipsis*, "Your grace, your virtue heightening: virtue, grace" (d.e., 108). The eulogy even pictures Somerset's mind as consisting of a *marriage* of contrary properties:

> The peacefull mixture then that meetes in yow
> (Most temperat Earl) that nought to rule doth ow:
> In which, as in a thorough kindled Fire,
> *Light* and *Heat* marrie *Judgement* and *Desire.*
>
> [*Andr.* d.e., 69–72]

Chapman allows no possibility of error; the qualities embodied by Perseus are the qualities he attributes to Somerset.

Having characterized the principals, Chapman next explains the process by which Perseus falls in love with Andromeda:

> "As to be lou'd, the fairest fittest are;
> "To loue so to, most apt are the most faire
> "Light like it selfe, transparent bodies makes
> "At ones act, th'other ioint impression takes.
>
> [*Andr.* 284–87]

In essence this is the doctrine proposed by Socrates in the *Symposium* and much amplified by Ficino: love is the desire for beauty. Chapman describes at considerable length the effect of love upon Perseus, the consequences of love, the seriousness of thwarted love, and, much more briefly, the dispatching of the sea monster. The narrative proper closes at the point of the marriage ceremony, the Parcarvm Epithalamion celebrates the union itself, prophesying "Progenie," and the Apodosis closes by moralizing generally on the implications of Perseus's triumphs.[44]

---

[44]For the rule that an epithalamion be divided into three parts, see George Puttenham, *The Arte of English Poesie*, ed. Gladys D. Willcock and Alice Walker (Cambridge, 1936), p. 51.

Since Schoell's source study revealed that key ideas in the last half of *Andromeda* originated in Ficino's *Commentarium in Convivum Platonis*,[45] this indebtedness frequently has been regarded as evidence of the feebleness of Chapman's poetic inspiration and proof of his surpassing pedantry. The tone of Jacquot's previously quoted appraisal is typical (see p. 196). Bartlett finds the passage concerning homicide (487–96) pertinent to the circumstances of the childless Essex marriage and so accepts it as the moral crux of the poem,[46] but makes no comment on the relevance of the other passages based on Ficino.

The first of these occurs following Perseus's realization of his love for Andromeda. Despite the impressive harmony of Perseus's character, it appears that he was deficient until fulfilled in love: "No wisdome, noblesse, force of armes, nor lawes, / Without loue, wins man, his compleat applause" (296–97). The process resulting in this completion is explained as the tempering of Mars's nature by Venus's, Mars being the culmination of masculine virtues and Venus of the feminine. She "tames" Mars, who is "Most full of fortitude (since he inspires / Men with most valour)." This domination of the male principal by love, exemplified by the Mars-Venus myth, is acted out on a cosmic scale by the planets which are named for the gods. Don Cameron Allen has noted the astrological correspondence which Chapman puts in verse (302–20).[47] This description of the planets' behavior, complete with harmonic implications ("*If Venus* neere him shine; she doth not let / His magnanimity, but in order set / The vice of Anger making *Mars* more milde"), comes directly from Ficino's elaboration upon Agathon's explanation of the virtues of love.[48]

The meaning of the Mars-Venus myth is discussed by Sandys, who tells us that the astrological sense of the legend "was invented to expresse the sympathy that is necessary in nature. . . . *Mars* likewise signifies strife and Venus friendship; which as the ancients held, were the parents of all things."[49] The ancients appropriated the legend of the adulterous passion between Mars and Venus to explain the contrary nature of things, Plato's principles of the Same and the Other.[50] The product of this union was Harmony (or Hermione),[51] who combined the qualities of her notable parents—*Harmonia est discordia concors*. This interpreta-

[45]Schoell, *Études*, pp. 1–20.

[46]Bartlett, *Poems*, p. 9.

[47]Don Cameron Allen, *The Star-Crossed Renaissance* (Durham, N.C., 1941), pp. 174–75.

[48]*Marsilio Ficino's Commentary on Plato's Symposium*, trans. Sears R. Jayne, University of Missouri Studies, 19 (Columbia, 1944), pp. 176–77.

[49]Sandys, *Ovid's Metamorphosis Englished*, p. 157. Cf. Lucretius, *De rerum natura* 1.30–41.

[50]In my exposition of this allegory I am much indebted to Edgar Wind, "Virtue Reconciled With Pleasure," in *Pagan Mysteries in the Renaissance* (New Haven, 1958), pp. 78–88.

[51]See Panofsky, *Studies in Iconology*, p. 163, n. 120.

tion of warlike contentiousness being tempered to harmony by love and friendship was commonplace in the Renaissance, and classical precedents were not hard to find. Schoell has found Chapman heavily indebted to Xylander's translation of Plutarch's *Moralia*; thus, the analysis of the myth in *De Homero* is very likely one that Chapman knew firsthand.[52] A more systematic and philosophic exposition of the allegory is provided by Pico della Mirandola, for whom *concordia discors* was the basis of an aesthetics:

> In these compositions the Union necessarily predominates over the contrariety; otherwise the Fabrick would be dissolved. Thus in the Fictions of Poets, *Venus* loves *Mars*; this Beauty cannot subsist without contrariety; she curbs and moderates him; this temperament allays the strife betwixt these contraries. And in Astrology, *Venus* is plac'd next *Mars*, to check his destructive influence. . . . If *Mars* were always subject to *Venus*, (the contrariety of principles to their due temper) nothing would ever be dissolved.[53]

It is this background of accepted interpretation that Chapman postulates to establish his own treatment of the Perseus-Andromeda myth. Perseus's mind, working in terms of correspondences, interprets his experience by means of the Mars-Venus relationship, revealing plainly enough the typological resemblances between their story and his own. Perseus and Andromeda are to be considered types of Mars and Venus, thus indicating that Chapman wishes the story to be read as a *concordia discors* allegory. The apparent contradiction that Perseus already embodies a concord of both masculine and feminine qualities (and, by implication, Andromeda does the same) makes perfect sense in the logic of the Renaissance mystagogues. The reproduction of the unity of the whole in the composition of its parts was an established platonic doctrine.[54]

Perseus has learned his Ficino well; he continues the analogical account of the planetary romance with a learned exposition of why Venus always dominates Mars:

> "Besides, *Mars* still doth after *Venus* moue
> "*Venus* not after *Mars*: because, of Loue
> "Boldnesse is hand-maid, Loue not so of her:
> "For not because men, bold affections beare

---

[52]"This is what the fable of Mars and Venus suggests, of whom the latter corresponds to Empedoclean friendship, the former to Empedoclean strife. . . . And with this agrees what is transmitted by other poets, that Harmony was born from the union of Mars and Venus: for when the contraries, high and deep, are tempered by a certain proportion, a marvellous consonance arises between them" (Wind, *Pagan Mysteries*, p. 82). See Schoell, *Études*, pp. 197–245, for Chapman's use of the *Moralia*.

[53]Pico della Mirandola, *A Platonick Discourse Upon Love*, 2.5, in *The Poems and Translations of Thomas Stanley*, ed. G. M. Crump (Oxford, 1962).

[54]See Wind, *Pagan Mysteries*, p. 87.

"Loues golden nets doth their affects enfold;
"But since men loue, they therefore are more bold
"And made to dare, euen *Death*, for their belou'd,
"And finally, Loues Fortitude is prou'd
"Past all, most cleerely; for this cause alone
"All things submit to Loue, but loue to none.

[*Andr.* 321–30]

The doctrine in the passage again emanates immediately from the *Commentarium*, in which it is explained that the myth invariably presents Venus dominating Mars through love;[55] since Mars cannot conquer, strife or war must always submit to amity and love. The triumph of Venus is a favorite theme in Renaissance iconography; Veronese portrays it as *Fortezza* submitting to *Carità*; Botticelli and Piero de Cosimo both reveal Mars, weary of the ardors of love, sleeping bereft of his armor; Francesco Cossa's fresco shows an enchained Mars, formally submissive to Venus.[56] It is this variant of the tradition that Shakespeare invokes in *Venus and Adonis* when Venus boasts of Mars, "Yet hath he been my captive and my slave" (1. 101), and that he uses for the mythic pattern of *Antony and Cleopatra*.[57]

Perseus's meditation completed and the necessary relationships established, the rescue itself is effected, with Chapman emphasizing the dangers concomitant. Not only is the monster to be dreaded, but the probable reaction of the multitude must be considered. Some acts are "too hie" for "Plebeian wit" to comprehend; therefore, Andromeda, exhibiting the fortitude of Mars, resolves to die rather than expose Perseus to the censure of the crowd, "for if he ouercame / The monstrous world would take the monsters part / So much the more" (388–90). Perseus, as a true lover, is above such concerns. He is, in fact, dead, "for he dies that loues." Closely following Ficino's argument,[58] Chapman maintains that the lover, not conscious of himself because "his euery thought, / (Himselfe forgot) in his belou'd is wrought" (401–2), can no longer properly be said to exist. Since the primary function of mind is consciousness, the mind that is unconscious of itself does not exist, function and existence being synonymous. As Chapman phrases it, "For, these two are in man ioynt properties, / To worke, and Be; for *Being* can be neuer / But *Operation*, is combined euer" (408–10). Therefore, no true lover is alive because he exists only in the object of his love—"whosoeuer is in loue is dead." Such a selfless lover has nothing to lose in venturing to combat monsters.

---

[55]*Commentary*, 5.8.

[56]Wind, *Pagan Mysteries*, pp. 84–85, discusses these paintings.

[57]See R. B. Waddington, "*Antony and Cleopatra*: 'What Venus did with Mars,'" *Shakespeare Studies*, 2 (1966): 210–27.

[58]*Commentary* 2.8.

The noble deed done, Chapman returns to his description of reciprocal love. Even though the individual lover must be considered as dead in himself, the loss is not total, for he recovers that self in the loved one: "Loue did both confer / To one in both: himselfe in her he found, / She with her selfe, in onely him was crownd" (454–56). Ficino explains the difference between the power of love and the strength of Mars:

> It is in this that the power of Cupid differs from the force of Mars; indeed it is in this way that military power and love differ: the general possesses others through himself; and the lover takes possession of himself through another, and the farther each of the lovers is from himself, the nearer he is to the other, and though he is dead in himself, he comes to life again in the other.[59]

This unity of opposites has been wrought in Perseus and Andromeda by their love:

O gaine, beyond which no desire can craue,
When two are so made one, that either is
For one made two, and doubled as in this:
Who one life had: one interuenient death
Makes him distinctly draw a two fold breath:
Jn mutuall Loue the wreake most iust is found,
When each so kill that each cure others wound.

[*Andr.* 480–86]

The succeeding passage includes the description of the person who frustrates procreation as a "homicide," which Bartlett takes to be a justification of Lady Frances's divorce and, thereby, the *raison d'être* of the poem. It is difficult to avoid seeing here an allusion to the Essex marriage, but the emphasis of the passage is on the impending union of Perseus and Andromeda. The offspring of Venus and Mars was Harmony, and, as the narrative comes to a close, Perseus focuses on the product of their own marriage:

All mortall good, defectiue is, and fraile;
Vnlesse in place of things, on point to faile,
We daily new beget. That things innate
May last, the languishing we re'create:
Jn generation, re'creation is,
And from the prosecution of this
Man his instinct of generation takes.
Since generation, in continuance, makes
Mortals, similitudes, of powers diuine,
Diuine worth doth in generation shine.

[*Andr.* 499–508]

59Ibid.

Thus, as the main poem ends with "admired Nuptialls" and "the rere banquet, that fore ranne the Bed," the song of the Fates picks up the generation motif:

> O you this kingdomes glory that shall be
> Parents to so renownd a Progenie
> As earth shall enuie, and heauen glory in,
> Accept of their liues threds, which Fates shal spin
> Their true spoke oracle, and liue to see
> Your sonnes sonnes enter such a *Progenie*,
> As to the last times of the world shall last.

[*Andr.* 531–37]

While the nuptial act, the supreme *concordia discors*, "which only two makes one" (596), is consummated, the attention remains on the life-thread of their "Progenie" through the refrain, "*Haste you that guide the web, haste spindles haste.*" Chapman's manipulation of the myth again parallels the Mars-Venus story with expectations about the fruit of the union: *Harmonia est concordia discors*.

Chapman's reasons for using the vehicle of the Mars-Venus allegory to honor the Somerset wedding are not difficult to guess. Beyond his own basic allegiance to the *concordia discors* conception of harmony, this particular myth was a favorite one for a nuptial occasion.[60] Astrologers believed the conjunction of Mars and Venus to be a favorable date for the wedding ceremony,[61] which leads to the typological identification of the participants. The whole treatment of marriage as a *concordia discors* probably owes still more impetus to parts of the *Symposium*, some of which have not yet been mentioned. Aristophanes' myth of the Androgyne, the round, double man that, severed by angry gods, continually seeks to reunite its halves, provides another fanciful explanation for the marital urge.[62] So Donne, hoping to form the small world of flesh, asks his mistress, "Where can we finde two better hemispheres?"

With good reasons, personal and conventional, for using the occasion to exemplify the reconciliation of opposites, it remains to be asked why Chapman did not employ the Mars-Venus legend directly rather than through a typological variation. The answer comes readily enough: the particular circumstances of this wedding render the desired myth sufficiently inappropriate that a substitute must be used. Chapman's loyalties in this marital triangle lay with the Somersets; it is his task to make

[60]See Panofsky's analysis of the Titian painting called the *Allegory of the Marquis D'Avolos* as a visualization of a newlywed couple in the guise of Venus and Mars (*Studies in Iconology*, pp. 160–63).

[61]See Allen, p. 175.

[62]On the Androgyne myth in the Renaissance, see p. 167, n. 44; also A. R. Cirillo, "The Fair Hermaphrodite: Love-Union in the poetry of Donne and Spenser," *Studies in English Literature*, 9 (1969): 81–95.

their case as sympathetic as possible. That the poet accomplished his purpose, perhaps too successfully, is evidenced by the *Free and Offenceles Ivstification of Andromeda Liberata*, wherein he is forced to disclaim any intention of allegorizing Essex as the "barraine rocke" to which Andrømeda is chained. Disingenuously the poet's mouthpiece, Theodines, protests: "As if that could applied be to a Man? / O barraine Malice! was it euer sayd / A man was barraine?" (122–24).

The Renaissance mythographers, interested primarily in utilizing the harmony of opposites implicit in the Venus-Mars affair, tend to isolate this phase of the goddess's life from the context of the whole, but they doubtless were aware of the more discordant passages as well. The tradition which emphasizes the fact of her marriage to Vulcan casts a somewhat different light on her passion for Mars. Panofsky has argued, on the basis of evidence in Hesiod and Pausanias, that the earliest version treated Mars as the legitimate husband of Venus and should take precedence over the account given by Homer, wherein Vulcan is cuckolded by Venus and Mars.[63] Whichever legend was the original, it is obvious that whenever Vulcan enters a narration of the romance with Mars, contradictory suggestions of discord arise. Chapman would have been particularly sensitive to the problem at this time, since when writing *Andromeda* he also must have been translating the *Odyssey*, which was published later the same year with a dedication to Somerset.

Homer's account admits a number of uncomfortably close parallels to the Essex-Somerset relationship. Adultery as the provocation of a ribald public scandal calls attention to the unsavory features surrounding the Essex divorce. Lady Frances's attachment to Somerset was open enough before the suit to provoke talk, and this was later intensified by her action of marrying Somerset with her hair unbound, the conventional token of virginity. Moreover, Frances's suit on the ground of Essex's alleged impotence provides an even more sensational parallel to Vulcan's situation, for his lameness is the cause of his own cuckoldry. Chapman translates Vulcan's complaint to the gods:

> Come
> And witnesse, how, when still I step from home
> (Lame that I am) Jove's daughter doth professe
> To do me all the shamefull offices,
> Indignities, despites, that can be thought;
> And loves this all-things-making-come-to-nought
> Since he is faire forsooth, foote-sound, and I
> Tooke in my braine a little, leg'd awrie—
> And no fault mine, but all my parents' fault
> Who should not get, if mocke me with my halt.[64]

---

[63]Panofsky, *Studies in Iconology*, pp. 163–64.

[64]From the *Odyssey* in *Chapman's Homer*, ed. Allardyce Nicoll (New York, 1956), 8.428–37.

The lameness clearly affects Vulcan's masculinity, and it takes no great stretch of the imagination to see lameness as a symbol for impotence; Vulcan's disability would have been subject to such an interpretation by Renaissance audiences.[65]

The themes of scandal, adultery, and impotence in the Venus-Vulcan myth not only bear too close a resemblance to the facts of the Essex imbroglio, but their treatment in Homer is designed to provoke sympathetic reactions directly contrary to the ones Chapman would desire. By using Perseus-Andromeda in place of Venus-Mars, however, Chapman can recast the same situation in terms favorable to the lovers. The adultery factor is eliminated entirely and the scandal and impotency motifs are so altered as to shift sympathy from injured husband to courageous lovers. When Venus, the promiscuous and lascivious wife, is unencumbered by marital ties, Chapman becomes free to treat her as *Venere Celeste* rather than *Venere Vulgare*, so she emerges as Andromeda, the "pious virgin." The public scandal is transformed from the just censure of Venus's peers to the malicious envy of Andromeda's inferiors.

The shifting of sympathy extends to Mars-Perseus as well. In the detached Mars-Venus story he is the culmination of manly virtues, but the Mars of the Vulcan episode is something of a laughingstock. His virility is no match for Vulcan's "shrewd mind;" the spectators of his humiliation comment humorously on the irony implicit in Mars's defeat: "The slow outgoes the swift. Lame Vulcan, knowne / To be the slowest of the Gods, outgoes / Mars the most swift" (*Odyssey* 8.459–61). Perseus, on the other hand, as the hero of a quest-romance with a dragon-killing theme, appears as an expressly English kind of hero, for the myth conforms to the typology of England's own St. George legend.[66] Therefore, by substituting the Perseus-Andromeda story for the Mars-Venus, Chapman can use the desired implications of the latter and dissociate the undesirable ones; in the process he reinterprets the salient features of the public scandal to the advantage of the Somersets. The substitution of the Perseus-Andromeda myth is both practically strategic and theoretically valid—theoretically in that it exemplifies as clearly as the more familiar Venus-Mars story the Empedoclean theory of according opposites.

The similarity of Perseus to St. George suggests the final level of meaning to be explored in the poem, that of political allegory. When

---

[65]Fraunce, for instance, in commenting upon the thigh wound of Adonis, allegorizes it as a nature-fertility myth, while taking for granted the sexual implications; see A. C. Hamilton, "Venus and Adonis," *Studies in English Literature*, 1 (1961): 6. As Northrop Frye remarks, "Adonis's traditional thigh-wound [is] as close to castration symbolically as it is anatomically" (*Anatomy of Criticism* [Princeton, 1957], p. 189).

[66]See Sir Thomas Browne, *Pseudodoxia Epidemica*, 6th ed.; (London, 1672), 5.17: "As for the story [of St. George] depending hereon, some conceive as lightly thereof, as of that of *Persius* and *Andromeda*; conjecturing the one to be the father of the other; and some too highly assert it. Others with better moderation, do either entertain the same as a fabulous addition unto the true and authentick story of St. *George*; or else conceive the literal ac-

Somerset is lauded poetically as hero and savior, this praise can be translated in practical terms into the only realm in which Somerset's accomplishment was notable. As in Spenser's version of the St. George myth, where the savior appears as Redcross Knight, it is impossible to ignore the political implications.[67]

Chapman's preference for the harmony resulting from the reconciliation of opposites predicates his theory of political organization, but the native factiousness of politics caused many of his contemporaries as well to envision the state as a *concordia discors* maintained by a ruler god-like in his wisdom. Bacon uses a familiar figure in commenting on Nero's failure: "*Nero could touch and tune the harp well, but in government sometimes he used to wind the pins too high, sometimes to let them down too low.* And certain it is that nothing destroyeth authority so much as the unequal and untimely interchange of power pressed too far, and relaxed too much."[68] Shakespeare presents another unsuccessful musician meditating on his own situation:

And here have I the daintiness of ear
To check time broke in a disordered string;
But for the concord of my state and time,
Had not an ear to hear my true time broke.

[*Rich. II* 5.5.45–48]

The image of the leader tuning the instrument of state is employed impartially by Royalist and Puritan; Marvell writes in honor of the *First Anniversary of the Government under O.C.*: "Such was that wondrous Order and Consent / When *Cromwell* tun'd the ruling Instrument."[69] In each formulation the ruler functions as the overriding agent that controls the balance of parts. The republican theory of mixed and balanced government reduces the ruler simply to one of the contraries,[70] but even with this reemphasis, the operative theory of government as a *concordia discors* remains the same. The use of the Mars-Venus myth to illustrate such a theory of political organization may be found in the most influential of *concordia discors* poems, Denham's *Coopers Hill*, in which

ception to be a misconstruction of the symbolical expression; apprehending a veritable history, in an Emblem or piece of Christian Poesie." The typology of the Perseus myth is considered at length by Edwin Sidney Hartland, *The Legend of Perseus*, 3 vols. (London, 1894–96); see 3: 38–49, for the relationship of the St. George legend.

[67]For some scattered but suggestive comments on this, see Angus Fletcher, *The Prophetic Moment: An Essay on Spenser* (Chicago, 1971).

[68]Sir Francis Bacon, "Of Empire," in *The Essayes*, ed. Ernest Rhys (London, 1906), pp. 57–58.

[69]*The Poems and Letters of Andrew Marvell*, ed. H. M. Margoliouth, 2d ed. (Oxford, 1952), 1: 105.

[70]See Zera S. Fink, *The Classical Republicans* (Evanston, Ill., 1945), p. 2 ff.

Windsor Hill is represented as the place "where *Mars* with *Venus* dwells / Beauty with strength" (39–40).[71]

To turn from seventeenth-century political theory in general to concerns immediate to Chapman's poems, one discovers that James I, among others, conceived his duty to be the maintenance of a harmony of opposing elements in the body politic. The union of England and Scotland, a subject of intense concern to James at the beginning of his reign, reveals the turn of mind. James's parliamentary speeches on the union employ the inevitable marriage metaphor: "What God hath conjoyned then let no man separate. I am the Husband, and all the whole Isle is my lawfull Wife." And again, "Union is a marriage." Indeed, marriage was such a natural metaphor for the political union that Ben Jonson took this as the theme for the allegory of his masque *Hymenaei*, which—ironically enough—celebrated the wedding of the Earl of Essex and Frances Howard, a uniting of political factions expected to be dynastic in result.[72]

The importance of the possible political realignment indicated by the marriage of Somerset to a Howard must have been obvious in court circles.[73] Robert Carr was the first Scot placed by James in the House of Lords, and upon the death of Salisbury in 1612 he became James's secretary, conducting all of the king's correspondence. Donne, another poet who lacked advancement, referred to Somerset as the "great instrument of God's providence in this Kingdom."[74] Frances was the daughter of Thomas Howard, earl of Suffolk, future commissioner of the treasury, and, more important, the grandniece of Henry Howard, earl of Northampton, then commissioner of the treasury, who seems personally to have played a considerable role in manipulating the marriage. The alliance, thus, was between James's most powerful favorite, a Protestant Scotsman, and the family that served as the leaders of the Catholic political group, dedicated to a pro-Spanish foreign policy.

James's equivocal foreign policies extended to the use of his children as counters. Upon the death of Prince Henry in 1612 the choice of a wife for Charles became of pressing importance. James had married his daughter Elizabeth to Frederick V, a German Protestant; no doubt thinking to harmonize the distribution of his children by balancing opposites, he determined to marry Charles to a Catholic, either Spanish or French.

[71]For an explication of the Mars-Venus passage, see Earl R. Wasserman, *The Subtler Language* (Baltimore, 1958), pp. 57–61.

[72]See D. J. Gordon, "*Hymenaei*: Ben Jonson's Masque of Union," *Journal of the Warburg and Courtauld Institutes*, 8 (1945): 107–45, especially pp. 127–28. For the quotations of James I, see p. 121.

[73]I have relied upon Gardiner, 2: 166–86, 304–63; and the pertinent *DNB* articles for the facts in the following account. See *DNB*, s.v. Robert Carr (Somerset), Henry Howard (Northumberland), Lord Thomas Howard (Suffolk), and Sir Thomas Overbury.

[74]Quoted by J. B. Leishman, *The Monarch of Wit*, 4th ed. (London, 1959), p. 35.

Somerset personally seems to have had no strong convictions about the matrimonial alliance at this stage, although Sir Thomas Overbury, who functioned as the intelligence of Somerset's sphere, as a matter of policy in Somerset's personal advancement did not want his man committed to any side, and—belatedly realizing the significance of a Howard marriage—opposed the match on this count. It probably cost him his life.

The Somerset wedding took place 26 December 1613. In the same month it had been discovered that a number of persons highly placed in James's court (among them Frances Howard's mother) had been receiving pensions from the Spanish government for furthering a pro-Spanish policy. Somerset, who had received no pension, remained in high favor with James; but in January he quarreled with the leading advocates of a French alliance and became an open supporter of the Spanish marriage. After the death of Northampton, Somerset was the leading advocate of Spanish policy, receiving in July 1615 permission to conduct a marriage treaty. Before a treaty could be effected, however, the story of Overbury's murder came to light in September 1615, ending Somerset's career.

The entry in the transcript of the Stationer's Register for Chapman's poem is suggestive:

> Laurence Lyle Entred for his Coppie vnder the handes of the Duke of Lennox, the earle of Sulfolke, the earle of Marr, Sir Julius Caesar, Master warden ffeild and master Adames a booke called Perseus and Andromeda by George Chapman. (16 Martii 1613[14])

Suffolk was, of course, Frances Howard's father and Caesar was a member of the commission that granted the Essex marriage nullity. It would seem that *Andromeda Liberata* was subscribed by the Howard faction.

Despite its title the poem shows full awareness of the primary importance of Somerset in the alliance. Perseus is described as "the man that next to Ioue comptrold / The triple world; got with a shoure of gold" (217–18). In view of the facts this hardly seems hyperbole; next to James, Somerset may well have been the ruler of the "triple world"—Great Britain and Ireland—and he almost literally was begotten with a "shoure of gold" (although here Chapman could not have intended the immediate association—Somerset's possession of Ralegh's estate was something of an embarrassment). Perseus is "Ioue's sonne" and, by extension, Somerset is James's.

The importance of James in the poem becomes increasingly evident as Chapman explains the source of Perseus's strength, "of *Ioue* he wanne / A power past all men els" (380–81). Perseus is the minister who imposes the order willed by Jove; their relationship is that of God the Creator and His Son, who becomes the instrument of God's will to restore the proper order. Here the typological similarity of Perseus to

Christ assumes prominence. Somerset, transformed to harmony in this marriage uniting contrary political elements, will be the means of enacting James's plan of peace through *concordia discors* on an international level. As it is "Ioue" who creates Perseus and endows him with extraordinary power, it is "Loue" that motivates Perseus to complete himself through Andromeda and slay the monster that is disorder personified;[75] and behind the roles of both divinities the identity of James I is perceptible.[76]

If in one sense the poem celebrates the wisdom and benevolence of James, who is the cause of all things political and whose design comes to fruition in the person of Somerset, it is also advice in the *Mirror for Magistrates* tradition. Chapman's dedication recommends to Somerset policy that steers a middle ground, befitting a temperate ruler: "true Policie / Windes like a serpent, through all Empery, / Her folds on both sides bounded, like a flood / With high shores listed" (d.e., 87–90). Reason, the regent of the soul, will bring order to the chaotic, natural political state:

Peace, *Concord, Order, Stay* proclaim'd, and *Law*
And none commanding, if not all in Awe,
Passion, and *Anger*, made to vnder lie,
And heere concludes, mans mortall Monarchie
In which, your Lordships milde Soule sits so hie
Yet cares so little to be seene, or heard,
That in the good thereof, her scope is Sphear'd.

[*Andr.* d.e., 145–51]

Chapman is well aware that the concord he envisions from Somerset's policies is only potential, as his emphasis on generation and the forthcoming "Progenie / As earth shall enuie, and heauen glory in" suggests. The Apodosis looks beyond the day of Somerset's favor and bids "you, that *Perseus* place supply / In our *Ioues* loue, get *Persean* victorie / Of our Land Whale" (610–12). Somerset's successors may order their policies on the pattern of *concordia discors* which produced the harmony celebrated in the poem.

It is futile to speculate on Chapman's naïveté or credulity in writing a poem to support Somerset and a Spanish alliance; his continued loyalty to Somerset eliminates simple favor-currying as a motive,[77] while other

---

[75]Cf. Frye, p. 189, "The ritual analogies of the myth suggest that the monster *is* the sterility of the land itself."

[76]There is a play upon the similarity of the names; the older use of *i* for *j* makes the visual identification nearly exact. Cf. Gordon's explication of the *Unio-Iuno* anagram in "*Hymenaei*" (pp. 114–17).

[77]Norma Dobie Solve, *Stuart Politics in Chapman's Tragedy of Chabot*, University of Michigan Publications in Language and Literature, vol. 4 (Ann Arbor, 1928), demonstrates the

of his poems indicate an affinity for James's policies of peacemaking.[78] The proper question to ask of a political prophet is not whether he was right or wrong, but whether he spoke when he felt the call. It may suffice that Chapman wrote a poem embodying his conception of the harmonious order of all things, exemplified through the principle of *concordia discors* on three corresponding levels—individual, governmental, and cosmic—by adapting platonic mythology to suit the particular circumstances of the occasion.

Andromeda Liberata was to be Chapman's last mythic narrative. As such, it becomes a doubly significant terminus for this study. First, coming after the disappointing sequence of funeral poems, *Andromeda* shows a great recovery to his best form of the 1590s; and, second, in the typicality of its themes and techniques, this last example proves ideal for summing up Chapman's achievement in this kind of poetry. *Andromeda* does not measure up to the best poems, *Hero and Leander* and *Ovids Banquet of Sence*, largely because of the undistinguished quality of the verse. Almost every other poem Chapman wrote has at least occasional brilliant, memorable flashes of poetry; even a part of *Eugenia* has been anthologized. Although M. Jacquot believes that "On peut cependant mentionner certains vers aux grâces précieuses,"[79] it seems doubtful that anyone ever felt compelled to learn by heart and recite aloud those verses. Admittedly, the theory underlying this mode of poetry does not require, and may even render suspect, such surface glitter, which is most prominent in the deliberately deceptive *Ovids Banquet*:

> the poet's idea or vision is the important thing; the allegory or poem has value insofar as it communicates this vision. It follows then that the critic must value poetry not for what it is but for what it stimulates—ecstasy and insight. The poet has as his task not the creation of art objects but the re-creation of vision within another person. It is not enough for an individual to regard a poem as an external spectacle in which he does not participate. If he does so, the poet has failed and provided mere entertainment.[80]

---

consistency of Chapman's adherence to Somerset's cause. Most scholars accept Solve's reading of *Chabot* as an allegory of the Somerset affair, although the date of the play remains unsettled. Irving Ribner has argued that *Chabot* dates from 1612 or 1413 and was rewritten sometime after 1621 by Chapman and Shirley to make it reflect Somerset's career; see "The Meaning of Chapman's *Tragedy of Chabot*," *Modern Language Review*, 55 (1960): 321–31.

[78]See *The Teares of Peace* and *Eugenia*, in which he expresses the hope that knowledge will "make our generall peace so circulare; / That Faith and Hope, at either end shall pull / And make it come: Round as the Moone at full" (939–41). On James's self-styled role as *Rex Pacificus* see D. H. Willson, *King James VI and I* (New York, 1956), pp. 271–87.

[79]Jacquot, p. 72.

[80]Murrin, *The Veil of Allegory*, p. 96.

The last thing of which Chapman could be accused is providing mere entertainment. But taken on its own terms—in its control, in the firmness of its design, and in the implementation of its central idea—*Andromeda Liberata* is a fine piece of work, exhibiting precisely that "architectonic power" in which Chapman so frequently has been thought wanting.[81]

Chapman began his first published poem by asserting a poetic theory based upon divine inspiration and memory (*Noct.* 1–20). As Michael Murrin explains, "Allegorical theory practically demands Platonism for its understanding" because "a poetic which places so much emphasis on memory would necessarily express itself philosophically in a system which similarly stresses memory and provides a rationale for it."[82] From the first, then, we should recognize the interdependence of the platonism in Chapman's thought and his poetics, which impelled him to develop a poetic mode capable of expressing that platonic vision. Just as *Andromeda Liberata*, with its direct indebtedness to Ficino and Comes, presents the later development of Chapman's platonism, so it will stand as an epitome of the poetic mode.

The narrator typically presents himself as hierophant and prophet, concealing his mysteries from the "rauenous Multitude" by allegory but also delivering the "true spoke oracle" of the Fates. He proclaims the meaning of his oracle through its form: the outer, conventional form of the epithalamion; the inner form or fictive body of the mythic narrative; and finally the "soul" of the poem, the platonic form of *concordia discors*. We are aided in interpreting the myth by the principle of correspondence in cosmic allegory which permits the extension of meaning from the microcosmic marriage of individuals, to the union of political factions, to the macrocosmic interaction of constellations, all governed by the pattern of *concordia discors*. Because again here Chapman draws his myth from Ovid's *Metamorphoses* we are not surprised to find his favorite motif of symbolic transformation; Perseus and Andromeda are rewarded for their virtue in expected fashion, "Both rapt to heau'n, did constellations reigne" (*Andr.* 602). As Chapman explains in his justification of *Andromeda*, poets enlarge or alter allegory "with inuentions and dispositions of their owne, to extend it to their present doctrinall and illustrous purposes" (*Poems*, p. 327). Perhaps the most impressive aspect of his mythic narratives is his skill at typological adaptation; and his handling of the Perseus-Andromeda fable equals his achievement with the technique in *Hero and Leander*.

Essentially the poet remains for Chapman the Orphic civilizer described in the *Hymnvs in Noctem*; his function is the reformation of reluctant mankind by restoring the memory of the good that once was. "Monsters kill the Man-informing Arts: / And like a lothed prodegie despise / The rapture that the Arts doth naturalise, / Creating and im-

[81]The phrase is Bush's; see *Mythology*, p. 218.

[82]Murrin, p. 90; see also pp. 85–97.

mortalising men" (*Andr.* 617–20). Because of that conception of his role, Chapman's poetry is, far more than has been realized, political in nature: sometimes in the specific sense of advocating or urging a policy, as he does in *The Shadow of Night, De Guiana,* and *Andromeda;* but almost always in the radical sense of concern with the orderly workings of society, its customs, rituals, ceremonies of innocence. Angus Fletcher has discussed the importance of marriage, the ultimate societal rite, for the prophetic poet in words that are relevant to Chapman:

> Prophecy requires the verbal or visionary expression of this contractual trust based on a betrothal. Because the betrothal is truly mutual, it accords with the dictates of conscience and it expresses the conscious choice, the deliberate wish, of the parties to the marriage. By its ceremonies of truth the prophetic poem shows that human bonds—the "bonds of society"—will have generative power.[83]

Society reconstitutes itself in the betrothal and regenerates itself in that simultaneously most personal and impersonal sexual act. Hymen, the blessed Hermaphrodite, presides over the ceremonial union of minds— "they must binde / In one selfe sacred knot each others minde"—as does the Androgyne over the union of bodies, that act "which only two makes one, / Flesh of each flesh and bone of eithers bone" (*Andr.* 596–97). The *concordia discors* of human love figures in little the form of societal relations and natural order which the poet remembers and to which he can envision a return. "And where Loues forme is, loue is, loue is forme." So is poetry.

[83]Fletcher, pp. 20–21.

INDEX

Achilles, 157, 183
Actaeon, 26, 57–60, 71, 83–86, 88–89, 129, 138, 178
Adam, 30, 33–34, 37–38, 53, 169–70
Ad Herennium, 172
Adlington, William, 60–61, 178
Adonis, 113, 124
Aemilius Paulus, 81
Aenesidemus, 147
Agathon, 201
Agrippa, Henry Cornelius, 61, 95, 97–104, 107, 142 n, 163–64
Alchemy, 93, 123, 137–41, 158
Alciati, Andrea, 70
Alcyone, 178–80
Alexander the Great, 113, 135
Allegory, 4–10, 16, 24–25, 33, 38, 40–45, 49–51, 56–59, 63–64, 66, 69, 100, 106, 155–58, 161, 165, 167, 173, 191, 193, 197, 202–3, 205–6, 212–13; political, 66, 72, 76–91, 109, 207–12
Allen, Don Cameron, 201
Alpheus, 67, 90
Alvarez, A., 4–5
Amalthea, 53, 98
Androgyne, 38 n, 44, 167, 205, 214
Andromeda, 43, 177, 197, 202, 207, 213
Antaeus, 21
Antichrist, 74, 80
Apelles, 148
Apollo, 106, 125, 129–32, 138
Apuleius, 57, 60–61, 178
Aquarius, 91
Argonauts, 32
Argus, 129
Ariosto, Ludovico, 60, 82, 131, 159, 178
Aristophanes, 44, 167, 205
Aristotle [Aristotelian], 116, 159, 168–70
Armada, 73, 76–77, 80, 87
Arnold, Matthew, 151
Astraea, 35, 78–80, 97, 187–88
Atalanta, 66
Augean stables, 21
Augustine, Saint, 24; City of God, 108

Bacon, Sir Francis; De Sapientia Veterum (Wisedom of the Ancients), 24–25, 27, 32–33, 65, 83–84, 108, 197 n; Of Adversity, 33; Of Empire, 208
Bacon, Roger, 147
Banquet, allegorical, 27–28, 67, 113, 115
Barker, Sir Ernest, 168
Bartlett, Phyllis Brooks, 115 n, 201, 204
Basilisk, 129, 135
Battenhouse, Roy W., 51, 59, 63–64, 72, 83, 87, 90
Berkeley, George (bishop), 147 n

Beroaldus, Philippus, 60
Bible, 7–8, 10, 16, 32, 66, 146 n, 158–59
Bloomfield, Morton W., 187
Boar, 56, 61–64, 100; Calydonian, 53, 59, 63, 67, 84, 86–87, 89
Boccaccio, Giovanni, 21, 24–25
Bocchi, Achille, 190–91
Bodin, Jean, 174 n
Body: fictive, 15–16, 19, 40, 192, 213; politics, 39, 82, 89–90, 209
Boethius, 182
Bosch, Hieronymus, 107
Botticelli, Sandro, 203
Bottrall, Margaret, 6 n
Bradbrook, Muriel C., 63, 72, 83, 87, 109
Brooke, Nicholas, 37
Browne, Sir Thomas; Garden of Cyrus, 164 n; Pseudodoxia Epidemica, 26, 207 n
Bruegel, Pieter, 107
Brueghel, Jan, 116 n
Bruno, Giordano, 61, 97
Burke, Kenneth, 125–26
Burton, Robert, 119 n, 120, 123
Bush, Douglas, 181, 196, 213 n

Caduceus, as emblem, 36
Caesar, Sir Julius, 210
Callimachus, 47–48
Calliope, 46
Callisto, 80
Campanella, Tommaso, 139 n
Cannon, Charles K., 2
Carew, Thomas, 17
Carey, George, second Lord Hunsdon, 92–93
Carr, Robert, earl of Somerset, 197, 200, 206–11
Cartari, Vincenzo, 36, 41, 62–63, 157, 163, 167
Casaubon, Isaac, 154 n
Cassirer, Ernst, 118
Cecil, William, Lord Burghley, 85, 92
Ceremony, 36, 44, 55, 68, 104, 111, 122, 161–63, 166–68, 170, 172–76, 182, 196, 200, 205, 214
Ceyx, 178–180
Chaos, 40, 52–53, 68, 198
Chapman, George, dramas of, 12, 19, 150, 181; Achilles Shield, 126, 127 n, 128, 157 n, 181; All Fools, 122–23; Andromeda Liberata, 43–44, 53, 112, 149 n, 169, 177, 196–214; Blind Beggar of Alexandria, 27 n; Bussy D'Ambois, 19–39, 42–43, 74–75, 122, 150, 183; Caesar and Pompey, 150, 176; Conspiracy of Byron, 78 n, 183; Coronet for his Mistresse Philosophie, 14, 39, 113, 142–43, 150, 182 n; Crowne of all Homer's Workes, 46; De Guiana, 25, 91, 94, 110–12,

128, 214; *Divine Poem of Musaeus*, 46, 153–54; *An Epicede*, 44, 149 n, 193–94; *Eugenia*, 22, 39–40, 44, 78, 122–23, 149 n, 193, 195, 212; *Free and Offenceles Ivstification*, 5–6, 17, 206; *Gentleman Usher*, 19 n, 26 n, 30; *Georgicks of Hesiod*, 24, 29, 46, 174–75; *Hero and Leander*, 3, 39, 43–44, 50, 56, 61, 68, 112–13, 122, 149 n, 153–80, 185, 188, 196, 199, 212–13; *Hymnes of Homer*, 78 n; *Hymne to Hymen*, 14, 43; *Hymne to our Sauiour*, 12, 39; *Hymnvs in Cynthiam*, 39, 43–44, 50–52, 55–72, 76–91, 92, 95, 98–102, 104–6, 109–10, 185; *Hymnvs in Noctem*, 2, 25, 35, 39, 46, 51–56, 58–59, 66, 79, 87–88, 95–99, 105–6, 109, 185, 190 n, 213; *Illiads*, 93, 127–28, 157, 181; *Memorable Maske*, 43, 110; *Monsieur D'Olive*, 19 n, 54; *Odysses*, 64, 206–7; *Ovids Banquet of Sence*, 12, 27, 44, 83, 93, 113–51, 185, 212; *Peristeros*, 39; *Petrarchs Seven Penitentiall Psalms*, 12, 165 n; *Pro Vere*, 78 n; *Revenge of Bussy D'Ambois*, 150, 183; *Shadow of Night*, 9, 12, 19 n, 24, 35, 39, 43, 45–112, 113, 128, 143, 149 n, 156, 191, 214; *Teares of Peace*, 7, 9, 12, 39, 43–44, 53, 149 n, 177, 180–193, 195, 212; *To my Admired and Sovle-Loved Friend . . . M. Harriots*, 126–27; *Tragedy of Chabot*, 122–23, 150, 211 n; *Virgils Epigram of this letter Y*, 165; *Whole Works of Homer*, 45, 153; *Widow's Tears*, 19 n, 57
Charles V, 82–83
Charles, Prince, 209
Chastel, André, 47–48
Chaucer, Geoffrey, 107, 182
Christ [Christian], 8, 21, 30, 33–34, 37–39, 47, 53–54, 80, 142 n, 158, 175, 195, 197, 210–11
Cicero, 147 n, 168, 172, 186 n
Cinthio, Giraldi, 159
Circle, 39, 59, 142 n
Comes, Natalis, 24–25, 28, 33, 41, 45, 51, 54, 57, 59, 61–63, 65, 70, 81, 83, 96–97, 99, 101, 103 n, 123–24, 129, 197, 213
Concordia discors, 35–39, 42–44, 52, 166–70, 196, 199–202, 205–9, 211–14
Cope, Jackson I., 2 n, 19 n
Correspondence, principle of, 16, 40, 51, 169, 201–2, 213. *See also* Macrocosm-microcosm
Cosimo, Piero de, 203
Cossa, Francesco, 203
Cressida, 153
Cydippe, 90
Cynthia, 44, 51–53, 55–60, 62, 66–72, 76–91, 94, 98–102, 104–6, 108, 138, 143, 187
Cytherea, 124–25

Dance, as metaphor, 35–36, 106
Dante, 69, 83; *De Monarchia*, 79–80, 90–91
Daphne, 125

Davenant, Sir William, *Gondibert*, 120
Davies, Sir John, 142; *Hymnes to Astraea*, 188; *Orchestra*, 36
Davis, Walter R., 60
Decorum, 173, 177 n
Della Porta, Giovanni Battista, 119 n, 139 n
Denham, Sir John, *Cooper's Hill*, 208–9
Derby. *See* Stanley, Ferdinando
Descartes, René, 128, 147 n
Devereux, Robert, second earl of Essex, 92, 94
Devereux, Robert, third earl of Essex, 197, 201, 204, 206–7, 209
Diana, 51–52, 57–59, 62–63, 65–67, 70–71, 78–80, 83–84, 87, 94, 96, 100, 108, 129, 131, 138
Digby, Sir Kenelm, 59
Dike, 174–76
Diogenes Laertius, 147, 164
Doctrina, 188–89
Donne, John, 1–5, 11–13, 16–17, 37–38, 119 n, 149, 195, 209; *Anniversaries*, 11, 16–17, 143–44, 195 n; *La Corona*, 142 n; *Death's Duell*, 195; *The Dissolution*, 140; *Elegies*, 156; *Epithalamion Made at Lincolnes Inne*, 11; *Goodfriday, 1613. Riding Westward*, 12, 38; *The Good-morrow*, 205; *Hero and Leander*, 155–56; *Hymne to God my God, in my sicknesse*, 38; *A nocturnall upon S. Lucies day*, 1; *Sermon Preached in the Evening of Christmas-Day, 1624*, 119 n; *Songs and Sonets*, 11; *To Mr. Tilman*, 38; *Upon the Annunciation and Passion*, 37–38; *Valediction forbidding mourning*, 169
Donno, Elizabeth S., 131, 156
Drake, Sir Francis, 82, 87
Drayton, Michael, 46, 121, 123, 154
Dream-vision, 12, 182–83, 186–89, 192
Drummond, William, 5, 121 n, 123, 138 n
Drury, Elizabeth, 16–17
Dudley, Robert, earl of Leicester, 74, 78, 80, 90, 92–93, 158

Eagle, 22–23, 91, 129
Ebreo, Leone, 55
Eden, 29, 159
Elegy: erotic, 114 n, 140, 143; funeral, 12, 140, 193–94
Eliot, T. S., 1–2, 13; *The Waste Land*, 45
Elizabeth, Princess (daughter of James I), 43, 110, 209
Elizabeth I, 35, 72–74, 76–81, 83–87, 89–91, 96, 108–11, 187–88; foreign policy of, 73–78, 84–91; motto of, 89; mythic roles of, 72–73, 78–81, 86; poem to Alençon, 76
Ellis, Havelock, 13
Eloquence, silent, 177, 189–92
Elyot, Sir Thomas, 160 n

Emblems, 23, 41, 75–76, 129, 134, 137 n, 141, 144–46, 160, 165, 167 n, 199

Empedocles, 52, 202 n, 207

Empire [imperialism], 79–91, 94, 98, 105, 108, 110–12, 187

Endymion, 69, 86, 90, 102, 106–7

Ennius, *Annales*, 186

Epic, 12, 20, 33, 35, 39, 111, 154, 156–60, 162, 177, 179, 186

Epigram, 155–56, 165

Epigraph, 142, 145, 176

Epimetheus, 28–29, 34

Epitaph, 193

Epithalamion, 11, 195–96, 200 n

Essex. *See* Devereux, Robert, second earl of Essex, and Devereux, Robert, third earl of Essex

Estienne, Henri, 49

Euippe, 143

Euripides, 148

Eurydice, 47, 53, 69

Eurynome, 174

Evans, Maurice, 42

Eve, 30, 37, 169–70

Fall, 52–54, 58, 66, 69

Farnese, Alessandro, duke of Parma, 73, 83

Fates, 170, 172, 174, 176, 205, 213

Fever, 44, 193–94

Ficino, Marsilio, 7, 25, 47–49, 65, 80 n, 95, 97–101, 103–4, 108, 116, 124 n, 193, 202, 213; academy of, 8, 47–50; *Commentary on Plato's Symposium*, 38 n, 40, 47 n, 68–69, 167, 196, 200–204

Fletcher, Angus, 43, 214

Form: mythic, 14–17, 19, 40, 42–44, 50–51, 105–6, 188–89, 192–93, 193, 197, 213; as number, 160–67, 176; outer or conventional, 10–14, 39, 42, 158, 181–82, 185, 193, 213; platonic, 7, 15–16, 40, 42–44, 212–14; as theme, 39, 43, 52–55, 58–69, 82–83, 105–6, 120, 161, 183, 185, 194–95

Fornari, Simon, 60

Fowler, Alastair, 145 n

Foxe, John, 80 n

François Hercule Valois, duke of Alençon, 73–76, 79–80, 83, 90; courtship of Elizabeth I of, 73–74, 90; reception of, in Netherlands, 75; sun emblem of, 75–76

Frank, Joseph, 2

Fraunce, Abraham, 57, 83, 197 n, 207 n

Frederick V, Elector Palatine, 43, 110, 209

Frye, Northrop, 30, 50, 52, 104, 109, 207 n

Fulgentius, 24, 57, 155

Fuller, Thomas, 147 n

Galileo, 128

Ganay, Germain de, 49

Ganymede, 56, 69–70, 90–91, 93 n, 106–7

Gellius, Aulus, 173, 187 n

Genre, 10–14, 42, 105, 153, 157–58, 181, 183, 187, 193, 196. *See also* Form, outer

George, Saint, 207–8

Golden Age, 20, 24, 29, 35, 54, 97, 110, 159

Golding, Arthur, 59, 75, 158–60, 177, 179

Gombrich, E. H., 41, 118 n, 121 n, 136, 148, 177 n

Gordon, D. J., 61–62, 68, 110, 153, 157, 161, 173

Gorgon, 121, 143, 197 n

Graces, 174

Greene, Thomas M., 196

Grenville, Sir Richard, 127

Guillén, Claudio, 124 n

Guss, Donald L., 11

Harington, Sir John, 60–61, 82–83, 178, 197 n

Harmony: of form, 14, 199; loss of, 52–53; in marriage, 168–70, 177, 201–3; of nature, 35, 72, 97, 171, 199–202; philosophic, 7–8; Pythagorean, 107, 166; social, 36, 97, 111, 168–70, 172, 176, 185, 188, 195; of the soul, 36, 52–53, 56, 94, 97–98, 105–7, 170, 183, 192; of the spheres, 36, 52–53, 94, 169, 173, 189–90. *See also Concordia discors*

Harmony (daughter of Mars and Venus), 201, 204–5

Harpocrates, 177, 190–92

Harriot, Thomas, 126–29, 148; *Briefe and True Report of the New Found Land of Virginia*, 127

Hawkins, Sir John, 87

Hawkins, Sherman, 58, 71

Hecate, 51, 72, 101–2, 106–8

Heninger, S. K., Jr., 1, 13, 160 n, 161 n

Henri III, 73, 80, 83

Henry, Prince of Wales, 44, 181, 183, 185, 193–94, 209

Heraclitus, 65

Herbert, George, 186

Hercules, 9, 21, 28, 30–34, 38–39, 42–43, 55–56, 113, 178; as champion of justice, 165, 191; choice of, 113, 165–66; Christian, 30; Gallic, 177, 191; labors of, 21, 191–92; pillars of, 82; as symbol of silent eloquence, 189–92; as wise man, 191–92

Hermaphrodite, 38, 44, 167 n, 199, 214

Hermes (Mercury), 190–91

Hermes Trismegistus, 9, 12, 48, 97, 183–84, 189–92

Hermetica, 154, 183, 190

Hermeticism, 7, 8 n, 97, 140–41, 177, 183–84, 190, 192

Hesiod, 13, 24–26, 45–46, 154, 174–75, 206; *Theogony*, 174; *Works and Days*, 24, 174–75

Heyns, Zacharias, 146 n

Heywood, Jasper, 186

Hieatt, A. Kent, 196

Hieroglyphics, 9, 41, 143

Hippomenes, 66
Hobbes, Thomas, 120
Holbein, Hans, *The Ambassadors*, 126, 134
Hollander, John, 103, 107
Homer, 10, 13, 15, 40, 45–48, 54, 61, 114, 128,
    148, 150, 154, 158, 181–86, 189–90, 192–93;
    Hymns, 47–48; *Odyssey*, 64, 66, 206–7
Hopkins, Gerard Manley, 197
Horace, *Ars poetica*, 151
Horapollo, 41
Hours, 174–76
Howard, Frances, countess of Somerset,
    197, 204, 206, 209–10
Howard, Henry, earl of Northampton, 209–10
Howard, Thomas, earl of Suffolk, 197, 209–
    10
Hunt, as allegory, 26, 44, 56–60, 63–64, 66–67,
    77, 83–87, 89, 100–102, 105
Hurstfield, Joel, 73
Hybris, 176–77, 180
Hydra, 21, 192
Hymen, 43–44, 68, 111, 161–63, 167–70, 178,
    214
Hymn, 12, 39, 45–51, 99, 104

Icarus, 132, 138
Iconography, 43, 100, 134, 190, 192, 203
Illusion, optical, 118–26, 130–32, 136–37, 141,
    144, 148–49
Imitation, doctrine of, 177
Inspiration, poetic, 7–10, 41, 105, 157, 182,
    185–86, 201, 213
Io, 121, 123, 125, 178
Iron Age, 24, 35
Isis, 164, 171

Jacquot, Jean, 1, 32, 36, 72, 117, 183, 186,
    192 n, 196, 201, 212
Jaeger, Werner, 175–76
James I, 181, 197, 209–12
Jamyn, Amadis, 55
Jeremiah, 10
Jewel, John, 80 n
Johnson, Samuel, 36
Jonson, Ben, 1, 6, 12, 15 n, 16, 121 n;
    Hymenaei, 209
Jove, 23, 26, 69–70, 210–11
Joyce, James, 2; *Finnegans Wake*, 14 n, 45
Julius Caesar, 113, 178
Juno, 132, 179
Jupiter, 22–23, 69
Justice, 23, 25, 35–36, 39, 41, 43, 161, 163–72,
    173–77, 180, 187–89; absolute, 171, 180;
    corrective, 168, 170; distributive, 168–70;
    equity as part of, 164–65, 170–72, 180;
    mercy as part of, 175, 180

Kargon, Robert, 128
Keats, John, 109
Kermode, Frank, 61, 113–15, 131

Keymis, Lawrence, 128
Knowles, Richard, 62 n
Kristeller, Paul O., 47–48

La Boderie, Guy Lefèvre de, 49, 108 n
Labyrinth, 43–44
Landino, Cristoforo, 47, 69–70
Latona, 131, 138, 143
Law, 22, 25, 168, 171, 173–75, 187–88, 198
Learning, 39, 41, 108, 182–86, 188, 191–92,
    195
Leicester. *See* Dudley, Robert
Lemmi, Charles W., 24, 33
Levin, Harry, 176
Levine, Jay Arnold, 140
Lewis, C. S., 109 n, 153, 157
Lindberg, David C., 131 n
Lion, 62–64, 66
Lohne, Johannes, 128
Lotis, 178
Love, 40, 48, 68–69, 105, 182, 204, 211, 214
Lucian, 64, 191
Lucretius, 116, 146, 186 n
Luna, 51, 62, 108, 139–40

Macedonians, 55, 81, 102
McKerrow, R. B., 145
MacLure, Millar, 1, 13, 97–98, 105, 110, 117,
    137, 142 n, 145, 158, 161 n, 181, 183, 186,
    195
Macrobius, 147 n
Macrocosm-microcosm, 15–16, 35, 38, 81–82,
    96, 105, 129, 132, 140, 160, 168–70, 187, 194,
    196, 213
Magic, 56, 106, 111; astrological, 95–97, 102,
    105; Hermetic, 97; lunary, 99–102, 107;
    Orphic, 12–13, 95–108
Manley, Frank, 16
Marlowe, Christopher, 12, 13, 132, 153–57,
    171, 176; *Hero and Leander*, 46, 142, 149 n,
    153–57, 170, 176, 185
Marriage, 43, 56, 68, 72–74, 76–79, 104, 110–
    12, 155, 161–64, 166–73, 177–80, 199–200,
    204–7, 213–14; alchemical, 139–41; as poli-
    tical metaphor, 209; Somerset-Howard,
    196–97, 205–7, 209–10
Mars, 43, 143, 169, 177, 201–9
Marston, John, 197
Marsyas, 106
Martin, L. C., 172
Marvell, Andrew; *Upon Appleton House*,
    121 n; *First Anniversary of the Govern-
    ment under O. C.*, 208
Mary, Queen of Scots, 84, 85 n, 86–87
Medici, Cosimo de, 48
Melancholy, 96–97, 103–5, 173
Memory, 213
Metamorphosis, 53–54, 58–61, 65, 69–70,
    86–88, 91, 100, 106, 125, 140, 143, 156,
    158–60, 177–80, 195 n, 213

Meyers, James P., Jr., 116, 132 n
Michelangelo, 70
Midas, 106, 178
Milton, John, 13–14, 29–30, 162, 186;
    L'Allegro, 98; Comus, 52, 63 n, 123, 178;
    Paradise Lost, 55, 64–65, 131, 157, 169–70,
    178, 180 n; Paradise Regained, 21, 119 n,
    123, 175; Il Penseroso, 97–98, 184
Mirror, as symbol, 134–35
Mirror for Magistrates, 211
Mode: dramatic, 148–50; Hypodorian, 103–4;
    in music, 102–5; poetic, 4–5, 11–13, 43–44,
    105, 107, 109, 116, 148–50, 155, 158, 212–
    213
Montaigne, Michel de, 147
Moon, 27–28, 52, 55, 70, 80, 82–83, 91, 94, 96,
    98–103, 105, 107–8, 138, 171; eclipse of,
    55–56, 73, 76–77, 79, 81, 89, 102
Moses, 7, 8, 158–59
Motley, John Lothrop, 74 n
Murrin, Michael, 4, 6, 16, 42, 193, 212–13
Musaeus, 39, 46, 154, 160; Hero and Leander,
    46, 153–56
Music, 36, 46, 52–54, 173; mode in, 102–5;
    Orphic, 53–54, 94, 97, 106; planetary, 95,
    102–3
Mutability, 28, 52–72, 88–89
Mysteries, 4–5, 8–10, 14, 16, 40–42, 45–51, 61,
    66, 98, 105, 107, 142, 160, 174, 183–85, 190,
    213
Myth [mythology], 5, 8–9, 14–17, 21–22, 24–
    28, 32, 35, 38, 41, 88–89, 107–8, 113–15, 129,
    131, 139, 141, 142 n, 153, 155, 157–60, 167,
    172, 174, 177–80, 190, 193, 195–98, 201–3,
    205–8, 212–13

Narcissus, 178
Narrative: mythic, 14–16, 19, 42–44, 49–51,
    56–57, 63, 66, 90, 104, 107, 109, 156, 181,
    186, 197, 212–13; technique of, 141–43,
    148–50
Neptune, 158, 172
Netherlands, 73–78, 181
Newton, Sir Isaac, 128
Nicèron, Jean François, 139 n
Nicholas of Cusa, 118–19
Nicolson, Marjorie, 16
Nijmegen, battle of, 73, 76, 78, 83, 86
Niobe, 123, 129–31, 136, 138, 141, 143, 178
Norris, Sir John, 78
Northumberland. See Percy, Henry
Numbers, symbolic, 145 n, 161–67, 196; two,
    99, 162–63, 167, 199; three, 162–63, 167,
    199; four, 163; five, 162–65, 167, 199;
    seven, 142 n; ten, 142 n, 163–64

Odysseus, 40, 183, 185
Optics, 128, 131, 135, 141, 147–48
Oracles, 6, 9–10, 14, 46, 184, 213
Order, 40, 53, 173, 187, 189, 198

Orion, 67, 90
Orpheus, 9, 12, 25, 45–54, 68–70, 94–108, 110,
    113, 154, 213; Argonautica, 47–48, 98; arts
    of, 52, 106; cult of, 47–49; magic, 12–13, 51,
    95–108; music, 53–54, 94, 97, 106; night,
    96–98; theology, 70
Orphic Hymns, 12, 47–51, 71, 95–96, 99, 104,
    108, 173–74; Hymn to Diana, 65, 96;
    Hymn to Nature, 49; Hymn to Night, 96;
    Hymn to Proteus, 65; Hymn to Themis,
    174 n; Hymn to the Moon, 71, 96
Osiris, 164, 171
Otis, Brooks, 158, 179
Overbury, Sir Thomas, 210
Ovid, 53, 57, 60, 63, 83, 93, 113–14, 125, 129,
    138, 142–43, 146 n, 156, 158–60, 177–79,
    193, 195; Amores, 114, 155–56; Ars Ama-
    toria, 114, 142; erotic poetry, 17, 113–14,
    140, 150, 155–56; exile of, 83, 114, 138;
    Heroides, 154–55, 177, 179; Metamor-
    phoses, 17, 59, 66, 69, 71, 84, 113–14, 140,
    156, 158–60, 162, 177–79, 213; mythological
    poetry, 17, 61; reputation of, 114, 140;
    Tristia, 83, 138

Pan, 70
Pandora, 26–29
Panofsky, Erwin, 206
Panther, 56, 61–64, 66, 84, 86, 100–101
Paracelsus, 143
Parma. See Farnese, Alessandro
Parrhasius, 136
Pausanias, 48, 63, 129–30, 136, 206
Peace, 87, 90, 108, 173–74, 182–84, 186, 188–
    92, 211–12
Peacham, Henry, 137, 145–47, 188–89
Pecham, John, 147
Pentagram, 102, 163
Percy, Henry, ninth earl of Northumber-
    land, 92–94, 127–28, 131
Perdrier, René, 49
Perseus, 43–44, 177, 197, 202, 207, 213
Persius, 145, 146 n, 186 n
Persona, 9–10, 12, 14, 16, 42, 104, 108, 141,
    186, 196, 213–14
Perspective, 44, 117–137, 141–44, 151, 173
Petowe, Henry, 180
Petrarch [Petrarchan], 12, 140
Phaeton, 58, 71, 132, 137–38
Phillips, James E., 180
Philo Judaeus, 147 n
Philosophy, 7, 108, 160, 177, 180, 184–85, 190,
    195
Phoenix, 39, 129, 132
Pico della Mirandola, 7–9, 12, 16, 47–50, 61,
    95; Conclusiones, 70; Heptaplus, 8, 16;
    Oration, 49–50, 65–66, 183–85, 190–91;
    Platonick Discourse Upon Love, 167, 202
Picus, 178
Pimander, 12, 183, 189, 192

Pintoricchio, 134
Plato, 5, 8, 64, 69, 97, 103, 116, 148–50, 184, 196, 201; *Laws*, 163 n; *Phaedrus*, 170; *Republic*, 21, 103, 146, 148–50, 188 n; *Symposium*, 200, 205
Platonism, 5 n, 7–9, 12, 15–16, 25, 38, 40–43, 47–51, 55, 60–61, 69–71, 95, 97, 103, 115, 124, 142, 156, 160, 164 n, 166–67, 173, 176, 181, 188, 190, 195–96, 202, 212–13
Pliny, 136
Plotinus, 8, 15, 25, 49, 98, 182
Plutarch, 41, 81, 163, 166–67, 202
Poetics, 5–17, 40–43, 97, 115, 117, 133, 177, 186, 195, 212–14
Policy, foreign, 73–91, 209–11
Politics [politician], 21, 36, 56, 88–96, 104, 207–12, 214
Poliziano, Angelo, 47, 193; *Elegia sive Epicedion*, 193–94; *Orfeo*, 47
Presson, Robert K., 182 n
Proclus, 48, 71
Prometheus, 21–22, 24–30, 32–34, 38, 42–43, 53, 106, 138
Prophecy [prophet], 7, 9–11, 14, 16, 29–30, 43–44, 46, 54, 65, 88, 97–98, 105, 110–11, 114, 158, 164, 173, 175, 200, 212–14
Proteus, 64–66, 68, 70, 88–89, 98
Pun, 133, 194, 195 n, 211
Puttenham, George, 119 n, 154
Pygmalion, 178
Pyramid, 130–31
Pyrrho, 147
Pythagoras, 7, 14, 94, 178; associated with justice, 164–66, 177; golden thigh of, 176; reputation of, 160, 165; as time, 176
Pythagoreanism, 60, 66, 105, 107, 124 n, 142 n, 177, 184, 186, 190; Pythagorean balance, 164–65, 170, 173; Pythagorean numerology, 160–67, 177; "Pythagorean oration" (*Metamorphoses* 15), 159–60; Pythagorean theory of harmony, 107, 166, 176–77; Pythagorean Y, 165–66, 175

quinque lineae amoris, 114
Quintilian, 117

Ralegh, Sir Walter, 91–94, 109–11, 127–28, 210
Religion, 44, 122, 195
Reynolds, Henry, 9, 12, 29 n
Rhetoric, 3–6, 9, 16, 42, 117, 129, 141, 172, 197, 200. *See also* Style
Ribner, Rhoda M., 144
Ripa, Cesare, 165–66, 192
Roche, Thomas P., Jr., 65
Roman, 50, 55, 81, 102, 128, 129, 158–59, 194
Roman de la Rose, 182
Ronsard, Pierre de, *Hercule chrestien*, 33–34, 38
Ross, Alexander, 63

Røstvig, Maren-Sofie, 183–184, 190
Roussel, Roy, 29 n
Roydon, Matthew, 92–94, 128, 142
Russell, William Lord, 193, 195

Sadler, Sir Ralph, 85–86
Salmacis, 90
Salutati, Coluccio, *De Laboribus Herculis*, 191
Sandys, George, 84–85, 143, 179, 197 n, 201
Satan, 21, 52, 55, 74, 131, 178
Satire, 3, 142, 156
Saturn, 23–24
Saul, 10
Scaliger, J. C., 154
Schoell, Franck L., 7, 44, 57, 61, 123, 130, 201–2
"School of Night," 92 n
Schrickx, W., 61, 87
Scrots, William, *Edward VI*, 126
Sea: of fortune, 20; of life, 32–33
Seneca, 147 n, 186; *Hercules Oetaeus*, 30, 32
Senses, deceptiveness of, 136, 146, 148–49, 151; hierarchy of, 115–16, 141, 151, 173
Servius, 24–25, 165
Sextus Empiricus, 147 n
Seymour, Edward, duke of Somerset, 90
Shakespeare, William, 93–94, 124–26; *All's Well that Ends Well*, 119 n; *Antony and Cleopatra*, 121, 141 n, 203; *A Midsummer Night's Dream*, 61, 125; *Othello*, 107; *Richard II*, 120, 135, 208; *Sonnet 86*, 185; *The Taming of the Shrew*, 124–25; *Twelfth Night*, 57, 121, 124–25; *Venus and Adonis*, 93, 113, 156, 203
Shelley, Percy Bysshe, 109
Sidney, Sir Philip, 90, 92, 115
Simon, Marcel, 38
Socrates, 13, 113, 200
Sol, 138–40
Sonnet, 11, 14, 39, 142 n
"Soul," of poem, 15–16, 213
Southampton. *See* Wriothesley, Henry
Spain, Spanish, 73, 77, 80, 83–86, 181, 209–11
Spenser, Edward, 3, 13, 98, 149, 162, 182; *Epithalamion*, 196; *Faerie Queene*, 35, 43, 44, 58–59, 67, 78, 90, 131, 164–65, 167 n, 168–69, 171, 175, 180, 182, 191–92, 208; *Mutabilitie Cantos*, 58, 71; *Shepheardes Calendar*, 45
Sphinx, 9
Stanley, Ferdinando, fifth earl of Derby, 92–93
Stapleton, Richard, 142, 145 n
Stick, bent in water, 145–49, 151
Strong, Roy, 126, 149
Structure, poetic, 10, 13, 19, 21, 32, 38, 42, 50–51, 57, 75, 115, 186
Stubbs, John, 74, 79–80

Style: allegorical, 4–6, 8–9, 104–5, 197; levels of, 11, 13; metaphysical, 1–2, 13–14, 137; obscurity in, 3–6, 8–9, 16, 49, 104, 109, 116; oratorical, 4–6, 9
Sun, 32–33, 55–56, 58, 63, 71, 75, 79–81, 83, 91, 96, 100, 106, 129–32, 137–41, 142 n, 171, 174
Svendsen, Kester, 55

Tantalus, 142 n
Taylor, F. Sherwood, 139
Taylor, Thomas, 50–51, 164–65
Temperance, 175, 183–85, 188–89, 191, 199–200, 202, 211
Temple, 43–44, 56, 67–68, 105–6, 194
Tennyson, Alfred Lord, 147 n
Tesauro, Emmanuele, 126 n
Themis, 173–76
Time, 175–77
Titans, the, 22–23, 26, 28, 32, 34
Tithonus, 195 n
Titian, 134
Torch, as symbol, 155–56, 163 n, 166
Transformation. See Metamorphosis
Troilus, 153
Trousson, Raymond, 33
"Turning pictures," 120–23, 143
Tuve, Rosemond, 2–3, 117
Typhon, 26
Typology, 15, 17, 33, 44, 54, 56, 58, 207; adaptation of, 17, 88–89, 115, 177, 191–93, 205, 212–13; of myth, 15, 29, 61, 202, 205, 208 n, 210–11

Ut pictura poesis, 117, 133, 136–37, 141, 145, 151

Valerius Flaccus, 32
Varro, 108

Venus, 43, 140, 161, 163 n, 169, 171–72, 177, 179–80, 201–9; triumph of, 203; Venere celeste, 207; Venere vulgare, 207
Vere, Sir Francis, 73, 78, 83
Vere, Sir Horatio, 78
Veronese, Paolo, 203
Virgil, 114, 146 n, 165, 175
Vision, 116–17, 129–37, 141, 145, 150, 173
Vulcan, 206–7

Waddington, Raymond B., 19 n, 141 n, 142 n, 190 n
Walker, D. P., 47, 49, 95, 101, 106–7
Wallerstein, Ruth, 8 n, 194
Walsingham, Lady Thomas, 156
Wasserman, Earl R., 43
Webster, John, 3
Wernham, R. B., 85
Weyden, Rogier van der, 118
Williams, Kathleen, 35
Wilson, E. C., 78–79
Wind, Edgar, 4, 8–9, 16, 43, 47, 70, 201 n
World body, 16, 40
World soul, 16, 40, 59, 81, 90, 98–99, 110
Wriothesley, Henry, earl of Southampton, 92–94

Xenophon, 69
Xylander, Guilielmus, 202

Yates, Frances A., 8 n, 48, 79–82, 92 n, 97, 184, 192 n

Zeus, 174
Zeuxis, 136, 148
Zincgreff, Julius Wilhelm, 146 n

The Johns Hopkins University Press

This book was composed in Chelmsford text and
Stettler display type by Jones Composition
Company from a design by Beverly Baum. It was
printed on 60 lb. Warren 1854 paper and bound in
Columbia Fictionette linen by The Maple Press
Company.

Library of Congress Cataloging in Publication Data

Waddington, Raymond B
   The mind's empire.

   Includes bibliographical references.
   1. Chapman, George, 1559?–1634—Poetic works.
2. Mythology in literature.   I. Title.
PR2457.P58W3   821'.3   74–6841
ISBN 0–8018–1546–0